A+ Certification: OS Technologies (2003 Objectives) Volume 1

Student Manual

THOMSON

COURSE TECHNOLOGY

Australia • Canada • Mexico • Singapore
Spain • United Kingdom • United States

A+ Certification: OS Technologies (2003 Objectives) Volume 1

VP and GM of Courseware:	Michael Springer
Series Product Managers:	Caryl Bahner-Guhin, Charles G. Blum, and Adam A. Wilcox
Developmental Editors:	Linda Long and Don Tremblay
Copyeditors:	Ken Maher, Cathy Albano, and Robert Tillett
Series Designer:	Adam A. Wilcox
Cover Designer:	Steve Deschene

For more information contact:

Course Technology
25 Thomson Place
Boston, MA 02210

Or find us on the Web at: www.course.com

For permission to use material from this text or product, contact us by

- Web: www.thomsonrights.com
- Phone: 1-800-730-2214
- Fax: 1-800-730-2215

Trademarks

Course ILT is a trademark of Course Technology.

Some of the product names and company names used in this book have been used for identification purposes only and may be trademarks or registered trademarks of their respective manufacturers and sellers.

Disclaimer

Course Technology reserves the right to revise this publication and make changes from time to time in its content without notice.

The logo of the CompTIA Authorized Curriculum Program and the status of this or other training material as "Authorized" under the CompTIA Authorized Curriculum Program signifies that, in CompTIA's opinion, such training material covers the content of the CompTIA's related certification exam. CompTIA has not reviewed or approved the accuracy of the contents of this training material and specifically disclaims any warranties of merchantability or fitness for a particular purpose. CompTIA makes no guarantee concerning the success of persons using any such "Authorized" or other training material in order to prepare for any CompTIA certification exam.

The contents of this training material were created for the CompTIA A+ Operating System Technologies exam covering CompTIA certification exam objectives that were current as of November 2003.

ISBN 1-4188-1510-1

Printed in the United States of America

4 5 PM 06 05

Contents

A+ Certification: OS Technologies (2003 Objectives)

Introduction

After reading this introduction, you will know how to:

A Use Course Technology ILT manuals in general.

B Use prerequisites, a target student description, course objectives, and a skills inventory to properly set your expectations for the course.

Topic A: About the manual

Course Technology ILT philosophy

Course Technology ILT manuals facilitate your learning by providing structured interaction with the software itself. While we provide text to explain difficult concepts, the hands-on activities are the focus of our courses. By paying close attention as your instructor leads you through these activities, you will learn the skills and concepts effectively.

We believe strongly in the instructor-led classroom. During class, focus on your instructor. Our manuals are designed and written to facilitate your interaction with your instructor, and not to call attention to manuals themselves.

We believe in the basic approach of setting expectations, delivering instruction, and providing summary and review afterwards. For this reason, lessons begin with objectives and end with summaries. We also provide overall course objectives and a course summary to provide both an introduction to and closure on the entire course.

Manual components

The manuals contain these major components:

- Table of contents
- Introduction
- Units
- Appendices
- Course summary
- Glossary
- Index

Each element is described below.

Table of contents

The table of contents acts as a learning roadmap.

Introduction

The introduction contains information about our training philosophy and our manual components, features, and conventions. It contains target student, prerequisite, objective, and setup information for the specific course.

Units

Units are the largest structural component of the course content. A unit begins with a title page that lists objectives for each major subdivision, or topic, within the unit. Within each topic, conceptual and explanatory information alternates with hands-on activities. Units conclude with a summary comprising one paragraph for each topic, and an independent practice activity that gives you an opportunity to practice the skills you've learned.

The conceptual information takes the form of text paragraphs, exhibits, lists, and tables. The activities are structured in two columns, one telling you what to do, the other providing explanations, descriptions, and graphics.

Appendices

An appendix is similar to a unit in that it contains objectives and conceptual explanations. However, an appendix does not include hands-on activities, a summary, or an independent practice activity.

Course summary

This section provides a text summary of the entire course. It is useful for providing closure at the end of the course. The course summary also indicates the next course in this series, if there is one, and lists additional resources you might find useful as you continue to learn about the software.

Glossary

The glossary provides definitions for all of the key terms used in this course.

Index

The index at the end of this manual makes it easy for you to find information about a particular software component, feature, or concept.

Manual conventions

We've tried to keep the number of elements and the types of formatting to a minimum in the manuals. This aids in clarity and makes the manuals more classically elegant looking. But there are some conventions and icons you should know about.

Convention	Description
Italic text	In conceptual text, indicates a new term or feature.
Bold text	In unit summaries, indicates a key term or concept. In an independent practice activity, indicates an explicit item that you select, choose, or type.
`Code font`	Indicates code or syntax.
`Longer strings of ▶ code will look ▶ like this.`	In the hands-on activities, any code that's too long to fit on a single line is divided into segments by one or more continuation characters (▶). This code should be entered as a continuous string of text.
Select **bold item**	In the left column of hands-on activities, bold sans-serif text indicates an explicit item that you select, choose, or type.
Keycaps like (↵ ENTER)	Indicate a key on the keyboard you must press.

Hands-on activities

The hands-on activities are the most important parts of our manuals. They are divided into two primary columns. The "Here's how" column gives short instructions to you about what to do. The "Here's why" column provides explanations, graphics, and clarifications. Here's a sample:

Do it!

A-1: Creating a commission formula

Here's how	Here's why
1 Open Sales	This is an oversimplified sales compensation worksheet. It shows sales totals, commissions, and incentives for five sales reps.
2 Observe the contents of cell F4	F4 ▼ = =E4*C_Rate

The commission rate formulas use the name "C_Rate" instead of a value for the commission rate. |

For these activities, we have provided a collection of data files designed to help you learn each skill in a real-world business context. As you work through the activities, you will modify and update these files. Of course, you might make a mistake and, therefore, want to re-key the activity starting from scratch. To make it easy to start over, you will rename each data file at the end of the first activity in which the file is modified. Our convention for renaming files is to add the word "My" to the beginning of the file name. In the above activity, for example, a file called "Sales" is being used for the first time. At the end of this activity, you would save the file as "My sales," thus leaving the "Sales" file unchanged. If you make a mistake, you can start over using the original "Sales" file.

In some activities, however, it may not be practical to rename the data file. If you want to retry one of these activities, ask your instructor for a fresh copy of the original data file.

Topic B: Setting your expectations

Properly setting your expectations is essential to your success. This topic will help you do that by providing:

- Prerequisites for this course
- A description of the target student at whom the course is aimed
- A list of the objectives for the course
- A skills assessment for the course

Course prerequisites

Before taking this course, you should be familiar with personal computers and the use of a keyboard and a mouse.

Target student

This course provides you with the skills and knowledge necessary to understand and support operating systems used on personal computers.

CompTIA certification

This course will also prepare you to pass CompTIA's A+ OS Technologies Exam. CompTIA is a non-profit information technology (IT) trade association. CompTIA's certifications are designed by subject matter experts from across the IT industry. Each CompTIA certification is vendor-neutral, covers multiple technologies, and requires demonstration of skills and knowledge widely sought after by the IT industry.

In order to become CompTIA certified you must:

1. Select a certification exam provider. For more information, you can visit www.comptia.org/certification/general_information/test_locations.asp.

2. Register for and schedule a time to take the CompTIA certification exam at a convenient location.

3. Read and sign the Candidate Agreement, which will be presented at the time of the exams. The text of the Candidate Agreement can be found at www.comptia.org/certification/general_information/candidate_agreement.asp.

4. Take and pass the CompTIA certification exam.

For additional information about CompTIA's certifications, such as their industry acceptance, benefits, or program news, visit www.comptia.org/certification.

To contact CompTIA with any questions or comments, call (630) 268-1818 or send an e-mail to questions@comptia.org.

Course objectives

These overall course objectives will give you an idea about what to expect from the course. It is also possible that they will help you see that this course is not the right one for you. If you think you either lack the prerequisite knowledge or already know most of the subject matter to be covered, you should let your instructor know that you think you are misplaced in the class.

After completing this course, you will know how to:

- Discuss the how operating systems works, the legacy of DOS, the various Windows operating systems, the differences between them and discuss advantages and disadvantages of common non-Windows operating systems.

- Relate an OS to hardware and to other software, and launch an OS application.

- Outline the steps to boot the computer, create and use Windows 9x rescue disks to troubleshoot and solve problems while booting Windows, view and manage memory in DOS and Windows 9x, use and manage floppy disks and hard drives in DOS and Windows 9x.

- Describe different versions and architecture of Windows 9x, install Windows 9x as a clean install and as an upgrade, use keystroke shortcuts, manage hard drives and floppy disks and desktop with Windows 9x, install hardware with Windows 9x, install applications with Windows 9x, and manage memory with Windows 9x.

- Discuss the Windows 9x startup process, troubleshoot the Windows 9x boot process, discuss the Windows 9x registry, its organization and the recovery procedure, discuss the tools used to monitor, control, and troubleshoot Windows 9x, troubleshoot hardware in Windows 9x, troubleshoot applications in Windows 9x and troubleshoot Windows 9x performance.

- Describe Windows NT architecture, install and customize Windows NT, use and support Windows NT, outline the Windows NT boot process, and create Windows NT setup and repair disks to repair a Windows NT system.

- Outline new features of Windows 2000 and understand basic and dynamic disks, plan and perform the Windows 2000 installation, manage and use Windows 2000 and install hardware and applications with Windows 2000.

- Outline the Windows 2000 boot process, troubleshoot the Windows 2000 boot process, and use tools for maintenance, troubleshooting, and performance monitoring in Windows.

- Outline the features and architecture of Windows XP, plan and perform Windows XP installation, customize the Windows XP desktop, manage audio and video, and allow multiple and remote logins under Windows XP, and install hardware and applications with Windows XP.

- Use Windows XP features to secure the PC, view and update the Windows NT/2000/XP/2003 registry, use tools for troubleshooting and maintaining Windows XP, and troubleshoot the Windows XP boot process.

- Support hard drives and take backups, identify computer viruses and infestations and protection against them.

- Outline the basics of networking, the different types of addresses used on networks, connect and share resources over a local area network and control a computer remotely.

- Discuss how the OSI model applies to TCP/IP networks, such as the Internet, connect to the Internet using a dial-up connection, connect to the Internet using a cable modem or DSL connections and support some common Internet clients: Web browsers, e-mail, and FTP.

- Discuss starting up, using, and supporting hardware in the Mac OS, outline the file structure of the Linux OS, usage of some Linux commands, outline Windows 98, Windows 2000 and Windows XP notebook features and describe power management in notebooks.

Skills inventory

Use the following form to gauge your skill level entering the class. For each skill listed, rate your familiarity from 1 to 5, with five being the most familiar. *This is not a test.* Rather, it is intended to provide you with an idea of where you're starting from at the beginning of class. If you're wholly unfamiliar with all the skills, you might not be ready for the class. If you think you already understand all of the skills, you might need to move on to the next course in the series. In either case, you should let your instructor know as soon as possible.

Skill	1	2	3	4	5
Describing the function and components of an operating system					
Discussing the legacy of DOS					
Discussing the various Windows operating systems and the differences between them					
Discussing advantages and disadvantages of common non-Windows operating systems					
Describing computer system hardware and the software needed to make it operate and perform tasks					
Describing how the operating system interacts with other software such as application software, the BIOS, and device drivers					
Explaining how the operating system loads, initializes, and starts application software					
Outlining the steps to boot the computer					
Creating and using Windows 9x rescue disks to troubleshoot and solve problems while booting Windows					
Viewing and managing memory in DOS and Windows 9x					
Using and managing floppy disks and hard drives in DOS and Windows 9x					
Describing different versions and architecture of Windows 9x					
Installing Windows 9x as a clean install and as an upgrade					
Using keystroke shortcuts, managing hard drives and floppy disks and desktop with Windows 9x					
Installing hardware with Windows 9x					

Skill	1	2	3	4	5
Installing applications with Windows 9x					
Managing memory with Windows 9x					
Discussing the Windows 9x startup process					
Troubleshooting the Windows 9x boot process					
Discussing the Windows 9x registry, its organization, and recovery procedures					
Discussing the tools used to monitor, control, and troubleshoot Windows 9x					
Troubleshooting hardware in Windows 9x					
Troubleshooting applications in Windows 9x					
Troubleshooting Windows 9x performance					
Describing Windows NT architecture					
Installing and customizing Windows NT					
Using and supporting Windows NT					
Outlining the Windows NT boot process					
Creating Windows NT setup and repair disks to repair a Windows NT system					
Outlining new features of Windows 2000 and understanding basic and dynamic disks					
Planning and performing the Windows 2000 installation					
Managing and using Windows 2000					
Installing hardware and applications with Windows 2000					
Outlining the Windows 2000 boot process					
Troubleshooting the Windows 2000 boot process					
Using tools for maintenance, troubleshooting, and performance monitoring in Windows					
Outlining the features and architecture of Windows XP					
Planning and performing Windows XP installation					

Skill	1	2	3	4	5
Customizing the desktop, managing audio and video, and allowing multiple and remote logins under Windows XP					
Installing hardware and applications with Windows XP					
Using Windows XP features to secure the PC					
Viewing and updating the Windows NT/2000/XP/2003 registry					
Using tools for troubleshooting and maintaining Windows XP					
Troubleshooting the Windows XP boot process					
Supporting hard drives and creating backups					
Identifying computer viruses and infections and protecting against them					
Outlining the basics of networking					
Describing different types of addresses used on networks					
Connecting and sharing resources over a local area network					
Controlling a computer remotely					
Discussing how the OSI model applies to TCP/IP networks, such as the Internet					
Connecting to the Internet using a dial-up connection					
Connecting to the Internet using a cable modem or DSL connections					
Supporting some common Internet clients such as Web browsers, e-mail, and FTP					
Discussing starting up, using, and supporting hardware in the Mac OS					
Outlining the file structure of the Linux OS and how to use some Linux commands					
Outlining Windows 98, Windows 2000 and Windows XP notebook features					
Describing power management in notebooks					

Topic C: Reviewing the course

This course is hardware and software intensive, and it would be impossible to recreate the classroom setup on your own. You can, however, review the coverage in this manual along with accompanying PowerPoint presentations.

Downloading the PowerPoint presentations

To download the PowerPoint presentations for this course:

1   Connect to www.courseilt.com/instructor_tools.html.
2   Click the link for A+ to display a page of course listings, and then click the link for A+ Certification: OS Technologies (2003 Objectives).
3   Click the link for downloading the PowerPoint presentations, and follow the instructions that appear on your screen.

CertBlaster exam preparation for CompTIA certification

If you are interested in attaining CompTIA A+ certification, you can download CertBlaster exam preparation software from the Course ILT Web site. To do so:

1   Go to www.courseilt.com/certblaster.
2   Click the link for A+.
3   Save the .EXE file to a folder on your hard drive. (**Note:** If you skip this step, the CertBlaster software will not install correctly.)
4   Click Start and choose Run.
5   Click Browse and then navigate to the folder that contains the .EXE file.
6   Select the .EXE file and click Open.
7   Click OK and follow the on-screen instructions. When prompted for the password, enter **c_a+**.

Unit 1

Operating systems overview

Unit time: 60 minutes

Complete this unit, and You want to know how to:

A Describe the function and components of an operating system.

B Explain the legacy of DOS.

C Describe the various Windows operating systems and explain differences between them.

D Discuss advantages and disadvantages of common non-Windows operating systems.

Topic A: Operating system fundamentals

Explanation

An *operating system* (OS) is a software program that enables the computer hardware to communicate and operate with other computer software. The operating system is the first software we see when we turn on the computer, and the last software we see when the computer is turned off. It's the software that enables all the programs we use.

A computer doesn't work unless a user controls it. Exhibit 1-1 shows how the user, the application software, and the operating system make the computer a functioning tool that can be used to accomplish a task. Without these components, the computer is nothing more than an interconnected assemblage of electronic and mechanical devices.

Exhibit 1-1: A user interacts with a computer

Common operating systems

The operating system is the most important and primary software used to control a computer. A computer might have several applications installed to meet various needs of the users, but it needs only one operating system. There are several operating systems that are commonly found on the market; each designed to support different types of hardware systems and user needs.

DOS/Windows 3.x

DOS (Disk Operating System) was the first operating system used for IBM computers and IBM-compatible computers. Because DOS was written for early PCs, it has significant limitations for today's computers.

Windows 3.1 and Windows for Workgroups 3.11 (collectively known as Windows 3.x) weren't operating systems. Rather, Windows 3.x was a graphical user interface (GUI) that used DOS as the operating system. Windows 3.x didn't perform any operations but simply served as a user-friendly intermediate program between DOS and the applications and the user.

Windows 9x

The more recent Windows 95, Windows 98, and Windows Millennium Edition, also known as Windows ME, are collectively called Windows 9x. Windows 9x is an operating system environment with a DOS core and a user-friendly interface. Unlike Windows 3.x, Windows 9x does perform operating system functions. Windows 9x provides a 32-bit operating system, which allows the computer to run faster and more efficiently. Windows 98 is the most popular operating system for desktop computers for home use. While, Windows ME wasn't a significant upgrade from Windows 98, it did provide a more stable system.

Windows NT, 2000, XP, and 2003

Windows NT comes in two versions, Windows NT Workstation for workstations and Windows NT Server to control a network. Windows NT 4.0 has the look and feel of Windows 95; however, it's a completely different operating system. Windows NT contains advanced security features, advanced network support, a full 32-bit operating system, advanced multitasking, user administration, and much more. While NT is a very advanced operating system, it lacks the support of drivers, features, and gaming available in Windows 9x. For this reason, even today, Windows NT is used primarily in business and technical fields.

Windows 2000 is an upgrade of Windows NT that was designed for reliability and stability. Windows 2000 also comes in several versions, some designed for the desktop and others designed for high-end servers. Windows 2000 Professional is now a popular operating system for the corporate desktop. Windows 2000 Server, Advanced Server, and Datacenter Server are networking server operating systems.

Windows XP is an upgrade of Windows 2000 Professional. Windows XP currently comes in two main versions: Windows XP Home and Windows XP Professional. Windows XP is expected to replace both Windows 9x and Windows 2000 Professional. Windows XP includes an interface with a new look. Windows XP can also automatically obtain updates from the Internet. In addition, Windows XP increases reliability when compared to previous versions of Microsoft Windows.

Windows Server 2003 is an upgrade of Windows 2000 Server and Windows NT Server. Windows Server 2003 includes all the functionality customers expect from a mission-critical Windows Server operating system, such as security, reliability, availability, and scalability. In addition, Microsoft has improved and extended the Windows server product family to enable organizations to experience the benefits of Microsoft.NET—a set of software for connecting information, people, systems, and devices.

UNIX

Bell Labs developed UNIX, which isn't an acronym, in the late 1960's. UNIX is a popular operating system used to control networks and to support applications used on the Internet. UNIX is primarily a command line-oriented operating system.

Linux

Linux is an operating system that was developed by Linus Torvalds and further elaborated by a number of developers throughout the world. Linux is a freely available multitasking and multi-user operating system. While similar to UNIX, Linux is available under a *General Public License* (GPL). The GPL allows open access to the operating system, so it can be distributed, used, and expanded free of charge. Developers have access to all of the source code, so they can easily integrate new functions or quickly find and eliminate programming bugs. Linux is often used for server applications. In recent years, it's also being used for desktop applications.

Mac OS

Apple Macintosh computers use a proprietary operating system called the Mac OS. This operating system is available only for Apple Macintosh computers and is often used for graphics applications and in educational settings.

OS/2

Microsoft and IBM jointly developed OS/2 to operate with Intel's microprocessors. OS/2 was originally a 16-bit operating system that was designed for use on home desktop PCs. Today, OS/2 is a 32-bit operating system that has a graphical interface similar to Windows and can be used as a server. OS/2 can also be run through command-line entries, such as DOS. In fact, many OS/2 and DOS commands are the same. OS/2 never became as popular as the other Microsoft operating systems, and software developers haven't created a substantial number of programs to run primarily under OS/2.

Operating system functions

Although there are important differences between various operating systems, all operating systems share the following four main functions:

Hardware management

1 Managing the BIOS (programs permanently stored on hardware devices)
2 Managing memory, which is a temporary place to store data and instructions as they're being processed
3 Diagnosing problems with software and hardware
4 Interfacing between hardware and software (that is, interpreting application software needs to the hardware and interpreting hardware needs to application software)

File management

1 Managing files on hard drives, floppy drives, CD-ROM drives, and other drives
2 Creating, storing, retrieving, deleting, and moving files

User interface

1 Performing housekeeping procedures requested by the user, often concerning secondary storage devices, such as formatting new disks, deleting files, copying files, and changing the system date
2 Providing a way for the user to manage the desktop, hardware, applications, and data

Application management

1 Installing and uninstalling applications
2 Running applications and managing the interface to the hardware on behalf of an application

In short, an operating system controls the hardware components that make up a computer and provides an interface that a user or an application can use. Exhibit 1-2 shows that an operating system must relate to the user, applications, and various hardware components. You can also see that the operating system must relate to these hardware devices by way of the *CPU (central processing unit)* , also called a *microprocessor*. The CPU is responsible for processing all data and instructions.

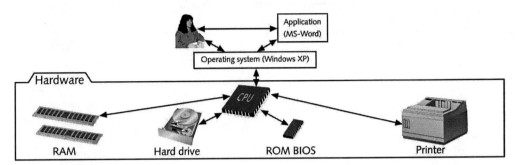

Exhibit 1-2: The OS relates users and applications to the hardware components

Operating system components

An operating system is made up of two main components as shown in Exhibit 1-3:

- Shell
- Kernel (or Core)

The *shell* is the portion of the operating system that relates to the user and to applications. The shell provides a command line environment, or menu, or icon interface to the user using various interface tools, such as Windows Explorer, the Control Panel, or My Computer.

The *kernel*, or core, of the operating system is responsible for interacting with hardware. It has more power to communicate with hardware devices than the shell. Application programs operating under the operating system are usually not allowed to access hardware devices directly. Instead all applications request the kernel to provide access to these devices. This structure provides for a more stable system.

An operating system needs a place to keep hardware and software configuration information, user preferences, and application settings that are used when the OS is first loaded and are accessed as needed by hardware, applications, and users. This information can be kept in a database or text files. Windows uses a database called the *registry* for most of this information. In addition, some data is kept in text configuration files called *initialization* (.ini) files.

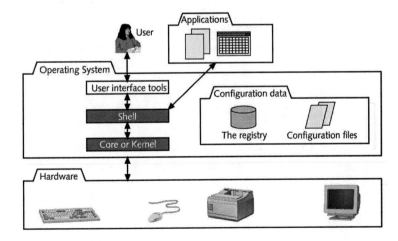

Exhibit 1-3: Inside an operating system

Do it!

A-1: Discussing operating system fundamentals

Questions and answers

1 What are some commonly found operating systems on the market today?

2 What four main functions do all operating systems share?

3 What is a shell?

4 The _____ of the operating system is responsible for interacting with hardware.

OS interfaces

Explanation

When a PC is first turned on, the operating system is loaded into memory with the help of a special program called a bootstrap loader. After the operating system is in control, it either automatically executes the shell or some other application software program.

If you're working with the operating system, you see a *user interface* on the monitor screen. A user interface allows a user to interact easily with the operating system. The user interface can be command-driven, menu-driven, or icon-based.

Command-driven interfaces

With a command-driven interface, you enter commands at a command prompt to tell the operating system to perform certain procedures. For example, Exhibit 1-4 shows the VER command, which is used to report the operating system version. DOS and UNIX use command-driven interfaces. Other operating systems might provide access to a command-driven interface as a secondary interface. For instance, Windows 9x provides a command-driven interface as an MS-DOS Prompt window. The command line in the MS-DOS Prompt window is called the C prompt, which can look like this:

```
C:\Windows> or C:\>
```

You can access the MS-DOS Prompt window on Windows 9x by clicking Start, and then choosing Programs, MS-DOS Prompt. In Windows 2000 and Windows XP, you can access the command prompt by clicking Start, then choosing All Programs, Accessories, Command Prompt. Computer technicians who are good typists and are very familiar with DOS-like commands often prefer a command-driven interface.

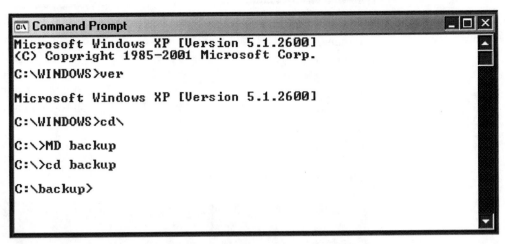

Exhibit 1-4: An operating system command-driven interface: a DOS box

Menu-driven interfaces

With a menu-driven interface, you choose a command from a list displayed on the screen. Windows Explorer, as shown in Exhibit 1-5, is an example of a menu-driven interface. Windows Explorer is used in Windows 9x, NT, 2000, and XP. You can use the menus to format disks, rename files, copy and delete files, and perform many other operations to manage files and storage devices. Note that Windows Explorer is a combination interface since it uses icons as well as menus.

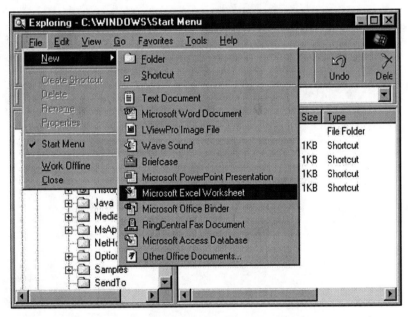

Exhibit 1-5: A menu-driven interface: Windows Explorer

Icon-driven interfaces

Today's operating systems are more likely to use an icon-driven interface than a command-driven one. With an icon-driven interface, sometimes called a *GUI (graphical user interface)*, you perform procedures by selecting icons (or pictures) on the screen. When an operating system that uses a GUI interface is first executed, the initial screen that appears, together with its menus, commands, and icons, is called the desktop. Exhibit 1-6 shows the Windows 2000 default desktop, which has an icon-driven interface. You double-click an icon with the mouse to execute an application software program or right-click an icon to see its shortcut menu. Just about all operating systems today offer a combination of menu- and icon-driven interfaces. One example is the Control Panel window shown in Exhibit 1-6, which includes both menus and icons.

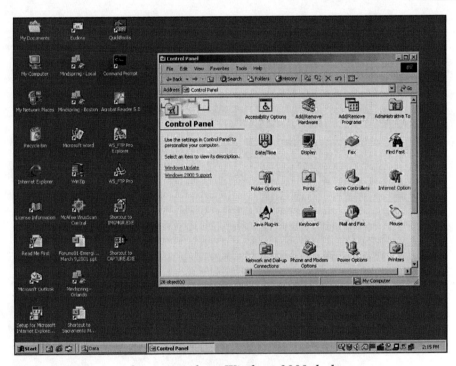

Exhibit 1-6: An icon-driven interface: Windows 2000 desktop

Do it!

A-2:   Comparing interfaces

Here's how	Here's why
1 Minimize all programs you have running	To see the desktop with its icons showing. You want to take screenshots of three different types of interfaces and compare them.
2 Press PRINT SCREEN	To copy an image of your screen onto the clipboard.
3 Click **Start**, choose **Programs**, **Accessories**, **Paint**	To start the Microsoft Paint program.

4 Choose **Edit**, **Paste** — To paste the image of your screen into Paint.

5 Choose **File**, **Save As...**

Navigate to the current unit folder — To save the image in the current unit folder.

In the File name box, enter **icon_interface** — To specify a name for the image.

Click **Save**

6 Choose **File**, **Print** — To print the screenshot.

7 Click **Start**, choose **Programs**, **MS-DOS Prompt** — If you're using Windows 2000 or XP, click Start, and then choose All Programs, Accessories, Command Prompt.

8 Press **Print Screen**, open **Paint**, and then choose **Edit**, **Paste** — To take a screenshot of the Command Prompt window.

Save the screenshot as **command_interface** — (Choose File, Save As.) To save the image in the current unit folder.

Print the screenshot

9 Right-click **Start**

Choose **Explore** — To open Windows Explorer.

Take a screenshot of Windows Explorer

Save the screenshot as **menu_interface**

Print the screenshot

10 Compare the printouts of the three different types of interface

What are the similarities and differences between the screenshots?

Besides menus, what other type of interface is Windows Explorer an example of?

Operating system features

Explanation

To make wise buying decisions and technical comparisons, you first need to learn some basic definitions for operating system features.

Threads

Each process that a CPU is aware of is called a *thread*.

Single tasking

Single tasking occurs when the CPU or an operating system can run only one program at a time. The CPU is aware of and is actively running only one thread. In Exhibit 1-7, DOS is a *single-tasking* OS, which can manage only one application at a time, passing a single thread to the CPU. All older CPUs used when DOS was written could handle only a single thread.

Multitasking

Multitasking is doing more than one thing at the same time. Exhibit 1-8 shows two applications open on the Windows 98 desktop, and you can move from one to the other by clicking your mouse on the appropriate window. In one sense, the operating system is multitasking, because it's supporting two applications at the same time. However, both applications can't use the CPU at the same time. For example, if you command Microsoft Excel to print a large spreadsheet and, before the printing is done, command Microsoft Word to save a large document, both applications request resources from the operating system at the same time. The OS multitasks by sharing its resources between the two applications, doing part of one task and part of the other, switching back and forth until both tasks are done. The OS and the CPU that the operating system uses aren't multitasking in the true sense of the word, because they're doing only one thing at a time. All operating systems today support some form of multitasking, so that two or more applications can be open at a time. The type of multitasking they use partly depends on the CPU. Some CPUs can perform two commands at the same time, each from a different thread, but in order to get a true multitasking system, you need two CPUs, each processing a separate thread at the same time. Having two or more CPUs in the same system is called *multiprocessing*.

Cooperative multitasking

Cooperative multitasking (see Exhibit 1-7) was used by Windows 3.x, which was designed for the older i386 and i486 CPUs by Intel. Cooperative multitasking is sometimes called *task switching* because it isn't true multitasking, in that the CPU is aware of only one program running at a time. But Windows 3.x switched back and forth between applications so that more than one application could be loaded at the same time. Also, Windows 3.x used DOS as the underlying OS. Windows 3.x passed one thread to DOS, which passed it to the CPU. DOS and the CPU weren't aware that more than one application was open. Using Windows 3.x, you could observe cooperative multitasking when you had two applications open, each in its own window. You didn't need to close one application before opening another. However, with cooperative multitasking, if one program was doing something (for example, when you saw the hourglass on the screen while the software was attempting to print or save a file), you couldn't click on another application and immediately switch to it.

Preemptive multitasking

Preemptive multitasking, also shown in Exhibit 1-7, is another type of pseudo-multitasking where the operating system allots CPU time to an application for a specified period called a *timeslice*. At the end of the process's timeslice, the process is forced to stop temporarily. The operating system then gives the CPU to another application. The end result is that the computer appears to be doing true multitasking. If two threads are running, the CPU can be aware of both, but still only one is active. Windows 95 was the first version of Windows to provide preemptive multitasking, and it requires the cooperation of the CPU.

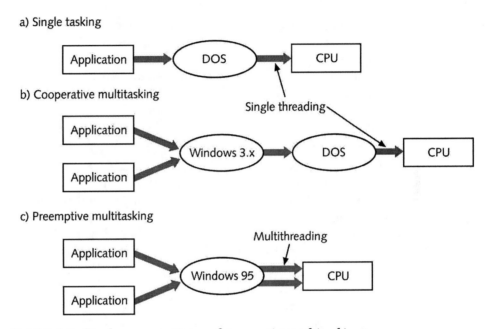

Exhibit 1-7: Single, cooperative, and preemptive multitasking

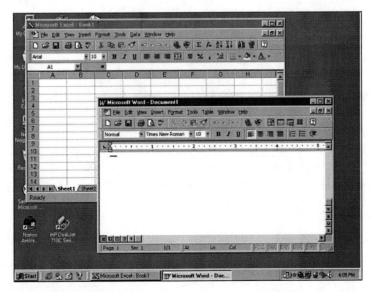

Exhibit 1-8: Multitasking allows two or more applications to run simultaneously

Environment

The type of support the operating system provides to the applications software is called the *environment*. For example, if you have an application that offers you a window with mouse movement, buttons to click, and icons to view, then that application must be supported by a GUI environment, such as Windows. Another example of an environment might be a DOS application that doesn't expect other applications to be running concurrently with it. This would be a single-tasking environment.

Modes

16-bit mode and *32-bit mode*, also called *real mode* and *protected mode*, respectively, have to do with whether the CPU processes 16 or 32 bits at a time. Operating systems, applications, and CPUs all operate in either 16-bit (real) or 32-bit modes. 16-bit operating systems support cooperative multitasking, and 32-bit operating systems support preemptive multitasking.

FAT

FAT (file allocation table) is a table on a hard drive or floppy disk that tracks the locations of files on a disk. A disk is composed of *tracks*, which are concentric circles on the disk surface, as shown in Exhibit 1-9. Each track is divided into several segments, called *sectors*. A *cluster* is the smallest unit of space on a disk for storing data and is made up of one or more sectors. The FAT contains a list of clusters and which clusters are used for each file stored on the disk. The most recent version of FAT, FAT32, is a more efficient method of organization for large drives than FAT16 (the earlier version).

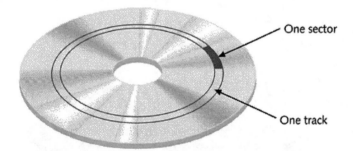

One sector

One track

Exhibit 1-9: A hard drive and floppy disk is divided into tracks and sectors

Ports

A computer provides several ports on the back of the computer case to connect different devices, such as a keyboard, mouse, or printer.

RAM

RAM (random access memory) is temporary memory stored on chips inside the computer. These chips are stored on memory modules, some of which are shown in Exhibit 1-10. *Memory* is a place for the CPU to store programs and data while it's processing both, and the information stored in RAM disappears when the computer is turned off. Because of hardware limitations at the time, DOS divides memory into categories called base memory, upper memory, high memory, expanded memory, and extended memory. Windows 9x still uses this same arrangement, although it makes better use of these categories. Windows NT/2000/XP uses an altogether new and more efficient form of memory paging. The goal of each operating system is the same: provide as much memory as possible for software to use without hindering software performance.

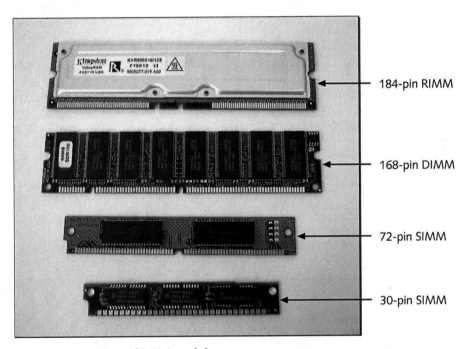

Exhibit 1-10: Types of RAM modules

Now that you've learned some basic terms relating to operating systems, answer the following questions when you're comparing operating systems:

- What kind of interface does the operating system provide for the user?
- Can the operating system support some form of multitasking?
- What kinds of applications are written to work with the operating system?
- What are the hardware requirements to make efficient use of the operating system
- What computer ports and other hardware devices and features does the operating system support?
- How does the operating system perform in a network?

Do it!

A-3:   Discussing operating system features

Questions and answers

1   What is it called when the CPU or an operating system can run only one program at a time?

2   What is multitasking?

3   What is multiprocessing?

4   What is preemptive multitasking?

5   What is RAM?

6   What categories does DOS use to divide its memory?

Topic B: DOS (Disk Operating System)

Explanation

DOS was the first operating system used by IBM microcomputers. For years, DOS remained the unchallenged standard for operating systems used by IBM and IBM-compatible machines. It's a simple operating system, and simple often means reliable. PC technicians should be familiar with DOS, because it can be very effective in troubleshooting situations when a more complex OS fails.

Legacy of DOS

With Windows 3.x, DOS ran in the background as the true OS and used Windows 3.x as a middle layer, or user interface, between the application and DOS. In this environment, users could interact with applications directly through Windows or directly through DOS. Windows 3.x supported cooperative multitasking, because it managed more than one open application by passing segments to DOS, which then, in turn, interfaced with hardware. However, DOS and Windows applications tended to conflict with each other when sharing hardware devices.

Note: Windows 3.11, called Windows for Workgroups, was the first Windows environment designed to interface with a network without depending on separate application software to do the job. Windows 3.x (3.1 and 3.11) is no longer in general use and has been replaced by Windows 9x.

DOS is still used in some proprietary systems where older hardware and software (sometimes called *legacy* hardware or software) are still doing the job and there's little reason to upgrade the system. Today, the primary use of DOS is as a troubleshooting tool. Windows 9x has a DOS core, and when the Windows 9x GUI interface fails to load, the only recourse is to fall back to the tried and true DOS portion of the operating system stored on floppy disks or the hard drive. Windows 2000 and Window XP both offer a recovery tool that includes a command prompt where you issue DOS-like commands.

The following table summarizes the advantages and disadvantages of DOS.

Advantages	Disadvantages
DOS runs on small, inexpensive microcomputers with a minimum amount of memory and hard drive space.	Memory management is awkward and sometimes slow
	DOS has no icon-driven interface
Text-based DOS programs are faster and more compact than comparable graphics-intensive GUI programs.	DOS does only single-tasking; that is, it supports only one application running at a time
Some older applications are still in use today that were written for DOS and older hardware, because DOS provides a much lower overhead for these applications when compared to newer ones used on modern operating systems.	DOS wasn't designed for use on networks. A separate software program is necessary for a DOS machine to access a network
DOS is still a viable option for some specialized applications using a dedicated computer that doesn't involve heavy user interaction, for example, a microcomputer dedicated to controlling an in-house phone system.	The last standalone version is DOS 6.22, which doesn't take advantage of the many new CPU features now available.
DOS can be used to boot up and troubleshoot a computer when a more sophisticated operating system is too cumbersome and has too much overhead.	

Do it!

B-1: Discussing DOS

Questions and answers
1 Legacy is a term that refers to _____ hardware and software.
2 Which operating system was the first one used by IBM microcomputers?
3 What is the primary use of DOS in computers today?
4 What type of task environment is DOS?

Topic C: Windows operating systems

Explanation

In this section, you'll learn more about the Windows family of operating systems (Windows 9x, NT, 2000, XP, and 2003.) You'll learn about the evolution of the Windows operating systems and some of the corresponding changes in the technology.

Windows 9x

Windows 95, Windows 98, and Windows Me (collectively referred to as Windows 9x) are true 32-bit operating systems; however, they don't completely eliminate DOS. Windows 95 is a combination of Windows for Workgroups (Windows 3.11) with an updated DOS core, as well as some completely new additions and improvements to the operating system. Windows 95 also introduced an improved and more automated method of installing new hardware devices, called Plug and Play.

Windows 98 and Window Me were updates to Windows 95. These operating systems added some new features, but both retain the fundamental DOS core and are a blend of low- and high-end technologies. These operating systems fulfill the Microsoft commitment to be *backward-compatible* with older software and hardware while still taking advantage of newer technology.

An example of a Windows 9x interface, a desktop for Windows 98 Second Edition (SE), is shown in Exhibit 1-11. This interface shows the Control Panel window, which provides a centralized location from which to administer hardware, software, and system settings. In addition, the Start and Programs menus are open. These features appear much the same on other Windows 9x desktops.

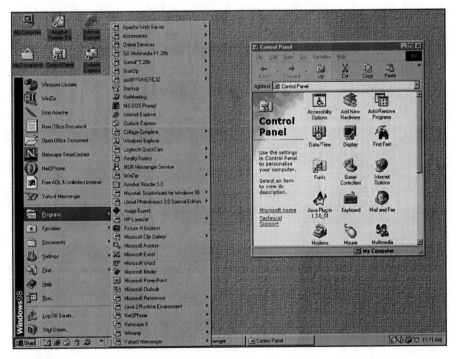

Exhibit 1-11: The Windows 98 SE desktop

Hardware requirements

The following table lists the hardware requirements of Windows 9x. Note that the table gives the recommended minimum to run each version of Windows 9x.

Hardware	Windows 95	Windows 98	Windows Me
Processor	486 or higher	Pentium	Pentium 150 MHz
RAM	8 MB	24 MB	32 MB
Free hard drive space	50 MB	195 MB	320 MB

Keep in mind that you might find different values in other documentation. System requirements can change depending on whether you're installing on a new system or upgrading an older system, as well as which features you choose to install. Also, sometimes Microsoft lists the minimum requirements to install an OS, which might be different from the requirements to run an OS.

The following table summarizes the advantages and disadvantages of Windows 9x.

Advantages	Disadvantages
Windows 9x offers a very user-friendly and intuitive GUI.	Because of its hardware requirements, Windows 9x can't be used on some older PCs.
Windows 9x offers almost complete backward-compatibility for applications written for DOS and earlier versions of Windows.	Because of the attempt to bridge older and newer technology, there are some problems with failures and errors created in this hybrid environment.
Windows 9x is a mix of older and newer OS technology and allows both older and newer software and hardware to run.	
Windows 9x offers the ability for one PC to talk with another over phone lines without additional software. It works well for low-end network use, such as when two users want to exchange files.	
Disk access time under Windows 9x is improved over DOS and Windows 3.x.	
Plug and Play (PnP) features make installing some new hardware devices easier than with earlier operating systems.	
Windows 9x supports preemptive multitasking. While the hourglass is showing on the window of an application, you can make another application active by clicking on its window.	
Because it's the most popular OS today, many users are comfortable with it and are reluctant to change.	

Windows 9x vs. Windows 3.x and DOS

Windows 9x is an operating system that bridges two worlds. In Exhibit 1-12, you see that Windows 3.x and DOS constitute a 16-bit world, with memory management centered around base, upper, and extended memory limitations. Windows 9x still has a DOS-based core, uses many 16-bit programs, and must manage memory in fundamentally the same way that DOS does. However, Windows 95 introduced 32-bit programming, a new form of memory paging, networking, and many other features available in Windows NT, 2000, and XP. Windows 9x includes hundreds of *device drivers*, some of which can be loaded as needed. Device drivers are software programs stored on the hard drive that are designed to run an input/output hardware device, such as a monitor or a mouse.

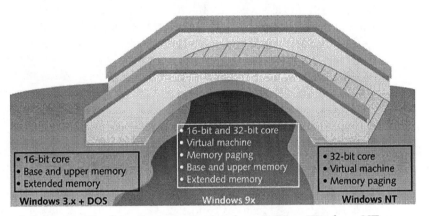

Exhibit 1-12: Windows 9x is the bridge from DOS to Windows NT

Windows 9x claims to be completely backward-compatible with older software and with hardware designed to work in a DOS and Windows 3.x environment. Windows 9x uses cooperative multitasking when supporting 16-bit applications and preemptive multitasking when supporting 32-bit applications.

Windows 98 and Windows Me

Windows 98 was an important upgrade to Windows 95. Windows 98 has significant updates, fixes, and support for new peripherals. Some of the new features included in Windows 98 include:

- **Protection:** Windows 98 includes additional protection for important files on your computer, such as backing up your registry automatically.

- **Improved support:** Improved support for new devices, such as AGP, Direct X, DVD, USB, and MMX.

- **FAT32:** Windows 98 has the capability of converting your drive to FAT32 without loosing any information.

- **Interface:** Windows 98 has the same easy interface that's used in Windows 95 and NT.

- **Plug and Play (PnP):** Improved PnP support, to detect devices even better than Windows 95 does.

- **Customizable taskbar:** Windows add many nice new features to the taskbar that Windows 95 and NT don't have.

- **Active Desktop:** Active Desktop allows users to customize their desktops with the look of the Internet.

Microsoft has produced two upgrades for Windows 98: Windows 98 Second Edition (Windows 98 SE) and Windows Millennium Edition (Windows Me). Each upgrade has significant enhancements over its predecessor.

Windows 98 SE includes several patches, or fixes, for the first edition of Windows 98, updates of existing components, and some new components. Most new features involve improved networking and Internet access. Improved support for ATM networks includes the addition of Point-to-Point Protocol (PPP) over ATM, which allows a dial-up connection over an ATM network. Security for a dial-up connection over regular phone lines is also upgraded. ATM is a high-speed network technology used by wide area networks.

A new feature is *Internet Connection Sharing* (ICS), which makes it possible for a Windows 98 PC to access the Internet through another computer on a local network, so that only one computer requires a direct connection to an ISP. This feature means that several PCs on a small home network can share the same access to an ISP without incurring additional charges and without installing third-party software. Support for modems that use a USB port and support for a wake-on-LAN connection are also included. (A *LAN*, or *local area network*, is a small computer network that's usually confined to a single building or some other geographically small area.) Wake-on-LAN means that a PC can go into a low-power state and then return to standard power when the network card detects activity from another computer on the network.

Note: Microsoft no longer supports Windows 98 and earlier operating systems.

Windows Me is one step closer to the merging of Windows 9x and Windows 2000 because it contains features from each OS, although, at its core, it's still a Windows 9x upgrade. It's designed for home users and not for businesses. It focuses on enhancements to multimedia features, such as support for video cameras, digital cameras, scanners, and a jukebox recorder. It includes a compression utility for video files and a video editor.

True to its goal as a home PC operating system, the OS is very user-friendly, including more informative error messages and troubleshooting utilities.

Note: To learn which version of Windows is installed, right-click the My Computer icon and select Properties from the shortcut menu. The System Properties window opens. Click the General tab.

When deciding to upgrade from one version of Windows 9x to another, if you have the hardware power to support it, you're better off upgrading from Windows 95 to Windows 98, because of the many tools and features that add to the stability of Windows 98. You don't necessarily need to upgrade from Windows 98 to Windows Me unless you need support for multimedia devices.

Windows NT

Windows NT (New Technology) has the look and feel of Windows 95; however, it's a completely different operating system. Although older applications written for DOS might work under Windows NT, Windows NT developers don't guarantee backward-compatibility. Windows NT takes an aggressive and altogether new approach toward managing hardware resources and interfacing with applications software. It completely eliminates the underlying relationship with DOS.

Windows NT supports preemptive multitasking and multiprocessing (two or more CPUs). Windows NT contains advanced security features and advanced network support. Computers called servers are configured to store programs and other computers, called clients, use data remotely.

With client/server arrangements, an organization's resources can be used more effectively, since computers are networked together to share the resources. Windows NT Workstation is designed to run on clients, and Windows NT Server to run servers. The following table summarizes the advantages and disadvantages of Windows NT:

Advantages	Disadvantages
Windows NT is designed to run in powerful client/server environments and targets both the client and the server market.	The hardware requirements of Windows NT eliminate it as a plausible option for older, low-end PCs.
Windows NT offers a completely new file management system, different from earlier Windows operating systems.	Windows NT isn't compatible with some older hardware and software.
Windows NT Workstation offers both networking over a LAN and dial-up connections over phone lines.	Windows NT doesn't use some of the technologies or have the newer features used by Windows 2000 and XP, including Safe Mode, Plug and Play, USB support, Device Manager, and FAT32.
Windows NT Server offers powerful security, both as a file server and for network administration.	Windows NT is largely outdated and replaced by Windows 2000.
Windows NT supports preemptive multitasking and multiprocessing.	

Goals of Windows NT

Windows NT was conceived when IBM and Microsoft collaborated in building OS/2. While IBM took over OS/2, Microsoft redesigned the original code and called the new operating system Windows NT. The next evolutions of the Windows NT operating system are Windows 2000, Windows XP, and Windows Server 2003. The Windows operating systems have many of the same objectives as UNIX and are considered the primary competitors to UNIX in the client/server industry. Because current versions of Windows also function on a LAN, Novell considers them competitors of NetWare software, which is popular for managing LANs. Finally, current versions of Windows compete for some of the standalone PC market, contending with Windows 9x, Linux, and the Mac OS.

In this discussion about the goals of Windows NT, the information given also applies to Windows 2000, Windows XP, and Windows Server 2003. For an operating system to contend for so many markets, it needs to meet many goals.

Expandability

Windows NT is designed for expandability, so it can more easily accommodate new hardware and software. The main way that NT does this is by using a modular approach to performing tasks. For example, DOS and Windows 9x allow applications to have direct access to memory, but Windows NT, 2000, XP, and 2003 don't allow an application direct access to memory or other hardware devices. Applications are required to pass their requests to NT, which processes them and gives the application as much memory as it requests, if that memory isn't currently being used by other applications. Because of this layer of protection between software and hardware, an application is insulated from hardware changes. When hardware requirements change, Windows NT manages the change.

A disadvantage to this approach is that Windows NT must have an interface with all new device drivers before any application operating under Windows NT can use a new device.

Portability to different platforms

Because of Windows NT's modular approach, it easily ports to various platforms or hardware configurations, including various CPU technologies. The Windows NT installation CD-ROM comes with three directories ready to accommodate three separate CPU technologies. For Intel-based CPUs, the directory on the CD is \i386. Windows NT can accommodate several CPU technologies, because it isolates some parts of the OS from other parts in a modular fashion.

The part of the operating system that interacts with the hardware is the *HAL* (*hardware abstraction layer*), which is the layer between the OS and the hardware. The HAL is available in various versions, each designed to address the specifics of a particular CPU technology. The HAL is the only part of the OS that has to change when platforms change. The other components of the OS don't need to be changed when the platform changes.

OS and legacy software compatibility

Generally, Windows NT doesn't support legacy devices, older computer devices that don't use current technology. As long as DOS applications don't attempt to access resources directly, they can run under Windows NT.

Security

Windows NT provides security similar to that of UNIX systems, which is greater than that found in Windows 9x. Windows NT security features include the following:

- The requirement that a user have a logon ID and password to gain access to the PC
- Security between users on the same PC, so that one user can block another user from data or software
- Auditing trails to identify security breaches
- Memory protection between different applications loaded at the same time

Performance and reliability

Although no operating system is fault-proof, the current versions of Windows provide a much more stable environment than many other operating systems, such as Windows 9x. These versions are less likely to hang or lock up than other PC operating systems are. If an application stalls, other applications also loaded are less likely to be affected.

Windows NT vs. Windows 9x

When comparing Windows NT and Windows 9x, remember the following two important points. First, if Windows NT is installed on a PC that isn't as powerful as the type of computer it's designed to run on, Windows NT doesn't perform as well as Windows 9x would on that PC. However, on a powerful workstation PC with a configuration recommended for Windows NT, Windows NT usually performs faster and better than Windows 9x. The second important point is that Windows NT isn't another evolution of DOS, Windows 3.x, and Windows 9x. In fact, the opposite is true. Windows NT was developed before Windows 95. Windows 95 and its upgrade, Windows 98, were built as a bridge between the old DOS with Windows 3.x and the new Windows NT.

While Windows 9x and Windows NT Workstation differ dramatically in underlying architecture and structure, they share many features, including a similar user interface, some of the same utilities, such as Internet Explorer and Microsoft Messaging, and other features, such as system policies, user profiles, and hardware profiles.

Windows NT Workstation offers higher performance, reliability, and security than does Windows 9x. On the other hand, Windows 9x has less demanding hardware requirements, offers broad application and device compatibility, and works well on notebook PCs because of better power management features and Plug and Play (PnP) capability.

The key to appreciating the advantage that Windows NT has over Windows 9x is in the platforms and settings that Windows NT targets. Windows NT is designed to satisfy the needs of powerful workstations networked in a corporate environment. Windows 9x, however, is used on low-end PCs dominating the home market, where multimedia application software and ease of installation are more of an issue than network security and high-end performance.

Note: As with Windows 98, Microsoft no longer supports Windows NT.

One major difference between Windows 9x and Windows NT is that Windows NT is a full 32-bit operating system, operating in protected mode as soon as it receives control from BIOS. Windows 9x begins the boot process in real mode and loads some real-mode components before shifting to protected mode. Windows 9x supports real-mode device drivers; Windows NT doesn't allow them. The following table lists the major differences between Windows NT and Windows 9x:

Feature	Windows 9x	Windows NT
Hardware requirements	Low, requiring a 486 PC with 8 to 16 MB of RAM	High, requiring a Pentium with 16 to 32 MB of RAM
Hardware compatibility	Supports most legacy devices	Supports most current devices, but doesn't claim backward-compatibility with legacy devices
Software compatibility	Fully backward-compatible with older DOS and Windows 3.x applications	No support for any application that attempts to access hardware directly
Installation	Offers Plug and Play capability	Does not offer Plug and Play and offers less device driver support
Power management	Built-in power management for laptops	None
Performance	Offers preemptive multitasking for 32-bit applications and cooperative multitasking for 16-bit applications	Also offers preemptive multitasking for 32-bit applications and cooperative multitasking for 16-bit applications. Has significantly better performance on systems with at least 32 MB of RAM
Reliability and stability	Much better than Windows 3.x	Very high reliability and stability; all applications run in protected memory space
Security	Provides increased security over Windows 3.x by offering user profiles and screensaver passwords.	Very high security down to the file level

Windows NT Workstation includes the following features:

- **Desktop performance:** Supports a powerful multitasking environment and multiple microprocessors.
- **Hardware profiles:** Can maintain separate hardware profiles for different hardware configurations on the same PC.
- **Internet Explorer:** Provides a built-in Web browser, Internet Explorer.
- **Peer Web services:** Provides a personal Web server.
- **Security:** Provides security for individual files, folders, and other resources. User access to a PC's resources can be controlled by user IDs and passwords on the standalone PC or managed from a network controller.
- **Stability:** Uses protective processing, which prevents applications from causing errors in other applications or in Windows NT itself.

Many of these same features, including Internet Explorer, hardware profiles, and user access, are available from Windows 9x as well.

Hardware requirements

The minimum hardware requirements for Windows NT on an IBM-compatible PC are listed below. However, even though Windows NT does run on this minimum hardware configuration, remember that you need a powerful high-end PC to experience the full benefits of Windows NT.

- Pentium-compatible processor or higher
- 16 MB of RAM (32 MB is recommended)
- 125 MB of hard disk space

While the minimum requirements listed above refer to IBM-compatible machines, Windows NT can run on other computers as well, providing the same interface and functionality. The main difference between Windows NT running on an Intel CPU and Windows NT on other microprocessors is in the HAL. The hardware platforms supported by Windows NT are listed below.

- Intel x86-based (486 or higher) processor
- MIPS R4x00-based processor
- Alpha AXP-based processor
- PReP-compliant PowerPC-based processor

Hardware supported by Windows NT

Windows NT doesn't support many hardware devices. For this reason, before you decide to install Windows NT, determine if all components on your PC will work under Windows NT. For instance, you might have to replace a network card, modem, video card, and so on, before these devices work with Windows NT. To determine if Windows NT supports a hardware component, see the *hardware compatibility list (HCL)* for Windows NT that comes with the software.

The most recent copy of the Windows NT HCL is available on the Microsoft Web site at:

```
https://winqual.microsoft.com/download/default.asp
```

The Windows NT HCL list shows the hardware category and then lists the supported hardware devices and manufacturer. If a device is not on the list, ask the manufacturer if there's a driver specifically for Windows NT, not just Windows 9x. If no driver exists, this device won't work under Windows NT.

The Windows NT desktop

Beginning with Windows NT 4.0, the Windows NT desktop took on a look and feel similar to that of Windows 9x. Exhibit 1-13 shows the Windows NT desktop with the Start menu and Control Panel, both of which work just as they do in Windows 9x, although some Control Panel icons are different.

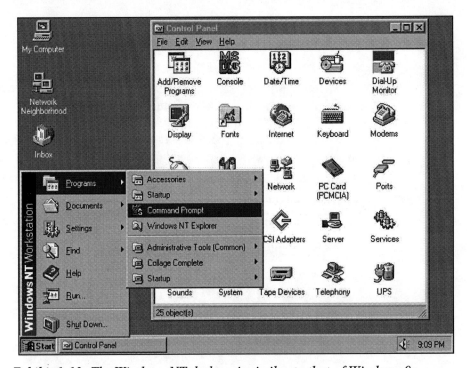

Exhibit 1-13: The Windows NT desktop is similar to that of Windows 9x

The Windows NT command prompt

Another similarity between Windows NT and Windows 9x is the command prompt that allows the user to enter DOS-like commands. To access the command prompt, click Start, and then choose Programs, Command Prompt, as shown in Exhibit 1-13. The Command Prompt window opens, as shown in Exhibit 1-14. From the command prompt, you can enter DOS-like commands.

In Windows 9x, the DOS prompt is actually accessing a version of DOS. In Windows NT, however, the Command Prompt interface is provided as a convenience for those wanting to use familiar DOS-like commands. There are no actual DOS programs underlying and running under Windows NT.

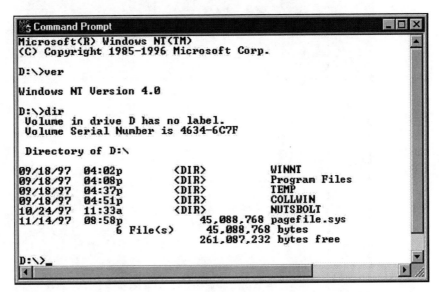

Exhibit 1-14: The Windows NT command prompt uses DOS-like commands

Choosing between Windows 9x and Windows NT

Although there's still a large installed base of Windows NT, it's now outdated, having been superseded by Windows 2000 and Windows XP. In most situations, you wouldn't choose to install Windows NT on a new system or upgrade from Windows 9x to Windows NT. Rather, you would be making the decision to choose between Windows 9x and Windows 2000 or Windows 9x and Windows XP. However, if you happen to be in a situation where you're forced to decide between Windows 9x and Windows NT as your PC OS, consider the following:

- Does Windows NT support all the hardware devices on your PC? Check the hardware compatibility list.

- Is the PC powerful and big enough to support Windows NT? See the hardware requirements listed, and then allow extra resources for your applications.

- Will the software you intend to use on the PC work better under Windows 98 or Windows NT? Running older DOS and Windows 16-bit applications might be a problem in a Windows NT environment. Verify that your current, older software works under Windows NT, or plan to replace the current software with 32-bit versions. Be aware, however, that some 32-bit programs written for Windows 9x might not work under Windows NT because of differences in the API calls to the operating system. An *API (application programming interface)* is a method by which one program calls another program to perform a task.

Windows 2000

Windows 2000 is actually a suite of operating systems, each designed for a different-sized computer system. The Windows 2000 desktop, as shown in Exhibit 1-15, is similar to the Windows 9x and NT desktops. Windows 2000 is built on the Windows NT architecture and was designed ultimately to replace both Windows 9x for low-end systems and Windows NT for midrange and high-end systems. For the most part, Windows 2000 has already replaced Windows NT, and Windows XP is slowly replacing Windows 2000 and Windows 9x.

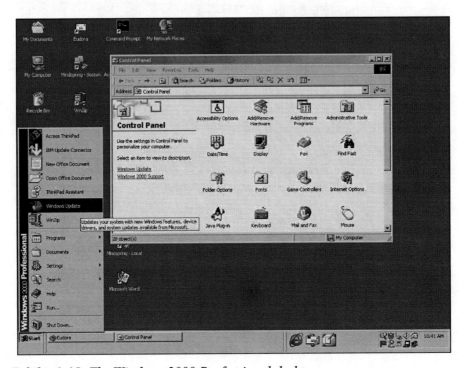

Exhibit 1-15: The Windows 2000 Professional desktop

Windows 2000 includes four operating systems:

- **Windows 2000 Professional:** This was designed to replace both Windows 9x and Windows NT Workstation as a personal computer desktop or notebook OS. It's an improved version of Windows NT Workstation, using the same new technological approach to hardware and software, and includes all the popular features of Windows 9x, including Plug and Play.

- **Windows 2000 Server:** This is the improved version of Windows NT Server and is designed as a network operating system for low-end servers.

- **Windows 2000 Advanced Server:** This is a network operating system that has the same features as Windows 2000 Server but is designed to run on more powerful servers.

- **Windows 2000 Datacenter Server:** This is a network operating system that's another step up from Windows 2000 Advanced Server. This operating system is used by large enterprise operations centers.

Hardware and software must qualify for all the Windows 2000 products, just as they must qualify for Windows NT. For hardware, check Hardware Compatibility at the following Web site:

```
www.microsoft.com/whdc/hcl/search.mspx
```

You can search by product and in product categories for hardware devices supported by Windows 2000 and Windows Me. If a device isn't on the list, ask the manufacturer if there's a driver specifically for Windows 2000.

For software applications, search the list of compatible software applications at the following Web site:

```
www.microsoft.com/windows2000/professional/howtobuy/upgrading/
compat/default.asp
```

The following table compares the hardware specifications for Windows 2000 products.

Hardware requirement category	Windows 2000 version			
	Professional	**Server**	**Advanced Server**	**Datacenter Server**
Minimum processor (CPU) required	133 MHz Pentium-compatible	133 MHz Pentium-compatible	133 MHz Pentium-compatible	133 MHz or higher
Minimum hard drive size	2 GB	2 GB	2 GB	2 GB
Minimum hard drive free space	650 MB	1 GB	1 GB	1 GB
Minimum RAM	64 MB	128 MB minimum supported; 256 MB minimum recommended	128 MB minimum supported; 256 MB minimum recommended	256 MB
Maximum RAM supported	4 GB	4 GB	8 GB	64 GB
Maximum CPUs in one system	2	4	8	32

Windows 2000 vs. Windows 98

Windows 2000 was built on Windows NT and is basically the next evolution of Windows NT with the added user-friendly features of Windows 98. In most cases, you would choose Windows XP rather than Windows 2000 for the corporate desktop or home market. However, if you must select between Windows 2000 and Windows 98, Windows 2000 is a better choice for the corporate desktop, and Windows 98 is the better choice for the home PC. Because of the power management improvements that Windows 2000 has over Windows 98, Windows 2000 is the best choice for notebook computers. For the business environment, Windows 2000 offers better support for very large hard drives, more security, and better reliability. For home users, Windows 98 works best with games, music, and video, and offers the best support for most hardware and software products.

The following table summarizes the advantages and disadvantages of Windows 2000:

Advantages	Disadvantages
Windows 2000 provides powerful support to a network, including advanced security for the network and the ability to organize access to network resources in a centralized location on the network called an Active Directory.	Just as with Windows NT, Windows 2000 hardware requirements disqualify it as an option for an older, low-end PC operating system.
Windows 2000 is backward-compatible with all Windows NT and Windows 9x applications and most Windows 3.x and DOS applications.	Windows 2000 is not scalable. Rather than having one OS that can easily handle a major computer system upgrade, the user must purchase one version of Windows 2000 for a small system and another to handle the upgraded system.
Windows 2000 is really four operating systems, each targeting a different-sized computer and different computing needs, thus making the OS suite extremely versatile.	Although the perception of Windows as a high-end network operating system is changing, traditionally Windows hasn't been as stable as the Unix operating system for large enterprise use.

Reliability

Windows 2000 is more reliable than Windows 98. The Windows File Protection feature of Windows 2000 prevents Windows system files and device drivers from being overwritten by faulty application installation programs or deleted by users, which prevents corruption and improves system reliability. By contrast, Windows 98 doesn't always ask for your permission before allowing an application to alter or overwrite a critical system file. Also, Windows 2000 has some new tools to help application developers build installation files for their products and troubleshoot application problems.

Security

Windows 2000 offers better security than previous operating systems. The *NTFS (NT file system)* developed for Windows NT and used by Windows 2000 and Windows XP gives better security. Windows 2000 has its own data encryption system and uses Kerberos (a security standard) to encrypt a user ID and password as the user logs on to the network from a Windows 2000 workstation. None of these features is available under Windows 98.

Personalized Start menu

Windows 2000 includes a personalized Start menu that shows only the applications used most often, so that the menus aren't cluttered with applications seldom used. See Exhibit 1-16. The down arrows indicate that there are more applications in the list but they're hidden from view. To see these applications, hold your mouse pointer over the menu for a brief moment.

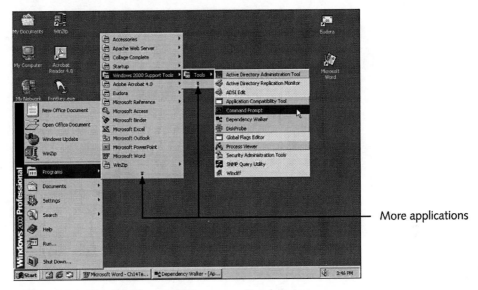

Exhibit 1-16: The Windows 2000 personalized Start menu

Power use

Windows 2000 and Windows 98 use the *Advanced Configuration and Power Interface (ACPI)*, which enables a computer to power down unused devices to conserve power and gives the user much more control over power to the system. The Windows 2000 ACPI features are improved over those of Windows 98. Both require the cooperation of an ACPI-compliant motherboard. For example, on a PC with an ACPI motherboard, to set the Power Options, open the Control Panel as shown in Exhibit 1-17.

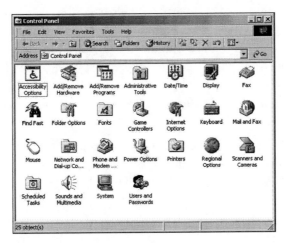

Exhibit 1-17: Windows 2000 Control Panel

Double-click the Power Options icon. The Power Options Properties dialog box opens. Click the Advanced tab, as shown in Exhibit 1-18. From the list of power options, select what happens when you press the power button on your computer case. For example, you can set the computer to change to Standby mode when you press the power button. On the Hibernate tab, you can also control when and how the system goes into hibernation, a state whereby little power is used but open applications are restored the next time you power up.

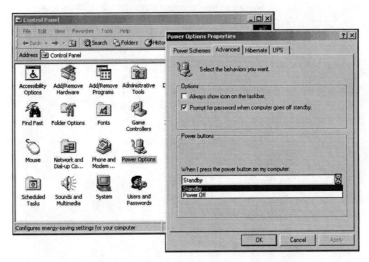

Exhibit 1-18: The Power Options properties dialog box

Compaq, Intel, Microsoft, Phoenix, and Toshiba developed the ACPI specifications to allow for reliable power management through hardware and software cooperation.

Added notebook computer features

The following features are available for notebook computers using Windows 2000 but are not a part of Windows 98:

- **Offline files and folders** – allow you to download files and folders from a network to the PC so you can work on them offline. When the PC is later connected to the network, the files and folders can be uploaded to the network so that any changes are kept current on the network.

- **Virtual private network technology** – allows a notebook user to work from home and connect to the corporate network over the Internet in a secure connection. To do so, Windows 2000 encrypts data before it's transmitted over the Internet.

- **Power management features** – allows notebook users to manage their power in a more efficient manner.

Windows 2000 Professional is designed as a desktop client computer operating system for a large network in a corporate or educational environment. Windows 98 is best used on a PC in a home or on a small network. Finally, for a notebook computer, Windows 2000 is the best choice.

Windows 2000 and Windows NT

Windows 2000 is the upgrade of Windows NT. It contains the same core technology and provides a number of new capabilities. Windows 2000 supports the FAT16, FAT32, and NTFS file systems. The Windows 2000 registry is organized and edited in the same way as the Windows NT registry. Utilities, such as Event Viewer and Dr. Watson, also work the same way with minor changes. Windows 2000 provides an encrypted file system for added security and support for virtual private networks, secure connections over the Internet between a person and a business or between two businesses. Windows 2000 Help and Troubleshooter utilities are much more comprehensive than the Windows NT or Windows 98 utilities. Windows 2000 supports multiple monitors, IEEE 1394 (FireWire), USB, and ACPI.

Windows NT doesn't support Plug and Play. Windows 2000 uses an advanced version of Plug and Play that does all the work for configuring a system and doesn't use the Plug and Play features of a motherboard.

Do it!

C-1: Comparing Windows versions

Here's how	Here's why
1 Open your browser	
Enter the following URL:	
`www.microsoft.com`	
2 What Product Families are listed?	
3 Choose **Support**, **Knowledge Base**	The Search the Knowledge Base page appears. The Microsoft Knowledge Base is a collection of information, grouped into articles, about different products and common errors.
4 From the Select a Microsoft Product list, select **Windows 98**	
5 In the Search for box, enter **troubleshooting**	
6 In the Using list, select **All of the words entered**	To specify the search options.
7 Leave all other options as they appear by default	
8 Click **Go**	

9 List the titles of the first three articles that appear as a result of your search

   Take a look at any of the articles

   Return to Microsoft home page   When you've finished examining the articles.

10 Under Product Families, Click **Windows**

   What versions of Windows are listed in the upper-left corner of the page?

11 Point to **Previous Versions**

   What Previous Versions of Windows do you see listed?

12 Click **Windows 95**

   Click **Get the latest info**

   Under Highlights & Top Issues, click **Before You Install**

13 Under Windows 95, click **Windows 95 Installation Requirements**

14 Click **Print** on the browser toolbar   To print the page information on the system requirements for Windows 95.

   Verify that the correct printer is selected

   Click **OK**

15 Search the system requirements for Windows XP   On the site.

   Print the information

16 Enter the following URL: In the address bar of your browser.

```
www.microsoft.com/whdc/hcl/default.mspx
```

To open the Windows Hardware and Driver Central site.

Click **Windows Millennium Edition and Windows 2000: See the Hardware Compatibility List (HCL)**

17 In the In list, select **Display**

Click **Search Now**

Observe the resulting list

18 What information is available in the HCL?

19 What are the minimum system requirements for Windows XP?

Windows XP

Explanation   Windows XP is an integration of Windows 9x and Windows 2000 Professional, while providing added support for digital and networking technologies. The two main versions are Windows XP Home and Windows XP Professional.

Both editions have these features, among others:

- A new user interface, as shown in Exhibit 1-19. Notice how different it looks from the desktops for earlier Windows versions such as Windows 9x and Windows 2000.
- The ability for two users to log on simultaneously, both with their own applications open
- Windows Media Player for Windows XP, which provides a centralized application for working with digital media
- Windows Messenger for instant messaging, conferencing, and application sharing
- An expanded Help feature
- Advanced security features

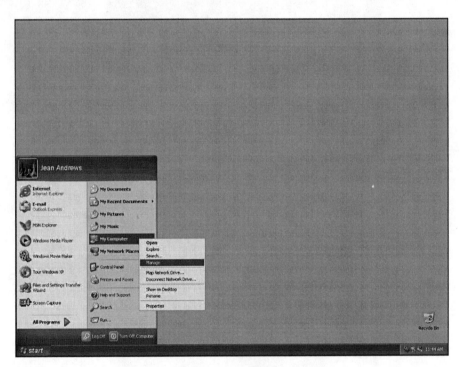

Exhibit 1-19: The Windows XP desktop and Start menu

Here are some of the features that Windows XP Professional adds to the home edition:

- Features for remote access, including remote desktop and roaming user profiles
- Additional security features
- Multilingual capabilities
- Support for new higher performance processors

There is also Windows XP 64-bit Edition designed to be used with a high-end CPU such as the Intel Itanium. This version of Windows XP is designed mostly for servers or heavily technical workstation users who need greater amounts of memory and higher performance than standard desktop users, for example, for scientific and engineering applications. For instance, an aircraft designer who needs to simulate how various conditions affect aircraft materials might use Windows XP on a system supporting resource-intensive simulation and animation applications.

Windows Internet Explorer, Windows Media Player, a firewall, and other Microsoft products are tightly integrated into the Windows XP operating system.

The minimum requirements for Windows XP Professional are:

- A minimum of 64 MB of RAM, with 128 MB recommended
- At least 1.5 GB of free hard drive space, with 2 GB recommended
- A CPU that runs at least 233 MHz, with a 300 MHz CPU recommended. Remember that Windows XP can support two CPUs.

Note: The requirements of an operating system vary, depending on which version you've installed and what applications and hardware you've installed with it.

Windows XP provides several enhancements over Windows 2000 and other earlier versions. The following table summarizes the advantages and disadvantages of Windows XP:

Advantages	Disadvantages
Provides better integration of Windows 9x and NT than Windows 2000 did	Requires nearly a gigabyte of hard drive space for the operating system itself, and at least a 233 MHz processor with 64 MB of RAM
Offers significant GUI enhancements over earlier versions of Windows	Programs used with Windows XP may require more than the minimum system specifications for the operating system
Adds features but uses only slightly more total memory for the OS than Windows 2000 does	
Adds advanced file sorting options, such as sorting pictures by resolution or sound files by artist	Nearly eliminates support for device drivers not approved by Microsoft
Includes built-in support for compressed files	Security concerns with centralized storage of online information in Microsoft Passport, a repository of the user IDs and passwords you use on the Internet
Has improved troubleshooting tools and is generally more stable than previous Windows operating systems	

Windows XP vs. previous Windows operating systems

Windows XP is replacing all previous versions of Windows in the home market and for the corporate desktop.

If your hardware and applications qualify, select Windows XP Home Edition for a home PC over Windows 98/Me. For a corporate environment, use Windows XP Professional over Windows NT/2000. The only exception to this is when Windows XP isn't compatible with older hardware and software.

The Windows Catalogs are replacing the HCL. You can view the Windows Catalog for Windows XP at the following Web site:

```
www.microsoft.com/windows/catalog/
```

The Windows XP Windows Catalog is shown in Exhibit 1-20.

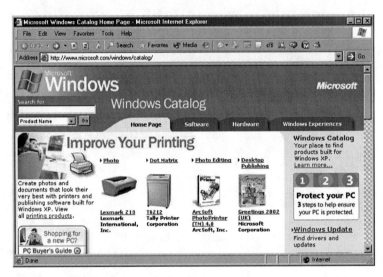

Exhibit 1-20: Windows Catalog

Click the Hardware tab and then select the type of hardware to see if your hardware is listed.

Do it!

C-2: Determining Windows XP hardware compatibility

Here's how	Here's why
1 Open **Control Panel**	You want to use Device Manager to inventory your system.
Double-click **System**	
2 Select the **Device Manager** tab for Windows 9x	The Device Manager window opens.
3 Click the **+** to the left of Display Adapters	To see what kind of video adapter is installed on your system. Devices are arranged by categories in Device Manager.

4 Select your video adapter

    Click **Properties**   Information about the adapter's model and manufacturer appears.

    Record the information

5 Use Device Manager to find similar information for your network adapter, modem card, or sound card

    Record the information

6 Open your browser   You want to check the Windows Catalog to determine if Windows XP supports these devices.

    Enter the following URL

    `www.microsoft.com/windows/catalog/`

    Click **Hardware**

7 Choose **Cameras and Video, Video Cards**

    Browse for your video card   If you don't find your card, Windows XP probably doesn't support it.

8 Check the other devices in your list

    Record whether they're compatible with Windows XP

9 Explain how to compile a list of devices installed on your system.

10 How are devices grouped in Device Manager?

11 What does HCL stand for?

12 What is replacing the HCL?

13 If a device isn't listed in the Windows Catalog, what are your options when installing Windows XP? List at least two possibilities.

14 Does the hardware in your system qualify for Windows XP? If it doesn't qualify, explain why.

Windows Server 2003

Explanation

Windows Server 2003 includes all the functionality customers expect from a mission-critical Windows Server operating system, such as security, reliability, availability, and scalability. In addition, Microsoft has improved and extended the Windows server product family to enable organizations to experience the benefits of Microsoft .NET—a set of software for connecting information, people, systems, and devices.

Editions

Windows Server 2003 is available in the following four editions:

- **Standard edition:** The ideal multipurpose network operating system for the everyday needs of organizations of all sizes, but especially small businesses and workgroups.
- **Enterprise edition:** This edition builds on the capabilities of the Standard edition by adding reliability features needed for business-critical applications.
- **Datacenter edition:** This edition is built for mission-critical applications that demand the highest levels of scalability, availability, and reliability.
- **Web edition:** This edition is designed for building and hosting Web applications, pages, and services and is available only through selected Microsoft partner channels.

In addition, Microsoft offers the following two special editions of Windows Server 2003:

- **64-bit versions:** The 64-bit versions of the Enterprise edition and Datacenter edition support larger amounts of memory and enable memory-intensive applications to achieve the highest levels of performance and scalability.
- **Windows Small Business Server 2003:** This edition integrates e-mail, fax, database, and shared Internet into one powerful platform that's easy to deploy.

System requirements

The following table describes the minimum and recommended system requirements needed to run each of the Windows Server 2003 editions.

Note: The 64-bit versions of Windows Server 2003, Enterprise edition and Windows Server 2003, Datacenter edition are compatible only with 64-bit Intel Itanium-based systems. They can't be successfully installed on 32-bit systems.

Hardware requirement category	Windows Server 2003 version			
	Standard	**Enterprise**	**Datacenter**	**Web**
Minimum CPU speed	133 MHz	133 MHz for x86-based computers	400 MHz for x86-based computers	133 MHz
		733 MHz for Itanium-based computers	733 MHz for Itanium-based computers	
Recommended CPU speed	550 MHz	733 MHz	733 MHz	550 MHz
Minimum RAM	128 MB	128 MB	512 MB	128 MB
Recommended minimum RAM	256 MB	256 MB	1 GB	256 MB
Maximum RAM	4 GB	32 GB for x86-based computers	64 GB for x86-based computers	2 GB
		64 GB for Itanium-based computers	512 GB for Itanium-based computers	
Multiprocessor support	Up to 4	Up to 8	Minimum 8-way capable machine required	Up to 2
			Maximum 64	
Disk space for setup	1.5 GB	1.5 GB for x86-based computers	1.5 GB for x86-based computers	1.5 GB
		2.0 GB for Itanium-based computers	2.0 GB for Itanium-based computers	

Upgrading to Windows Server 2003

Built on the reliable Windows 2000 Server family, Windows Server 2003 integrates a powerful application environment to develop innovative XML Web services and improved applications that dramatically improve process efficiency. Here are the major new features and improvements for organizations considering upgrading to Windows Server 2003 from Windows 2000 Server.

Active Directory improvements

Introduced in Windows 2000, the Microsoft Active Directory service simplifies the administration of complex network directories and makes it easy for users to locate resources on even the largest networks. This enterprise-class directory service is scalable and fully integrated at the operating-system level in Windows Server 2003, Standard, Enterprise, and Datacenter editions.

Windows Server 2003 provides new Active Directory features including cross-forest trusts, the ability to rename domains, and the ability to deactivate attributes and classes in the schema so that their definitions can be changed.

Group Policy Management Console

Administrators can use Group Policy to define the settings and allowed actions for users and computers. In contrast with local policy, organizations can use Group Policy to set policies that apply across a given site, domain, or organizational unit in Active Directory. The Group Policy Management Console (GPMC), a Windows Server 2003 add-in component, provides the new framework for managing Group Policy.

Resultant Set of Policy

The Resultant Set of Policy (RSoP) tool, a set of Microsoft Management Console (MMS) snap-ins, allows administrators to see the effect of Group Policy on a targeted user or computer. With RSoP, organizations have a powerful and flexible base-level tool to plan, monitor, and troubleshoot Group Policy.

Volume Shadow Copy service

The Volume Shadow Copy service lets administrators configure point-in-time copies of critical data volumes without interrupting service. These copies can then be used for service restoration or archival purposes. Users can retrieve archived versions of their documents that are invisibly maintained on the server.

Internet Information Services 6.0

Internet Information Services (IIS) 6.0 is a full-featured Web server that enables Web applications and XML Web services. Now, IIS can isolate an individual Web application or multiple sites into a self-contained process, called an application pool, that communicates directly with the operating system kernel

Integrated .NET Framework

The Microsoft .NET Framework is the programming model of Microsoft .NET-connected software and technologies for building, deploying, and running Web applications, smart client applications, and XML Web services that expose their functionality programmatically over a network using standard protocols such as SOAP, XML, and HTTP. With the .NET Framework fully integrated into the Windows Server 2003 operating system, developers are freed from writing "plumbing" code and can instead focus their efforts on delivering real business code.

Command-line management

The Windows Server 2003 family provides a significantly enhanced command-line infrastructure, letting administrators perform most management tasks without using a graphical user interface. Of special importance is the ability to perform a wide range of tasks by accessing the information store enabled by Windows Management Instrumentation (WMI). This WMI command-line (WMIC) feature provides a simple command-line interface that interoperates with existing shells and utility commands and can be easily extended by scripts or other administration-oriented applications.

Overall, the greater command-line functionality in the Windows Server 2003 family, combined with ready-to-use scripts, rivals the power of other operating systems often associated with higher cost of ownership. Administrators accustomed to using the command line to manage UNIX or Linux systems can continue managing from the command line in the Windows Server 2003 family.

Clustering (eight-node support)

Clustering is available only in Windows Server 2003, Enterprise and Datacenter editions. This service provides high availability and scalability for mission-critical applications, such as databases, messaging systems, and file and print services. Clustering works by enabling multiple servers, or nodes, to remain in constant communication. If one of the nodes in a cluster becomes unavailable as a result of failure or maintenance, another node immediately begins providing service, a process known as failover. Users who are accessing the service continue their activities, unaware that service is now being provided from a different server (node).

Emergency Management Services: Headless Server Support

"Headless server" capabilities allow IT administrators to install and manage a computer without a monitor, VGA display adaptor, keyboard, or mouse. Emergency Management Services is a new feature allowing IT administrators to perform remote-management and system recovery tasks when the server is unavailable through the network or other standard remote-administration tools and mechanisms.

Do it!

C-3:   Discussing Windows Server 2003

Questions and answers

1 What Windows Server 2003 editions would you use if you need clustering?

2 What Windows Server 2003 edition would you use if you needed to integrate e-mail, fax, database, and a shared Internet connection?

3 What's the minimum amount of disk space required for setting up Windows Server 2003 Web edition?

4 What's the recommended CPU speed required for Windows Server 2003 Standard edition?

5 What new Active Directory features does Windows Server 2003 provide?

6 What are Headless server capabilities?

Topic D: Other operating systems

Explanation

The following sections compare the other well-known non-Windows operating systems, including their advantages and disadvantages. When choosing an operating system you should consider all the criteria discussed. Your choice should be determined by the size and type of your microcomputer system, your familiarity with the various operating systems, and the application software you plan to use. As you read these sections, keep in mind the four main functions of an operating system (managing hardware, providing a user interface, working with files, and running applications), and notice how each operating system performs these functions differently. As a PC technician, you're likely to see a variety of operating systems on all kinds of personal computers. Windows and non-Windows operating systems share many of the same functions and goals.

In this topic, you'll learn more about UNIX, Linux, OS/2, and Mac OS.

Pay close attention to the advantages and disadvantages of each, as well as comparisons between the technologies.

UNIX

UNIX was originally developed at Bell Laboratories as a private research project by a small group of people starting in 1969. UNIX was originally written for mainframe computers. However, it's now available for many different kinds of computers, including PCs.

In 1984, the University of California at Berkeley released version 4.2BSD, which included a complete implementation of the TCP/IP networking protocols. Systems based on this and later BSD releases provided a multi-vendor networking capability based on Ethernet networking.

As UNIX was ported onto more and more various types of computer hardware, the UNIX networking allowed many different types of systems to share and mutually use data. Networks consisting of many different systems could be used as a large distributed system. As a result, UNIX computers are often used for Internet support. Because there are many versions of UNIX, most problems tend to stem from the lack of consistency from one vendor's version to another. Hardware requirements for UNIX vary widely depending on the version installed.

The following table summarizes the advantages and disadvantages of the UNIX operating system, including comparisons of UNIX and Windows.

Advantages	Disadvantages
UNIX was written for powerful microcomputer systems and has strong multitasking capability, including preemptive multitasking.	UNIX industry standards aren't uniform, making it difficult for UNIX developers, administrators, and users to move from one UNIX vendor to another.
UNIX manages large quantities of memory well.	UNIX requires a powerful, large microcomputer system.
UNIX performs very well in a networking environment.	Few business application software packages are written for UNIX for PCs, although there are several very powerful database packages available under UNIX, such as Informix and Oracle.
UNIX doesn't require as much memory or processor time as Windows does.	
UNIX systems generally don't crash as frequently as Windows systems.	UNIX doesn't include some of the customized applications development and Web publishing features that Windows has.
Design and implementation of UNIX include support for remote management.	

Linux

Linux is an operating system, based on UNIX that was developed by Linus Torvalds and further elaborated by a number of developers throughout the world. Linux is a freely available multitasking and multi-user operating system. While similar to UNIX, Linux is available under a *General Public License* (GPL). The GPL allows open access to the operating system, so it can be distributed, used, and expanded free of charge. Developers have access to all of the source code, so they can easily integrate new functions or quickly find and eliminate programming bugs.

Like UNIX, several companies distribute versions of Linux. Linux versions are called *distributions*. The following companies make popular distributions of Linux:

- SuSE (www.suse.com)
- RedHat (www.redhat.com)
- SCO, formerly Caldera (www.sco.com)
- Mandrake (www.mandrakelinux.com)
- TurboLinux (www.turbolinux.com)

Linux can be used both as a server platform and a desktop platform, but its greatest popularity has come in the server market. Hardware requirements for Linux vary widely, depending on the distribution and version installed.

Note: For more information on Linux, see www.linux.org, as well as the Web sites of the different distributors of Linux.

The following table summarizes the advantages and disadvantages of Linux.

Advantages	Disadvantages
Linux rarely crashes.	Linux can be difficult to install, particularly for users who aren't familiar with UNIX commands.
Basic versions can be downloaded and installed free of charge.	Documentation can be difficult to find.
Linux distributions that include technical support and software packages are available at a lower cost than other operating systems.	Linux can be difficult for casual users to operate.
	Optimizing a Linux system can take a significant investment of time and research.
Linux generally handles network connections better than Windows does.	Not as many applications are available for Linux on the desktop as for Windows.
Source code is available to users, enabling customization of the development environment.	
Linux on an inexpensive PC is an excellent training tool for learning UNIX.	

A computer running the Linux operating system often provides network services, such as a Web server or e-mail server. Linux is well suited to support various types of servers. Because Linux is very reliable and doesn't require a lot of computing power, it's sometimes used as a desktop OS. As a PC support technician, you should know a little about Linux, including a few basic commands.

Because many users prefer a Windows-style desktop, several applications have been written to provide a GUI shell for UNIX and Linux. These shells are called X Windows. A typical X Windows screen (as shown in Exhibit 1-21).

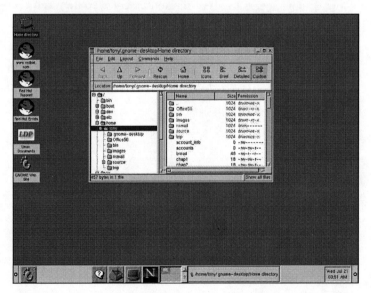

Exhibit 1-21: X Windows software provides a GUI shell for Linux and UNIX users

Do it!

D-1: Investigating Linux

Here's how	Here's why
1 Open your browser	
Enter the following URL	
`www.linux.org`	
Explore the site on your own	
Return to the main page	
2 Click **General Info** on the navigation bar	Answer the following questions using the information on the What is Linux page.
What's the current, full-featured version of Linux?	
Who's credited with inventing the Linux kernel?	
How is Linux licensed?	
Read the GNU General Public License. Give a brief description of its terms and conditions	
How much does Linux cost?	
3 Click **Applications** on the navigation bar	The various types of applications written for Linux are listed by category.
Will the business be able to send faxes from a Linux machine?	
List two Web browsers suitable for Linux	
How many anti-virus software packages are available for Linux? List at least two	
Searching under Office and Word Processor, list at least three word-processing applications that are available for Linux	
How many accounting applications are available for Linux? List at least two and tell where you found them	

4 Click **Documentation** on the
   navigation bar

   Read about the Linux
   Documentation Project

5 Use the information displayed on
   the Linux Web site and answer
   the following questions:

   Give a brief description of the
   Linux Documentation Project

   Who's responsible for writing the
   documentation for the Linux
   Operating System?

6 Return to the Home page

   Scroll down to display the heading
   Linux 101

   Click **more**   To explore the site's Linux tutorial.

7 Click **Getting Started with
   Linux**

   Browse through this tutorial and
   answer the following questions:

   What are the distributions
   (flavors) of Linux, and how are
   they categorized?

   Can you install Linux on a
   computer that has another
   operating system already
   installed? Print the Web page
   supporting your answer

   When preparing to install Linux,
   what's a good computer-use
   practice?

8 Click **Distributions**

Notice that a link to the source code for Linux kernels is available on this page. Also notice the Distribution search area. When searching for a distribution of Linux, if you don't narrow your search, you return a large number of distributions.

From the Language list, select **English**

From the Category list, select **Mainstream/General Public**

From the Platform list, select **Intel compatible**

Click **Go**

9 Record how many distributions you see listed

10 Browse through the list of distributions, looking specifically for Suse, TurboLinux, Linux Mandrake, and Red Hat

List which one claims that it's the most popular distribution

List what user level it's geared for

11 Can Linux be used on systems other than those that run Intel-compatible processors?

Print the Web page supporting your answer

12 What's the least amount of money that you pay for Linux?

13 What's one advantage of using Linux on a desktop rather than a Windows operating system?

14 Based on what you learned from the Linux Web site, how do you think companies that provide Linux make the most profit?

OS/2

Explanation

OS/2, written by IBM in collaboration with Microsoft Corporation, was designed as a replacement for DOS. OS/2 requires at least a 286 processor, 12-16 MB of RAM, and 32 MB of free hard drive space, depending on which features are installed. Many airline ticketing systems, worldwide and local banks, prisons, railroad systems, and U.S. government branches use OS/2. OS/2 never gained popularity for individual PC users. Although some people have predicted the downfall of OS/2 for years, its use continues, and applications are still being written for it. IBM adapted OS/2 for use with Web business solutions, including support for Web server software, Web protocols, and database interaction. The following table summarizes the advantages and disadvantages of OS/2.

Advantages	Disadvantages
OS/2 supports preemptive multitasking.	Relatively few application software packages are written for OS/2.
OS/2 can handle large quantities of memory directly and quickly.	Many microcomputer users aren't familiar with OS/2 and avoid it for that reason.
OS/2 runs many DOS applications better than DOS. It also ran Windows programs better than Windows.	
OS/2 has an icon-driven interface.	
OS/2 works well in a networking environment.	
Software designed for OS/2 sometimes runs more efficiently than comparable Windows programs.	

Macintosh operating system (Mac OS)

The Mac OS is available only on Macintosh computers. Both the computers and the OS were first introduced in 1984. Several versions of the Macintosh OS have been written since, the latest being Mac OS X (ten), which offers easy access to the Internet and allows any Macintosh computer to become a Web server for a small network. Because it's easy to use, the Mac OS has been popular in educational environments from elementary school through the university level. It also provides excellent support for graphics and multimedia applications. Mac OS X requires at least 128 MB of RAM and 1.5 GB of hard drive space.

The Mac OS X interface is significantly different from that of the Mac OS 9, including two new features called the dock and the toolbar, as shown in Exhibit 1-22. When a Mac is turned on, a program called the Finder is automatically launched. This is the program that provides the desktop, which functions as the GUI for the Mac OS. Generally, under normal Mac OS operation, you can't quit the Finder program.

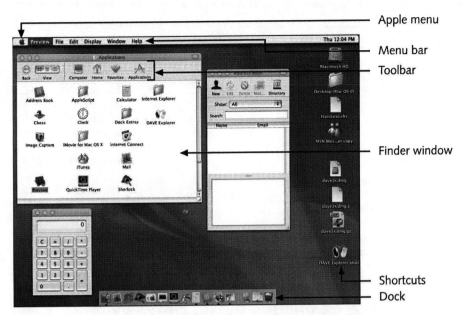

Exhibit 1-22: The Mac OS desktop is intuitive and easy to use

Windows are used to navigate among files and applications in the Mac. The Mac windows function similarly to windows in Microsoft operating systems, in that they can be minimized or maximized, icons can be moved around within them, and the window on top is active when several are open. You can work within one window, using buttons and menu options to navigate between applications and views, or you can open each application or view in a new Finder window.

Before Apple introduced the iMac, most of the Mac OS was permanently stored in Apple ROM, and only Apple had access to that code. This prevented other companies from manufacturing computers to run Macintosh software. With the iMac, Apple moved most of the OS code into an upgradeable file called Mac OS ROM, stored on the hard drive, but it still stores some startup code in a smaller ROM chip. The Mac OS X ROM file contains programs called managers that perform specific system functions, such as keeping track of windows, organizing menus, allocating system resources, and many others. Another important difference between Mac OS X and earlier versions is that the Mac OS X provides support for preemptive multitasking and is thus less likely to freeze versions when several applications are running simultaneously.

The Mac OS X tries to make user interaction with the OS as smooth and as minimal as possible by providing superior Plug and Play capabilities, so that new hardware devices can be added easily and are automatically recognized by the OS. Additionally, the Mac OS doesn't allow users to interact directly with the OS code as some other operating systems do. This can be an advantage because the Mac OS automatically performs certain functions that the user has to perform with other operating systems.

Note: Although the initial cost of setting up a Macintosh system is generally higher than for a comparable IBM-compatible system, the cost of support and maintenance is generally lower for the Mac.

The following table summarizes the advantages and disadvantages of the Macintosh OS.

Advantages	Disadvantages
The Mac OS has an excellent icon-driven interface, and it's easy to learn and use.	Historically, the Macintosh wasn't viewed as a professional computer but rather was relegated to education and game playing. Then the Mac gained a significant place in the professional desktop publishing and graphics markets. Most recently, the availability of more powerful IBM-compatible PCs and operating systems to handle the high demands of graphics has reduced the demand for the Mac.
The Mac OS has supported a GUI interface and Plug and Play devices since it was first developed.	
The Mac OS manages large quantities of memory.	
Many applications exist for the Mac OS to create and edit graphics, build Web sites, and manage multimedia.	Because IBM-compatible PCs have a larger share of the market than Macintosh computers, software compatible with the Mac OS isn't always as readily available.
Mac OS systems are generally less prone to crashing than Windows systems.	

Do it!

D-2: Exploring the Macintosh world

Here's how	Here's why
1 Open your browser	
Enter the following URL:	
`www.apple.com`	
Explore the site on your own	
Return to the main page	
2 Use the various links on the Apple Web site to answer the following questions:	
3 What versions of the Mac operating system currently come preinstalled on the iMac?	
4 What's the cost of upgrading your operating system from OS 9 to OS X?	
5 What are the current speeds or frequencies of the iMac processors?	

6   How much does the iMac (classic design) cost?

7   What software comes bundled with the new iMac?

8   What's an iBook?

9   How much does the most expensive iBook cost?

10 What features are included with the least expensive iBook?

11 Describe the features of the Apple Pro Mouse.

12 What's the function of an AirPort card?

13 What Apple computer can use the AirPort card?

14 What's the purpose of QuickTime software?

15 Describe what AppleWorks software does

16 Describe the purposes of iMovie software

17 What's one advantage of using an Apple computer compared to using a PC?

18 What type of user do you think Apple applications are intended for?

19 Why do you think it's easier for Apple to provide compatibility between its hardware and operating system than it is for Microsoft or Linux to provide similar compatibility?

20 What type of user is the iMac intended for?

Unit summary: Operating systems overview

Topic A   In this topic, you learned the any **operating system** provides four main functions including **hardware management**, **file management**, **user interface**, and **application management**. You learned about the commonly found operating systems, such as **DOS**, **Windows**, **UNIX**, **Linux**, and **Mac OS**. You learned that **shell** and **kernel** are the two main **OS components**. You then learned about some features, such as **multitasking**, **modes**, **environment**, and **files systems**. Next, you learned about different types of user interfaces: **command-driven**, **menu-driven**, and **icon-driven** interfaces.

Topic B   In this topic, you learned about the **Disk Operating System (DOS).** You learned how DOS is now used mostly as a **troubleshooting** tool.

Topic C   In this topic, you learned about various Windows operating systems: **Windows 9x**, **Windows NT**, **Windows 2000**, **Windows XP**, and **Windows Server 2003**. You learned that, although Windows 9x is a complete OS, it retains its **DOS core**. You also learned how Windows 9x uses **multitasking**. You learned the **features**, **advantages**, and **disadvantages** for the various Windows operating systems. You also learned how to check for **hardware compatibility** for Windows NT, 2000, and XP.

Topic D   In this topic, you learned about other operating systems, such as **UNIX**, **Linux**, **OS/2**, and **Macintosh**. You learned about the **features**, **advantages**, and **disadvantages** for each of these operating systems.

Review questions

1 What are the four main functions of an operating system?

2 Name three types of user interfaces.

3 Which Microsoft operating system supports only single tasking?

4 Which Microsoft OS first supported preemptive multitasking?

5 Windows _____ used DOS as its underlying OS, Windows _____ is a true OS but bases its core functions on DOS, and Windows _____ was the first Windows version to sever the connection fully with DOS and create an altogether new OS core.

6 Which Windows OS uses only 16-bit processing?

7 Which Windows operating system uses some 16-bit and some 32-bit processing?

8 Which Windows operating systems use 32-bit processing?

9 Can any versions of Windows use 64-bit processing?

10 A software program stored on the hard drive that's used by the OS to run an input/output hardware device is called a _____.

11 Windows Me is an upgrade of Windows ____.

12 Why doesn't Windows NT guarantee backward compatibility with applications written with older Windows versions?

13 Which Windows operating system doesn't support Plug and Play?

    A Windows 95

    B Windows NT

    C Windows 2000

    D Windows XP

14 What kind of multitasking does Windows NT support?

15 What information can you find on the HCL?

16 What's replacing the HCL for Windows XP?

17 Name the four operating systems in the Windows 2000 suite.

18 Which is a better choice for networks: Windows 9x or Windows 2000?

19 What file systems used to organize a hard drive does Windows 2000 support?

20 What's the name of the Windows database used to hold configuration information?

21 Which is the best choice for notebook computers: Windows 9x, NT, or 2000? Why?

22 Under what circumstances is Windows 98 a better choice for a home computer user than Windows 2000?

23 Name at least two advantages of Windows XP over earlier versions of Windows.

24 Name two Windows operating systems that support USB ports. Name one Windows OS that doesn't support USB.

25 In documentation, why is there sometimes a discrepancy in the hardware requirements listed for an OS?

26 What was UNIX originally written for? How is it used today?

27 How is true multitasking achieved?

28 Name an OS that doesn't have a built-in GUI.

29 What are two features on the Mac OS X desktop that weren't present in OS 9?

30 What are two popular uses for Mac OS?

31 What type of multi-tasking was performed by Windows 3.x?

32 What versions of Windows are referred to by the term Windows 9x?

33 Software programs stored on the hard drive that are designed to run input/output hardware devices are known as _____.

34 In Windows NT, the NT stands for _____.

35 Windows NT utilizes plug and play technology. True or False?

36 Home PC users generally should choose Windows 98 over Windows NT for home use. True or False?

37 What's the name of the latest version of the Windows operating system for desktop PCs?

38 What editions are available for Windows Server 2003?

39 What user-friendly feature helps install hardware in Windows 2000 and XP?

40 The latest version of the Windows operating system requires at least 1.5GB of free hard disk space. True or False?

Unit 2

Hardware and software management

Unit time: 90 minutes

Complete this unit, and you'll know how to:

A Describe computer system hardware and the software needed to make it operate and perform tasks.

B Describe how the operating system interacts with other software, such as application software, the BIOS, and device drivers.

C Explain how the operating system loads, initializes, and starts application software.

Topic A: Hardware management

Explanation

As shown in Exhibit 2-1, software controls hardware at the direction of a user. There are several layers of software needed to make a computer system operate and perform tasks. You see these in Exhibit 2-1 as application software, the operating system, and BIOS and device drivers.

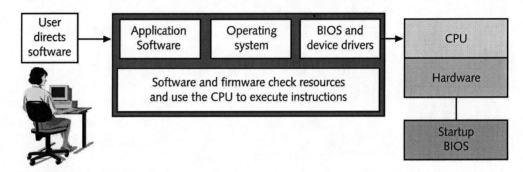

Exhibit 2-1: Software needed to make computer hardware operate

Device drivers and BIOS are software written to interface with specific hardware devices. The *BIOS (basic input/output system)* is permanently stored on microchips.

The BIOS that the operating system uses to help manage the system is called *system BIOS* and is stored on a BIOS chip on the motherboard. Device drivers are stored on the hard drive until needed and are generally first added to the system as part of the device installation process.

Device drivers can come from a device manufacturer, or an operating system can use its own device drivers, as shown in Exhibit 2-2.

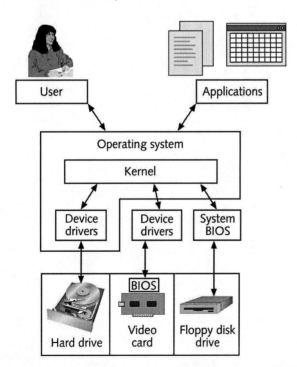

Exhibit 2-2: An OS relates to hardware by way of BIOS or device drivers

One advantage of using BIOS and device drivers as an interface with hardware is that it frees the operating system and application software from having to know the specifics of how to communicate with a device.

For example, various printers understand data and commands according to various sets of rules and standards called protocols. Application software and the operating system can pass print requests to the printer driver, which communicates with the printer, as shown in Exhibit 2-3. With the device drivers doing the interpreting, application software developers don't have to include the specific protocol and standards for every printer that might be used by the applications they write.

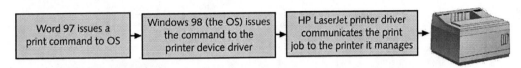

Exhibit 2-3: Application software and the OS passing print requests to the printer

The application software doesn't even need to know which printer is being used, because Windows keeps track of the default printer. The application sends print jobs to Windows for printing. Windows uses the default printer, unless the user selects a different one from the Windows printer list. Windows knows which device driver to call to execute the print job, because the device driver was assigned to that printer when the printer was installed.

It's difficult to describe what an application, operating system, BIOS, and device drivers do unless you know something about computer hardware. So first, you want to learn about several hardware components common to most systems.

The motherboard

The *motherboard*, as shown in Exhibit 2-4, is the largest and most complex circuit board inside a computer case. Because the CPU is central to all operations by hardware and software, all devices must somehow connect to the CPU, and they do this by way of the motherboard. In order to allow for and manage this communication, the motherboard has several slots, connections, embedded wires, microchips, and ports.

When you look on the back of a computer case, you can see some ports that are connected directly to the motherboard. These provide a way for external components to connect to the CPU.

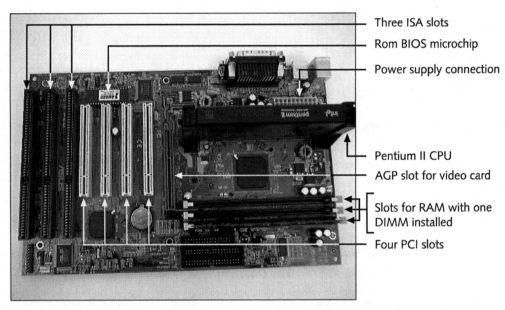

Exhibit 2-4: The motherboard is the largest circuit board inside a computer case

Exhibit 2-5 shows the ports provided to the outside of the case by this motherboard: a keyboard port, a mouse port, two serial ports, two USB ports, and a parallel port. A *serial port* is called a serial port because data travels serially, that is, one bit follows the next. This port is often used for an external modem or serial mouse, a mouse that uses a serial port. A *parallel port* carries data in parallel and is most often used by a printer. A *USB (universal serial bus)* port is a newer port used by many input/output devices, such as a keyboard, printer, scanner, or mouse. You want to learn how the OS configures and manages each of these ports and the devices that use them.

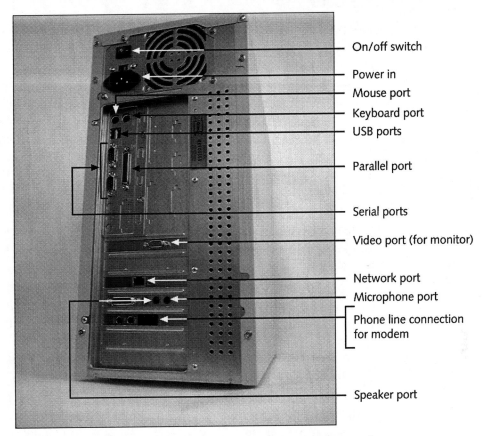

Exhibit 2-5: Input/output devices connect to the computer case by ports

Listed below are the major components found on all motherboards, some of which are labeled in Exhibit 2-4.

- Central processing unit (CPU)
- Random access memory (RAM)
- Traces or wires
- Expansion slots
- ROM BIOS memory chip
- CMOS configuration chip
- Power supply connections

The CPU

The CPU is central to all processing done by a computer. Every command from the operating system is passed to the CPU, which controls all the hardware components in the computer.

The CPU is installed in a slot or socket on the motherboard (refer back to Exhibit 2-4). All x86 CPUs today operate in one of two modes: real mode and protected mode. When the CPU operates in *real mode,* the CPU can address only up to approximately 1MB of RAM and doesn't provide any features to prevent errant applications from interfering with memory that belongs to another application. When the CPU operates in *protected mode*, the CPU allows the operating system to use features that protect one application from another.

Today, all CPUs for personal computers begin processing in real mode when they're first turned on and must be instructed to change over to protected mode. DOS stays in real mode, if the EMM386.exe isn't loaded. Other operating systems quickly switch to protected mode, which is much faster than real mode.

The speed of a CPU is partly determined by how much data it can process at one time and how much data it can send or receive at one time. Every CPU has lines coming to it that are embedded on the motherboard and collectively called a *bus*, as shown in Exhibit 2-6. These lines are devoted to various purposes. Some lines on the bus are designated to carry data, and they're called the *data bus* or *data path*.

Early CPUs used an 8-bit data path and processed 16 bits at a time. Today's CPUs can use one size for the data path but another for internal processing. For example, the Pentium III CPU uses a 64-bit data path coming to and from the CPU, but internally, it processes 32 bits at a time. Other lines on a bus are used for addresses, control signals, and voltage.

Note: A new CPU, the Intel Itanium, operates in 64-bit mode. The 64-bit versions of Windows XP and Windows Server 2003 Enterprise and Datacenter editions are designed to use this type of CPU.

Exhibit 2-6: On the bottom of the motherboard, bus lines ending at the CPU socket

Memory or RAM

PCs use *RAM (random access memory)* for short-term storage of data and programs. RAM microchips are used to hold data and instructions temporarily while the CPU processes both. These microchips are stored on tiny circuit boards called *memory modules*. Memory modules can be SIMMs, DIMMs, or RIMMs. The most common module for today's motherboards is a DIMM. A memory module is installed in memory slots on the motherboard designed to hold a particular type and speed of module, as shown in Exhibit 2-4.

Using Windows 9x, you can find out what type of CPU and how much memory you've installed by right-clicking the My Computer icon on your desktop, choosing Properties from the shortcut menu, and clicking the General tab. Exhibit 2-7 shows the information displayed on the General tab.

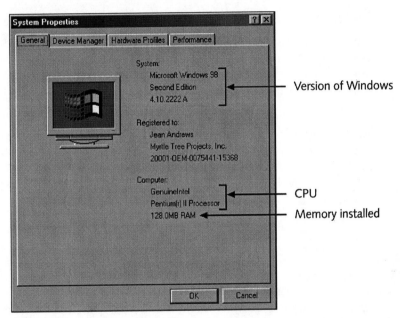

Exhibit 2-7: Memory information on the General tab of the System Properties window

Memory is useless to the system until it has been assigned addresses that the operating system, device drivers, and BIOS can use to communicate with it. These *memory addresses* are numbers assigned to each usable cell of memory, and the assignments are normally made when the OS is first loaded.

Buses on the motherboard

All hardware devices are directly or indirectly connected to the motherboard, because they're all dependent on the CPU on the motherboard for processing their data. Each bus provides a way for devices to connect to the motherboard and, ultimately, to the CPU. Sometimes a bus provides a port on the outside of the computer case for an external device to connect to by way of a cable or cord, or the bus might provide a slot on the motherboard into which a circuit board fits. In any case, a device always connects to a single bus on the motherboard. A motherboard can have several different buses; each type of bus has data lines, address lines, and control lines. An operating system relates to the bus, so the OS must support it in order for it to be used by the system.

Next you want to learn about some common buses and the expansion slots they support.

ISA bus

The first motherboards of the 1980s only had one bus, the *system bus*, which supported several *ISA (Industry Standard Architecture)* slots. The first ISA slot had only eight lines for data and was called the 8-bit ISA slot. It had 20 address lines and ran at 4.77 MHz, which means that data was transferred on the bus at a rate of 4,770,000 transfers per second.

Later, the 8-bit ISA slot was improved by adding an additional 8 lines for data, and this version is known as the 16-bit ISA slot. This slot runs at 8.33 MHz and has 24 lines for the address bus. All operating systems for personal computers today support the 16-bit ISA slot, although its use is diminishing in favor of faster I/O buses. You can see three ISA slots in Exhibit 2-8. An 8-bit expansion card, as shown in the exhibit, can use the first part of the 16-bit slot.

System buses

Today's system buses run up to 400 MHz and have a 64-bit wide data path and a 36-bit or wider address path. These system buses, sometimes called *memory buses*, *front-side buses*, or *local buses*, always connect directly to the CPU and memory, but are much too fast to support the slow ISA slots, which connect to the system bus by way of slower I/O buses that act as intermediaries.

PCI bus

The PCI (*Peripheral Component Interconnect*) bus was invented for devices that are faster than the 16-bit ISA bus but can't run as fast as the system bus between memory and the CPU. The PCI bus runs in sync with the system bus at one-third or one-half the speed. PCI uses a 32- or 64 bit path for data transfer. The maximum throughput of 32-bit operation is 132 MBps, whereas maximum throughput for 64-bit operation is 264 MBps. All Windows operating systems support PCI. In addition, the PCI bus is processor-independent, which means that it can be used for many non-Intel systems, such as the Apple Macintosh.

AGP bus

The *AGP (Accelerated Graphics Port) bus* was designed to accommodate a fast video card, which is a circuit board that controls the monitor. A motherboard has only a single AGP slot to accommodate one monitor. Rather than using the PCI bus for graphics data, AGP introduces a dedicated point-to-point channel between the graphics controller and the main memory. The AGP bus is based on the PCI specification, which is 32 bits wide. AGP has several versions, which support the following transfer rates:

AGP version	Transfer rate
AGP 1x	266 MBps
AGP 2x	533 MBps
AGP 4x	1.07 GBps
AGP 8x	2.13 GBps

Windows 98, Me, 2000, XP, and 2003 support AGP.

USB

USB (*Universal Serial Bus*) is designed to provide ports off the motherboard for slower external devices, such as a mouse, keyboard, scanner, video camera, or digital telephone. You saw two USB ports on the back of a computer case in Exhibit 2-5. The USB bus supports up to 127 devices, which can be daisy chained together and connected to a single USB port on a motherboard. Windows 95 Service Release 1 has limited support for USB. USB is fully supported in Windows 98, Me, 2000, XP, and 2003.

IEEE 1394 FireWire

IEEE 1394, also known as *FireWire*, is a new bus developed for high-bandwidth devices such as digital cameras, digital camcorders, and videodisc players. IEEE 1394 adheres to the Win32 Driver Model (WDM) by using the OpenHCI standard.

IEEE 1394 allows the direct connection of up to 63 devices. However, if splitters, bridges, and repeaters are used, then IEEE1394 can connect up to 1,023 buses, which allow for the connection of 64,000 devices. Windows 98/Me/NT/2000/XP/2003 support FireWire.

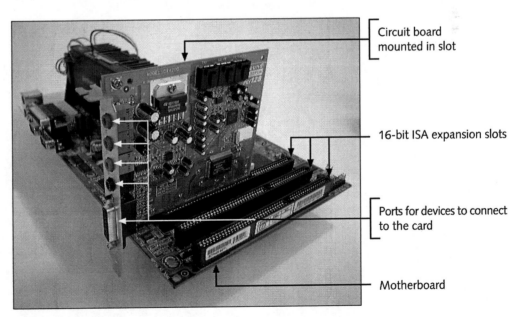

Exhibit 2-8: Three ISA slots

Managing buses

Device Manager under Windows 9x and Windows 2000/XP/2003 (Windows NT doesn't have a Device Manager) is the primary tool used to manage bus resources and the devices that use them. To access Device Manager using Windows 9x, right-click the My Computer icon on the desktop, choose Properties from the shortcut menu, and click on the Device Manager tab. For Windows 2000, from the System Properties window, click on the Hardware tab, and then click Device Manager. The Device Manager tab of the System Properties window for Windows 98 is shown in Exhibit 2-9. You can see two PCI devices, a modem, a network card, and the AGP video card listed in the window. The USB controller is also shown.

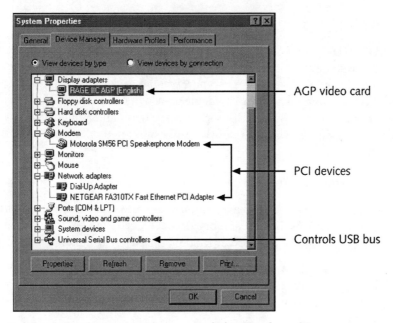

Exhibit 2-9: The Device Manager tab for Windows 98

Do it!

A-1: Discussing the motherboard

Exercises

1 The device in a computer that ultimately connects all hardware devices to the CPU is known as the _____.

2 Name three types of memory modules.

3 Which one of the following buses is designed to accommodate a fast video card?

A   ISA

B   PCI

C   AGP

D   FireWire

4 How many devices can be directly connected using FireWire?

5 What's the primary tool you use in Windows 98/2000/XP to manage buses?

Motherboard system resources

Explanation

Software has resources to control hardware, and hardware has resources to alert software that it needs attention. Think of a system resource as a tool that either hardware or software uses to communicate with the other.

There are four types of system resources: memory addresses, I/O addresses, interrupt request numbers (IRQs), and direct memory access (DMA) channels. The following table shows these system resources used by software and hardware and defines each:

System resource	Purpose
Memory addresses	Numbers that are assigned to physical memory located either in RAM or ROM chips. Software can access this memory by using these addresses. On the motherboard, memory addresses are transferred on the address bus.
IRQ	A control line of a motherboard bus that a hardware device can use to signal the CPU that the device needs attention. Some lines have a higher priority for attention than others. Each IRQ line is assigned a number (0 to 15) to identify it.
I/O Addresses	Numbers assigned to hardware devices that software uses to command a device. Each device "listens" for these numbers and responds to the ones assigned to it. On the motherboard, I/O addresses are transferred on the same address lines used by memory addresses.
DMA channel	A number designating a channel through which the device can pass data to memory without involving the CPU. Think of a DMA channel as a shortcut for data moving to/from the device and memory. Physically, DMA channels are lines on the motherboard.

System resource communications

Hardware devices signal the CPU for attention using an IRQ. The operating system addresses a device by one of its I/O addresses. The OS looks at memory as a hardware device and addresses it with memory addresses, and DMA channels are used to pass data back and forth between a hardware device and memory. As you read about these system resources, you might be interested in examining your own computer to see how the system resources are used. In Windows 98, go to Device Manager, right-click Computer, and then choose Properties. The Computer Properties window is displayed. In Windows 2000, go to Device Manager and, from the menu, click View, Resources by type. The system resources are displayed as shown in Exhibit 2-10.

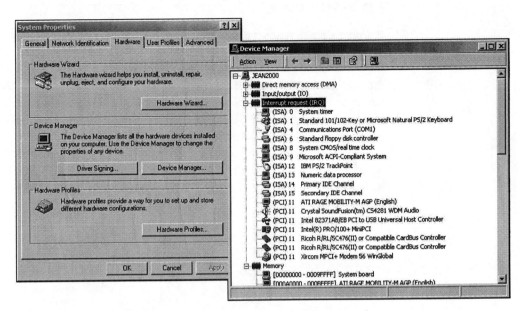

Exhibit 2-10: Device manager shows the current assignments for system resources

Interrupt request number (IRQ)

When a hardware device needs the CPU to do something, such as when the keyboard needs the CPU to process a keystroke after a key is pressed, the device needs a way to get the CPU's attention, and the CPU must know what to do once its attention is turned to the device. These interruptions to the CPU are called *hardware interrupts*, in which the device initiates an interrupt by placing voltage on the designated IRQ line assigned to it. This voltage on the line serves as a signal to the CPU that the device has a request that needs processing. Often, a hardware device that needs attention from the CPU is referred to as needing servicing. Many processes that the CPU carries out are initiated by interrupts and are said to be interrupt-driven. Software can also issue an interrupt to the CPU, so that the software can have access to a device.

Exhibit 2-10 shows IRQ 11, which is being shared by several devices on a Windows 2000 system. Look to the left of the IRQ number and see that the ISA bus controller is managing some of these IRQs and that the PCI bus controller manages the others. ISA-managed IRQs can't be shared, but PCI-managed IRQs can be shared. Also notice that the secondary IDE channel uses IRQ 15, and the primary IDE channel uses IRQ 14. IDE channels are used to connect hard drives, CD-ROM drives, Zip drives, and DVD drives to the motherboard.

With interrupts, the hardware device or the software initiates communication by sending a signal to the CPU, but a device can be serviced in another way, called *polling*. With polling, software is constantly running that has the CPU periodically check the hardware device to see if service is needed. Not very many devices use polling as the method of communication; most hardware devices use interrupts. A joystick is one example of a device that uses polling. Software that's written to manage a joystick has the CPU check the joystick periodically to see if the device has data to communicate, which is why a joystick doesn't need an IRQ to work.

I/O addresses

Another system resource that's made available to hardware devices is input/output addresses, or I/O addresses. *I/O addresses*, or *port addresses*, sometimes simply called *ports*, are numbers that the CPU can use to access hardware devices. The address bus on the motherboard sometimes carries memory addresses and sometimes carries I/O addresses. If the address bus is set to carry I/O addresses, then each device is listening to this bus, as shown in Exhibit 2-11. If the address belongs to it, then it responds; otherwise it ignores the request for information. In short, the CPU knows a hardware device as a group of I/O addresses. If it wants to know the status of a printer or a floppy drive, for example, it passes a particular I/O address down the address bus on the motherboard.

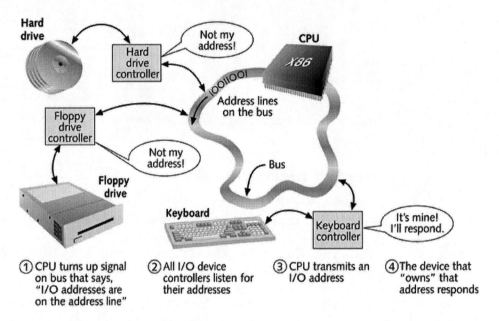

Exhibit 2-11: How I/O address lines on a bus work

A few common assignments for I/O addresses are listed in the following table.

IRQ	I/O address	Device
0	0040-005F	System timer
1	0060-006F	Keyboard controller
2	00A0-00AF	Access to IRQ above 7
3	02F8-02FF	COM2
3	02E8-02EF	COM4
4	03F8-03FF	COM1
4	03E8-03EF	COM3
5	0278-027F	Sound card or parallel port LPT2

IRQ	I/O address	Device
6	03F0-03F7	Floppy drive controller
7	0378-037F	Printer parallel port LPT1
8	0070-007F	Real-time clock
9-10		Available
11		SCSI or available (SCSI is a bus system often used for fast hard drives)
12	238-23F	System board mass
13	0F8-0FF	Math coprocessor
14	1F0-1F7	IDE hard drive
15	170-170	Secondary IDE hard drive or available

Because IBM made many address assignments when the first PC was manufactured in the late 1970s, common devices such as hard drives, floppy drives, and keyboards have no problem with I/O addresses. Their controllers can simply be programmed to use these standard addresses. Devices such as scanners or network cards that weren't assigned I/O addresses in the original IBM list can be configured to use more than one group of addresses, depending on how they're set up during either the installation process or during the startup (boot) process. Exhibit 2-12 shows how I/O addresses are assigned on a Windows 98 computer.

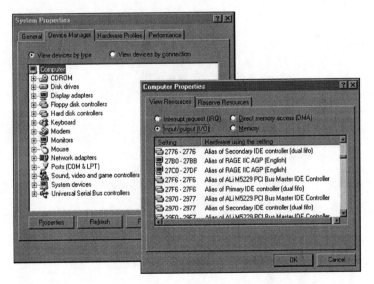

Exhibit 2-12:Windows 98 I/O address assignments

COM and LPT assignments

In the previous table, notice the COM and LPT assignments. COM1 and COM2 are preconfigured assignments that can be made to serial devices such as modems, and LPT1 and LPT2 are preconfigured assignments that can be made to parallel devices such as printers. For example, rather than assigning an IRQ and some I/O addresses to a modem, the modem is configured to use the assignments previously made to COM2, making it easier to configure the modem and to avoid conflicts with other devices that also need an IRQ and some I/O addresses.

It's common for a system to assign COM1 or COM2 to a serial port and LPT1 or LPT2 to a parallel port, as shown in Exhibit 2-5. When an external modem connects to a serial port that's assigned COM1, the modem is using the system resources assigned to COM1. If a printer is connected to the parallel port assigned to LPT1, it's using the system resources assigned to LPT1.

Memory addresses

An operating system relates to memory as a long list of cells that it can use to hold data and instructions, somewhat like a one-dimensional spreadsheet. Each memory location or cell is assigned a number beginning with zero. These number assignments are made when the OS is first loaded and are called *memory addresses*. Think of a memory address as a seat number in a theatre, as illustrated in Exhibit 2-13. Each seat is assigned a number regardless if it has someone sitting in it. The person sitting in a seat can be data or instructions, and the OS doesn't refer to the person by name but only by the seat number. For example, the OS might say, "I want to print the data in memory addresses 500 through 650."

Exhibit 2-13: Memory addresses are assigned like seats in a theatre

These addresses are most often displayed on the screen as hexadecimal (base 16 or hex) numbers in segment/offset form. For example, C800:5 in decimal is 819,205. Let's first look at how memory addresses are assigned and then turn our attention to how the CPU makes use of them.

Assigning memory addresses

Remember that the CPU uses lines coming to and from it to receive and send data. It has another group of lines called the address bus that it uses to send and receive the memory addresses that it uses to access memory. For example, if it wants to read the data in memory address 819,205, it must send the value 819,205 to memory to say to memory, "Send me the data stored in cell 819,205." It does this by sending the binary value for 819,205 on the address bus, which is 11001000000000000101. Each line on the address bus must hold one of the bits for this number. In this case, 20 lines are required. Therefore, the largest memory address the CPU can use is limited by the number of lines on the motherboard devoted to the address bus.

Note: Windows offers a calculator that can quickly convert numbers in binary, digital, and hexadecimal. You can use it to follow along with the conversions used here. Enter a number in one number system, and then click another number system to make the conversion. To access the calculator in Windows 9x or Windows NT/2000/XP, click Start, and then choose Programs, Accessories, Calculator.

Early CPUs had only 20 lines on the bus available to handle addresses, so the largest memory address the CPU could use was 11111111111111111111, which is 1,048,575 or 1,024K or 1 MB of memory. This 1 MB of memory was used by DOS and divided up according to the scheme shown in the following table:

Range of memory addresses	Range of memory addresses in hex	Type of memory
0 to 640K	0 to 9FFFF	Conventional or base memory
640K to 1024K	A0000 to FFFFF	Upper memory (A through F ranges)
Above 1024K	100000 and up	Extended memory

DOS and applications use the first 640K of memory, while the BIOS and device drivers use the addresses from 640K up to 1024K. Then newer CPUs and motherboards were developed with 24 address lines and more, so that memory addresses above 1024K became available. This is called *extended memory.* Windows 9x still uses these same divisions of memory, although it makes more use of extended memory. Memory addresses are expressed using hexadecimal notation. Because the hex numbers in upper memory begin with A through F, the divisions of upper memory are often referred to as the A range, B range, C range, and so on, up to the F range.

The previous table applies only to DOS and Windows 9x. Windows NT/2000/XP/2003 use an altogether different memory-mapping design, in which there's no conventional, upper, or extended memory; it's all just memory.

Using Windows 9x Device Manager, see how the first 1 MB of memory addresses are assigned, as shown in Exhibit 2-14. To view the list, select Computer and click Properties, then click Memory. Notice in Exhibit 2-14 that the system BIOS is assigned memory addresses in the F range of upper memory. This F range is always reserved for motherboard BIOS and is never requested by other programs. When the CPU is first turned on and needs a program to know how to boot up, it begins with the instructions stored on the ROM BIOS chip that are assigned to these memory addresses.

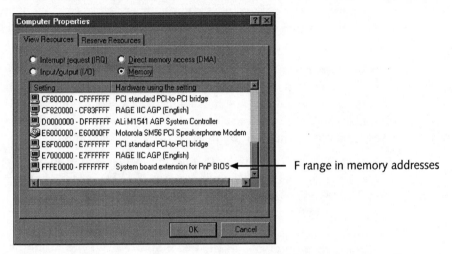

Exhibit 2-14: How the 1st megabyte of memory addresses is assigned

Using memory addresses

Once memory addresses have been assigned to memory, they can be used for communication with all software layers. As you saw in Exhibit 2-2, BIOS, device drivers, OS, and application software are working when a computer is running. During output operations, application software must pass information to the OS, which in turn passes that information to a device driver or to the BIOS. The BIOS and device drivers managing input devices must pass information to the OS, which passes it to the application software.

These layers of software all identify the data they want to share by referring to the memory address of the data, as illustrated in Exhibit 2-15.

Exhibit 2-15: Applications, the OS, and drivers passing data

Direct memory access (DMA) channels

Another system resource used by hardware and software is a *DMA (direct memory access) channel*, a shortcut method whereby an I/O device can send data directly to memory, bypassing the CPU. Some devices, such as hard drives or sound cards, are designed to use DMA channels. Others, such as the mouse, are not. Those that use the channels might be able to use only a certain channel, say channel 3, and no other. Alternately, the BIOS might have the option of changing a DMA channel number to avoid conflicts with other devices. Conflicts occur when more than one device uses the same channel. DMA channels aren't as popular as they once were, because their design makes them slower than newer methods. However, slower devices such as floppy drives, sound cards, and tape drives may still use DMA channels.

As shown in Exhibit 2-16, you can use Device Manager to show the current DMA assignments. Notice that, in this Windows 98 system, a sound card uses DMA1, and a floppy drive uses DMA2. DMA3 is available for a printer, and DMA4 is designated for access by the DMA controller for the higher DMA channels.

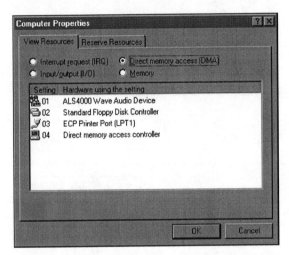

Exhibit 2-16: DMA channel assignments

Using system resources

Now let's look at examples of how the system resources help carry out hardware and software interrupts. This helps show how the resources work together.

Hardware interrupts

Once the CPU is interrupted by an IRQ, the job of the IRQ is over, and the CPU must handle the interruption. To do that, the CPU must use a program designed to interface with the device. This program to process an interrupt is called the *request handler* or *interrupt handler*. The program is either a part of the total BIOS in a system or is a device driver that had previously been installed on the hard drive.

To see how the process of handling an interrupt works, let's use the example of a keyboard that uses an IRQ to request attention from the CPU. Exhibit 2-17 shows the process it uses.

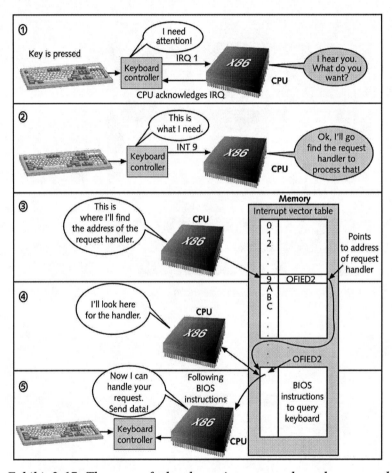

Exhibit 2-17: The story of a hardware interrupt, where the request handler is BIOS

When a keyboard uses an IRQ to request attention from the CPU, the following steps are performed:

1   A key is pressed on the keyboard. The keyboard controller puts voltage on its assigned IRQ 1 to the CPU, saying, "I need attention." The CPU sees the IRQ, acknowledges it, and turns its attention to servicing it. By sending the acknowledgment, it's requesting that the device controller send a number called an interrupt (abbreviated INT) that tells the CPU what service the device needs.

2   The keyboard controller sends INT 9 to the CPU, saying that it has a pressed key to process. The CPU uses this value to locate the program to handle this interrupt.

3   The CPU looks to a table in RAM called the *interrupt vector table*, or *vector table,* that contains a list of memory address locations of interrupt handlers. The INT value passed to the CPU by the controller points to a row in the interrupt vector table. This row stores the memory address for the instructions to service the keyboard, a portion of system BIOS.

4   The CPU looks to the location in memory of the request handler and begins to follow the instructions there.

5   The CPU, following the interrupt handler instructions, processes the keystroke.

Note: The BIOS and operating system initialize the interrupt vector table during booting, but later another program can modify the vector table to change the interrupt handler location to execute another program instead. This is a common method that a virus uses to propagate itself.

Software interrupts

In the hardware interrupt example, two of the four system resources were used (memory addresses and an IRQ). The keyboard controller used an IRQ to initiate communication. When the software initiates communication, such as when the user of word processing software gives the command to save a file to the hard drive, this is known as a *software interrupt*, which is illustrated in Exhibit 2-18. Both hardware and software interrupts use the same numeric INT (interrupt) values to communicate their requests to the CPU. The interrupt value for a call to the hard drive for I/O interaction is INT 13.

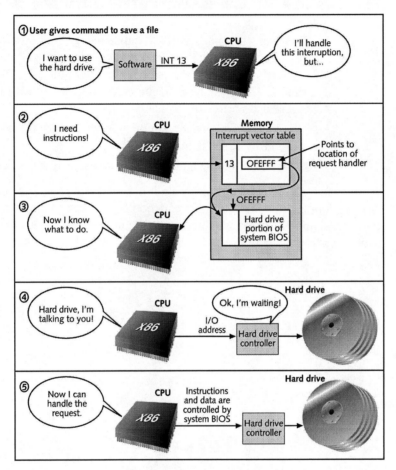

Exhibit 2-18: The story of a software interrupt

The software interrupt process, as shown in Exhibit 2-18, uses the following steps:

1 The CPU receives the software interrupt, INT 13.

2 The CPU turns to the interrupt vector table, using the INT value to locate the correct request handler.

3 The CPU locates the handler in memory.

4 The CPU alerts the hard drive that instructions are forthcoming by sending one of the hard drive's I/O addresses over the address bus.

5 The CPU follows the instructions of the request handler, in this case, system BIOS, to manage the hard drive.

BIOS on the motherboard and other circuit boards

The BIOS is a hybrid of two worlds. It's technically both hardware and software, since it's the intersection point of the two and must communicate with both, as shown in Exhibit 2-2. Because this software is permanently stored on a microchip, it's called *firmware*, and the chip is called *a ROM (read-only memory) BIOS chip*. The motherboard and other hardware devices contain ROM BIOS chips. The motherboard contains a vital ROM BIOS chip, as shown in Exhibit 2-19, that contains the programming necessary to start the computer, called *startup BIOS*. The motherboard also contains other fundamental BIOS programs to control I/O devices, such as the floppy disk drive and the keyboard, called *system BIOS*.

In addition, some complex hardware devices contain BIOS software embedded directly on the card.

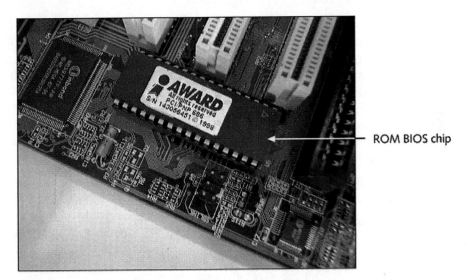

— ROM BIOS chip

Exhibit 2-19: The ROM BIOS chip on the motherboard

Advanced configuration and power interface (ACPI)

Some types of BIOS on the motherboard and operating systems support a power saving feature using the standards developed by Intel, Microsoft, and Toshiba, called *the Advanced Configuration and Power Interface (ACPI) standards*. Using ACPI, a system can be powered up by an external device, such as a keyboard. Windows 9x and Windows 2000 support ACPI, as do most newer motherboard BIOS. Microsoft calls an ACPI-compliant BIOS a "good" BIOS. To see if your BIOS is ACPI compliant, check this Microsoft URL:

```
www.microsoft.com/windows2000/professional/howtobuy/
upgrading/compat
```

Plug and play

Another feature of both the BIOS and the OS is *Plug and Play (PnP)*, a standard designed to make the installation of new hardware devices easier. If the BIOS is Plug and Play, then it begins the process of configuring hardware devices in the system. It gathers information about the devices and then passes that information to the operating system. If the operating system is also Plug and Play compliant, it uses that information to complete the hardware configuration process. For a system to be fully Plug and Play, the BIOS, the operating system and all devices must be Plug and Play.

Windows 9x and Windows 2000/XP/2003 support Plug and Play, but Windows NT doesn't. However, Windows 2000/XP/2003 Plug and Play is more advanced than the Windows 9x version and doesn't use the startup BIOS to help with Plug and Play configurations. Therefore, on a Windows 2000/XP/2003 system, it isn't important if the motherboard BIOS is Plug and Play.

The Plug and Play standard applies to the operating system, to BIOS on the motherboard, and to BIOS on devices. Plug and Play under Windows or the motherboard BIOS doesn't assign resources to a device if the device doesn't allow it. For example, if a legacy sound card requires a certain group of upper memory addresses that are hard-coded into its on-board BIOS, there's nothing that Plug and Play can do about that. (Hard-coded is computer jargon for something being coded so that it can't be changed.) Plug and Play simply tries to work around the problem as best it can. If two non-Plug and Play hardware devices require the same resource, and their BIOS doesn't provide for accepting a substitute, these two devices can't coexist on the same PC.

Newer devices that contain BIOS that is Plug and Play compliant are more cooperative. At startup, they simply send a request and then wait for the OS to assign the resources they need to work. Startup BIOS that is Plug and Play does some of the up-front work for Windows 9x, but Windows 2000/2003 does all its Plug and Play configuration without the help of BIOS.

Note: A Plug and Play hardware device has something like Windows 9x Ready or Windows 9x Compliant written on the box.

ESCD (extended system configuration data) Plug and Play BIOS is an enhanced version of Plug and Play that creates a list of all the things you've done manually to the configuration that Plug and Play doesn't do on its own. This ESCD list is written to the BIOS chip, so that the next time you boot, the startup BIOS can faithfully relay that information to Windows 9x. The BIOS chip for ESCD BIOS is a special RAM chip called *Permanent RAM*, or *PRAM*, that can hold data written to it without the benefit of a battery, which the CMOS setup chip requires.

CMOS setup chip

Another chip on the motherboard, called the *CMOS configuration chip*, *CMOS setup chip*, or *CMOS RAM chip*, contains a very small amount of memory, or RAM, enough to hold configuration or setup information about the computer. This chip is responsible for remembering the current date and time, which hard drives and floppy drives are present, how the serial and parallel ports are configured, and so forth. When the computer is first turned on, it looks to the CMOS chip to find out what hardware it can expect to find. The CMOS chip is powered by a trickle of electricity from a small battery located on the motherboard or computer case, usually close to the CMOS chip itself so that, when the computer is turned off, the CMOS chip still retains its data.

The program to change CMOS setup is stored in the ROM BIOS chip and can be accessed during the startup process. The keystrokes to enter CMOS setup are displayed somewhere on the screen during startup in a statement such as "Press the Del key to enter setup." Different types of BIOS use different keystrokes. The CMOS setup doesn't normally need to be changed, except when there's a problem with hardware, a new floppy drive is installed, or a power-saving feature needs to be disabled or enabled. The CMOS setup can also hold a power-on password to help secure a system. Know that this password isn't the same password that can be required by a Windows OS at startup.

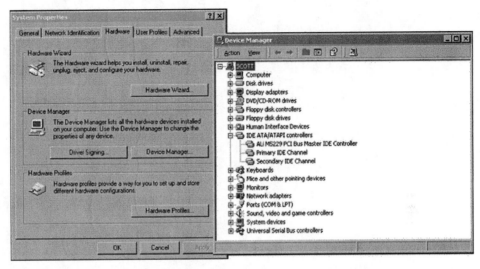

Exhibit 2-20: Device Manager Window

Do it!

A-2: Examining system resources with Device Manager

Here's how	Here's why
1 Click the **Start** button	To display the Start menu.
Choose **Settings, Control Panel**	To open the Control Panel.
Double-click **System**	To open the System Properties dialog box.
2 If you're using Windows 9x, activate the **Device Manager** tab	
If you're using Windows 2000, activate the **Hardware** tab and click **Device Manager**	
3 Observe the output	In both Windows 9x and Windows 2000, the Device Manager appears similar to Exhibit 2-20. You can right-click an item in the list and then choose Properties from the shortcut menu to view information about that item, or you can view the item's Properties by double-clicking the item.

4	Click the plus sign (+) next to **Network Adapters**	When you click the + sign to the left of an item, a list of the installed devices for that item appears beneath the item.
5	In the Network adapters list, double-click any device	The open the Properties dialog box for the selected device.
6	Activate the **Resources** tab	This tab shows all resources used by the selected device.
7	Using the information on the Resources tab, answer the following questions: What IRQ is assigned to the network adapter? What's the I/O range of the network adapter? What Memory Addresses are available to the network adapter?	
8	Close the Properties dialog box	To return to the Device Manager.
9	If you're using Windows 9x, click **View resources by connection** Click the plus sign (+) next to **Plug and Play BIOS**	(If you're using Windows 2000, skip ahead to the step 10.) Notice that the groupings change. To view the devices managed by the Plug and Play BIOS.
10	If you're using Windows 2000, choose **View**, **Resources by type** Click the plus sign (+) next to **Interrupt request (IRQ)**	(If you're using Windows 9x, skip ahead to step 11.) Notice that information is now grouped into four categories. To see which device is assigned to each IRQ line.
11	If you're using Windows 9x, print a system summary as follows: Click **Print** Select **System summary** Click **OK**	If you're using Windows 2000, skip ahead to the step 12. If necessary.

12 If you're using Windows 2000, print a system summary as follows:

If you're using Windows 9x, skip ahead to step 13.

Choose **View**, **Print**

Under Report type, select **System summary**

If necessary.

Click **Print**

13 Name the Windows operating systems that don't include the Device Manager.

14 How do you display individual devices under the group headings?

15 What are two ways to view device properties in Device Manager?

16 What are the four types of system resources?

17 What three options are available for printing in Device Manager?

Hard drives and other secondary storage devices

Explanation

A hard drive is an example of a *secondary storage* device, which is a device that can hold data and instructions, but the data and instructions can only be stored there and not processed there by the CPU. Before the instructions can be processed, they must be copied from a secondary storage device to a *primary storage* device, which is memory. In other words, you store files that contain data and programs on a hard drive, but to use these data and programs, they must be copied into memory.

Another difference between secondary and primary storage devices is that secondary devices hold data permanently, and primary devices hold data temporarily. What's stored on your hard drive remains there, even when the PC is turned off, but what's stored in memory is lost as soon as you turn off your PC. The most common secondary storage devices are hard drives, floppy disk drives, CD-ROM drives, DVD drives, and Zip drives. Exhibit 2-21 shows a hard drive subsystem.

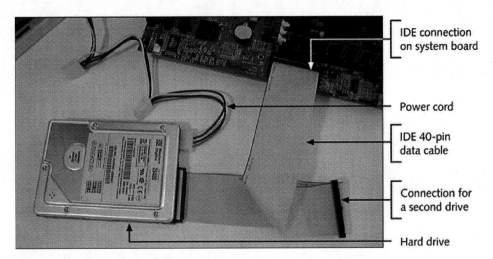

Exhibit 2-21: A PC's hard drive subsystem

Most motherboards offer two *EIDE (Enhanced Integrated Drive Electronics)* connections. *IDE (Integrated Drive Electronics)* is a group of standards that governs how a hard drive works, and EIDE is a group of standards that governs how a secondary storage device, such as a hard drive, CD-ROM drive, or Zip drive, can interface with a system. In the industry, you most often use the term IDE for both IDE and EIDE. The connections for the two IDE channels on the motherboard are called the primary and secondary channels. Each cable or channel can accommodate two IDE devices, such as a hard drive and a CD-ROM drive, for a total of four IDE devices in one system. Power to the hard drive comes through a power cable from the PC's power supply.

Directory structures and file names

The operating system is responsible for storing the files and folders on a secondary storage device, such as a hard drive, using organizational methods called a *file system*. Windows uses several different file systems.

Regardless of the file system used, every OS manages a hard drive by using directories (Windows calls these folders), subdirectories, and files. A *directory table* is a list of files and subdirectories. On Microsoft operating systems, when a hard drive is first installed and formatted, there's a single directory table on the drive called the *root directory*. For a logical drive C, the root directory is written as C:\. **Note:** A physical hard drive can be divided into logical partitions, sometimes called volumes.

This root directory can hold files or other directories, as shown in Exhibit 2-22, which can have names such as C:\Tools. These directories, called *subdirectories*, *child directories*, or *folders*, can, in turn, have other directories listed in them. Any directory can have files and/or other directories listed in it, for example, C:\wp\data\myfile.txt, in Exhibit 2-22. The C: identifies the drive. If the directory had been on a floppy disk, it would have been either A: or B:. When you write the drive and directories pointing to the location of the file, as in this example, the drive and directories are called the *path* to the file. The first part of the file before the period is called the *file name* (myfile), and the part after the period is called the *file extension (txt)*, which, for Windows and DOS, always have three characters or fewer. The file extension identifies the type of file, such as .doc for Microsoft Word document files or .xls for Microsoft Excel spreadsheet files.

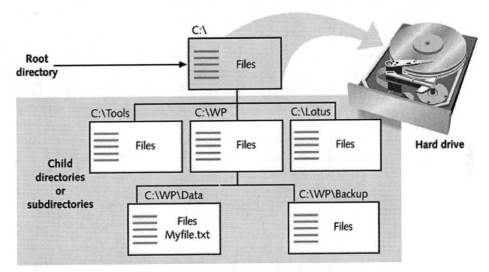

Exhibit 2-22: Root directory can hold files or other directories

File naming conventions

Because Windows 9x is built on a DOS core, you need to understand how to name files under DOS. Under DOS, a file name can contain up to eight characters and the file extension can contain up to three characters, which are separated by a period, like this: filename.ext. Characters used can be the letters a through z, the numbers 0 through 9, or the following characters: _, ^, $, ~, !, #, %, &, - {, } , (,), @, ', `. Be sure not to use a space, period, asterisk (*), question mark (?), or backslash (\) in a file name or file extension. Acceptable file extensions for program files are .com, .sys, .bat, and .exe. A *program file* contains a list of instructions for the OS to follow. For example, the DOS utility program to display information about the system is Msd.exe.

Under Windows 95 and later Windows operating systems, file names can be as long as 255 characters and can contain spaces. Before Windows 95, only the Macintosh OS and UNIX used these long file names. When using long file names in Windows 9x, remember that the DOS portion of the system can understand only eight-character file names with three-character extensions. When the DOS part of the system is operating, it truncates long file names and assigns new eight-character ones. Windows NT/2000/XP/2003 doesn't have a DOS core and therefore does a better job of managing long file names.

File organization

By creating various directories on a hard drive, you can organize your program files and data files by placing programs in one directory and files created by those programs in a second directory. This organization is comparable to keeping paper records in separate folders. You can also organize files on other secondary storage media, such as floppy disks or Zip drives.

Note: When representing directories, Windows uses a backslash, as in this example: C:\Tools. However, UNIX uses a forward slash to represent directories. The root directory in UNIX is written / and subdirectories are written as /etc or /bin. Also, Windows doesn't care if directory names and file names are uppercase or lowercase, but UNIX is case-sensitive: /Bin is a different directory from /bin.

The FAT file system

The FAT (*file allocation table*) file system, is based on a table that's a very long list of all the entries on a hard drive that can hold data. Two FAT file systems used by Windows for hard drives are FAT16 and FAT32. The 16 or 32 stands for the size of each number in the table – 16 bits or 32 bits – although, for FAT32, only 28 of them are used to hold a number. There's one entry in the FAT for each cluster on the hard drive. A cluster is the smallest unit of space on the hard drive used to hold data that's addressed by the OS. An OS puts files on the hard drive in increments of whole clusters. All clusters on a hard drive are assigned a single number, the first useable cluster number is two. The OS identifies a cluster by this number and knows how many bytes or characters of data a cluster can hold. All clusters on a logical drive hold the same number of bytes.

Exhibit 2-23 shows that the OS relates to the hard drive by using two tables, the FAT and the directory table. A logical drive, such as drive C, has two copies of FAT but can have several directory tables, one for each subdirectory on the drive. The directory table tells the OS the name of a file and the first cluster number for that file. All the other cluster numbers for the file are kept in the FAT. For example, let's say a file named Mydata.txt begins at cluster 5 and requires three clusters to hold the file. The OS reads the file using the following steps. The first three are numbered in Exhibit 2-23:

1 The OS goes to the directory and reads the name of the file (Mydata.txt) and the first cluster number (5).

2 The OS retrieves the contents of cluster 5 on the hard drive, which is the first segment of the file.

3 The OS turns to the FAT, looks at the fifth position in the FAT, and reads 6, which says that the next segment of the file is in cluster 6.

4 It retrieves the second segment of the file from cluster 6 on the hard drive.

5 The OS then turns to the sixth position in the FAT and reads 10, which says the next segment of the file is in cluster 10.

6 It retrieves the third segment of the file from cluster 10 on the hard drive.

7 The OS turns to the 10th position in the FAT and reads all 1s in the FAT entry, which says that this is the last cluster in the file. (If the FAT is FAT16, then an entry of 16 ones is written in the FAT. If it's FAT32, then an entry of 28 ones is written.)

There are other organizational tables and entries that an OS uses to manage a hard drive besides the FAT and directory tables.

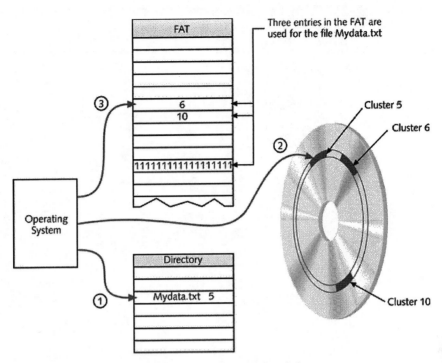

Exhibit 2-23: How an OS reads a file from the hard drive

3rd party system utilities

You can also use 3rd party system utilities to gather and report system information. One of these programs is SANDRA, which provides a quick, comprehensive review of your entire PC system, as shown in Exhibit 2-24. SANDRA also includes benchmarking and reporting tools. Next, you can use SANDRA to examine your system.

Exhibit 2-25: SiSoft Sandra main Window

Do it!

A-3:   Using shareware to examine a computer

Here's how	Here's why
1 Open Web browser Enter the following URL: www.3bsoftware.com	
2 Choose **Downloads**, **Trial Versions**	
3 Under SANDRA Standard, click **Download STANDARD**	You're routed to C/Net Download.com.
4 After the File Download dialog box appears, save the file, **san_897a.zip**, to your PC Desktop	Note tha,t if you can't find SANDRA on the C|Net Web site, you can use a search engine to locate the shareware. Also, note that later versions of SANDRA might have different file names for the zip file.
5 Double-click **san_897a.zip** on your desktop Extract all the files, including Setup.exe with its components	You want to decompress the SANDRA file and install the utility on your PC.
6 Run **Setup.exe**	To create a new program in your Program Group and add an icon to your desktop.
7 Run **SiSoftware Sandra 2002**	You see a screen similar to the one shown in Exhibit 2-25.
8 Double-click **System Summary**	You want to execute each of the utilities, in turn, by double-clicking the icons, or you can create a composite report of the results of each selection. The System Summary utility launches and gathers information about your system before displaying it in a format similar to Device Manager, with devices listed by type.
9 Press (ESC)	To close the System Summary utility.

10 Open Windows Information

Scroll down and note the listed information types

According to this utility list, what version of Windows are you using?

What's the path to the Temporary Folder on your system

11 Press (ESC)   To close the Windows Information utility.

12 Open Drives Information   The utility begins to gather information regarding your drives. Don't move the mouse or touch the keyboard while this is in progress.

Record the following information:

How much Total Space does the hard drive contain?

How much Free Space does the hard drive contain?

What type of File System does the hard drive use?

13 Press (ESC)   To quit the Drives Information utility.

14 Open DMA Settings

Why are you unable to view the DMA Settings information?

15 Close DMA Settings

16 Choose **File**, **Create a Report Wizard...** on the SiSoft Sandra menu bar   You want to create a composite report of your system using SANDRA.

17 Click **Next**   In the wizard introduction window.

18 Click **Clear All**   In the Step 1 of 8 window.

Check **System summary**

Click **Next**   To continue.

19	Click **Clear All**	In the Step 2 of 8 window.
	Click **Next**	To continue.
20	Click **Clear All**	In the Step 3 of 8 window.
	Click **Next**	To continue.
21	Click **Clear All**	In the Step 4 of 8 window.
	Click **Next**	To continue.
22	Add any comments that you desire	In the Step 5 of 8 window.
	Click **Next**	To continue.
23	Click **Print it or Fax it**	In the Step 6 of 8 window.
	Click **Next**	To continue.
24	Click **OK**	In the print dialog box.
25	Click **Finish**	
	Collect your report from the printer	
26	Continue to explore each utility in SANDRA	
	Close SANDRA	
27	Enter the following URL:	
	`www.zdnet.com`	
	Find SANDRA	
28	Is the program available through this avenue as well?	
	Print the Web page or pages to support your answer	

29 What URL can you use to find a
    link to download SANDRA?

30 Is SANDRA capable of only
    hardware diagnostics?

31 What two of the four system
    resources aren't you able to view
    with the version of SANDRA you
    downloaded and why?

32 Based on your experience with the
    labs in this chapter, which do you
    think is better at analyzing your
    system, SANDRA or Device
    Manager? Why?

33 What type of software is
    SANDRA considered?

Topic B: Software management

Explanation

Next, you want to learn how the OS interfaces with other software, including BIOS, device drivers, and applications. Because the CPU operates in two modes, real mode and protected mode, the OS boot loader must be able to operate in each mode. This dual modality also affects the mode that an application uses. Therefore, we begin our discussion of software by looking more carefully at each of these modes.

Real and protected operating modes

Remember that the two modes a CPU can operate in are real mode and protected mode. There are several differences between real mode and protected mode, but the fundamental difference is that, in real mode, there's no memory/instruction protection from errant applications. In protected mode, such protection is available. Privileged instructions may not be executed by ordinary applications.

In real mode, as shown in Exhibit 2-26, a CPU assumes that only one application or program is running at a time. This is called single tasking, so it gives that program direct access to all hardware devices including memory. It uses a 16-bit data path and 1 MB of memory addresses, unless a *memory extender* is used. A memory extender is an OS utility program that provides an OS with memory addresses above 1 MB, called *extended memory*.

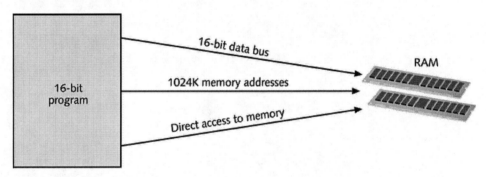

Exhibit 2-26: Real mode or MS mode provides single tasking

Note: Real mode is 8086 compatibility mode. Therefore, it's limited to 16-bit data processing. Originally the data path was only 8 bits wide. However, the processor could process 16-bits at a time, and two fetches were needed from the 8 bit data path.

In protected mode, more than one program can run at the same time, which is a type of multitasking. In protected mode, each program can be safely contained within its own range of resources. Here lies the meaning behind the two terms, real and protected. Real mode means that the software has "real" access to the hardware, and protected mode means that more than one program can be running and each one is "protected" from the other(s).

In protected mode, as shown in Exhibit 2-27, more than one program can run, and the programs have access to memory addresses of 4096 MB or 4 GB, depending on the motherboard, CPU, and OS being used, or sometimes more. In protected mode, the OS doesn't allow a program direct access to RAM but works as the mediator between memory and programs. This allows the OS some latitude in how it uses RAM. If the OS is low on RAM, it can store some data on the hard drive. This method of using the hard drive as though it were RAM is called *virtual memory*, and data stored in virtual memory is stored in a file on the hard drive called *a swap file* or *page file*. The OS manages the entire process, and the applications know nothing about this substitution of hardware resources for RAM. The programs running in protected mode see only memory addresses and have no idea where they're located.

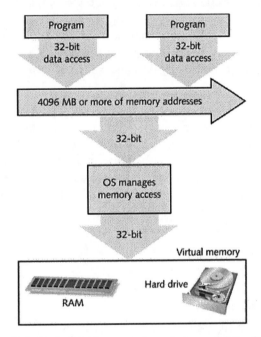

Exhibit 2-27: Protected mode is a multitasking program

Even after protected mode became available, hardware and software needed to be backward-compatible, that is, able to support older technology. So real mode is still supported by today's CPUs and operating systems. In fact, the CPU starts in real mode and must be told to switch to protected mode. For this reason, an OS starts in real mode and commands the CPU to switch to protected mode before allowing user interaction or loading an application. DOS and the MS-DOS mode of Windows 9x operate in real mode. Windows 9x and Windows NT/2000/XP/2003 start out in real mode and then switch to protected mode. The following table summarizes the differences between real mode and protected mode.

Real mode	Protected mode
16-bit data path	16 or 32-bit data path
Only one program runs at a time	Several programs can be loaded and running
The CPU can access up to 1 MB of memory unless a memory extender is used	The CPU can access more than 1 MB to 4 GB or more of memory
Programs have direct access to hardware	Programs access hardware by way of the operating system

How an OS uses real and protected modes

The OS must be in sync with the CPU, using the same mode it's using. Not only must the OS be in sync with the CPU, but applications must be compiled to run in either real or protected mode. In addition, there's a mode that's a hybrid of real and protected mode that was used by older software written for Windows 3.x. In this hybrid mode, the mode is real but the intent is to run more than one program in a pseudo-protected environment. This unique situation that occurred with Windows 3.x is important, because it helps to make clear the different ways in which an OS can manage applications.

Windows 3.x wasn't really an OS, but neither did it act like normal application software. It used DOS as its operating system and, therefore, is considered to be a DOS application. Windows 3.x provided an operating environment, which refers to the overall support that it provided to application software, and applications were installed under Windows 3.x. The two primary things that Windows 3.x provided that DOS didn't were a graphical user interface (GUI) and a limited form of multitasking.

16-bit and 32-bit software

Applications and device drivers written for Windows 3.x are called *16-bit Windows software*. Data access is 16 bits at a time, and each program is written so that it should not infringe on the resources of other applications that might be running. Software applications written for Windows 95 and higher are called *32-bit drivers or 32-bit applications*. In short, there are four general types of software that run on PCs:

- 16-bit DOS software is designed to run in real mode as the only program running and expecting direct access to hardware. Under DOS, an application might attempt to serve as its own device driver. These programs could use only the first 1 MB of memory.

- 32-bit DOS uses a 32-bit DOS extended mode program, which could run using the full available range of memory.

- 16-bit Windows software is designed for Windows 3.x to run where other programs might also be running. These applications might or might not attempt to access hardware resources directly and could most likely use extended memory.

- 32-bit Windows software is designed to run in protected mode with other software and can be loaded in extended memory. These applications never attempt to access hardware directly.

Nearly all applications and device drivers written today are 32-bit, although 16-bit software still exists, and you must know how to support it in a Windows environment.

DOS, with or without Windows 3.x, is a real mode OS. Windows 9x is a hybrid operating system. Some of Windows 9x uses 16-bit data access (called *16-bit programs*) and some uses 32-bit data access (called *32-bit programs*). The Windows 9x 16-bit components exist primarily for backward-compatibility with older hardware and software. Because the 32-bit programs access twice as much data at one time as 16-bit programs do, the 32-bit programs are faster. This fact largely explains why Windows 9x is faster than DOS. Windows NT/2000/XP/2003 are true 32-bit operating systems; all OS programs are written using 32-bit coding methods.

A 32-bit OS allows a 16-bit program to run by providing it with an environment that appears to the program to be a 16-bit environment. This technique is called *virtual real mode*.

After Windows 9x is loaded, you can switch to real mode by using the Shut Down menu. Click Start, Shut Down, and then select Restart in MS-DOS mode from the menu. You get a C prompt and a full screen from which you can run DOS commands or applications. Windows 2000, Windows XP, and Me don't support accessing real mode while the OS is loaded, although recovery procedures using these operating systems sometimes are done in real mode.

Do it!

B-1: Observing Windows 9x in real mode

Here's how	Here's why
1 Boot into MS-DOS real mode	Using Windows 9x.
2 Make drive C, root directory the default drive and directory	From the command prompt.
Verify that the prompt is C:\>	
3 Enter **DIR**	To get a list of files on C:\.
Does the hard drive contain Autoexec.bat and Config.sys files in the root directory?	
Print the files using a local printer by using one of the following methods:	If the hard drive contains Autoexec.bat and Config.sys files in the root directory.
C:\> TYPE filename.ext > PRN	
C:\> PRINT filename.ext	
C:\> COPY filename.ext PRN	
C:\> COPY filename.ext LPT1	
4 At the DOS prompt, enter **PROMPT $P $G**	To customize the DOS command prompt. The space between $P and $G can contain any text, for example $PThisIsAPrompt$G.
What prompt did you get?	
5 By examining the prompt, guess what $P in the command line accomplishes and what $G accomplishes	
Test the theory by changing the PROMPT command, leaving first $P and then $G out of the command line	You want to test the theory that, without the appropriate PATH command, you can't execute software stored on one drive or directory while you're in another.

6 Make drive C, the root directory,
   the default drive and directory

7 Enter the Msd command

   Does the command work?

   What error message do you see?

8 What are the current paths your
   system knows?

   Enter the Path command without   To find out what paths your system knows.
   any paths following

How an OS uses BIOS and device drivers

Explanation

Looking back at Exhibit 2-2, you can see that an operating system uses programs designed to interact with specific hardware devices. There are two kinds of programs used for this purpose, BIOS and device drivers. In Exhibit 2-2, you can see that some device drivers belong to the OS, and others don't. You can also see that the total BIOS in a system can be located in several places in the system. The OS communicates with simple devices, such as floppy drives or keyboards, through BIOS, and with more complex devices, such as digital cameras or CD-ROM drives, through device drivers and BIOS. We first want to look at the BIOS and then turn our attention to device drivers.

How an OS uses system BIOS

System BIOS contains the programming instructions to run the simple hardware devices that are common to every system, specifically the keyboard, floppy disk drive, hard disk drive, and monitor. In addition, system BIOS can be used to access the hard drive. In the case of any hardware device, an OS has a choice of using system BIOS or device drivers. Most often it uses device drivers, because they're faster. One reason device drivers are faster than system BIOS is that device drivers are executed from RAM, and BIOS is stored in ROM. RAM access is faster than ROM access. However, sometimes the OS virtualizes the hard drive and makes it available when older software requires it.

Note: There's a good way to determine whether the BIOS or a device driver is controlling a device. If the device is configured using CMOS setup, most likely system BIOS controls it. If the device is configured using the OS, most likely a driver controls it.

For example, in Exhibit 2-28, the setup main menu for an Award BIOS system. It shows the ability to configure, or set, the system date and time, the Supervisor Password (power-on password), floppy drive diskettes, the hard drive, and the keyboard.

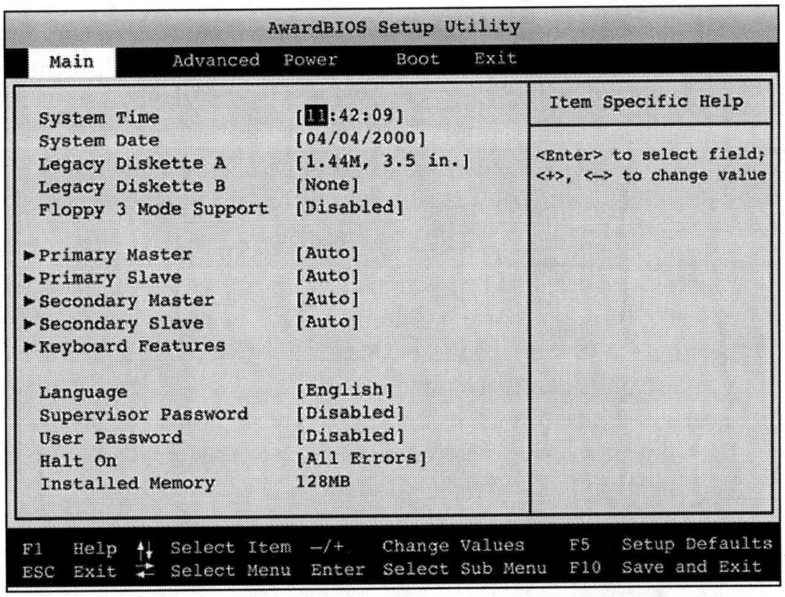

```
                    AwardBIOS Setup Utility
  ┌──────────────────────────────────────────────────────────┐
  │  Main   Advanced  Power    Boot   Exit                    │
  ├──────────────────────────────────────┬───────────────────┤
  │                                       │ Item Specific Help│
  │  System Time          [11:42:09]      │                   │
  │  System Date          [04/04/2000]    │<Enter> to select  │
  │  Legacy Diskette A    [1.44M, 3.5 in.]│         field;    │
  │  Legacy Diskette B    [None]          │<+>, <-> to change │
  │  Floppy 3 Mode Support [Disabled]     │         value     │
  │                                       │                   │
  │ ►Primary Master       [Auto]          │                   │
  │ ►Primary Slave        [Auto]          │                   │
  │ ►Secondary Master     [Auto]          │                   │
  │ ►Secondary Slave      [Auto]          │                   │
  │ ►Keyboard Features                    │                   │
  │                                       │                   │
  │  Language             [English]       │                   │
  │  Supervisor Password  [Disabled]      │                   │
  │  User Password        [Disabled]      │                   │
  │  Halt On              [All Errors]    │                   │
  │  Installed Memory     128MB           │                   │
  │                                       │                   │
  ├───────────────────────────────────────────────────────────┤
  │ F1  Help  ↑↓ Select Item  -/+  Change Values  F5  Setup Defaults│
  │ ESC Exit  ⇄  Select Menu  Enter Select Sub Menu F10 Save and Exit│
  └───────────────────────────────────────────────────────────┘
```

Exhibit 2-28: The Setup Utility menu for an Award BIOS system

Exhibit 2-29 shows another setup window for BIOS that can configure serial ports, an infrared port, and a parallel port. All these devices can be controlled by system BIOS. On the other hand, there's no setup window in this BIOS to control the DVD drive or Zip drive that are installed on this system. The BIOS isn't aware of these devices. Instead, device drivers control these devices.

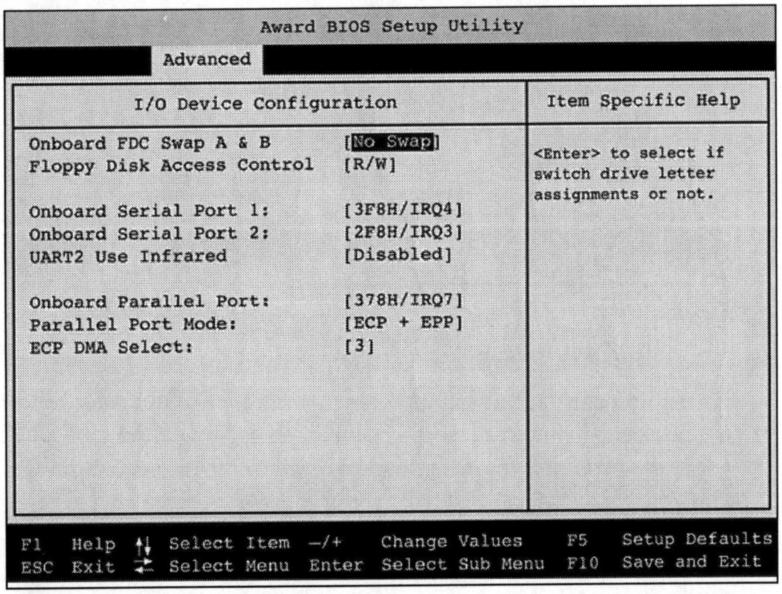

```
                    Award BIOS Setup Utility
  ┌──────────────────────────────────────────────────────────┐
  │       Advanced                                            │
  ├──────────────────────────────────────┬───────────────────┤
  │       I/O Device Configuration        │ Item Specific Help│
  │                                       │                   │
  │  Onboard FDC Swap A & B    [No Swap]  │<Enter> to select if│
  │  Floppy Disk Access Control [R/W]     │ switch drive letter│
  │                                       │ assignments or not.│
  │  Onboard Serial Port 1:  [3F8H/IRQ4]  │                   │
  │  Onboard Serial Port 2:  [2F8H/IRQ3]  │                   │
  │  UART2 Use Infrared      [Disabled]   │                   │
  │                                       │                   │
  │  Onboard Parallel Port:  [378H/IRQ7]  │                   │
  │  Parallel Port Mode:     [ECP + EPP]  │                   │
  │  ECP DMA Select:         [3]          │                   │
  │                                       │                   │
  ├───────────────────────────────────────────────────────────┤
  │ F1  Help  ↑↓ Select Item  -/+  Change Values  F5  Setup Defaults│
  │ ESC Exit  ⇄  Select Menu  Enter Select Sub Menu F10 Save and Exit│
  └───────────────────────────────────────────────────────────┘
```

Exhibit 2-29: Award BIOS setup window that configure I/O devices including ports

Note: CMOS setup windows are accessed during startup. A system displays a message at the bottom of the screen saying something like, "Press Del to enter setup." Pressing the indicated key launches a program stored on the ROM BIOS microchip to change the contents of CMOS RAM. This BIOS setup program provides windows such as those in Exhibit 2-28 and Exhibit 2-29.

How device drivers control hardware

Device drivers, which are software designed to interface with specific hardware devices, serve the same functions as BIOS programs. However, they're stored on the hard drive rather than on ROM chips, as BIOS is. The OS provides some device drivers, and the manufacturer of the specific hardware device with which they're designed to interface provides other device drivers. In either case, unlike BIOS, device drivers are usually written for a particular OS and must be rewritten to be used with another.

When you purchase a printer, DVD drive, Zip drive, digital camera, scanner, or other hardware device, bundled with the device is a set of floppy disks or CDs that contain the device drivers, as shown in Exhibit 2-30. You must install these device drivers under the operating system so it has the necessary software to control the device. In most cases, you install the device and then install the device drivers. There are a few exceptions, such as a digital camera using a serial port to download pictures. In this case, you install the software to drive the digital camera before you plug in the camera. See the device documentation to learn what to do first.

Exhibit 2-30: CD-ROM device with floppy disk containing device drivers

Note: You can find device drivers in a number of sources. Some come with and are part of the operating system, some come with hardware devices when they're purchased, and some are provided for download over the Internet from a device manufacturer's Web site.

There are two kinds of device drivers: 16-bit real-mode drivers and 32-bit protected-mode drivers. Windows 9x supports both, but Windows NT/2000/XP/2003 use only 32-bit drivers.

Device drivers under Windows 9x

Windows 9x comes with 32-bit drivers for hundreds of hardware devices. Windows automatically loads these drivers into extended memory (memory above 1024K) at startup or when the device first needs them. However, Windows drivers don't support all older devices, so a system might sometimes need to use an older 16-bit real-mode device driver. These 16-bit drivers are loaded by entries in the *Config.sys*, *Autoexec.bat*, and *System.ini* files, text files used to configure DOS and Windows 3.x that are supported by Windows 9x for backward-compatibility. These drivers use upper memory addresses. When the driver is installed, the driver installation program makes appropriate entries in these files.

Note: Under DOS, when any program, such as a device driver, stays in memory until the CPU needs it is called *a terminate*-and-*stay-resident (TSR) program*. The term is seldom used today, except when talking about real mode programs.

Windows uses Autoexec.bat and Config.sys, in order to be backward-compatible with DOS, and uses System.ini, in order to be backward-compatible with Windows 3x. However, using 16-bit drivers can slow performance, so to get the most out of Windows 9x, use 32-bit protected-mode drivers designed for Windows 9x. When selecting a driver to install, be sure the driver claims to be Windows 9x compatible, which means that it's a 32-bit driver and you can install the driver using the Add New Hardware Wizard. If the driver must be installed using a setup program provided by the driver manufacturer and can't be installed using the Add New Hardware Wizard, then it's a 16-bit driver.

Windows 9x keeps information about 32-bit drivers in the Windows *registry*, a database of hardware and software settings, Windows configuration settings, user parameters, and application settings. Windows 32-bit drivers are sometimes called *dynamic drivers,* because they can be loaded into memory when the device is accessed and then unloaded to conserve memory when the device is disconnected or turned off. Drivers that always remain in memory are called *static drivers*.

Sometimes, to address bugs, make improvements, or add features, manufacturers release device drivers that are more recent than those included with Windows. Whenever possible, it's best to use the latest driver available for a device provided by the device manufacturer. You can usually download these updated drivers from the manufacturer's Web site. For example, let's say you just borrowed a printer from a friend but you forgot to borrow the CD with the printer drivers on it. You can go to the printer manufacturer's Web site, download the drivers to a folder on your PC, and install the driver under Windows

Sixteen-bit drivers under Windows 9x can cause slow performance, so use 32-bit drivers whenever possible. Sometimes, it can be difficult to determine whether a device driver is 16-bit or 32-bit. One way to identify whether Windows 9x is using a 16-bit driver is to go into Device Manager and look for an exclamation point beside the device. This indicates that the driver has a problem. This might indicate that the driver is a 16-bit driver. If a driver is loaded from Config.sys or Autoexec.bat, it's a 16-bit driver; if it's loaded from the registry, it's a 32-bit driver. System.ini can contain both types. The following table summarizes basic information about device drivers under Windows 9x.

Characteristics	16-bit device drivers	32-bit device drivers
Operating mode	Real mode	Protected mode
Use of memory	May use upper memory addresses	Stored in extended memory
How loaded	Loaded by a command line in Config.sys, Autoexec.bat, or System.ini	Automatically loaded from the registry by Windows 9x at startup or when the device is used
How changed	Edit the Config.sys or Autoexec.bat files	From Device Manager, select the device and use the Properties, Driver tab
How to identify the type	In Device Manager, look for an exclamation point beside the device name	Look to see how the driver is loaded, from the registry System.ini, Autoexec.bat, or Config.sys
When to use this type	Use a 16-bit driver under Windows only when a 32-bit driver isn't available. When operating under DOS, 16-bit drivers are required	When you can, always use 32-bit drivers, because they're faster and give fewer configuration problems

Device drivers under Windows 2000

Windows 2000 installs protected-mode drivers in the same way as Windows 9x, but Windows 2000 doesn't claim to support 16-bit device drivers. For Windows 2000, always check the hardware compatibility list (HCL) to determine if a driver works under Windows 2000. Go to the following Microsoft Web site and search for your device:

```
www.microsoft.com/windows2000/professional/howtobuy/
upgrading/compat
```

If the device doesn't install properly or produces errors, check the manufacturer's Web site for a driver that the manufacturer says is compatible with Windows 2000.

Do it!

B-2: Using Device Manager

Here's how	Here's why
1 Right-click **My Computer** on the desktop	To access Device Manager using Windows 9x.
Choose **Properties**	From the shortcut menu.
Click the **Device Manager** tab	
2 From the System Properties window, click the **Hardware** tab	For Windows 2000.
Click **Device Manager**	
3 Record the following information:	
Does your computer have a network card installed? If so, what's the name of the card?	
What are three settings that can be changed under Device Manager?	
What are all the hardware devices that Device Manager recognizes as present?	

Topic C: Application management

Explanation

Most application software fits into the following eight categories:

- Word processing
- Spreadsheets
- Database management
- Graphics
- Communications
- Games
- Mathematical modeling
- Software development

Each software category contains many different products. For example, some popular database management packages include Access, Paradox, and Filemaker, and two popular word-processing packages include Word and WordPerfect. Some application software manufacturers produce suites of software, which combine a word-processing program and spreadsheet program and usually include a database management program, a presentation package, an e-mail package, and a World Wide Web browser package. Suites have many advantages, including providing similar user interfaces. The programs are designed to make it easy to move data from one suite program to another, and files within a suite's programs can be linked, so that updates to data or text are automatically recorded in all linked files.

Application software is designed to work on a particular OS. An application depends on an OS to provide access to hardware resources, manage its data in memory and in secondary storage, and perform many other background tasks. For example, consider an application running on Windows 98. Windows 98 loads the application and executes it. The application can't run or load itself without Windows 98. Windows 98 stays available to the application for the entire time the application is running. The application passes certain functions to Windows 98, such as reading from a CD-ROM or printing.

An application written to work with one OS, such as Windows 98, doesn't necessarily work with another, such as a Macintosh system. There are, however, some exceptions. For instance, OS/2 is written so that any application designed to work with DOS also works with OS/2, an early selling point for OS/2. However, to take full advantage of an operating system's power and an application's power, buy application software written specifically for your OS.

Application software is available on floppy disks and CD-ROMs, or it can be downloaded from the Internet. The application usually must be installed on a hard drive in order to run. During the installation, the install program creates folders on the hard drive and copies files to them. For Windows, it also makes entries in the Windows registry and puts files in the folder and subfolders that it later uses as software components to perform various tasks. It can also place icons on the desktop and add entries to the Start menu. Because the install program does all the work for you, installing a software package usually is very easy.

Loading and initializing application software

Opening an application is a simple task for the user. For example, in Windows, you click the shortcut icon on the desktop, and the application window opens ready for use. But what happens behind the scenes between your click and the appearance of the application? Software or programs are stored in program files on a secondary storage device, such as a hard drive or CD, until needed. Before they can be executed, they must first be copied or loaded into RAM and assigned memory addresses, as shown in Exhibit 2-31.

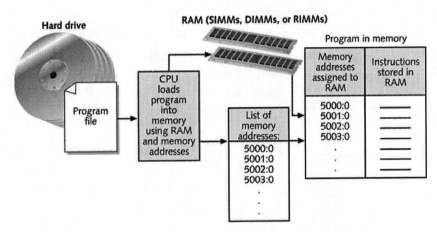

Exhibit 2-31: RAM is a hardware resource; memory addresses are system resources

Even the operating system programs must be copied from the hard drive into memory before these programs are executed. The following process is illustrated in Exhibit 2-32:

1   The OS program files are copied into memory and assigned memory addresses and then executed.
2   The OS copies a program file into memory, which is executed.
3   The program requests data from the hard drive, which is copied into memory, and then the program uses that data.

In Exhibit 2-32, you can see that memory is used by the OS, the applications, and data. In addition, BIOS and device drivers are also using memory and are executed from memory as the OS needs them.

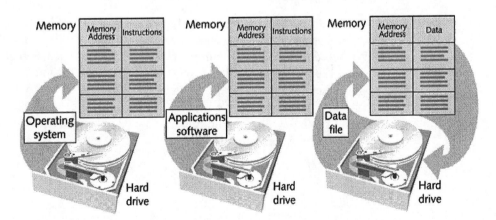

Exhibit 2-32: Memory is used by the OS, the applications, and data

Understanding the process of loading and initializing software is important to people responsible for supporting PCs. Listed below are the major steps that must take place.

1 The OS receives the command to execute the application.

2 The OS locates the program file for the application.

3 The OS loads the program file into memory.

4 The OS gives control to the program.

5 The program requests memory addresses from the OS for its data.

6 The program initializes itself and possibly requests that data from secondary storage be loaded into memory.

7 The program turns to the user for its first instruction.

Begin with Windows 98 in MS-DOS mode as our OS. Before we discuss the specific command to load software in real mode, let's first look at the command prompt the user sees and the information it provides. If you boot a Windows 98 PC from a floppy disk into command prompt mode, the MS-DOS prompt looks like this:

```
A:\>
```

This prompt is called the A prompt. The MS-DOS prompt (A:\>) displayed immediately after booting means that the OS was copied from drive A, which is where the startup disk containing enough of the OS to load in real mode is stored. Drive A then becomes the default drive and default directory, sometimes called the current working drive and directory, which the OS automatically uses to save and retrieve files. The colon following the letter identifies the letter as the name of a drive, and the backslash identifies the directory on the drive as the root or main directory. The > symbol is the prompt symbol that the OS uses to say, "Enter your command here." To make the hard drive (drive C) the default drive, enter C: at the A prompt.

The prompt now looks like this:

```
C:\>
```

Recall that when an OS first formats a hard drive for use, the format procedure creates a single directory on the drive, called the root directory. This directory is written in the OS command lines as a single backslash (\), or forward slash in the case of UNIX, with no other directory name following. In the preceding OS prompt, the backslash indicates that it's the root directory.

Starting a program

At the command prompt, when you type a single group of letters with no spaces, the OS assumes that you want to execute a program that has the file name that you just typed and is stored in a program file in the current directory. The OS first attempts to find the program file by that name, then copies the file into RAM, and then executes the program. Let's use the program, Mem.exe, a Windows 9x utility to display how memory is currently allocated, as our example. The program file, Mem.exe, is stored on the hard drive in C:\Windows\command folder. Note what happens in Exhibit 2-33 when you type mem at the A: prompt, like this:

```
A:\>mem
```

```
A:\>mem
Bad command or file name

A:\>c:

C:\>cd\windows\command

C:\WINDOWS\COMMAND>mem

Memory Type          Total      Used      Free
- - - - - - - - - -  - - - - - -  - - - -  - - - - - -
Conventional          640K      160K      480K
Upper                   0K        0K        0K
Reserved                0K        0K        0K
Extended (XMS)      130,036K   2,112K   127,924K

Total memory        130,676K   2,272K   128,404K

Total under 1 MB      640K      160K      480K

Largest executable program size         479K (490, 816 bytes)
Largest free upper memory block           0K        (0 bytes)
MS-DOS is resident in the high memory area.

C:\WINDOWS\COMMAND>
```

Exhibit 2-33: Finding a program file

The OS says it can't find the program to execute. It looked only on the floppy disk (drive A) for Mem.com, Mem.exe, or Mem.bat, the three file extensions that MS-DOS recognizes for programs. If the OS doesn't find any of these files in the current directory, it stops looking and displays the error message:

```
Bad command or file name
```

To help the OS locate the program file, you must first change the default drive to the hard drive by giving the command:

```
A:\> C:
```

Notice, in Exhibit 2-33, that the prompt changes to C:\>, indicating that the logical drive C on the hard drive is the default drive. Now you change the default directory on the hard drive to \Windows\Command using the *CD (change directory)* command like this:

```
C:\>CD\windows\command
```

Remember that DOS and Windows commands aren't case-sensitive, so it makes no difference whether you type CD, Cd, or cd. The prompt now looks like this:

```
C:\WINDOWS\COMMAND>
```

Next, in Exhibit 2-33, we enter the mem command again, and this time the OS locates and executes the program file.

There's another way to tell the OS where to look to find program files. As part of the boot procedure, you can give the OS a list of paths in which to look for executable program files beyond the default directory, by using the Path command. You can cause the Path command to be executed automatically during the boot process by storing the command in the Autoexec.bat file. You can also execute the Path command at any time after booting. The last Path command you execute overrides any previous ones.

To see the list of paths that are presently active, type Path at the command prompt, and then press Enter, as shown in the first Path command in Exhibit 2-34. To enter a new list of paths, type Path followed by each path name, separating one path from the next by a semicolon, as shown in the second Path command in Exhibit 2-34.

```
C:\>path
PATH=F:\;A:\;G:\

C:\>path F:\;A:\G:\C:\;C:\Windows\Command

C:\>path
PATH=F:\;A:\G:\C:\;C\WINDOWS\COMMAND

C:\>
```

Exhibit 2-34: The path command

In Exhibit 2-34, the first Path command displays the list of active paths, which are three logical drives, F, A, and G. The second Path command changes this list; giving the OS the same three logical drives as well as the drive C root directory and the C:\Windows\Command directory. The last Path command displays the new list of active paths.

When you tell the OS to execute a program, you can also include the path to that program file as part of the command line. For example, if the Mem.exe file is stored in the directory C:\Windows\Command, you can execute the program by typing the following:

```
A:\> C:\Windows\Command\Mem.exe
```

Here, you're telling the OS that the name of the program file is Mem.exe and that its location is in the directory \Windows\Command on drive C. With this method, the directory and drive that contains the Mem program need not be the defaults, nor do you need to use the Path command.

In summary, using the MS-DOS mode of Windows 9x, the OS searches for executable program files using the following rules:

1 If no path is given before the file name, the OS looks in the current directory.

2 If there's a path given in front of the file name in the command line, the OS looks in that path.

3 If no path is given, and the file isn't in the current directory, the OS looks in the paths given to it by the last Path command executed.

If you've an Autoexec.bat file in your root directory when Windows 9x starts, it reads the Path command stored in that file. You can also store DOS commands in batch files and execute them from Windows 9x by double-clicking the file name of the batch file in Explorer.

If you don't have an Autoexec.bat file with a Path command, Windows 9x uses a default path:

```
C:\Windows; C:\Windows\Command
```

Copying the program into memory

Recall that once the OS finds the program file, it copies the file into memory (RAM) in a location that the OS chooses, as shown in Exhibit 2-35. After it copies the program into memory, the OS goes to the first address in memory occupied by the program to receive its first instruction. If the program requests some memory for its data, and most will, the OS decides which memory addresses to give the program, usually the memory after the program.

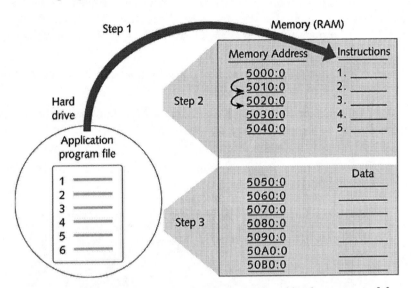

Exhibit 2-35: Applications software is stored in files but executed from memory

If the program wants to write or read data to or from memory, the OS manages these tasks. If the program needs to print, display something on the screen, or read from or write to the hard drive or a floppy disk, the OS does the work and returns to the program when finished. In other words, the OS is the software behind the software, doing the background tasks for an application or utility program.

Do it!

C-1: Discussing execution of applications

Questions	Answers
1 If the command prompt is A:\> and you want the default drive to be drive C, what command do you use?	
2 What's the command to change the default directory to \Windows?	
3 If you enter the command MEM at the command prompt, what file names and extensions does the OS look for to execute a program?	

Starting an application in Windows

Explanation

When using the Windows GUI, once an application is installed, there are four ways to execute software:

- Double-click a shortcut icon on the desktop. You can place a shortcut icon directly on the desktop for the applications you use often and want to get to quickly. These shortcuts contain the command line used to execute the application. To view this command line, right-click an application icon. From the menu that appears, select Properties. The icon's Properties box appears, as shown in Exhibit 2-36. From this box, you can view the complete command line that the icon represents.

- Click the Start button, choose Programs, and then choose the program from the list of installed software.

- Use the Run command: Click the Start button, and then choose Run to display the Run dialog box, as shown in Exhibit 2-37. In this box, enter a command line or click Browse to search for a program file to execute.

- Execute a program or launch an application file by double-clicking the file name in Windows Explorer or My Computer.

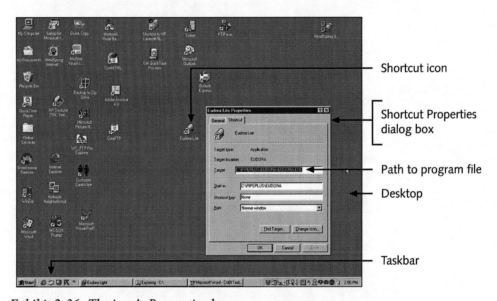

Shortcut icon

Shortcut Properties dialog box

Path to program file

Desktop

Taskbar

Exhibit 2-36: The icon's Properties box

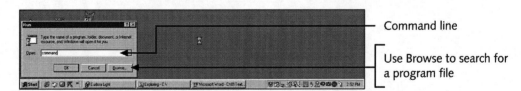

Command line

Use Browse to search for a program file

Exhibit 2-37: The Windows Run dialog box allows entering DOS-like commands

Do it! **C-2: Installing Windows components**

Here's how	Here's why
1 Open Control Panel	
Double-click **Add/Remove Programs**	
2 Click the **Windows Setup** tab	
Verify that there are several categories of Windows components listed in the Components field	
3 Click **Accessories**	
Click **Details**	A window opens displaying Windows components in the Accessories category.
4 Check **Desktop Wallpaper**	
Click **OK**	To close the window.
5 Click **Apply**	
6 Click **OK**	When prompted.
Type the path to the Windows setup files	
Click **OK**	Windows installs the files containing the new desktop wallpaper.
7 After the installation of the files containing the new desktop wallpaper is complete, click **OK**	To exit the Add/Remove Programs utility.
8 Double-click **Display**	In the Control Panel.

9 Click the **Background** tab

Browse through the various wallpapers

Experiment with the Tile, Center, and Stretch options in the dropdown menu

Observe the preview of your wallpaper selections in the Background tab

10 Select a background combination you like

Click **Apply**

Click **OK**   To close the Display utility.

11 Close any other open windows

Observe your new desktop wallpaper

12 What collection of files is needed to install a new Windows component?

13 Which utility is used to install new Windows components?

14 What category of components is Desktop Wallpaper part of?

15 What utility did you use to select a wallpaper for your system?

16 Is it necessary to apply the Display properties before you see what a wallpaper looks like?

Unit summary: Hardware and software management

Topic A   In this topic, you learned how an OS and other software manage system **hardware**. You learned about the **motherboard, CPU,** and **memory**. You learned about the different types of **buses**, such as **ISA, PCI, AGP, USB,** and **FireWire**. Then you learned about **system resources**, such as **memory addresses, IRQ, I/O addresses,** and **DMA channels**. You learned how to identify the **BIOS** on the motherboard. You also learned about the **CMOS** setup chip and hard drives and other **secondary storage devices**.

Topic B   In this topic, you learned how an OS interacts with other software such as the **BIOS** and **device drivers**. You learned about the **real** and **protected** operating modes. Then you learned how an OS uses BIOS. You also learned how device drivers control hardware.

Topic C   In this topic, you learned how an OS **loads** and **initializes** an **application**. You learned how an application is **started in DOS**. You then learned how the application is **copied into memory**. You also learned how to **start** an application using the Windows GUI.

Review questions

1 How does firmware differ from a software program stored on the hard drive?

2 Which Windows operating systems don't support Plug and Play?

3 Memory above 1024K is called _____.

4 Real mode allows programs direct access to _____, but protected mode doesn't.

5 List four system resources that software uses to manage hardware.

6 What Windows 9x utility allows you to see the IRQ assignments made to devices?

7 What must happen to a program that's stored on a hard drive before it can be executed?

8 How is a software interrupt initiated?

9 How is a hardware interrupt initiated?

10 Describe a request handler. Where in memory can you find a list of addresses where request handlers are located?

11 When the mouse initiates a hardware interrupt to the CPU, how does the CPU know where to find a program to service the mouse?

12 If memory addresses are used by the CPU to access memory, then what are I/O addresses used for?

13 What is the I/O address range for the keyboard?

14 Why are DMA channels not as popular as they once were with high-speed devices?

15 Name a device that uses polling in order to be serviced by the CPU.

16 Which Windows operating systems use Plug and Play, but don't depend on BIOS Plug and Play to aid in the configuration process?

17 What's the name of the memory extender program used by DOS and Windows 9x?

18 When an OS uses part of a hard drive to act like memory, what's the file on the hard drive called that's used for this virtual memory?

19 List three text files that Windows 9x supports for loading device drivers in order to remain backward-compatible with DOS and Windows 3.x.

20 Name one way BIOS and device drivers are the same. Name one way they're different.

21 Where in memory are 32-bit device drivers stored?

22 Describe how you can change the contents of the CMOS RAM setup chip.

23 Is a mouse more likely to be controlled by a device driver or by system BIOS?

24 What do the letters IRQ represent?

25 What are 3 common types of ports available for hardware devices on a computer?

26 What do the letters BIOS represent?

27 What do the letters CMOS represent?

28 A hard drive is categorized as a primary storage device. True or false?

29 How many characters can be in a file name using Windows 95 or later?

30 The letters FAT represent:

31 What does the term "protected-mode" actually mean?

32 Name one device that's likely to be controlled by system BIOS.

33 Using Device Manager, what do you look for to indicate that a device driver is likely to be 16-bit software?

34 What makes BIOS a "good" BIOS according to Microsoft?

35 What's a device driver?

36 List four ways an application can be launched from the Windows desktop.

Independent practice activity

The Microsoft Diagnostics (MSD) utility, which is included with both DOS and all versions of Windows, examines your system and displays useful information about ports, devices, memory, and the like. You want to install and use MSD. Before you can begin using MSD, you need to copy the program file to your hard disk.

1 Insert the Windows 98 installation CD into your CD-ROM drive or access the setup files at another location.

2 Copy the file **MSD.EXE** from the Windows 98 Tools/OldMSDOS directory to your hard drive, storing it in a folder named **Tools**.

You'll use MSD in a real mode environment.

1 Reboot your computer using the bootable floppy disk or a Windows 98 startup disk to boot your PC into real mode and provide a command prompt.

2 Choose **Start**

3 Click **Shut Down**

4 Click **Restart Computer in MS-DOS mode**.

5 At the command prompt, type **C:\TOOLS\MSD.EXE**. Press Enter.

6 Note that this is a way to execute a program file located in a directory other than the one you're working in. You told the computer the exact path, called an absolute path, to the file you wanted to execute. At this point, your screen should look similar Exhibit 2-38.

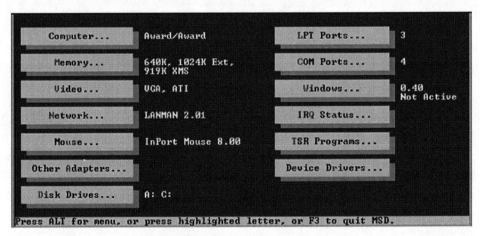

Exhibit 2-38: The MSD screen

7 Study all the MSD menu options and record the following information.

8 What categories of information are available in MSD?

9 What version of the operating system are you running?

10 What COM ports are available on the system?

11 What IRQ and Port Address are associated with COM1?

12 How far does the MEMORY map extend?

13 What's the Address Range at 1024K?

14 Save the information you noted so that you can compare it with the information you obtain from MSD in the next set of steps.

15 Click **File** on the MSD menu bar.

16 Click **Exit**.

17 Remove the floppy disk.

18 Reboot your system to the Windows desktop.

19 Using Windows Explorer, double-click the **MSD.EXE** file to start it again.

20 With MSD open, answer the following questions:

21 What categories of information are available in MSD?

22 What version of the operating system are you running?

23 What COM ports are available on the system?

24 What IRQ and Port Address are associated with COM1?

25 How far does the MEMORY map extend?

26 What is the Address Range at 1024K?

27 Compare the information obtained the first time you used MSD with the information you obtained the second time.

28 Record the following information.

29 How does your first set of answers compare to your second set of answers?

30 How do you explain the differences?

31 What key can you press to exit MSD?

32 Close MSD.

Unit 3

The boot process and command line management

Unit time: 120 minutes

Complete this unit, and you'll know how to:

A Describe the steps to boot the computer.

B Create and use Windows 9x rescue disks to troubleshoot and solve problems while booting Windows.

C View and manage memory in DOS and Windows 9x.

D Use the command line to use and manage floppy disks and hard drives in DOS and Windows 9x.

Topic A: The boot process

Explanation

An OS and a CPU can operate in either real mode or protected mode. In this unit, you'll learn how to use the command line in real mode under Windows 9x, which is called MS-DOS mode. Real mode can be used to boot the computer and troubleshoot problems with Windows when a computer cannot boot to the Windows desktop.

Windows 9x uses DOS-like core components, so if you learn and understand MS-DOS mode commands you will have a better understanding of the foundation of Windows. In addition, you'll learn many commands that can also be used with the Recovery Console tool, which can be used to troubleshoot booting problems in Windows 2000/XP.

Booting up your computer

Understanding what happens when you first turn on your PC and boot up to an operating system interface is essential to learning to troubleshoot problems with the operating system.

The term *booting up* comes from the phrase "lifting yourself up by your bootstraps" and refers to the computer bringing itself up to an operable state without user intervention. Booting up can refer to either a soft boot or hard boot. A *hard boot*, also known as a *cold boot*, involves initially turning on the power with the on/off switch. A *soft boot*, also known as a *warm boot*, involves using the operating system to restart the computer. For DOS, pressing the three keys Ctrl, Alt, and Del at the same time performs a soft boot. For Windows 9x and Windows NT/2000/XP, one way to soft boot is to choose Start, Shut Down, select Restart from the Shut Down list, and then click OK. You can also press Ctrl + Alt + Del and then select Shut Down from the Close Program dialog box.

A hard boot is more stressful on your machine than a soft boot.

Also, a soft boot is faster. Always use the soft boot method to restart unless the soft boot method doesn't work. If you must power down, avoid turning off the power switch and immediately turning it back on without a pause, because this can damage the machine. Some PCs have a reset button on the front of the case. Pressing the reset button starts the booting process at an earlier point than does the operating-system soft boot and is, therefore, a little slower but might work when the OS soft boot fails. For newer motherboards, pressing the reset button restarts the system without actually powering off and thus avoids the stress to the system caused by the initial power surge when the power first comes on.

Boot process overview

A successful boot process depends on the hardware, the BIOS, and the operating system all performing without errors. If errors occur, they could stall or lock the boot process.

The boot process can be divided into four main steps:

- BIOS checking hardware
- Loading the operating system
- Initializing the operating system
- Loading and executing an application

We will examine the first three steps in detail and get a brief overview of the final step. Startup BIOS is in control for the first step; control is turned over to the OS in the second step.

Step 1: BIOS checking hardware

When you turn on the power to a PC, the CPU begins the boot process by initializing itself and then turning to the ROM BIOS for instructions. The ROM BIOS then performs the *power-on self test (POST)*. Listed below are the key steps in this process.

- When the power is first turned on, the system clock begins to generate clock pulses.
- The CPU begins working and initializes itself (resetting its internal values).
- The CPU turns to memory address FFFF0h, which is the memory address always assigned to the first instruction in the ROM BIOS startup program.
- This instruction directs the CPU to run POST.
- POST first checks the BIOS program operating it and then tests CMOS RAM.
- A test determines that there has not been a battery failure.
- Hardware interrupts are disabled. (This means that pressing a key on the keyboard or using another input device at this point will not affect anything.)
- Tests are run on the CPU, and it is initialized further.
- A check determines if this is a cold boot. If so, the first 16 KB of RAM is tested.
- Hardware devices installed on the computer are inventoried and compared to configuration information.
- Video cards, memory, keyboard, floppy disks, hard drives, ports, and other hardware devices are tested and configured. IRQ, I/O addresses, and DMA assignments are made. The OS will later complete this process.
- Some devices are set up to go into "sleep mode" to conserve electricity.
- The DMA controller is checked.
- Interrupt vectors are moved into the interrupt vector table.
- The interrupt controller is checked.
- CMOS setup (a BIOS program to change CMOS configuration data) is run if requested.
- The BIOS begins its search for an OS.

During POST, before the CPU has checked the video system, errors are communicated by beeps. Short and long beeps indicate an error. After POST checks and verifies the video controller card, POST can use the monitor to display its progress.

Note: POST does not check to see if a monitor is present or working.

After checking video, POST checks RAM by writing and reading data. A running count of RAM is displayed on the monitor during this phase.

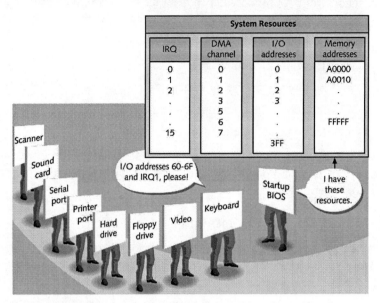

Exhibit 3-1: BIOS checking hardware

Next, the keyboard is checked, and with some types of BIOS if you press and hold any keys at this point an error occurs. Secondary storage is also checked, which includes floppy disk drives and hard drives. The hardware that POST finds is checked against the data stored in the CMOS chip, jumpers, and/or DIP switches to determine if they agree.

System resources are assigned to devices by more than one method. Jumpers and DIP switches might be set to request a resource (for example, a jumper might be set "on" if IRQ 5 is requested or "off" if IRQ 7 is requested), or the resources needed might simply be hard-coded into the BIOS as part of the ROM programming that cannot be changed.

On earlier computers, system resources were always assigned to the device during the boot process, as shown in Exhibit 3-1. Think of the process as a dialog. First, the startup BIOS recognizes that a hardware device is present. The BIOS asks the device, "What resources do you need?" The device says, "I need this IRQ, these I/O addresses, this DMA channel, and these addresses in upper memory for my BIOS." For legacy hardware, a device is the sole owner of these resources and problems occur when more than one device attempts to use the same resource. However, some newer buses allow more than one device to share the same IRQ and newer protected-mode types of BIOS don't require upper memory addresses. Today, more flexible plug and play devices simply say, "I need one IRQ, some I/O addresses, and this many memory addresses for my BIOS. Please tell me the resources I can use."

If a computer takes full advantage of the Windows 9x OS, its BIOS is plug and play BIOS, which means that BIOS configures the plug and play devices before it loads Windows 9x. A plug and play device allows BIOS to select the device's computer resources, such as an IRQ, an I/O address, and DMA channels. BIOS first enables the devices that are not plug and play, and then tries to make the plug and play devices use the leftover resources. The BIOS then turns this information over to Windows 9x when it loads, which completes the assignment of resources. Windows 2000 and Windows XP use an advanced version of plug and play that does not use the BIOS plug and play. Windows NT does not support plug and play.

Step 2: Loading the operating system

Once POST and the first pass at assignment of resources is complete, the next step is to load an OS. Most often the OS is loaded from logical drive C on the hard drive. The minimum information required on the hard drive to load an OS is listed below. You can see some of these items labeled in Exhibit 3-2.

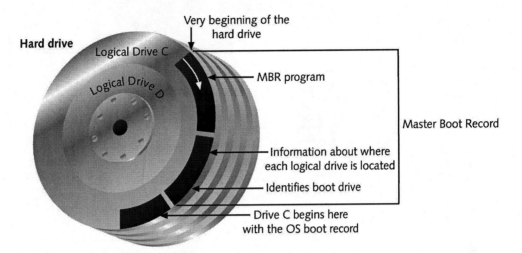

Exhibit 3-2: A logical hard drive

- A sector at the very beginning of the hard drive, called the *Master Boot Record (MBR)*, contains a program needed to locate the beginning of the OS.
- A *partition table* contains a map to the logical drives on the hard drive, including how many partitions and logical drives there are, which drive is the boot drive (the *active partition*), and where each logical drive begins and ends.
- At the beginning of the boot drive is the OS boot record that loads the first program file of the OS. For Windows 9x, that program is *Io.sys*.
- For Windows 9x, *Msdos.sys* is needed next, followed by *Command.com*. These two files, plus Io.sys, are the core components of the real-mode portion of Windows 9x. The Windows NT/2000/XP/2003 operating systems have a different set of startup files.

One logical drive on the hard drive, usually drive C, is designated as the boot drive, and the OS is stored on it. At the beginning of this logical drive is the OS boot record, which contains the *bootstrap loader*, a program that knows the names of the files that contain the core programs of the OS.

Step 2 begins with BIOS looking to CMOS setup to find out which secondary storage device should have the OS. (See Exhibit 3-3.)

Setup might instruct the BIOS to first look on drive C and if no OS is found there, then try drive A. Or the BIOS might look on drive A and then drive C. If BIOS looks first to drive A and does not find a disk in the drive, it turns to drive C. If it first looks to drive A and finds a disk in the drive, but the disk does not contain the OS (for Windows 9x, that means the OS boot record, Io.sys, Msdos.sys, and Command.com), then this or a similar error message appears:

```
Non-system disk or disk error, press any key to continue
```

You must replace the disk with one that contains the OS or simply remove the disk to force the BIOS to continue on to the next drive to find the OS.

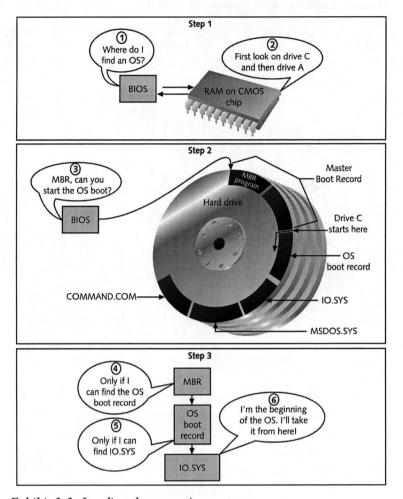

Exhibit 3-3: Loading the operating system

Step 3: Initializing the operating system

The operating system configures the system and completes its own loading. The OS checks some of the same things that startup BIOS checked, such as available memory and whether that memory is reliable. Additionally, the OS continues beyond that by loading the software to control a mouse, CD-ROM, scanner, and other peripheral devices. These devices generally have device drivers stored on the hard drive.

Step 4: Loading and executing an application

In the forth step, the user executes application software. When you tell the OS to execute an application, the OS first must find the application software on the hard drive, CD-ROM, or other secondary storage device, copy the software into memory, and then turn control over to it. Finally, you can command the application software, which makes requests to the OS, which, in turn, uses the system resources, system BIOS, and device drivers to interface with and control the hardware. At this point, the user is like the passenger in the back seat of the car with the chauffeur at the wheel. The trip has begun!

Loading the Windows 9x MS-DOS core

When booting, if only the MS-DOS core of Windows 9x is loaded, the OS goes to a real-mode command prompt similar to a DOS command prompt. It's important for a PC technician to understand this real-mode DOS core, because it is often used as a troubleshooting tool when the hard drive fails. You can boot to a command prompt in several ways, including booting from a Windows startup disk or using the Windows startup menu.

In Step 2 of Exhibit 3-3, the BIOS locates the MBR on the hard drive, which looks to the partition table to determine where the logical boot drive is physically located on the drive. It then turns to the OS boot record of that logical drive.

The operating system *boot record* is simply the boot sector of the partition and is a very short program. It loads just one *hidden file*, which makes up the DOS core, into memory, as shown in Exhibit 3-3 Step 3 and Exhibit 3-4). A hidden file is a file that is not displayed in the directory list. The operating system boot record program knows the file name, which is Io.sys. The Io.sys file contains the basic I/O software for real mode and requires that the Msdos.sys file be present. Msdos.sys is a text file that contains some parameters and switches that can be set to affect the way the OS boots.

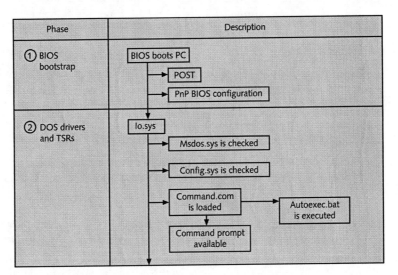

Exhibit 3-4: Boot step 3

Note: The three OS files that are necessary in Windows 9x to boot to a command prompt are Io.sys, Msdos.sys, and Command.com. Config.sys and Autoexec.bat are not required but are used if they are present.

Once Io.sys is loaded into memory, the boot record program is no longer needed, and control is turned over to Io.sys. This program looks for Msdos.sys, reads it, and uses the settings in it. Io.sys then looks on the hard drive for a file named Config.sys. This configuration file contains commands that tell Io.sys how many files it can open at any one time (Files=) and how many file buffers to create (Buffers=). (A *buffer* is a temporary holding area for files.) Config.sys also includes the commands to load device drivers (Device=) as well as other information. An example of a typical command in Config.sys is the following command, which gives real-mode Io.sys access to memory above 1 MB, called extended memory:

```
Device=himem.sys
```

Several drivers can be loaded into memory from commands in Config.sys. Io.sys puts these programs in memory wherever it chooses. However, a program can request that it be put in a certain memory location.

Sometimes Config.sys is used to create a *RAM drive*. A RAM drive is an area of memory that looks and acts like a hard drive. However, a RAM drive is much faster than a hard drive because it is memory. A RAM drive is sometimes used to speed up access to often-used software. Windows creates a RAM drive when booting from the startup disk, to hold files after they have been uncompressed. This eliminates the need for access to the hard drive and provides space for those files that might not fit on a floppy disk. An example of a command in Config.sys to create a RAM drive is:

```
device=ramdrive.sys 2048
```

The command tells the operating system to create a RAM drive that is 2048 K in size.

After Config.sys is processed, Io.sys looks for another OS file, named Command.com. This file has three functions: managing I/O, directing internal OS commands such as Copy and Dir, and locating the Autoexec.bat file.

Note: Some OS commands are *internal commands*, which means they are embedded in the Command.com file. Others are *external commands*, meaning they have their own program files. An example of an external command is Format, stored in the file Format.com.

Command.com looks for Autoexec.bat on the drive used to boot the OS. If Autoexec.bat is found, then Command.com executes it. The file name Autoexec.bat stands for "automatically executed batch file." A *batch file* is a text file that contains a series of commands that are executed in order. Autoexec.bat lists OS commands that execute automatically each time the OS is loaded. The following commands are examples of commands that might be found in the Autoexec.bat file:

- The Path command lists paths to various hard drive locations, separated by semicolons.

  ```
  PATH C:\;C:\Windows;
  ```

- The Set command is used to create and assign a value to an environmental variable that can later be read by an application. A software installation program might add a Set command to your Autoexec.bat file. Later, the software will use the environmental variable in the program. An example of a Set command assigning a path to the variable Mypath is:

  ```
  Set Mypath=C:\VERT
  ```

- The Temp environment variable lets applications know where temporary files will be stored. By default, DOS stores temporary files in `C:\Temp`, Windows 9x uses `C:\Windows\Temp`, Windows NT uses `C:\Temp`, and Windows 2000/XP uses `%USERPROFILE%\Local Settings\Temp`. Add the Temp command to Autoexec.bat if applications are putting temporary files in strange locations.

  ```
  Temp=C:\Temp
  ```

- The Echo command turns on and off the displaying of commands and messages. Use it in a batch file to control output to screen.

  ```
  Echo off
  ```

The boot process with a command prompt is completed after Autoexec.bat has finished executing. At this point, Command.com is the program in charge, providing you with a command prompt and waiting for your command. On the other hand, if a program or menu was executed from Autoexec.bat, the program might present an interface to you.

The command prompt will indicate the drive that loaded the OS. If the OS files were loaded from a floppy disk, the command prompt will be A:\>, and if the OS was loaded from the hard drive, the command prompt will be C:\>. This drive and root directory are now the default drive and default directory, sometimes called the current working drive or directory.

If you want to load Windows, use the Win command. Enter this command at the C prompt:

```
C:\> WIN
```

Note: Commands used at a command prompt are not case sensitive; that is, you can enter WIN, Win, or win.

Do it!

A-1:   Observing the boot process

Here's how	Here's why
1 Perform the following steps if your computer has a reset button	
Press the reset button	
Record what happens	
2 Perform the following steps if your computer does not have a reset button:	
Turn off your system	
Turn your system back on	After few seconds.
3 Record every beep and light that goes on or off, and every message on the screen that you notice	
Compare your information with others	To verify that you are not overlooking something.

4   Record the following information after observing the boot process

    What type of video card are you using?

    Who is the BIOS vendor and what version of the BIOS are you using?

    As the computer boots, memory is counted. Observe the memory count and record the amount of memory detected. What number system is used to count this memory?

5   Unplug the keyboard

    Reboot the computer

    Record what happens that is different

6   Plug the keyboard back in

    Unplug the monitor

    Reboot the system

    Plug the monitor in   After you reboot.

    Record if the computer knew the monitor was missing

7   Put a floppy disk that is not bootable in drive A

    Reboot the system

    Record what you observe

    Record what caused the PC to not   If you booted to the desktop as normal.
    look to the floppy disk to load the
    OS

CMOS setup

CMOS contains a very small amount of memory, or RAM–enough to hold configuration or setup information about the computer. CMOS is responsible for remembering the current date and time, which hard drives and floppy drives are present, how the serial and parallel ports are configured, and so forth. When the computer is first turned on, it looks to the CMOS to find out what hardware it should expect to find.

The program to change the CMOS setup is stored in the ROM BIOS chip and can be accessed during the startup process. The keystrokes to enter CMOS setup are displayed somewhere on the screen during startup in a statement such as "Press the Del key to enter setup." Different types of BIOS use different keystrokes, as shown in the following table.

BIOS	Method for entering CMOS setup
AMI BIOS	Boot the computer, and then press the Delete key.
Award BIOS	Boot the computer, and then press the Delete key.
Older Phoenix BIOS	Boot the computer, and then press the Ctrl + Alt + Esc or Ctrl + Alt + S key combination.
Newer Phoenix BIOS	Boot the computer, and then press the F2 or F1 key.
Dell Computers with Phoenix BIOS	Boot the computer, and then press the Ctrl + Alt + Enter key combination.
Older Compaq computers such as the Deskpro 286 or 386	Place the diagnostics disk in the drive, reboot the system, and choose Computer Setup from the menu.
Newer Compaq computers like the Prolinea, Deskpro, DeskproXL, Deskpro LE, or Presario	Boot the computer and wait for two beeps. When the cursor is in the upper-right corner of the screen, press the F10 key.
All other older computers	Use the setup program on the floppy disk that came with the PC. If the floppy disk is lost, contact the motherboard manufacturer to obtain a replacement.

Note: For Compaq computers, the CMOS setup program is stored on the hard drive in a small, non-DOS partition of about 3 MB. If this partition becomes corrupted or the computer is an older model, you must run setup from a diagnostic disk. If you cannot run setup by pressing F10 at startup, it's likely that a damaged partition or a virus is taking up space in conventional memory.

The CMOS setup does not normally need to be changed except when there is a problem with hardware, a new floppy drive is installed, or a power-saving feature needs to be disabled or enabled. The CMOS setup can also hold a power-on password to help secure a system. Know that this password is not the same password that can be required by a Windows OS at startup.

Do it!

A-2: Examining and adjusting CMOS settings

Here's how	Here's why
1 Double-click the clock on the taskbar	To record the exact date and time as indicated by your computer's internal clock.
Record the date and time	
2 Close the Date/Time Properties window	
3 Start **SANDRA**	
Double-click **CPU & BIOS Information**	To determine which version of BIOS is installed on your computer.
4 From **Device**, choose **System BIOS**	
5 Record the manufacturer and version information for your BIOS	
6 Close **SANDRA**	
7 Using the information recorded in step 5, consult the CMOS/BIOS table to find out how to enter your system's setup utility	Alternately, you can look for a message on your screen when you first turn on the PC, which might read something like "Press F2 to access setup."
8 Insert a floppy disk	If a floppy disk is necessary to enter the CMOS setup utility.
9 Restart the computer	
10 Enter the setup utility by using the correct method for your computer	After the system restarts.
Observe the output	Notice that the CMOS utility groups settings by function. For example, all the power management features will be grouped in a Power Management window.
11 Select a category named **Standard CMOS Setup**	The main screen usually has a Help section describing how to make selections and exit the utility. Typically, you can use the arrow keys or Tab key to highlight options. After you have highlighted your selection, you usually need to press the Enter key, Page Down key, or the Spacebar. The main screen may or may not display a short summary of the highlighted category.

12 Verify that you see some or all of the following settings and list the current setting for each

In the Standard CMOS Setup screen.

Date:

Time:

For IDE hard drives, a table listing drive size and mode of operation, cylinder, head and sector information:

Floppy drive setup information, including drive letter and type:

Halt on error setup (the type of error that will halt the boot process):

Memory summary (summary of system memory divisions):

Boot sequence (drives the BIOS searches for an OS):

13 Exit the Standard CMOS setup screen

Return to the main page

Select a section named **Chipset Features Setup**

14 Record settings for the following, as well as any other settings in this section:

RAM setup options:

AGP setup options:

CPU-specific setup options:

Settings for serial and parallel ports:

Provisions for enabling/disabling onboard drive controllers and other embedded devices:

15 Exit to the CMOS setup main screen

To see options for loading CMOS defaults (which restores everything to factory settings and can be helpful in troubleshooting) as well as options for exiting with or without saving changes. There probably will be an option to set user and supervisor passwords as well as a utility to automatically detect IDE hard disk drives.

16 Return to the Standard CMOS setup screen

To change the date and time settings.

17 Highlight the time field(s)

Set the time ahead one hour

18 Move to the date field(s)

Set the date ahead one year

19 Return to the main CMOS setup screen

Select an option named **Save Settings and Exit**

Verify that you do want to save the settings

If prompted.

20 Wait while the system reboots

Allow Windows to load

21 Check the time and date

At the desktop.

Record if your CMOS setup changes are reflected in Windows

22 Reboot the system

Return to CMOS setup

Change to the correct time and date

23 Verify that the changes are again reflected in Windows

24 Propose a change that you could make to CMOS setup that would prevent a computer from booting successfully

Record what change you propose

25 Record if your instructor has approved the change

Some changes might cause information written to the hard drive to be lost, making it difficult to recover from the problem without reloading the hard drive.

26 Now go to another team's computer

Make the change to CMOS setup while they make a change to your system

27 Return to your computer

Troubleshoot the problem

Record the problem as a user would describe it

28 Record the steps you went through to discover the source of the problem and fix it

29 If you were to encounter this same problem in the future, what might you do differently to troubleshoot it?

30 Do all systems use the same method to enter CMOS setup? Can you enter CMOS setup after the system has booted?

31 How are settings usually grouped in the CMOS setup utility?

32 In what section will you usually find the time and date setup located in the CMOS setup utility?

33 What types of options are shown on the CMOS setup main screen?

34 What automatically happens after you exit CMOS setup?

35 What tool in SANDRA can you use to find information on your version of the BIOS?

36 Why does a computer need CMOS?

37 When troubleshooting a computer, when might you have to enter CMOS setup? List at least three reasons.

Topic B: Emergency startup disks

Explanation

Although you normally boot from a hard drive, problems with the hard drive sometimes make it necessary to boot from a floppy disk. A floppy disk that has enough software on it to load an operating system is called a *bootable disk*, or *system disk*. A bootable disk that has some utility programs on it to troubleshoot a failed hard drive is called a *rescue disk*, an *emergency startup disk (ESD)*, or a *startup disk*.

Having a rescue disk or rescue CD available for an emergency is very important, and a PC technician should always have one or more on hand. For DOS, you have to create your own rescue disk, making sure it includes the necessary system files and any utilities that you might need in an emergency.

Beginning with Windows 95, the OS provides an automated method to create a rescue floppy. This rescue disk is created under the Control Panel, Add/Remove Programs group. The files on the rescue disk vary with the version of Windows 9x. You can also create your own bootable disk or add your own utilities to the rescue disk created by Windows. In addition, in some situations, you'll need a startup disk, which you can use to boot up a PC for the first time after a new hard drive has been installed when the hard drive has nothing written on it.

You'll learn several ways to create these startup disks and then, you'll learn to use many of the utilities that Windows puts on these disks.

Windows 9x startup disks

Windows 9x can create a startup disk for you, complete with everything you need to troubleshoot a failed hard drive or prepare a new hard drive for use. The disk does not need to be created on the same computer that will use it, although in most cases you should use the same version of Windows that's used by the computer that will be using the disk. Follow these directions to create a startup disk for Windows 9x.

1   From the Taskbar, choose Start, point to Settings, and then click Control Panel.

2   In the Control Panel window, double-click the Add/Remove Programs icon.

3   Click the Startup Disk tab, and then click the Create Disk button. (See Exhibit 3-5.)

4   Windows might need the Windows CD to create the disk. Insert the CD if it is requested. The startup disk will then be created.

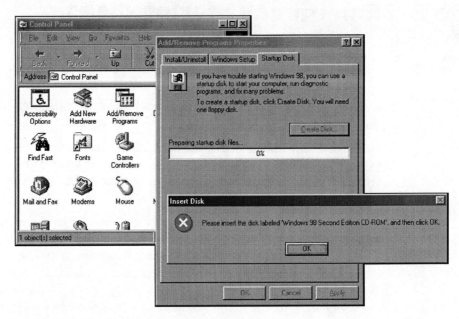

Exhibit 3-5: Windows might use the Windows CD to create a startup disk

The following table lists the files included on the startup disk for Windows 98, Second Edition (Windows 98 SE). Other versions of Windows 9x contain some, but not all, of these files.

File	Description
Aspi2dos.sys	Real-mode Adaptec CD-ROM driver
Aspi4dos.sys	Real-mode Adaptec CD-ROM driver
Aspi8dos.sys	Real-mode Adaptec CD-ROM driver
Aspi8u2.sys	Real-mode Adaptec CD-ROM driver
Aspicd.sys	Real-mode Adaptec CD-ROM driver
Autoexec.bat	Batch file that contains commands executed at startup
Btcdrom.sys	Mylex/BusLogic CD-ROM driver
Btdosm.sys	Mylex/BusLogic CD-ROM driver
Command.com	Command interpreter
Config.sys	Loads device drivers
Drvspace.bin	Used to access compressed hard drive
Ebd.cab	Cabinet file containing other utility program files
Ebd.sys	Identifies the startup disk

File	Description
Extract.exe	Used to uncompress the Ebd.cab file
Fdisk.exe	Partitions the hard drive
Findramd.exe	Locates the RAM drive during startup
Flashpt.sys	Mylex/BusLogic CD-ROM driver
Himem.sys	Extended Memory Manager
Io.sys	System boot file
Msdos.sys	Contains boot parameters
Oakcdrom.sys	Generic device driver for CD-ROM drives
Ramdrive.sys	Creates a RAM drive at startup
Readme.txt	Information about the startup disk
Setramd.bat	Searches for a drive letter to assign the RAM drive

The file Ebd.cab is a compressed file, called a *cabinet file*, which contains several compressed files that are listed in the following table. During startup, the contents of the cabinet file are uncompressed and copied to the RAM drive because there is not enough space for them on the floppy disk, and the startup disk assumes the hard drive might not be accessible. You can also use the Extract command to extract specific files when the RAM drive is not active.

File	Description
Attrib.exe	Changes file attributes
Chkdsk.exe	Determines the status of a disk and repairs it
Debug.exe	Debugging utility used to view contents of memory
Edit.com	Text editor used from a command prompt
Extract.exe	Extracts files from a cabinet file
Format.com	Formats a hard drive
Mscdex.exe	Microsoft utility to interface with a CD-ROM driver
Scandisk.exe	Checks and repairs hard drives
Scandisk.ini	Contains parameters for Scandisk.exe
Sys.com	Copies system files to a disk, making the disk bootable

Creating a bootable rescue disk for Windows 9x

By using Windows Explorer, you can create a system disk (Windows terminology for a bootable disk) and then copy program files to the disk that you might need in an emergency. The first step is to format the disk, which writes tracks on the disk and puts a file system on the disk. To format a floppy disk in Windows 9x, follow these steps.

1 Click the Start button on the Taskbar, point to Programs, and then click Windows Explorer. Right-click either drive A or drive B. The shortcut menu in Exhibit 3-6 appears.

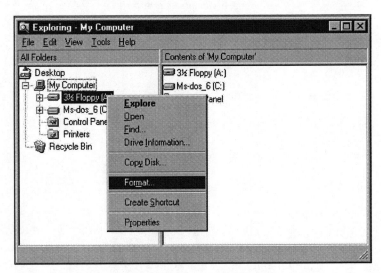

Exhibit 3-6: Menu for managing a floppy disk

2 Click Format on the menu. The dialog box shown in Exhibit 3-7 opens. Notice that there are three format options: Quick format (does not overwrite existing tracks), Full format (writes new tracks and sector markings), and an option to copy just the system files, files that are needed to make the disk bootable, to the disk. (Io.sys, Msdos.sys, and Command.com are copied to the disk.)

Exhibit 3-7: Format a disk in Microsoft Windows 9x

3 If the disk has been preformatted at the factory, you can select the third option, to copy system files only; but if the disk has never been formatted, select Full. Then choose Start.

From a command prompt, you can create your own bootable rescue disk and manually copy OS utility files to it. To make a bootable rescue disk for Windows 9x, from the command prompt, type:

```
Format A:/S
```

The command erases any files currently on the disk in drive A, and the /S switch copies the two hidden files, Io.sys and Msdos.sys, and Command.com to the disk in drive A, making the disk bootable.

You might also want to put some utility programs on the disk to help in troubleshooting. In addition to the files listed in the earlier tables, other files you might need are Xcopy.exe, MSD.exe, Mem.exe, and More.com.

Editing Autoexec.bat and Config.sys

You can change Config.sys and Autoexec.bat to configure your OS environment or troubleshoot boot problems. Use any text editor to edit the files. For example, from a command prompt, use EDIT, a full-screen text editor, and from Windows, use Notepad, WordPad, or Sysedit. From Windows, Sysedit is the preferred method.

If you make a mistake when editing Autoexec.bat or Config.sys, you can cause a boot problem. Before editing these files on your hard drive, always make a rescue disk. If you're editing one of these files on a rescue disk, you can make a backup copy of the file before you edit it or use the F5 or F8 keys to bypass the errors or have a second rescue disk ready just in case.

Note: Do not use word-processing software such as Word or Word-Perfect to edit Autoexec.bat or Config.sys, unless you use the ASCII text mode, because word-processing applications place control characters in their document files that prevent the OS from interpreting the file correctly.

Use the following steps to edit the Autoexec.bat and Config.sys files at the command prompt. Follow these steps to use Edit.com to edit the Autoexec.bat file on a rescue disk:

1 Boot to the command prompt and make drive A the default drive, as follows:

```
C:\> A:
```

2 If the default directory is not the root directory, make it so, using the CD (Change Directory) command, as follows:

```
A:\DOS> CD\
```

The prompt at the root directory of drive A should look like this:

```
A:\>
```

No matter what the default directory was (in this example, it was \DOS), the backslash (\) in the prompt indicates that the root is now the default.

3 If Autoexec.bat exists on the floppy disk, back it up, as follows:

```
A:\> Copy Autoexec.bat Autoexec.bk
```

4 Edit the file, as follows:

```
A:\> Edit Autoexec.bat
```

Your screen should be similar to the one shown in Exhibit 3-8. After you've made your changes, to exit from the editor, press the Alt key to activate the menus, and choose Exit from the File menu. When asked if you want to save your changes, respond Yes to exit the editor and save any changes.

```
  File  Edit  Search  View  Options  Help
                        a :\AUTOEXEC.BAT
@ECHO OFF
set EXPAND=YES
SET DIRCMD=/O :N
set LglDrv=27 * 26 Z 25 Y 24 X 23 W 22 V 21 U 20 T 19 S 18 R 17 Q 16 P 15
set LglDrv=%LglDrv% O 14 N 13 M 12 L 11 K 10 J 9 I 8 H 7 G 6 F 5 E 4 D 3 C
cls
call setramd.bat %LglDrv%
set temp=c :\
set tmp=c :\
path=%RAMD% :\;a :\;%CDROM% :\
copy command.com %RAMD% :\ > NUL
set comspec=%RAMD% :\command.com
copy extract.exe %RAMD% :\ > NUL
copy readme.txt %RAMD% :\ > NUL


:ERROR
IF EXIST ebd.cab GOTO EXT
echo Please insert Windows 98 Startup Disk 2
echo.
pause
GOTO ERROR

F1=Help                               Line :1      Col :1
```

Exhibit 3-8: Edit Autoexec.bat

5   You can reboot your computer (Ctrl + Alt + Del) to execute the new
    Autoexec.bat file, or you can type Autoexec.bat at the command prompt. If the
    computer stalls during the boot, use another startup disk to reboot. You can also
    press the F5 key to bypass the startup files during the boot.

Accessing a command prompt

There are several ways to get to the command prompt. From the Windows desktop, you
can access a command prompt by choosing Start, and then choosing Programs, MS-
DOS Prompt. A command prompt window, sometimes called a *DOS box*, appears, as
shown in Exhibit 3-9. In it you can enter DOS-like commands. To exit the window, type
Exit at the command prompt. This DOS box is not actually operating in real mode, but
is operating in the virtual real mode provided by Windows. In fact, Windows sees this
DOS box as the window provided for the 16-bit program Command.com. Every
Windows OS offers this command window.

You can also get a DOS box by this alternate method: Choose Start, Run and enter
Command.com in the Run dialog box. Because you're not using true real mode and
Windows is still running in the background, some commands entered from a DOS box
might not work correctly or might even produce errors.

You can use other means to get a true real-mode environment. The easiest way is to
choose Start, Shut Down, and select Restart in MS-DOS mode from the Shut Down
dialog box. This method works only for Windows 95 and Windows 98. Windows ME,
NT, 2000, XP, and 2003 do not support accessing real mode in this way. For Windows
ME and Windows XP, create an MS-DOS startup disk, insert it in the floppy disk drive,
and boot from that disk. The startup BIOS boot sequence must be drive A first and then
drive C for you to be able to do this. Windows NT and Windows 2000 do not offer the
option to create an MS-DOS startup disk, but, in a pinch, you can use one created on
another PC to boot a Windows NT/2000 computer to a DOS prompt.

For Windows 9x, you can also boot to a command prompt by holding down the Ctrl key
or the F8 key while booting, which causes the OS to display a startup menu. From the
menu, select Command prompt only.

In some situations, it is appropriate to use a startup disk created by one OS to boot a failed system that has a different OS installed. For example, suppose Windows NT/2000/XP refuses to boot. By using a different PC, you can create a startup disk under Windows 98 and then use it to boot the Windows NT/2000/XP PC. For Windows Server 2003, you can create a startup disk by using Windows NT/2000/XP. If you can successfully boot to an A prompt, you've demonstrated that the hard drive or files stored on it is the source of the problem. However, it is best to use recovery procedures and disks native to the OS installed.

Suppose there is an important data file on the Windows NT/2000/XP computer and you don't have the proper recovery disks for the OS. You might be able to use the Windows 98 startup disk to recover the file. There are special considerations for Windows NT/2000/XP. These operating systems support more than one file system, and a Windows 9x startup disk supports only FAT16 or FAT32. If a Windows NT/2000/XP hard drive has a different file system installed, such as NTFS (New Technology File System), then the Windows 9x startup disk will not be able to read that file system. In this situation, you can work from an A prompt (A:\>), but you won't be able to access the hard drive. The solution is to create rescue disks under these operating systems that can read the file system.

Note: When Windows 9x (including Windows ME) creates a startup disk, it copies files to the disk from the \Windows\Command\EBD folder. You can also copy these files to a formatted disk to manually create a startup disk.

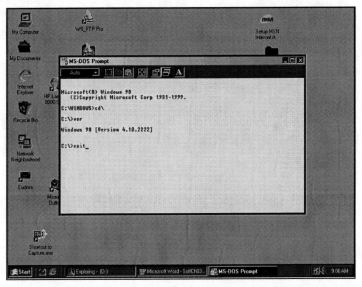

Exhibit 3-9: An MS-DOS prompt window in virtual mode provided by Windows 9x

By looking at the list of files in the earlier tables that are stored on a Windows 98 startup disk, you can see several files needed to manage memory and hard drives, two hardware devices that are essential to successfully booting a PC into Windows. Before you discuss how to use a startup disk to troubleshoot a failed Windows boot, let's look at these programs on the startup disk and how the MS-DOS portion of Windows 9x uses them to manage memory and hard drives. These same methods also affect the way Windows 9x manages memory and a hard drive, even when the desktop is loaded.

Do it!

B-1:   Creating a startup disk using Windows 9x

Here's how	Here's why
1 Create a startup disk in Windows 9x	
Test the startup disk by rebooting the computer with the disk still in the drive	
2 Record the following information using the Readme.txt file on the startup disk	
What command line is recommended to check your hard drive for errors?	
At what point in the boot process is the RAM drive created?	
If you reboot your PC after booting from the startup disk, will the RAM drive remain in memory?	
3 Use Windows Explorer to create a system disk on a second disk	
Compare the contents of the two disks	

Topic C: DOS/Windows 9x memory management

Explanation

Memory management under DOS and Windows 9x can seem complicated because of the way the process has evolved over the past 20 years or so. Decisions made by IBM and Microsoft in the early 1980s still significantly affect, and in some cases limit, the way memory is used under Windows 9x. Because Windows NT, followed by Windows 2000, XP, and 2003, have had the luxury of being designed from the ground up, they are free of those limitations.

Earlier versions of DOS operated completely in real mode, which initially allowed access to only the first 1 MB of memory addresses. Later, DOS added a memory extender, *Himem.sys*, which allowed access to memory addresses above 1 MB. Early versions of Windows 3.x working with DOS could keep more than one program loaded at the same time by swapping them in and out of memory; this was called standard mode, but was actually real mode with some fancy maneuvering. Later versions of Windows 3.x let 16-bit programs share memory in a "virtual DOS machine" in a 386 enhanced mode. Windows 3.x could also perform virtual memory management by creating a swap file stored on the hard drive and using it as if it were memory.

Windows 95 was the first OS in the evolution of Windows operating systems to support 32-bit protected-mode applications software. Most of the OS code is written in 32-bit protected mode. It still allows 16-bit real-mode device drivers, and 16-bit software can run in a *virtual DOS machine (VDM)*, just as with Windows 3.x, or can run in real mode. A VDM is an environment that a 32-bit protected-mode OS provides for a real-mode program to operate in.

Windows NT made a break with the past. All its code is written in protected mode, and it does not allow other software to operate in real mode. Instead other software operates in a virtual real mode, which the NT operating system controls tightly. This makes Windows NT a much more stable OS than Windows 9x.

The following table summarizes the evolution of operating systems and software as it applies to memory. Notice that Windows NT is the first Microsoft OS to resolve many issues involving real mode, particularly the 1024-K limitation imposed by real mode. With DOS and Windows 3.x, this limitation directly affected managing memory resources and, in some cases, can still be significant with Windows 9x.

OS	Real mode	Protected mode
DOS	Operates totally in real mode, but later offered Himem.sys, a device driver that allows programs access to extended memory.	NA
DOS with Windows 2.x	Operated totally in real mode but managed the process of switching programs in and out of memory.	NA
DOS with Windows 3.x	Real mode was called standard mode. Allows only one 16-bit application at a time in memory.	Protected mode is called 386 enhanced mode. Multiple applications can share memory.
Windows 9x	Allows real-mode drivers to be loaded during startup; 16-bit DOS applications are allowed a real-mode session.	Switches back and forth between real mode and protected mode as necessary. Supports both 16-bit and 32-bit applications in a virtual machine.
Windows NT/2000/XP/2003	NA	All work is done in protected mode. Supports 32-bit applications. 16-bit applications can operate in a virtual machine only.

Physical memory and memory addresses

To understand how memory uses evolved, beginning with DOS and moving to Windows NT, you must understand basic memory concepts.

A memory address is a number the CPU assigns to ROM or RAM to track the memory it can use. A CPU has a limited number of memory addresses that it can assign to physical memory, determined by the number of memory address lines available on the memory bus.

Some older 16-bit programs work only when they can use certain memory addresses, such as a hexadecimal number like C80000. This address is part of the physical memory's ROM programming; no other address works for it.

An example of this kind of memory is a ROM chip on an older video card. Some memory, usually ROM chips on expansion boards, must be assigned one of two, or sometimes three, sets of addresses. You make the choice by setting jumpers or DIP switches on the board or, in more recent cases, when you run an installation program for the board. New plug and play boards don't have this restriction. Their ROM code can be assigned any values chosen by the OS or system BIOS. Plug and play cards are required to use whatever memory addresses are assigned to them. The system is free to assign any address it chooses to this physical memory.

Both RAM and ROM must be assigned memory addresses so the CPU can access this memory. System BIOS stored on motherboard ROM chips must be assigned addresses by the CPU so that the CPU can access that programming. The assigning of addresses to both RAM and ROM occurs during booting, and is sometimes called memory mapping. In Exhibit 3-10, the memory addresses available to the CPU are listed on the left, and the physical RAM and ROM that need these addresses are on the right. These RAM modules are located on the motherboard, and ROM chips are found on a sound card, network card, and video card in this example. RAM is holding several device drivers, applications, and the OS.

Memory Addresses	Physical Location of Memory	Contents
8 MB		
	RAM	32-bit application's data
		32-bit application
		32-bit BIOS and device drivers
		portion of OS
1024K		
	ROM	system BIOS and startup BIOS
	RAM	16-bit sound card device driver
	ROM	16-bit network card BIOS
	ROM	16-bit video ROM
640K	RAM	16-bit video RAM
		16-bit application's data
		16-bit application
		16-bit mouse device driver
	RAM	
		operating system
0		data used by BIOS and OS

Exhibit 3-10: Areas of the memory map

Programming that's stored on ROM chips is not usually copied into RAM. It's simply assigned memory addresses by the CPU. These ROM programs become part of the total memory available to the CPU, and do not use up part of total RAM. The resources they use are memory addresses. The RAM memory is still available to be assigned other addresses. There is an exception, called *shadowing ROM*, in which programs stored on ROM are copied to RAM to improve performance.

Finally, memory management in DOS and Windows 9x presents limitations not so much because of the operating systems themselves, but because applications, device drivers, and BIOS used the architectures presented to the industry when DOS was first introduced, and these standards are still in effect today. Compared to that of other operating systems, memory management in DOS and Windows 9x is handicapped because DOS has existed longer than most other operating systems. Therefore, DOS must maintain compatibility with software and devices that have been around for a long time. Also, Microsoft made the commitment with Windows 9x that it, too, would be compatible with older software and BIOS written for DOS and Windows 3.x using DOS. Probably the greatest limitation of Windows 9x today is this commitment to maintain backward compatibility with older software and hardware.

Areas of the memory map

There are several types of memory that the OS manages: conventional, upper, and extended memory.

These memory types are logical divisions or categories rather than physical ones, and the divisions are determined by their memory addresses rather than by their physical location. The following sections cover this logical memory management. A segment of RAM can be assigned memory addresses in the upper memory range today but be assigned a range of addresses in extended memory tomorrow. It's still just RAM, no matter what address it's assigned. The difference is the way the CPU can use this memory because of the addresses assigned to it.

To get a clear picture of this memory-addressing schema, consider the memory map shown in Exhibit 3-11. The memory addresses up to the first 640 K are called *conventional memory*, or base memory. The memory addresses from 640 K up to 1024 K are called *upper memory*. Memory above 1024 K is called extended memory. The first 64 K of extended memory is called the *high memory area (HMA)*.

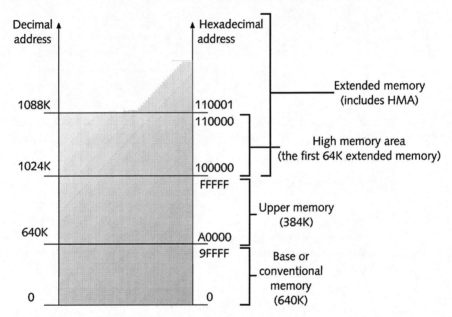

Exhibit 3-11: Memory address map

Conventional memory

In the early 1980s, when IBM and Microsoft were designing the original PCs, they decided to make 640 K of memory addresses available to the user, thinking that this was plenty for anything the user would ever want to do. This 640 K of addresses was intended to hold the OS, the applications software, and the data being processed. At that time, 640 K of memory addresses was more than enough to handle all the applications available. Today, 640 K of memory addresses is inadequate, for the following reasons:

- Many applications are very large programs, requiring a considerable number of memory addresses to hold the programs as well as the data.

- Often, more than one application runs at the same time, each of which requires its own memory area for the program and data. Also, sometimes computers in a network serve more than one user at a time. In the early 1980s, a PC was expected to be used by a single user, operating one application at a time.

- Users expect software to provide a friendly graphical user interface, or GUI. Graphical user interfaces provide icons, graphics, and windows on a screen, all requiring large amounts of memory.

Future versions of DOS could have solved the problems resulting from restricting the number of memory addresses available to the user to 640 K by simply providing more addresses. However, another original design decision ruled this out. The next group of memory addresses, 384 K above conventional memory, called upper memory, was assigned to utility operations for the system. The system requires memory addresses to communicate with peripherals. The programs (such as BIOS on a video card or on the motherboard) and data are assigned memory addresses in this upper memory area. For example, the video BIOS and video RAM BIOS routines and programs placed in the very first part of upper memory, the area from 640 K to 832 K. All ROM written for DOS-based computers assumes that this memory address range is assigned only for this purpose. Also, many DOS and Windows applications interact directly with video ROM and RAM in this address range.

Programs almost always expect data to be written into memory directly above the addresses for the program itself, an important fact for understanding memory management. Thus, if a program begins storing its data above its location in conventional memory, eventually it will "hit the ceiling," the beginning of upper memory assigned to video ROM. The major reason that applications have a 640 K memory limit is that video ROM begins at 640 K. If DOS and Windows 9x allowed applications into these upper memory addresses, all DOS-compatible video ROM would need to be rewritten, and many DOS applications that access these video addresses would not work.

The Windows NT/2000/XP/2003 operating systems are not backward-compatible with older hardware and software because they do not manage memory in the same way. You'll learn more about how these operating systems manage memory later.

Upper memory

The memory map in Exhibit 3-11 shows that the memory addresses from 640 K up to (but not including) 1024 K are called upper memory. In the hexadecimal number system, upper memory begins at A0000 and goes through FFFFF. Video ROM and RAM are stored in the first part of upper memory, hex A0000 through CFFFF (the A, B, and C areas of memory). Sixteen-bit BIOS programs for other legacy expansion boards are assigned memory addresses in the remaining portions of upper memory. BIOS on the motherboard (system BIOS) is assigned the top part of upper memory, from F0000 through FFFFF (the F area of upper memory). Upper memory often has unassigned addresses, depending on which boards are present in the system. Managing memory effectively involves gaining access to these unused addresses in upper memory and using them to store device drivers and TSR (terminate-and-stay-resident) programs.

Exhibit 3-12 shows that video memory addresses fall between A0000 and CFFFF. For VGA and Super VGA video, the A and B areas hold data sent to the video card, and the C area contains the video BIOS.

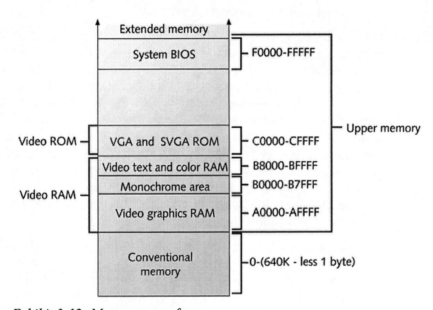

Exhibit 3-12: Memory map of upper memory

Extended memory and the high memory area

Memory above 1 MB is called extended memory. The first 64 K of extended memory is called the high memory area, which exists because a bug in the programming for the older 286 CPU (the first CPU to use extended memory) produced this small pocket of unused memory addresses. Beginning with DOS 5, the OS capitalized on this feature by storing portions of itself in the high memory area, thus freeing some conventional memory where DOS had been stored. This method of storing part of DOS in the high memory area is called "loading DOS high."

Extended memory is actually managed by the OS as a device (the device is memory) that is controlled by a device driver. To access extended memory, you need the device driver (called a memory extender) that controls it, and you must use applications that have been written to use the extended memory. The amount of extended memory you can have on your computer is limited by the amount of RAM that can be installed on your motherboard and the number of memory addresses the CPU and the memory bus can support.

Utilities that manage memory

The two utilities used by Windows 9x to manage memory above 640 K are *Himem.sys* and *Emm386.exe*.

Himem.sys is the device driver for all memory above 640 K. The program file Emm386.exe contains the software that loads device drivers and other programs into upper memory. Himem.sys is automatically loaded by Windows 9x during the boot process, but can also be loaded by an entry in Config.sys. Emm386.exe is not loaded automatically by Windows 9x, but you can load it by an entry in Config.sys.

Using Himem.sys

Himem.sys is considered a device driver because it manages memory as a device. It can be executed by the Device= command in Config.sys. Exhibit 3-13 shows an example of a very simple Config.sys file on a floppy disk that loads Himem.sys. The Config.sys file is being edited by the Edit.com text editor utility.

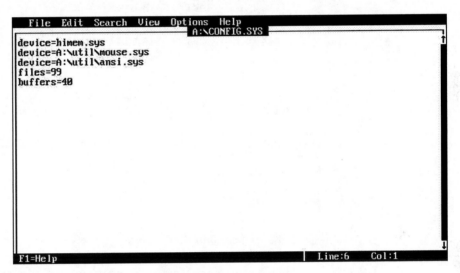

Exhibit 3-13: Config.sys set to use memory above 640 K

To create the file on a floppy disk, you can use either of these two methods:

- Make drive A the default drive and enter this command:

    `A:\> Edit Config.sys`

- Make drive C the default drive and enter this command:

    `C:\> Edit A:Config.sys`

The second line in the Config.sys file, `device=A:\util\mouse.sys`, tells DOS to load into memory a device driver that is found on the floppy disk in the \Util directory, which allows you to use the mouse while in MS-DOS mode.

The third line in the Config.sys file, `device=A:\util\ansi.sys`, tells DOS to load the device driver Ansi.sys into memory. Ansi.sys helps control the keyboard and monitor, providing color on the monitor and an additional set of characters to the ASCII character set.

Using Emm386.exe

In DOS and Windows 9x, Emm386.exe manages the memory addresses in upper memory. Before you see how to use it, let's begin by examining memory when upper memory addresses are not available. To do that, you use the MEM command, which lets us view how memory is currently allocated. Use the /C option to get a complete list and include the |MORE option to page the results on your screen. Exhibit 3-14 was produced by using this command:

```
MEM /C |MORE
```

```
Modules using memory below 1 MB:

    Name       Total           Conventional      Upper Memory
    ---------  --------------  ---------------   ----------------
    MSDOS       18,672  (18K)   18,672  (18K)        0    (0K)
    HIMEM        1,168   (1K)    1,168   (1K)        0    (0K)
    DBLBUFF      2,976   (3K)    2,976   (3K)        0    (0K)
    IFSHLP       2,864   (3K)    2,864   (3K)        0    (0K)
    WIN          3,616   (4K)    3,616   (4K)        0    (0K)
    COMMAND      8,416   (8K)    8,416   (8K)        0    (0K)
    SAVE        72,768  (71K)   72,768  (71K)        0    (0K)
    Free       544,720 (532K)  544,720 (532K)        0    (0K)

Memory Summary:

    Type of Memory        Total         Used          Free
    ----------------   -----------   -----------   -----------
    Conventional          655,360       110,640       544,720
    Upper                       0             0             0
    Reserved                    0             0             0
    Extended (XMS)    133,156,864        69,632   133,087,232
    ----------------   -----------   -----------   -----------
-- More --
```

Exhibit 3-14: MEM report with /C option on a PC not using upper memory

In Exhibit 3-14, the first column shows the programs currently loaded in memory. The second column shows the total amount of memory used by each program. The columns labeled Conventional and Upper Memory show the amount of memory being used by each program in each of these categories. This PC is not making use of upper memory for any of its programs. At the bottom of the screen is the total amount of free conventional memory (544,720 bytes) that is available to new programs to be loaded. Making this value as high as possible is the subject of this section.

Creating and using upper memory blocks

Exhibit 3-15 shows an example of a Config.sys file that is set to use upper memory addresses. The first line loads the Himem.sys driver. The second line loads the Emm386.exe file. Emm386.exe assigns addresses in upper memory to memory made available by the Himem.sys driver. The NOEMS switch at the end of the command line says to Windows, "Do not create any simulated expanded memory." Expanded memory is an older type of memory above 1 MB that is no longer used by software. The command to load Emm386.exe must appear after the command to load Himem.sys in the Config.sys file.

The command DOS=HIGH,UMB serves two purposes. The one command line can be broken into two commands like this:

```
DOS=HIGH

DOS=UMB
```

The DOS=HIGH portion tells the OS to load part of the DOS core into the high memory area ("loading DOS high"). Remember that the high memory area is the first 64 K of extended memory. This memory is usually unused unless you choose to store part of DOS in it with this command line. Including this command in Config.sys frees some conventional memory that would have been used by the OS.

The second part of the command, DOS=UMB, creates upper memory blocks. An *upper memory block (UMB)* is a group of consecutive memory addresses in the upper memory area that has had physical memory assigned to it. The OS identifies blocks that are currently not being used by system ROM or expansion boards, and the memory manager makes these blocks available for use. This command, DOS=UMB, enables the OS to access these upper memory blocks. After the UMBs are created, they can be used in these ways:

- Devicehigh= command in Config.sys

- Loadhigh command in Autoexec.bat

- Loadhigh command at the command prompt

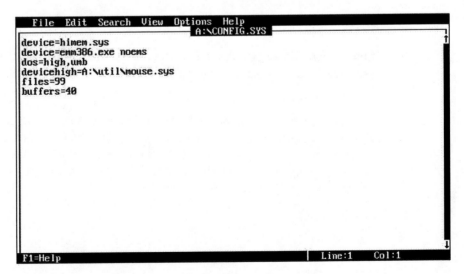

Exhibit 3-15: Config.sys set to use upper memory

The next line in the Config.sys file in Exhibit 3-15 attempts to use a UMB. The command `Devicehigh=A:\Util\Mouse.sys` tells the OS to load the mouse device driver into one of the upper memory blocks created and made available by the previous three lines. This process of loading a program into upper memory addresses is called loading high.

Loading Device Drivers High

Using the Devicehigh= command in Config.sys, rather than the Device= command, causes the driver to load high. With the Devicehigh= command, the OS stores these drivers in UMBs by using the largest UMB first, then the next largest, and so on until all are loaded. Therefore, to make sure there is enough room to hold them all in upper memory, order the Devicehigh= command lines in Config.sys so that the largest drivers are loaded first.

You can determine the amount of memory a device driver allocates for itself and its data by using the MEM command with the /M file name option:

```
MEM /M file name
```

The file name is the name of the device driver without the file extension.

You can also use a UMB from Autoexec.bat by using the Loadhigh (LH) command. For example, to load high Mscdex.exe, a utility to access a CD-ROM drive, use either command:

```
LH Mscdex.exe
```

-or-

```
Loadhigh Mscdex.exe
```

In either case, the program is loaded into the largest UMB available and does not use up more precious conventional memory. Note that before the Loadhigh command will work, the program files Himem.sys and Emm386.exe must be available to the OS and these three lines must be added to Config.sys and executed by booting the computer:

```
Device=HIMEM.SYS
Device=EMM386.EXE NOEMS
DOS=UMB
```

If the Himem.sys and Emm386.exe files are not in the root directory of the boot device, you must include the path to the file name in the Device= line, like this:

```
Device=C:\DOS\HIMEM.SYS
```

Note: When a program is loaded high, two things can go wrong. Either the program might not work from upper memory, causing problems during execution, or there might not be enough room in upper memory for the program and its data. If the program causes the computer to hang when you attempt to run it, or if it simply refuses to work correctly, remove it from upper memory.

Some Windows default settings

You've just seen how Windows MS-DOS mode uses Config.sys and Autoexec.bat. Most of the settings that once were put into Config.sys under DOS are now embedded into the Windows 9x Io.sys file. If Config.sys or Autoexec.bat are present, the entries in those files override the default entries in Io.sys. The entries in Io.sys cannot be changed and are listed in the following table.

Entry	Description
Buffers=30	Specifies the number of file buffers to create.
DOS=HIGH	Loads the DOS core of Windows 9x into the HMA.
Files=60	Specifies the number of files that can be open at one time under 16-bit applications.
Himem.sys	Loads Himem.sys to manage extended memory in Windows 9x.
Lastdrive=Z	Specifies the last letter that can be assigned to a logical drive.
Setver.exe	Executes a program that tells DOS applications that the version of DOS they are looking for is the version they are using. The program allows some older DOS applications to run that might otherwise hang.
Shell=Command.com /P	Loads Command.com and executes Autoexec.bat.
Stacks=9,256	Specifies the number of frames of instructions that can be held in memory in a queue at one time. Used for backward compatibility with older applications.

Do it!   ## C-1:   Discussing memory management

Exercises

1   What Windows OS allows applications to run in either real mode or protected mode? What Windows OS was the first to force 16-bit applications to run in virtual real mode?

2   What are the three types of memory that Windows 9x manages? What are the memory address ranges for each?

3   What is the hexadecimal address range for upper memory?

4   Name the two utilities that Windows uses to manage memory above 640 K. Give a brief description of each.

5   The latest versions of Windows (NT/2000/XP/2003) never allow for applications to run in real (true 16-bit) mode. True or false?

6   Conventional memory includes that memory in the first _____ of RAM.

7   What is one way that Windows 9x attempts to gain maximum usage of its conventional memory?

Topic D: DOS/Windows 9x disk management

Explanation

When a hard drive (sometimes called the HDD) is first installed, it has nothing written on it except empty track markings put there at the factory. A floppy disk is completely blank and does not even have these track markings.

The OS must prepare both these media for use by putting track markings on a floppy disk and putting a file system on both floppy disk and hard drive. In addition, the OS is responsible for managing the file system, including creating, deleting, copying, and moving directories and files.

This section looks at the commands to do all this from a command prompt under Windows 9x. Except for writing a new file system to a hard drive, these same functions can also be done from within Windows by using Windows Explorer.

Before we get into how to use specific commands, you'll learn about how data is organized on floppy disks and hard drives.

How data is stored logically on a floppy disk

When a floppy disk is first formatted, sector and track markings are written to the disk. Tracks are concentric circles on the disk and a segment of a track, called a sector, always holds 512 bytes of data.

All floppy disks, no matter what size or density, and hard drives are divided into tracks and sectors, and each sector holds 512 bytes of data.

A cluster, sometimes called a file allocation unit, is a group of sectors that is the smallest unit on a disk used to hold a file or a portion of a file. The term sector refers to how data is physically stored on a disk, while the term cluster describes how data is logically organized. The BIOS manages the disk as physical sectors, but the OS considers the disk only as a long list of clusters that can each hold a fixed amount of data. (See Exhibit 3-16.)

The OS keeps that list of clusters in the file allocation table (FAT).

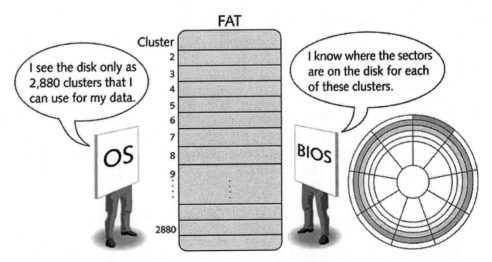

Exhibit 3-16: Cluster or FAT units are managed by the OS

There are several variations of floppy disks including the older 5 ¼" floppy disk, the 3.5" double-density floppy disk, and the most current floppy disk, the 3.5" high-density disk, which holds 1.44 MB of data. Let's see how this disk holds that data.

The 5 ¼" floppy disk was single-sided and had a capacity of only 160 KB. Today, the 3.5" floppy disk has replaced the 5 ¼" floppy disk. The 3.5"high-density floppy disk has 80 tracks and 18 sectors per track on each side, for a total of 1,440 sectors. This type of disk has only one sector per cluster, making 1,440 x 2 sides, or 2,880 clusters. Because each cluster holds 512 bytes (one sector) of data, a 3.5" high-density floppy disk has 2,880 x 512 = 1,474,560 bytes of data. Divide this number by 1,024 to convert bytes to kilobytes. The storage capacity of this disk is 1,440 KB. Divide by 1,000 to convert kilobytes to megabytes, and the storage is 1.44 MB.

Note: There is a discrepancy in the computer industry regarding the definition of a megabyte. Sometimes 1 megabyte = 1,000 kilobytes; at other times, you use the relationship of 1 megabyte = 1,024 kilobytes.

Formatting a floppy disk

The formatting of all floppy disks is similar, no matter what their size or density. During formatting, the Format command, without added options, performs the following steps:

- Creates the tracks and sectors by writing tracks as necessary and marks the place on each track where the first sector begins
- Creates the boot record
- Creates two copies of the FAT
- Creates the root directory

These basic steps are described in detail next.

Creating the tracks and sectors

The Format command prepares a disk for use. The first step in the formatting process erases any data on the disk. In its simplest form, without adding any parameters, the Format command always overwrites all data on the disk.

The boot record

At the beginning of each floppy disk, the first sector contains basic information about how the disk is organized, including the number of sectors, the number of sectors per cluster, the number of bits in each FAT entry, and other basic information that an OS or BIOS needs in order to read the data on the disk.

This information is stored in the first sector on the disk called the *boot sector*, or *boot record*. At the end of the boot record is a small program, called the *bootstrap loader*, which can be used to boot from the disk. The following list shows the layout of the boot record and its contents:

1 Bytes per sector
2 Sectors per cluster
3 Number of FATs
4 Size of the root directory
5 Number of sectors
6 Medium descriptor byte
7 Size of the FAT
8 Sectors per track
9 Number of heads (always two)
10 Number of hidden sectors
11 Program to load the OS

The boot record indicates which version of DOS or Windows was used to format the disk, and is always located at the beginning of the disk at track 0, sector 1 (bottom of the disk, outermost track). This uniformity of layout and content allows any version of DOS or Windows to read any DOS or Windows disk.

The ninth item in the list is the number of heads. A head refers to the read/write head that is a part of the physical components of the drive. Because the disk always has only one top and one bottom with a read/write head assigned to each, the number of heads is always two. The last item in the table is the program that searches for and loads Io.sys if it is present on the disk. If Io.sys, Msdos.sys, and Command.com are on the disk, the disk is said to be bootable.

All boot records, however, are the same, whether or not the disk is bootable. When the PC is looking for a bootable disk during POST, if a disk is in the drive, the program stored in the boot record is executed. If this program does not find Io.sys, then the disk is not bootable and a message appears, such as the following:

```
Non-system disk or disk error...Replace and strike any key
when ready...Disk boot failure
```

POST stops until the user intervenes. Only the program in the boot record can determine if the disk is bootable.

The File Allocation Table (FAT)

When formatting a floppy disk, after the boot record is created, the next step is to write two copies of the FAT to the disk. The FAT lists the location of files on the disk in a one-column table. Because the width of each entry in the column is 12 bits, the FAT is called a 12-bit FAT or *FAT12*.

The FAT lists how each cluster or file allocation unit on the disk is currently used. A file is stored in one or more clusters that do not have to be contiguous on the disk. If a file is not stored in consecutive clusters, it is called a *fragmented file*. In the FAT, some clusters might be marked as bad (the 12 bits to mark a bad cluster are FF7h). These bits can be entered in the FAT when the disk is formatted or added later with the Recover command. An extra copy of the FAT is kept immediately following the first. If the first is damaged, sometimes you can recover your data and files by using the second copy.

The root directory

After creating the file allocation tables, the formatting process sets up the root directory. The root directory, or main directory, is a table listing all the files assigned to this table. The root directory contains a fixed number of rows to accommodate a predetermined number of files and subdirectories; the number of available rows depends on the disk type. A 3.5" high-density floppy disk has 224 entries in the root directory.

The root directory will later contain information about each file and subdirectory stored in it. Each directory entry is 32 bytes long, although only 22 bytes are used. The following table lists how the 22 bytes are used.

Notice that the root directory contains only the starting cluster number. To find out what other clusters store the file, look in the FAT. By dividing the size of the file by the number of bytes per cluster and rounding up to the nearest whole number, you can determine how many clusters the file occupies.

Root directory bytes	Usage
8	Name of file
3	File extension
1	Attribute byte (special meaning for each bit)
10	Not used
2	Time of creation or last update
2	Date of creation or last update
2	Starting cluster number in binary
4	Size of file in binary

Also note that there is no place for the period (often referred to as "dot") that you normally see between the file name and the file extension in OS command lines. The period is not stored in directories and is used only in OS command lines to indicate where the file name ends and the file extension begins. For the long file names in Windows 9x and Windows NT/2000/XP/2003, more room in the directory is required. This is provided by using more than one entry in the directory for a single file, enough to accommodate the length of the file name. Both the long file name and the DOS version short file name are stored in the directory.

The time and date of creation or last update are stored in a coded form that is converted to a recognizable form when displayed on the screen. The date and time come from the system date and time, which the OS gets from the real-time clock during the boot. At the command prompt, you can change these with the Date and Time commands. If you are using the Windows desktop, change the date and time in the Control Panel. The earliest possible date allowed for both is 1/1/1980.

The file attributes are used for various purposes. One file attribute byte is broken into bits; and each bit has a specific meaning. The last two bits right-to-left are not used. The meanings of the other six bits are listed in the following table, beginning with the rightmost bit in the byte and moving to the left.

Bit	Info	Bit=0	Bit=1
6,7	Not used		
5	Archive bit	Not to be Archived	To be Archived
4	Directory status	File	Subdirectory
3	Volume label	Not volume label	Is volume label
2	System file	Not system file	Is system file
1	Hidden file	Not hidden	Hidden
0	Read-only file	Read/write	Read-only

Note: Bit 5, the archive bit, is a switch used to indicate whether the file has been changed since the last backup and should be backed up the next time a backup is made.

The root directory and all subdirectories contain the same information about each file. Only the root directory has a limitation on the number of entries. Subdirectories can have as many entries as disk space allows. Because long file names require more room in a directory than short file names, assigning long file names reduces the number of files that can be stored in the root directory.

In summary, the Format command writes tracks and sectors on the disk, and creates a boot record, an empty FAT, and an empty root directory. If you include the /S option in the Format line, you add Io.sys, Msdos.sys, and Command.com, which together make a disk bootable. The three files are referenced in the FAT and in the root directory. The two hidden files have their file attribute bit 1, the hidden bit, set to 1 (hidden). When you make a Windows 9x rescue disk or use Windows Explorer to format as a system disk, these three files are copied to the disk to make the disk bootable.

Do it!

D-1: Discussing floppy disk data organization

Questions	Answers
1 How many bytes are contained in a sector?	
2 What is the name of the first sector on a floppy disk? What information is contained in this sector?	
3 How many bytes long is each entry in the root directory?	
4 A file can become a hidden file or a read-only file by changing its _____.	

How a hard drive is organized logically to hold data

Explanation

Today's hard drives come from the factory already low-level formatted (that is, with track and sector markings already in place). During installation, after the hard drive is physically installed, the next step is to partition the drive into manageable areas. The high-level divisions are called partitions, and within the partitions, the drive is divided further into logical drives or volumes. This section discusses the different types of divisions, how they are organized and used by the OS, and how to use OS commands to partition and format a hard drive for first use.

Preparing a hard drive to hold data requires the following three steps:

1 **Low-level format.** This physically formats the hard drive and creates the tracks and sectors. For hard drives today, this has already been done by the time you buy the drive, and does not involve an OS.

2 **Partitioning the hard drive.** Even if only one partition is used, this step is still required. The DOS and Windows 9x Fdisk program sets up a partition table at the beginning of the hard drive. Within each partition, Fdisk also creates logical drives, assigning letters to these drives. Windows NT/2000/XP/2003 uses the Diskpart program at the command prompt or the Disk Management utility from within Windows to create and delete partitions and logical drives.

3 **High-level format.** This must be done by the OS for each logical drive on the hard drive. As each logical drive is formatted, the OS creates an OS boot record, a root directory, and two copies of VFAT for the logical drive, just as it does for a floppy disk. DOS and Windows 9x use the Format.com program to do the job, and Windows NT/2000/XP uses Diskmgmt.msc or Disk Management.

Although you might have a 10 GB hard drive that is only a single physical drive, an OS can divide this single physical drive into more than one logical drive. Exhibit 3-17 shows several divisions of a hard drive.

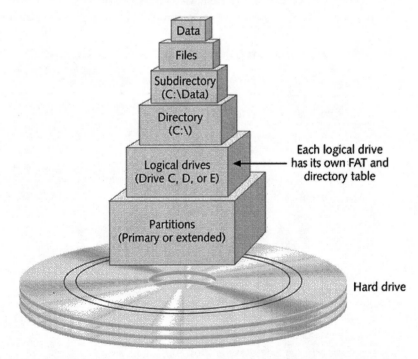

Exhibit 3-17: A hard drive is divided and organized at several levels

When you use Fdisk or any disk management tool to partition the drive, two kinds of divisions take place.

First, the physical drive is divided into one or more partitions, and then each partition is divided further into logical drives or volumes.

(A logical drive is sometimes called a logical partition; don't let the two uses of the term "partition" confuse you; partitions and logical partitions are divisions at different levels.) Exhibit 3-18 shows a typical example; the hard drive is divided into two partitions. The first partition contains one logical drive (drive C), and the second partition is divided into two logical drives (D and E). The partition table at the very beginning of the drive records all these divisions. The partition table is located in the first sector of the hard drive on head 0, track 0, sector 1, which is the MBR that was introduced earlier.

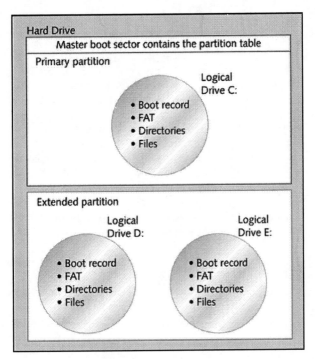

Exhibit 3-18: A hard drive is divided into one or more partitions

The following table lists the contents of a partition table. Don't confuse this first physical sector of the hard drive with sector 1 as Windows knows it. The operating system's sector 1 comes after the physical sector 1 and is the first sector in the logical drive C.

Partition	Bytes used	Description
1	446 bytes	Program that calls the boot program on the OS boot record
2	16-byte total	Description of first partition
	1 byte	Is this the bootable partition? (Yes = 90h, No = 00h)
	3 byte	Beginning location of the partition
	1 byte	System indicator; possible values are:
		0 = Not a DOS partition 1 = DOS with a 12-bit FAT 4 = DOS with a 16-bit FAT 5 = Not the first partition 6 = Partition larger than 32 MB
	3 bytes	Ending location of partition
	4 bytes	First sector of the partition table relative to the beginning of the disk
	4 bytes	Number of sectors in the partition
3	16 bytes	Describes the second partition by using the same format as first partition
4	16 bytes	Describes the third partition by using same format as first partition
5	16 bytes	Describes the fourth partition by using same format as first partition
6	2 bytes	Signature of the partition table; always AA55

The partition table is exactly 512 bytes long. During POST, the partition table program, which is stored at the beginning of the MBR, executes and checks the integrity of the partition table itself. If it finds any corruption, it refuses to continue execution, and the disk is unusable. Sometimes the MBR is the target of a *boot sector virus*, which can cause problems with the boot process and data retrieval. The DOS and Windows 9x Fdisk/MBR command or the Windows 2000/XP Fixmbr command is used to repair damage to the MBR.

If the table entries are valid, the partition table program looks in the table to determine which partition is the active partition, and it executes the bootstrap loader program in the boot record of that partition.

With DOS or Windows 9x, a hard drive can have only one *primary partition* and one *extended partition*, although the partition table can contain four partitions. Also, the primary partition can have only a single logical drive. In that case, the one logical drive in the primary partition is the only logical drive on the hard drive that can boot the operating system and is the active partition. The extended partition can have several logical drives. With Windows NT/2000/XP/2003, the drive can have up to four partitions, but only one of them can be an extended partition.

How many and what kind of logical drives

After the hard drive is formatted and ready for use, you're not usually aware that the several logical drives on the hard drive all belong to the same hard drive. For example, Exhibit 3-19 shows three drives, C, D, and E, which are logical drives on one hard drive. If you right-click the icon for one drive, such as drive D in the exhibit, and select Properties from the shortcut menu, you can see the amount of space allotted to this logical drive and how much of it is currently used. Also note that in the exhibit, drive D is formatted with the FAT32 file system. It is possible for one logical drive to be formatted with one file system and other logical drives on the same hard drive be formatted with a different file system such as FAT16 or NTFS.

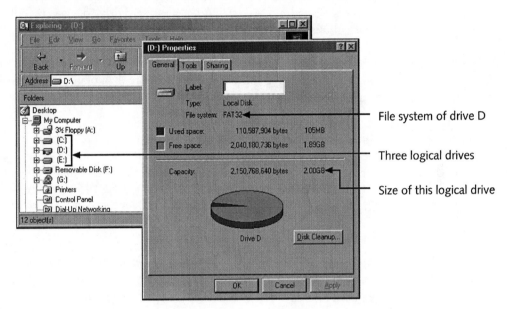

Exhibit 3-19: This hard drive contains three logical drives

DOS and all versions of Windows support the FAT16 file system. Windows 95 offers a slightly improved file system called VFAT that supports long file names, and Windows 95, Service Release 2 (sometimes called Windows 95b or Windows 95 OSR2), introduced the FAT32 file system.

This and all later versions of Windows 9x, Windows 2000, and Windows XP support FAT32. Windows NT introduced the NTFS file system, which is also supported by Windows 2000/XP/2003. You'll learn about the different versions of NTFS. With these file systems, the primary goal is to reduce the size of one cluster so as to not waste space on the hard drive for short files that don't need large clusters.

FAT16

DOS and all versions of Windows support the FAT16 file system, which uses 16 bits for each cluster entry in the FAT. With FAT16, the smallest cluster size is four sectors. Each cluster is 512 bytes/sector times 4 sectors/cluster, or 2,048 bytes. A one-character file takes up 2,048 bytes of space on a hard drive. For larger drives, the number of sectors in one cluster is even larger.

Virtual File Allocation (VFAT)

Windows 95 and Windows for Workgroups feature some improved methods of hard drive access, called *VFAT*, or *virtual file allocation table*. These enable Windows to use 32-bit protected-mode device drivers for hard drive access. In Windows for Workgroups, VFAT is called 32-bit file access. Windows 95 supports file names up to 255 characters. The file name and extension are stored in the root directory or in a subdirectory list. Each entry in the directory is 32 bytes long, and each 32-byte entry is called a block. Long file names require more than one block in the directory. The FAT is not affected, but still uses 16 bits per cluster entry. VFAT has been rendered outdated by FAT32.

Note: Some DOS-based disk utility programs can damage the entries in a directory in these additional blocks because they are not programmed to manage the extra blocks used to hold long file names. Even a simple DEL command under DOS can leave the extra blocks in the directory used to hold the long file name unavailable for later use. The Windows 9x ScanDisk utility can recover these unreleased blocks.

FAT32

Beginning with Windows 95 OSR2, Microsoft offered a FAT that contains 32 bits per FAT entry instead of the older 12-bit or 16-bit FAT entries. Actually, only 28 of the bits are used to hold a cluster number; the remaining 4 bits are reserved.

FAT32 is recommended for hard drives larger than 512 MB and is efficient for drives up to 16 GB. In this range, the cluster size is 8 K. After that, the cluster size increases to about 16 K for drives in the 16 GB to 32 GB range. You're then reaching a hard drive size that warrants a more powerful file management system than FAT32, such as NTFS, supported by Windows NT/2000/XP/2003.

Note: If you're currently using FAT16 and are considering switching to FAT32, you can use PartitionMagic by PowerQuest Corporation (www.powerquest.com), to scan your hard drive and tell you how much of the drive is used for slack space. Knowing this can help you decide if the change will yield more usable drive space.

How many logical drives?

When you partition a hard drive and create logical drives, you decide how many logical drives you want and how large each drive will be. Some people prefer to use more than one logical drive to organize their hard drives, especially if they plan to have more than one OS on the same drive. However, the main reason you need multiple logical drives is to optimize space and access time to the drive. The larger the logical drive, the larger the cluster size, and the more slack or wasted space. When deciding how to allocate space to logical drives, the goal is to use as few logical drives as possible and still keep cluster size to a minimum. For Windows 9x, you can use FAT32 in order to get the smaller cluster size.

The following table gives the information you need to decide how to divide your drive. Notice that the largest logical drive possible using FAT16 is 2 GB. (This limitation is rooted in the largest cluster number that can be stored in a 16-bit FAT entry.) However, you can see from the table that, to make a drive that big, the cluster size must be huge. Also, the largest hard drive that FAT16 can support is 8.4 GB; if the drive is larger than that, you must use FAT32.

File system	Size of logical drive	Size of cluster
FAT16	Up to 128 MB	4 sectors per cluster
	128 to 256 MB	8 sectors per cluster
	256 to 512 MB	16 sectors per cluster
	512 MB to 1 GB	32 sectors per cluster
	1 GB to 2 GB	64 sectors per cluster
FAT32	512 MB to 8 GB	4 sectors per cluster
	8 GB to 16 GB	8 sectors per cluster
	16 GB to 32 GB	16 sectors per cluster
	More than 32 GB	32 sectors per cluster
NTFS	Up to 512 MB	1 sectors per cluster
	512 MB to 1 GB	2 sectors per cluster
	More than 1 GB	4 sectors per cluster

When to partition a drive

There are several reasons to partition a drive.

When you first install a new hard drive, you must partition it to prepare it for use. Also, if an existing hard drive is giving errors, you can repartition the drive and reformat each logical drive to begin fresh. If you suspect that a virus has attacked the drive, you can repartition it to begin with a clean drive. Also, if you want to wipe a hard drive clean and install a new OS, you can repartition a drive in preparation for formatting it with a new file system.

When installing Windows 9x, before you can use the Windows 9x CD for Windows 9x upgrades, you can boot from a bootable disk and use Fdisk to partition the hard drive and install enough of a previous version of Windows on it to boot from it. When using the Windows 98 Upgrade CD, you'll also need the first Window 3.x setup disk or Windows 95 setup CD because Windows 98 upgrade setup asks for it during the Windows 9x installation. During a Windows 9x installation, if the drive is not partitioned, the install procedure automatically executes Fdisk to partition the drive.

You can use Fdisk to partition a drive or use third-party software such as PartitionMagic. Fdisk is simple and easy to use, but PartitionMagic has some advantages over Fdisk. A major advantage is that when Fdisk partitions a drive, it erases all data on the existing partitions that it changes or overwrites, but PartitionMagic protects data when it changes the partitions on the drive. Also, PartitionMagic has a user-friendly GUI interface.

There are times that you should not use Fdisk to partition a drive. If the drive has already been partitioned by third-party software such as Disk Manager or Storage Dimensions' SpeedStor, you should use the same third-party product to repartition the drive. This is because these products implement a type of drive translation that is used to enable a large hard drive to exist in a system whose system BIOS does not support such large drives. To know if a large hard drive has been partitioned to do disk translation, look for entries in the Config.sys file that point to third-party software to manage the drive. Examples of these command lines are Dmdrvr.bin, Sstor.sys, Harddrive.sys, and Evdisk.sys. If you find lines with these file names mentioned, use the same third-party software to repartition the drive.

Do it!

D-2: Calculating the size of a cluster

Here's how	Here's why
1 Record how much space is available on your hard drive	By using the Dir command.
2 Create a text file containing only a single character	By using Edit or Notepad.
3 In the command prompt, enter **Dir**	
Record how much disk space is available	
Compare the two values, before and after a single one-character file is written to the disk	The difference in the two values is the size of one cluster, which is the smallest amount that can be allocated to a file.
4 Verify your calculations by using Chkdsk	

Using Fdisk to partition a drive

Explanation

Windows 9x and DOS use Fdisk to partition a drive. To use Fdisk, boot from a startup disk that has the Fdisk.exe utility on it and enter Fdisk at the command prompt.

Note: Do not use Fdisk if the drive has already been partitioned by third-party software.

The Fdisk opening menu, shown in Exhibit 3-20 appears.

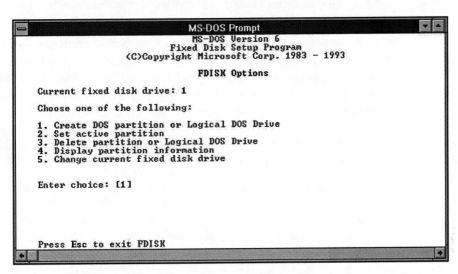

Exhibit 3-20: Fixed disk setup program (FDISK) menu

Select option 1 to create the first partition. The menu in Exhibit 3-21 appears. Use option 1 to create the primary DOS partition. If you plan to install Windows 9x later, be sure this partition is at least 500 MB, and preferably more. Make this first partition the active partition, which is the partition that is used to boot the OS. Fdisk automatically makes this partition drive C.

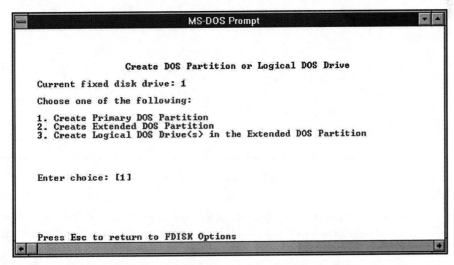

Exhibit 3-21: FDISK menu to create partitions and logical drives

Note: In order for a hard drive to be bootable, it must have an active primary partition, which Fdisk will designate as drive C.

Next, use option 2 shown in Exhibit 3-21 to create an extended DOS partition using the remainder of the hard drive, then use option 3 to create logical drives in the extended partition.

When you're creating logical drives, you decide how large you want each drive to be. If you have at least 512 MB available for the drive, a message appears asking, "Do you wish to enable large disk support (Y/N)?" If you respond Y, then Fdisk assigns the FAT32 file system to the drive; otherwise, it uses FAT16.

Fdisk also assigns a drive letter to the logical drive. For a primary partition, drive C is assigned to the one volume and drives D, E, and so forth are assigned to volumes in the extended partition. However, if a second hard drive is installed in a system, Fdisk takes this into account when assigning drive letters. Drive D is assigned to the one volume in the primary partition of the second hard drive, leaving drive letters E, F, G, H, and so forth for the volumes in the extended partitions of both hard drives. For example, in a two-hard-drive system, in which each hard drive has three logical drives, the drive letters for the first hard drive will be C, E, and F and the drive letters for the second hard drive will be D, G, and H.

When Fdisk is completed, the hard drive's partition table is updated to show the active and extended partitions, and the logical drives within these partitions. As seen in Exhibit 3-20, you can choose option 4 of Fdisk to display partition information. (See Exhibit 3-22.) After you exit the Fdisk window, reboot the PC before you format the logical drives.

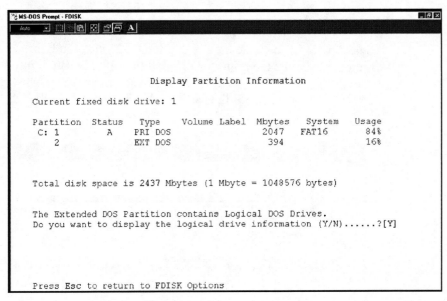

Exhibit 3-22: FDISK displays partitions information

Now that the hard drive is partitioned and logical drives are created and assigned drive letters, the next step is to format each logical drive. For the configuration, the three commands used to format these three logical drives are:

```
Format C:/S
Format D:
Format E:
```

In the Format command line, the /S option makes the drive bootable, and the drive letter tells the OS which drive to format.

The OS format for each logical drive creates these file system items at the beginning of each logical drive, which are similar to the file system items used on floppy disks:

- Boot record
- FAT
- Root directory

The boot record

A boot record is used during the boot process to inform the OS how a logical drive is organized. If the logical drive is the boot device, the boot program at the end of the boot record will load the first Windows hidden file, Io.sys, which requires that Msdos.sys and Command.com be present. The following table shows the complete record layout for the boot record.

Description	Number of bytes
Machine code	11
Bytes per sector	2
Sectors per cluster	1
Reserved	2
Number of FATs	1
Number of root directory entries	2
Number of logical sectors	2
Medium descriptor byte	1
Sectors per FAT	2
Sectors per track	2
Heads	2
Number of hidden sectors	2
Total sectors in logical volume	4
Physical drive number	1
Reserved	1
Extended boot signature record	1
32-bit binary volume ID	4
Volume label	11
Type of file system (FAT12, FAT16, or FAT32)	8
Program to load operating system (boot strap loader)	Remainder of the sector

The medium descriptor byte tells the OS what type of disk this is. The values of this descriptor byte are given in the following table.

Disk type	Descriptor byte
3.5" double-density floppy disk, 720 K	F9
3.5" high-density floppy disk, 1.44 MB	F0
Hard disk	F8

The FAT and the root directory

The purpose of the FAT and how it is used have already been discussed in detail and will not be repeated here. The layout of the root directory is the same for hard drives as for floppy disks. The total number of bytes for each file entry in a directory is 32.

Note: Although earlier versions of Windows did limit the number of entries in the root directory, Windows 98 does not. Note, however, that the OS manuals recommend that you keep only about 150 entries in any one directory. Having any more entries slows access to the directory.

Do it!

D-3:   Discussing creating partitions using Fdisk

Questions and answers
1   What is the /S switch used for with the Format command? The /V switch? The /F:size switch?
2   Name the Windows 98 command that is used to partition a hard drive. When should you not use this command?

Using commands to manage a floppy disk or hard drive

Explanation

You can use several OS commands to manage a floppy disk and hard drive. A number of commands are described with some of their more common options. For more information about these and other OS commands, type the command name at a command prompt followed by /? (slash and a question mark).

There are two wildcards you can use with file names to execute a command on a group of files or a file for which you do not know the entire name. The question mark (?) is a wildcard for one character, and the asterisk (*) is a wildcard for more than one character. For example, if you wanted to find all files in a directory that start with A and have a three-letter file extension, you would use the following command:

```
dir a*.???
```

One other thing you need to be aware of when using commands at the command line is how DOS restricts the length of file names. DOS allows only eight characters for a file name and three for the extension; this is often called the 8.3 format. For file names that do not meet this format, such as the file name Mydocument.doc, DOS will display the file name with the first few letters and a tilde (~) character followed by a number:

```
MyDocu~1.doc
```

If you've two documents that would have the same name if truncated in this manner, DOS will also add an identifying number. For example, if you've a document named Mydocument.doc and one named Mydocumentnew.doc, in a list of files, DOS will truncate these as follows:

```
Mydocu~1.doc
Mydocu~2.doc
```

If you're entering a long file or folder name in a command line, you can enclose the file name in double quotes, like this: "My long file name.doc".

Fdisk/Status/MBR

The Fdisk command creates partitions and logical drives on a hard drive, displays partition information, and restores a damaged MBR. The following table shows options for this command.

Fdisk command option	Description
/MBR	Repairs a damaged MBR program stored at the beginning of the partition table
/Status	Displays partition information for all hard drives in the system

Note: Many real-mode commands, such as Fdisk/MBR, have equivalent commands in the Windows 2000 Recovery Console. The Recovery Console is also available with Windows XP and Windows Server 2003.

Format drive: /S /V:Volumename /Q /U /Autotest

The Format command is used to format a disk or a hard drive. For a hard drive, first run Fdisk to partition the drive and create each logical drive. Then use Format to format each logical drive. The following table shows options for this command.

Format command option	Description
/V	Allows you to enter a volume label only once when formatting several disks. The same volume label is used for all disks. A volume label is displayed at the top of the directory list to help you identify the disk.
/S	Stores the system files on the disk after formatting. Writes the two hidden files and Command.com to the disk, making the disk bootable.
/Q	Recreates the root directory and FATs if you want to quickly format a previously formatted disk that is in good condition. /Q does not read or write to any other part of the disk.
/F:size	Specifies the size of a floppy disk. If the size is not specified, the default for that drive is used. The common values for size are: /F:360 is 360 K, double-density 5 ¼" disk /F:1.2 is 1.2 MB, high-density 5 ¼" disk /F:720 is 720 K, double-density 3.5" disk /F:1.44 is 1.44 MB, high-density 3.5" disk
/U	Allows for an unconditional format of the disk, which does a more thorough job of formatting the disk by erasing all data. Use this option when you've been getting read/write errors on the disk
/Autotest	Does not prompt the user before and during the format

Dir

Use this command to list files and directories. Some examples are shown in the following table:

Command	Description
DIR /P	List one screen at a time.
DIR /W	Use wide format, where details are omitted and files and folders are listed in columns on the screen.
DIR *.txt	Use wildcard character.
DIR Myfile.txt	Check that a single file is present.

Type

The Type command displays on screen the contents of a text file. Some examples are shown in the following table:

Command	Description
Type Myfile.txt	Displays file contents
Type Myfile.txt >PRN	Redirects output to the printer
Type Myfile.txt |More	Displays output one screen at a time

Del or erase

The Del or Erase command erases files or groups of files. Where the command does not include drive and directory information, like the following examples, the OS uses the default drive and directory when executing the command.

For example, use the following command to erase all the files in the A:\DOCS directory:

```
C:\> ERASE A:\DOCS\*.*
```

To erase all the files in the current default directory, use the following command:

```
A:\DOCS> DEL *.*
```

To erase all files in the current directory that have no file extension, use the following command:

```
A:\DOCS> DEL *.
```

To erase the file named Myfile.txt, use the following command:

```
A:\> DEL MYFILE.TXT
```

Undelete

The Undelete command attempts to recover files that have been deleted. Following are some variations of the Undelete command. The Undelete command is not included in Windows 9x.

To list the files that can be undeleted, without actually undeleting them, use the following command:

```
A:\>UNDELETE /list
```

To recover deleted files without prompting for confirmation on each file, use the following command:

```
A:\>UNDELETE /all
```

Recover

The Recover command attempts to recover a file from damaged sectors on a disk. Always specify the drive, path, and file name of the file you want to recover with the Recover command. If you want to recover several files, use the command on one file at a time. The Recover command is not available in Windows 9x.

To recover the file named Myfile.txt on a floppy disk, use the following command:

```
RECOVER A:\DOCS\MYFILE.TXT
```

Whatever portion of the file that the Recover command can read is stored in the root directory and named A:FILE0000.REC (or the next available number). Copy this file to another disk before trying to recover the second file.

Because the Recover command might mark clusters as bad in the FAT, first use the Diskcopy or Copy command before using Recover. Data that might have been saved by other methods can sometimes be destroyed by the Recover command.

Diskcopy

The Diskcopy command makes an exact duplicate (sector by sector) of one floppy disk (called the source disk) to another disk of the same size and type (called the target disk).

To duplicate a floppy disk using only a single drive, use the following command:

```
C:\>DISKCOPY A: A:
```

The OS prompts you as many times as necessary to insert the source disk and then insert the target disk to make the exact copy. Data is copied from one disk to the other, byte by byte, including any hidden files, bad sectors, fragmented files, or other contents; everything is copied as is. For this reason, the copy can be faulty if the target disk has bad sectors. Diskcopy ignores the fact that a sector is marked as bad in the FAT and copies to it anyway. The Diskcopy command copies formatting information, so the target disk does not need to be formatted before executing the copy.

Copy

The Copy command copies a single file or group of files. The original files are not altered.

To copy a file from one drive to another, use the following command:

```
A:\>COPY drive:\path\file name.ext drive:\path\file name.ext
```

The drive, path, and file name of the original source file immediately follow the Copy command, and the drive, path, and file name of the destination file follow the source file name. If you do not specify the file name of the copy, the OS assigns the original name of the file. If you omit the drive or path of the source or the destination, then the OS uses the current default drive and path.

To copy the file Myfile.txt from the root directory of drive C to drive A, use the following command:

```
C:\>COPY MYFILE.TXT A:
```

Because a drive or path is not indicated before the file name Myfile.txt, the OS assumes that the file is in the default drive and path.

To copy all files in the C:\DOCS directory to the floppy disk in drive A, use the following command:

```
C:\>COPY C:\DOCS\*.* A:
```

To make a backup file named System.bak of the System.ini file in the \Windows directory of the hard drive, use the following command:

```
C:\WINDOWS> COPY SYSTEM.INI SYSTEM.BAK
```

If you use the Copy command to duplicate multiple files, the files are assigned the names of the original files. When duplicating multiple files, no file name can be listed in the destination portion of the command line.

Xcopy /C /S /Y /D:

The Xcopy command is more powerful than the Copy command. It follows the same general command-source-destination format as the Copy command, but it offers several more options, as outlined next, with a couple of useful examples.

Use the /S option with the Xcopy command to copy all files in the directory \DOCS, as well as all subdirectories under \DOCS and their files, to the disk in drive A. Use the following command:

```
C:\>XCOPY C:\DOCS\*.* A: /S
```

To copy all files from the directory C:\DOCS created or modified on March 14, 2002, use the /D switch, as in the following command:

```
XCOPY C:\DOCS\*.* A: /D:03/14/02
```

Use the /Y option to overwrite existing files without prompting and use the /C option to keep copying even when there is an error.

Deltree

The Deltree command deletes the directory tree beginning with the subdirectory you specify, including all subdirectories and all files in all subdirectories in that tree. Use it with caution.

```
C:\>DELTREE [drive:]path
```

Mkdir [drive:]path or MD [drive:]path

The Mkdir (abbreviated MD, for make directory) command creates a subdirectory entry in a directory. To create a directory named \GAME on drive C, use this command:

```
MKDIR C:\GAME
```

The backslash indicates that the directory is under the root directory. To create a directory named CHESS under the \GAME directory, use this command:

```
MKDIR C:\GAME\CHESS
```

The OS requires that the parent directory GAME already exist before it creates the child directory CHESS.

Exhibit 3-23 shows the result of the Dir command on the directory \GAME. Note the two initial entries in the directory table, the . (dot) and the .. (dot, dot) entries. These two entries are created by the Mkdir command when the OS initially sets up the directory. You cannot edit these entries with normal OS commands, and they must remain in the directory for the directory's lifetime. The . entry points to the subdirectory itself, and the .. entry points to the parent directory, in this case, the root directory.

```
C:\>DIR \GAME /P

Volume in drive C has no label
Volume Serial Number is 0F52-09FC
Directory of C:\GAME

.              <DIR>      02-18-93   4:50a
..             <DIR>      02-18-93   4:50a
CHESS          <DIR>      02-18-93   4:50a
NUKE           <DIR>      02-18-93   4:51a
PENTE          <DIR>      02-18-93   4:52a
NETRIS         <DIR>      02-18-93   4:54a
BEYOND         <DIR>      02-18-93   4:54a
        7 file(s)              0 bytes
                       9273344 bytes free

C:\>
```

Exhibit 3-23: Dir of the \Game directory

Chdir [drive:]path or CD [drive:]path or CD..

The Chdir (abbreviated CD, for change directory) command changes the current default directory. By using its easiest-to-follow form, you simply state the drive and the entire path that you want to be current:

```
CD C:\GAME\CHESS
```

The command prompt now looks like this:

```
C:\GAME\CHESS>
```

To move from a child directory to its parent directory, use the .. variation of the command:

```
C:\GAME\CHESS> CD..
C:\GAME>
```

Remember that .. always means the parent directory. You can move from a parent directory to one of its child directories simply by stating the name of the child directory:

```
C:\GAME> CD CHESS
C:\GAME\CHESS>
```

Do not put a backslash in front of the child directory name; doing so tells DOS to go to a directory named CHESS that is directly under the root directory.

Rmdir [drive:]path or RD [drive:]path

The Rmdir command (abbreviated RD, for remove directory) removes a subdirectory. Before you can use the Rmdir command, three things must be true:

- The directory must contain no files.
- The directory must contain no subdirectories.
- The directory must not be the current directory.

The . and .. entries are present when a directory is ready for removal. For example, to remove the \GAME directory in the above example, the CHESS directory must first be removed:

```
C:\> RMDIR C:\GAME\CHESS
```

Or, if the \GAME directory is the current directory, use this command:

```
C:\GAME> RD CHESS
```

Once you remove the CHESS directory, you can remove the \GAME directory. You must first leave the \GAME directory like this:

```
C:\GAME>CD..
C:\> RD \GAME
```

Attrib

The Attrib command displays or changes the read-only, archive, system, and hidden attributes assigned to files. Example Attrib commands are shown in the following table:

Command	Description
ATTRIB MYFILE.TXT	Displays the attributes of the file MYFILE.TXT
ATTRIB +H MYFILE.TXT	Hides the file
ATTRIB -H MYFILE.TXT	Removes the hide status of the file
ATTRIB +R MYFILE.TXT	Makes the file a read-only file
ATTRIB -R MYFILE.TXT	Removes the read-only status of the file
ATTRIB +A MYFILE.TXT	Turns the archive bit on
ATTRIB -A MYFILE.TXT	Turns the archive bit off

Unformat

The Unformat command might be able to reverse the effect of an accidental format. To unformat a disk, use this command:

```
UNFORMAT C:
```

Path

The Path command lists where the OS should look to find executable program files. This command is discussed here again to make the list of commands more complete. A sample Path command is

```
PATH C:\;C:\DOS;C:\WINDOWS;C:\UTILITY
```

Each path is separated from the next with a semicolon. You should put the most-used paths at the beginning of the line, because the OS searches the paths listed in the Path command line from left to right. The Path command goes in the Autoexec.bat file and can be executed from the OS prompt.

Sys Drive:

The Sys command copies the system files needed to boot to a disk or hard drive. Use the command if the system files on a drive are corrupted. You can access the drive, but you cannot boot from it. The command to copy system files to the hard drive is:

```
SYS C:
```

Chkdsk [drive:] /F /V

The Chkdsk command reports information about a disk. Use the /F option to have Chkdsk fix errors it finds, including errors in the FAT caused by clusters marked as being used but that do not belong to a particular file (called lost allocation units) and clusters that are marked in the FAT as belonging to more than one file (called cross-linked clusters).

To check the hard drive for errors and repair them, use this command:

```
CHKDSK C: /F
```

To redirect the output from the Chkdsk command to a file that you can later print, use this command:

```
CHKDSK C: >Myfile.txt
```

The /V option of the Chkdsk command displays all path and file name information for all files on a disk:

```
CHKDSK C: /V
```

Chkdsk is useful when using a startup disk; otherwise, use Scandisk or disk error-checking from the Windows desktop.

Scandisk Drive: /A /N /P

The Scandisk command scans a hard drive for errors and repairs them if possible. Scandisk checks the FAT, long file names, lost and cross-linked clusters, directory tree structure, bad sectors, and compressed structure if the drive has been compressed using Windows DriveSpace or DoubleSpace.

The /A parameter is used to scan all nonremovable local drives. Use this command only to display information without fixing the drive:

```
SCANDISK C: /P
```

Use this command to display information and fix errors:

```
SCANDISK C:
```

Use this command to start and stop Scandisk automatically:

```
Scandisk C: /N
```

If you use the above command, Scandisk will still stop to report errors.

Defrag drive: /S

The Defrag command examines a hard drive or disk for fragmented files (files written to a disk in noncontiguous clusters) and rewrites these files to the disk or drive in contiguous clusters. Use this command to optimize a hard drive, improving the hard drive performance.

Use the /S:N option to sort the files on the disk in alphabetical order by file name.

```
DEFRAG C: /S:N
```

Use the /S:D option to sort the files on the disk by date and time.

```
DEFRAG C: /S:D
```

Ver

Use the Ver command to display the version of the operating system in use.

Scanreg /Restore /Fix /Backup

The Scanreg command restores or repairs the Windows 98 registry. It uses backups of the registry that Windows 98 Registry Checker automatically makes each day. To restore the registry from a previous backup, use this command:

```
SCANREG /RESTORE
```

A menu appears asking you which backup to use.

To repair a corrupted registry, use this command:

```
SCANREG /FIX
```

To create a new backup of the registry, use this command:

```
SCANREG /BACKUP
```

Don't use this last command if you're having problems with the registry.

Extract file name.cab file1.ext /D

The Extract command extracts files from a cabinet file such as the Ebd.cab file on the Windows 98 startup disk. To list the files that are contained in the cabinet file, use this command:

```
EXTRACT EBD.CAB /D
```

To extract the file Debug.exe from the Ebd.cab file, use this command:

```
EXTRACT EBD.CAB DEBUG.EXE
```

To extract all files from the Ebd.cab cabinet file, use this command:

```
EXTRACT EBD.CAB *.*
```

Debug

The Debug program is an editor that can view and manipulate the components of a file system on floppy disks and hard drives, including the FAT, directories, and boot records. It can also be used to view the contents of memory and hexadecimal memory addresses. To access Debug, enter the command Debug at the command prompt.

Edit [path][file name]

The Edit program (Edit.com) is a text editor to edit Autoexec.bat and Config.sys files. It is a handy, "quick and dirty" way to edit text files while working at a command prompt. To edit the file Autoexec.bat on a floppy disk, use this command:

```
EDIT A:\AUTOEXEC.BAT
```

If the file does not already exist, Edit will create the file.

Note: With older versions of DOS, Qbasic.exe was required for Edit.com to work correctly.

Do it!

D-4: Working from the command line

Here's how	Here's why
1 Double-click **My Computer**	(On the Windows desktop.) You'll create a new folder and text file from within My Computer.
Double-click the drive **C:** icon	Note that if you are using Windows XP, the My Computer icon might not be on the desktop. In this case, choose Start and click My Computer.
2 Right-click anywhere in the blank area of the drive C: window	
Choose **New, Folder**	(From the shortcut menu.) A new folder icon appears with "New Folder" highlighted, ready for you to rename it.
3 Enter **Tools**	To rename the folder as "Tools."
4 Double-click the **Tools** folder icon	To create a file in the Tools folder.
Right-click anywhere in the blank area of the Tools window	
Choose **New, Text Document**	(In the shortcut menu.) A new file icon appears in the Tools window with "New Text Document.txt" highlighted, ready for you to rename it.
5 Double-click **New Text Document.txt**	(In \Tools.) The file opens in Notepad.
6 Choose **File, Save As...**	On the Notepad menu bar.
7 Name the file **Deleteme**	In the Save As dialog box.
Verify that the Save as type: is Text Documents	
Click **Save**	To save the file.
8 Close Notepad	
9 Right-click **New Text Document.txt**	
Choose **Delete**	From the shortcut menu.
Click **Yes**	(To confirm the deletion.) The file is deleted.
10 Close all open windows	

11 Choose **Start**, **Programs**, **Accessories**	(On the taskbar to open the command line window in Windows 2000). You'll practice using the command line environment. To open the command line window in Windows 9x, choose Start on the taskbar, then choose Programs, MS-DOS Prompt. To open the command line window in Windows XP, choose Start on the taskbar, then choose All Programs, Accessories, Command Prompt.
Click **Command Prompt**	To open a command line window.
Observe the command line window	The title bar of this window differs with different versions of Windows. Below the title bar, a command prompt like the following appears in Windows 9x:C:\WINDOWS>. In Windows 2000, the following command prompt appears instead: C:\>. The Windows XP command prompt depends on the user name of the person currently logged in, for example: C:\Documents and Settings\Jean Andrews>.
	The command prompt indicates the working drive (drive C) and working directory (either the \Windows directory, the root directory indicated by the backslash, or the Documents and Settings directory of the current user). Commands issued from this prompt apply to this folder unless you indicate otherwise.
12 Enter **DIR**	Remember that DIR is the command used to list the contents of a directory.
Verify that a list of files and directories appears in the command line window	The list may be too large to fit within one screen, in which case you will see only the last entries.
13 Enter **DIR /?**	(To display Help information for the directory command. You can obtain Help information for any command by entering the command followed by the /? switch.) You'll learn more about displaying lists of files in the command line environment.
14 Enter **DIR /W**	
Record the results	
15 Enter **DIR /P**	
Record the results	
16 Enter **DIR /OS**	
Record the results	

17 Enter **DIR /O-S**

Record the results

What do you think the hyphen between O and S accomplishes?

18 Insert a blank disk into the floppy drive

Enter **A:**

Verify that the resulting prompt looks like: A:\>

19 Record the following information:

What does the A: indicate?

What do you think you would see if you executed the DIR command at this prompt?

20 Enter **DIR**

Do you see what you expected to see?

21 Enter **C:**   To return to the C: drive.

22 Enter **DIR C:\Tools**   To display a list of the contents of a specific directory without actually changing to that directory.

Verify that the Deleteme.txt file appears in the resulting file list

23 Enter **DEL Deleteme.txt**   To instruct the computer to delete that file.

Verify that a message appears, indicating that the file could not be found   This is because the system assumes commands refer to the working directory unless a specific path is given.

What command do you think you could use to delete the file without changing to that directory?

24 Enter **CD**   The resulting prompt is C:\> for Windows 9x, Windows 2000, and Windows XP. The \ in the command you typed indicates the root directory.

25 Enter **CD Tools**   The prompt now ends with "Tools>," (indicating that Tools is the current working directory).

26 Enter **DEL Deleteme.txt /p**

Observe the output

You'll be prompted to type "Y" for yes or "N" for no. If you do not enter the /p switch to Prompt for Verification, the file is deleted automatically without a confirmation message. It is a good practice to use the Prompt for Verification switch, especially when deleting multiple files with wildcard characters. Also, when you delete a file from the command line, the file does not go to the Recycle Bin, as it would if you deleted it from Windows Explorer or My Computer, therefore making it more difficult to recover accidentally deleted files.

27 Type **Y**

To delete the Deleteme.txt file.

Verify that you are returned to the Tools directory

28 Return to the root directory

Record the command you have used

29 Enter **DIR *.***

Record how many files are displayed

30 Enter **DIR C*.***

Record how many files are displayed

31 Explain why the results differed in the previous two steps

32 Copy the program file notepad.exe from \WINNT or \Windows directory in Windows 2000/XP to the \Tools directory

To practice using additional commands at the command prompt.

What command did you use?

33 Rename the file in the \Tools directory as **Newfile.exe**

What command did you use?

34 Change the attributes of
Newfile.exe to make it a hidden
file

What command did you use?

35 Enter **DIR**

Record if the Newfile.exe file is
displayed

36 Unhide **Newfile.exe**

What command did you use?

37 List all files in the \Windows or
\WINNT directory that have an
.exe file extension

What command did you use?

38 Create a new directory named
\New in \Windows or \WINNT

Copy **Newfile.exe**   To the \New directory.

What command did you use?

39 Delete the **\New** directory   By using the /p switch to prompt for
verification.

What command did you use?

40 What command/switch can you
use to view Help information for
the DIR command?

41 What do you add to the DIR
command to list the contents of a
directory that is not the current
working directory?

42 What command can you use to
change directories?

43 What command can you use to
delete a file?

44 What command can you use to
switch from drive A to drive C?

Using batch files

Suppose you have a list of OS commands that you want to execute several times. Perhaps you have some data files to distribute to several PCs in your office, and, having no LAN, you must walk from one PC to another, doing the same job repeatedly. A solution is to store the list of commands in a batch file on disk and then execute the batch file at each PC.

Windows requires that the batch file have a .bat file extension. For example, store these five OS commands on a disk in a file named MYLOAD.BAT

```
C:
MD\UTILITY
MD\UTILITY\TOOLS
CD\UTILITY\TOOLS
COPY A:\TOOLS\*.*
```

From the command prompt, you execute the batch file, just as you do other program files, by entering the name of the file, with or without the file extension:

```
A:\>MYLOAD
```

All the commands listed in the file will be executed, beginning at the top of the list. The batch file above will create a subdirectory under the C: drive called Utility\Tools; change to that directory as the default directory, and copy all files from the \Tools directory in drive A into that new subdirectory. Look at any good book on DOS to find examples of the very useful ways you can elaborate on batch files, including adding user menus.

File extensions

The following table lists common file extensions with their corresponding file types. In Windows, one icon represents files with the same extension.

File extension	File type
.txt	Text
.exe	Executable
.com	Command
.sys	System
.cab	Cabinet (contains compressed installation or setup files)

Do it!   **D-5:   Learning file naming conventions**

Here's how	Here's why
1 Open **Windows Explorer**	
Choose **Tools**, **Folder Options**	On the menu bar.
2 Clear **Hide file extensions for known file types**	On the View tab.
Click **Apply**	
Click **OK**	The Folder Options dialog box closes.
3 In Explorer, browse through several folders	
Record the file extensions	The previous table listed common file extensions with their corresponding file types. Note that in Windows, the same icon represents files with the same extension.
4 Open a command prompt window	You'll create a directory on the hard drive and store a file in it by using the DOS naming convention.
Change directories to the root of the C: drive	
5 Enter **MD Test**	The MD command instructs the system to make a directory, in this case one called Test.
6 Enter **DIR /AD /P**	To verify that this new directory exists.
7 Type **CD Test**	To change to the Test directory.
8 Enter **Edit Test.txt**	This edit command opens a DOS text editor called Edit, and creates a file named Test.txt. By using this program, you can create and edit text files.
9 Type **This is a test. This file was created with Edit.**	
10 Press (ALT) + **F** + **S**	To save the file.
11 Press (ALT) + **F** + **X**	To exit Edit and leave the command window.
12 By using Windows Explorer, find the Test folder	You'll use Notepad to create a file with a long file name.

13	Double-click **Test.txt**	(Note that this fairly short file name is identical in Explorer and in the command prompt environment.) The file opens in Notepad, which is the default text editor for Windows.
14	Choose **File**, **New**	In Notepad on the menu bar.
	Type **This is a test. This file was created in Notepad with a long file name**	
15	Choose **File**, **Save as…**	On the menu bar.
	Name the file as **Longnametest.txt**	
	Click **Save**	
	Do not close Notepad	
16	Look at the file name in Explorer	Note that the name appears exactly as you typed it in the Save As dialog box. Note also that the file is represented by the same icon as the Test.txt file.
17	Return to the DOS command window	To see how DOS displays the long file name.
	Verify to see \Test as the current working directory	
	Enter **DIR**	
	Record the short names and long names of the files listed	Now you're ready to create another file with a long file name.
18	Use Notepad to amend the text to read **This is the second file created in Notepad with a long file name**	
	Save the file as **Longnametestagain.txt**	
19	In the command prompt window, enter **DIR**	
	Verify that you see two files other than Test.txt	These files are named Longna~1.txt and Longna~2.txt. As you can see, DOS changes long file names to the 8.3 format by leaving the first six characters and adding a ~ (tilde) and a number indicating the alphabetical instance (beyond the sixth character) of that file.

20 Compare the way the file Longnametest.txt was displayed earlier, when it was the only file other than Test.txt, and the way it is displayed now

21 Use the command prompt to make C: root the current directory   At the command prompt.

Enter **DIR /O /P**

Record the way DOS lists the Program Files directory, which does not follow the 8.3 DOS naming convention for files and directories   The directory is listed by DOS as Progra~1.

22 Enter **CD Progra~1**   (To make the Progra~1 directory the current directory.) If you want to use a long (that is, unabbreviated) directory name with the CD command, you need to enclose the directory name in quotation marks

23 Enter **CD**   This makes the C: root the current directory.

24 Enter **CD "Program Files"**   Program Files is now the current directory.

25 What does 8.3 mean in the context of naming conventions?

26 How does the Windows OS graphically depict file types?

27 What type of file ends in .exe?

28 How is a long file name represented at the DOS prompt?

29 How can you use long names at the DOS prompt?

Unit summary: The boot process and command line management

Topic A

In this topic, you learned the steps for **booting** the computer. You learned how startup **BIOS** controls the beginning of the boot process and how the **MS-DOS core** of Windows 9x is loaded.

Topic B

In this topic, you learned about the **emergency startup disks**. You learned how to create your own Windows 9x **bootable rescue disk** and how to access the **command prompt**.

Topic C

In this topic, you learned how DOS and Windows 9x view and manage **memory**. You learned the basics of physical memory and **memory addresses** and learned about the various utilities that manage memory, **Himem.sys** and **Emm386.exe**. You also learned about some default settings used by Windows.

Topic D

In this topic, you learned about managing floppy disks and hard drives. You learned how data is logically stored on a **floppy disk** and how a **hard drive** is logically organized to hold data. You also learned about the **formatting** process for a floppy disk and how to use **Fdisk** to partition the hard drive. You learned the various commands to manage a floppy disk or hard drive, such as **Dir, Type, Del, Recover, Diskcopy**, and so on. Finally, you learned how to use the **batch files**.

Review questions

1 What is the difference between a hard boot and a soft boot?

2 What are the four main parts of the boot process?

3 Give the memory address that is always assigned to the first instruction in the ROM BIOS startup program.

4 Name the program that is needed to locate the beginning of the OS on a drive.

5 Which file systems for a hard drive does Windows 98 support?

6 Which version of Windows introduced the VFAT file system? The FAT32 file system?

7   What three OS files are necessary to boot to MS-DOS mode? What is the function of each? What additional two files are not required but are used if they are present?

8   Name at least three program files that are included in the Ebd.cab file.

9   Why is it important not to edit Autoexec.bat with word-processing software such as Microsoft Word or WordPerfect?

10 Give two ways to access a command prompt from Windows 9x.

11 What Windows OS introduced the NTFS file system?

12 The _____ command changes the operating system name assigned to a hard drive, and the _____ command erases files or groups of files.

13 What command line would you use to list files that can be undeleted without actually undeleting them?

14 Explain the difference between the Diskcopy command, the Copy command, and the Xcopy command.

15 What command is used to create a subdirectory? To change the current directory? To remove a subdirectory?

16 The _____ command displays or changes the read-only, archive, system, and hidden characteristics of files.

17 Name the file that DOS uses to access memory addresses above 1 MB.

18 What command is used to list where the OS should look to find executable program files?

19 Explain the difference between the Chkdsk and Scandisk commands.

20 What is a hidden file? Name a Windows 9x file that is hidden.

21 What improvement did VFAT offer when it was introduced? Which file system replaced it?

22 What is the purpose of the Ebd.cab file on the Windows 98 startup disk?

23 FAT32 is recommended for hard drives larger than _____ and is efficient for drives up to _____.

24 When using Fdisk, what is the question that the software asks you that will cause it to use the FAT32 file system?

25 The term cold boot is used to describe when a computer is powered up from being turned completely off. True or false?

26 What does POST stand for?

27 Name one of the two system (.sys) files needed by Windows 9x to boot properly.

28 Hidden files are files that are hidden from what?

29 What is a batch file?

30 Editing files like Autoexec.bat and Config.sys can be done with any word processor or text editor. True or false?

31 One hard drive can contain more than one logical drive. True or false?

32 Why isn't it a good idea to use increasingly larger hard drives for the FAT16 file management system?

Independent practice activity

Follow these steps to prepare a hard drive for a new installation of Windows 9x:

1 Boot from a Windows 9x startup disk.

2 Use Fdisk to create primary and extended partitions on the drive. The primary partition will contain drive C.

3 If there is room on the drive, create two logical drives in the extended partition.

4 Format all three logical drives, placing system files on drive C.

5 Verify that you can boot to drive C.

6 Get a C: prompt and verify that all three drives are accessible.

7 Use the Dir command to print a directory of each drive to a local printer.

8 Use these or similar commands: DIR C:>PRN, DIR D:>PRN, and DIR E:>PRN

9 Use Scandisk to scan each logical drive disk surface for errors.

Follow these steps to use Windows Explorer to open the Autoexec.bat and Config.sys files:

1 Choose **Start** on the taskbar.

2 Choose **Programs**.

3 Click **Windows Explorer** (or right-click the **Start** button on the taskbar and then choose **Explore**).

4 Insert the startup disk you created.

5 In the left pane of Windows Explorer, click the icon for **drive A:**. The drive is highlighted in the left pane, and the right pane displays a list of folders and files stored on the floppy disk.

6 If necessary, scroll down the right pane until you can see the Autoexec.bat file.

7 Right-click **Autoexec.bat**.

8 Choose **Edit** from the shortcut menu. The file opens in a text editor (Notepad by default), ready for you to modify it. Autoexec.bat is a batch file that contains a list of commands for tasks that you want the system to execute each time it starts up. Your system might contain other batch files, but only Autoexec.bat is run by default each time the system boots.

9 Look for entries in the Autoexec.bat file similar to the entry shown in Exhibit 3-24. The Autoexec.bat file instructs the OS where to look for executable files. Virus protection software and any drivers that are loaded for DOS compatibility can also be referenced in Autoexec.bat.

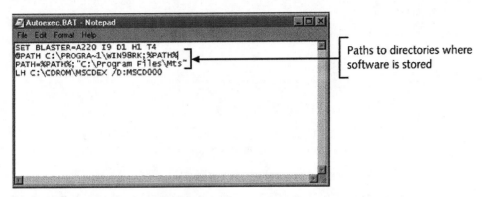

Exhibit 3-24: Sample Autoexec.bat file

10 Close the file. If you had made any changes, you would be asked whether you wanted to save them. Do not save any changes at this time.

11 In Windows Explorer, locate the Config.sys file on the A: drive.

12 Right-click **Config.sys**, choose **Open With…** from the shortcut menu. The Open With dialog box appears.

13 In the Open With dialog box, scroll down and select **Notepad**, deselect the **Always use this program to open this file** check box, and then click **OK**. Config.sys opens in Notepad.

14 Note that the Config.sys file contains configuration instructions as well. An example is shown in Exhibit 3-25. Yours may have instructions for loading device drivers to high memory to free up conventional memory for DOS applications.

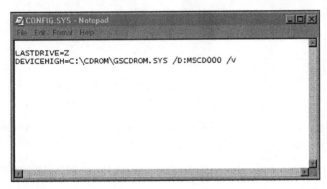

Exhibit 3-25: Sample Config.sys file

15 Close Config.sys. If you made any changes, do not save them.

16 Record the following information

17 What is the purpose of configuration files?

18 On either a startup disk or on a hard drive, in what directory are Autoexec.bat and Config.sys located?

19 Are other batch files besides Autoexec.bat automatically processed during the boot process?

20 Which configuration file can contain a path statement?

21 Which configuration file can instruct DOS drivers to load in high memory?

Follow these steps on a Windows 9x PC to create a bootable floppy disk and to copy a file to the disk.

1 Choose **Start** from the taskbar.

2 Choose **Programs.**

3 Click **MS-DOS Prompt**.

4 Insert a blank floppy disk.

5 Enter **FORMAT A: /S.** The following prompt appears: "Insert new diskette for drive A: and press Enter when ready."

6 Press **Enter** to start formatting the disk.

7 Watch as the floppy disk is formatted and the system files are transferred to the floppy disk.

8 When prompted, enter a volume name if you wish (or simply press **Enter** to bypass this step entirely).

9 When asked if you want to format another disk, Enter **N.** (Note that if your disk was already formatted, you could have used the SYS A: command to copy system files to the disk.)

Follow these steps to copy some configuration files to the boot disk.

1 Insert the Windows 9x CD into the CD drive, enter **Copy D:\tools\oldmsdos\msd.exe A:\.** (If you don't have access to the Windows 9x CD, your instructor can give you an alternate location for the file. If your CD has a drive letter other than D, substitute the appropriate drive letter.)

2 Repeat the above step for the mouse driver file and the text editor, Edit.com, in the location specified by your instructor. The mouse driver file will be named Mouse.com, Mouse.sys, or a similar name.

3 Close the command prompt window.

4 Shut down the system.

Follow these steps to boot the PC using the boot disk and verify that the mouse is not available.

1 With the floppy disk still in the drive, boot the system. A message is displayed on your screen.

2 To use the Microsoft Diagnostic Utility, at the command prompt, enter **MSD.EXE**.

3 Move the mouse around. Does the mouse work as you would expect?

4 Press **F3** to exit MSD.

Follow these steps to use the Edit program to create and edit an Autoexec.bat file.

1 At the A prompt, type **Edit Autoexec.bat**. The Edit window opens and the Autoexec.bat file is created.

2 Enter the command to load the mouse driver, using the file name of the driver such as Mouse.com.

3 To exit the editor, save your changes, press the **Alt** key, and use your arrow keys to choose **Exit** from the **Exit** menu.

4 When asked if you want to save your changes to the file, select **Yes**.

Follow these steps to test your floppy disk to see if it provides mouse support.

1 With the boot disk still in the floppy drive, reboot.

2 Run the MSD program.

3 Record if you observe any change when you moved the mouse.

4 Click **Exit** on the File menu to close MSD.

5 Remove the floppy disk and reboot the PC.

6 Record the following information.

7 When formatting a disk, what command can you use to make the floppy disk a boot disk?

8 If you have a formatted floppy, what command other than **Format a: /s** can you use to transfer the system files to the floppy disk?

9 Which configuration file did you modify to cause the mouse to be automatically supported?

10 Did you notice a difference in the boot process after you changed a configuration file?

11 When booting from a floppy disk, how would you automatically load a program to provide support for your CD-ROM drive?

Unit 4

Installing and using Windows 9x

Unit time: 90 minutes

Complete this unit, and you'll know how to:

A Describe various versions and architecture of Windows 9x.

B Install Windows 9x as a clean installation and as an upgrade.

C Use keystroke shortcuts and manage hard drives, floppy disks, and the desktop with Windows 9x.

D Install hardware with Windows 9x.

E Install applications with Windows 9x.

F Manage memory with Windows 9x.

Topic A: Versions and architecture

Explanation

As a PC support technician, you need to know how to install, use, and troubleshoot the Windows operating systems commonly used today. You need to have a general knowledge of how hardware works and a detailed knowledge of how Windows and other types of software work. You learned how hardware and software work together. This unit covers how Windows 9x is structured, how it's used, and how it works with various software programs and hardware devices. Windows 9x has had several releases, including Windows 95, Windows 95 Service Release 2 (SR2), Windows 98, Windows 98 Second Edition (SE), and Windows Me (Millennium Edition). Each of these operating systems uses the same basic architectural structure, and each release has improvements over previous versions plus new features.

How Windows 98 differs from Windows 95

Windows 98 is basically the same operating system as Windows 95, with the same core components and the same fundamental services to software, hardware, and the user. However, it does offer some added features and improved performance over Windows 95. Some of these added features became available with Windows 95 Release 2, such as support for FAT32, USB, and DVD. Windows 98 also includes some new system tools to monitor and improve system performance, new hardware support, and additional Web tools.

Note: FAT32 isn't compatible with Windows NT or disk compression, including the use of DoubleSpace under Windows 98. To use disk compression or to have a file system compatible with Windows NT, use FAT16. Windows 2000/XP supports FAT32.

Windows 95 and Windows 98 load, run, and install very much the same way. The following table summarizes the changes that took place from Windows 95 to Windows 98.

Feature	Description
Troubleshooting utilities	Windows 95 had a few troubleshooting utilities, but the utilities that come with Windows 98 are more interactive.
Update Wizard	The Update Wizard connects to the Microsoft Web site and automatically downloads any new drivers or fixes.
Maintenance Wizard	The Maintenance Wizard can be used to schedule several regular maintenance tasks, which include running Disk Defragmenter and Scandisk.
DriveSpace 3	An improved version of DriveSpace for Windows 95, it includes a third level of data compression, called UltraPack, which takes up less space per file than does the regular compression utility, called HiPack.
Power management	Windows 98 supports some power management features, if both hardware and software are present to use them.
Registry Checker	Backs up and restores the registry.
Web tools and features	Several Windows 98 features take on an Internet look and feel. Windows 98 also supports viewing TV and interactive programs. You need a special TV interface card to do it.
FAT32	FAT32 is a file system that allows for a smaller cluster size on large drives than does the earlier FAT16.
New hardware support	With 1,200 device drivers, Windows 98 supports many more hardware devices than Windows 95. Also, Windows 98 supports USB, DVD drives, and multiple video cards supporting multiple monitors and faster data throughput for CD-ROM drives.
Win32 Driver Model (WDM)	A new device driver model, also used by Windows NT, makes it possible for the same device driver to be used by both operating systems, making it easier for device manufactures to supply drivers for their devices.

Windows Me

Windows Me, the last Windows 9x upgrade, has a desktop that looks more like Windows 2000 than Windows 98 SE. Like Windows 2000, Windows Me doesn't include the option to boot to the DOS command prompt in the Start menu. That means that you can't boot Windows Me from the hard drive in true real mode, although you do have an MS-DOS Command Prompt window. If you want to get a true real-mode command prompt using Windows Me, create a blank formatted floppy disk and copy Io.sys and Command.com from the \Windows\Command\EBD folder to the disk, and then boot from that disk.

Windows Me doesn't allow real-mode device drivers and TSRs to be loaded from Config.sys and Autoexec.bat, as do earlier versions of Windows 9x. If you want to run these 16-bit programs, your only option is to load them after Windows Me loads. One way to do this is to include them in a batch file that's listed in the Properties tab of the MS-DOS Command Prompt shortcut.

Troubleshooting tools new to Windows Me include:

- **System Restore:** Automatically backs up the registry and other system files when the system is idle, after about every 10 hours of operating time. When needed, the System Restore Wizard can be used to choose between earlier versions of the saved system.

- **System File Protection:** Prevents system files from being deleted. For example, if you attempt to delete files in the Program Files folder where applications are normally stored, the utility works in the background to compress and save these files in case you need them later. The utility also prevents an application installation from overwriting newer DLL files with older or nonstandard versions.

Windows 9x architecture

Like other operating systems, Windows 9x has a shell and a kernel. The two most important parts of the shell are the *user component* and the *GDI (Graphics Device Interface)*. The user component manages input from the keyboard and other user devices, output from the user interface, and the GDI. The GDI is a component of the OS responsible for presenting the graphical interface to the user and providing graphics support to output devices. The purposes of each component are listed in the following table:

Component	Component files	Functions
Kernel	Kernel32.dll, Krnl386.exe	Handles the basic OS functions, such as managing memory, file I/O, and loading and executing programs.
User	User32.dll, User.exe	Controls the mouse, keyboard, ports, and desktop, including the position of windows, icons, and dialog boxes.
GDI	GDI32.dll, GDI.exe	Draws screens, graphics, and lines and prints them.

Exhibit 4-1 shows the three core portions of the Windows 9x OS. In Exhibit 4-1, you can see that the basic Windows 9x core component, the kernel, uses mostly 32-bit code. The 16-bit code is retained only to provide entry points into the kernel from 16-bit application programs. The user portion uses mostly 16-bit code, primarily because it uses less memory than the 32-bit equivalent and doesn't have a need for significant speed. The GDI core uses a mix of 16-bit and 32-bit code in order to maintain compatibility with 16-bit application programs.

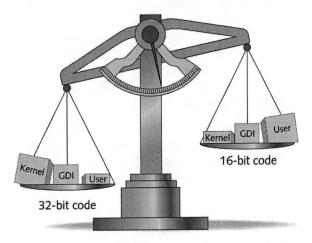

Exhibit 4-1: Core components of Windows 9X

The Windows 9x core relates to users, software, and hardware by way of several modules, as seen in Exhibit 4-2. Just as DOS and Windows 3.x each provides a shell for the user to interface with the OS, Windows 9x provides a group of user interface tools and a shell for applications. Configuration data stored in Windows 3.x ini files is stored in the Windows 9x registry, a database that also contains the initialization information for applications, a database of hardware and software settings, Windows configuration settings, user parameters, and application settings.

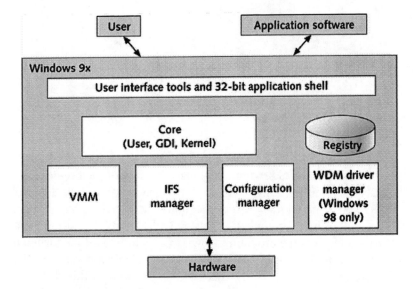

Exhibit 4-2: The Windows9x architecture

Virtual machines

Before we look at the various components in Exhibit 4-2, we need to understand how these components relate to applications and hardware. Recall that DOS allows applications direct access to hardware but, beginning with Windows 95, the Windows operating system manages hardware for applications. Applications call on the OS to access hardware or other software by using an *application programming interface (API) call*. When applications are first loaded by Windows 9x, the methods to access hardware and software are made available to the software through an interface called a *virtual machine*. An application sees a virtual machine as a set of resources made available to it through these predefined APIs. An OS can provide a virtual machine to a single application that commands all the resources of that virtual machine, or the OS can assign a virtual machine to be shared by two or more applications. Think of virtual machines as multiple logical machines within one physical machine, similar in concept to several logical drives within one physical drive.

Exhibit 4-3 shows several virtual machines that Windows 9x can provide. The system virtual machine (system VM) is the most important VM under Windows 9x and is where all the OS processes run. It can also support 32-bit and 16-bit Windows application programs, but DOS programs run in their own virtual machines.

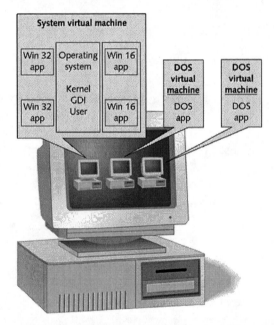

Exhibit 4-3: Windows 9x uses the virtual machine concept

A DOS program expects to control directly the hardware of the entire PC, memory included. If a DOS program begins to use memory addresses not assigned to it, errors occur in a multitasking environment. Windows 9x solves this problem by providing the DOS program with its own virtual machine. In effect, the application program says, "I want all of memory and all of this and all of that." Windows 9x says, "OK, here they are," and gives the program its own PC, including all the virtual memory addresses it wants from 0 to 4 GB, as well as its own virtual hardware! As far as the DOS program is concerned, it can go anywhere and do anything within its own PC. The DOS application program doesn't try to communicate with any other application program or to access the data of another program, because it thinks there are no other programs; it controls its entire world, and it's the only program in it. That's a virtual machine.

Note: One important result of running DOS programs in individual virtual machines is that when a DOS program makes an error, the virtual machine it's using hangs. However, other programs and the OS are isolated from the problem and aren't affected by it.

Windows 16-bit application programs offer a slightly different challenge to Windows 9x. These programs make some of the same mistakes that DOS programs do and can cause the system to hang. However, they also sometimes expect to access other programs and their data. The 16-bit Windows programs don't expect to control the hardware directly and are content to route their requests to Windows. Windows 9x places these programs within the system virtual machine because they communicate with hardware through the OS, but Windows 9x puts these programs together in their own memory space, so they can share memory addresses.

The result of this arrangement is that, when a 16-bit Windows program causes an error, called a Windows Protection Error or a General Protection Fault, it can disturb other 16-bit programs, causing them to fail. However, it doesn't disturb DOS programs in their own virtual machine or 32-bit programs that don't share their virtual memory addresses.

Components of Windows 9x

We now turn our attention back to the OS components that create, configure, and manage the virtual machines used by software and the OS. Exhibit 4-2 serves as a simple but complete reference point for all the components of Windows 9x, illustrating how they relate to the user, the hardware, the software, and each other. As you can see, Windows 9x architecture uses a modular approach that divides functions into separate program groups, making each component easier to update and implement.

One component in Exhibit 4-2 is the *Virtual Machine Manager (VMM)*, which is responsible for managing virtual machines and all the resources needed by each application running in them. One hardware device that all applications require is memory, and the VMM manages memory and virtual memory for applications. Virtual memory uses hard drive space, so that it acts like memory. Windows stores virtual memory in a file called a swap file. The purpose of virtual memory is to increase the amount of memory available. Of course, because a hard drive is much slower than RAM, virtual memory works at a considerably slower speed than real memory. For example, a hard drive may have a data access time of 10 ms (10/1,000 second or 10 milliseconds), whereas RAM speed may be 60 ns (60/1,000,000,000 second or 60 nanoseconds).

Another component, called *the Installable File System (IFS)* manager, is responsible for all disk access. The *Configuration Manager* is responsible for the Plug and Play features of Windows 9x and other hardware configuration tasks, such as providing system resources to hardware devices. In Exhibit 4-2, the only component that's found in Windows 98 but not in Windows 95 is the Win32 Driver Model (WDM) driver manager. This component is responsible for managing device drivers. The WDM makes it possible for device drivers written for Windows 98 to work also with Windows NT.

Note: Keep in mind that Windows 9x is a compromise OS, attempting to bridge the 16-bit world and the 32-bit world. It makes many compromises between these two worlds.

Although Windows 9x supports 16-bit device drivers and applications, it's preferable to use 32-bit drivers and 32-bit applications for four main reasons:

- 32-bit drivers and applications are generally much faster than 16-bit software.
- 32-bit drivers and applications can be stored in extended memory, releasing more of the first megabyte of memory.
- 32-bit drivers can be dynamically loaded, meaning that they're loaded into memory when they're needed and then removed when not needed, thus conserving memory. In contrast, 16-bit drivers must be stored in conventional or upper memory and remain there as long as the OS is running.
- 32-bit applications can share data with other 32-bit applications and are generally better designed, making better use of OS resources.

Note: When windows 9x is installed over DOS, it searches for 16-bit drivers and replaces them with 32-bit drivers, if it can.

Do it!

A-1: Discussing versions and architecture

Exercises

1 Name one Windows 9x release that doesn't support USB.

2 What are the three core components of Windows 9x?

3 _____ uses hard drive space, so that it acts like memory.

4 Give three reasons why it's preferable to use 32-bit drivers over older 16-bit drivers.

5 What's a virtual machine? How does Windows 9x use virtual machines differently from Windows 3.x to handle DOS applications and 16-bit Windows applications?

Topic B: Installation

Explanation

You want to learn to install Windows 9x after booting a computer to a C prompt on a working hard drive. There are separate CDs for installing Windows 9x on a PC without Windows (Windows 9x for a New PC) and for installing Windows 9x on a PC with an earlier version of Windows (Windows 9x Upgrade). The CDs for installing Windows 9x on a new PC are significantly more expensive than the upgrade CDs. To use the upgrade CDs, you must have a previous version of Windows installed on your hard drive.

A problem arises if you have just replaced a failed hard drive with a new hard drive and you want to do a fresh installation using a Windows 9x Upgrade CD. During the OS installation, the upgrade CD asks you to provide a Microsoft floppy disk or CD from an earlier version of Windows. If you can't provide the CD or floppy, the upgrade installation terminates, and you must use the more expensive version, Windows 9x for a New PC.

First, let's look at what's on the Windows 9x installation CD and how to prepare your hard drive for installation.

Windows 9x installation CD

The Windows 9x installation CD contains all the files you need to complete installation of the OS, as well as some system administration tools, instructions, tutorials, and other utilities. The CD includes a setup wizard that guides you through the process of installation and doesn't require you to work directly with the OS files.

The Windows 9x installation CD includes files you can use for the following tasks:

- Installing the OS
- Customizing configuration of the operating system
- Configuring and optimizing your desktop
- Network administration
- Diagnosing and troubleshooting system errors
- File management

Exhibit 4-4 shows the opening screen of the Windows 98 CD. It provides links to find information on software available with Windows 98, play video clips showing the multimedia features of Windows 98, browse the CD for a particular file or program, and add or remove software.

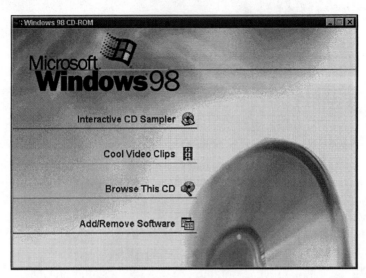

Exhibit 4-4: The opening screen of the Windows 98 CD

Important folders on the CD and their contents include the following:

- CD sample – contains subfolders that provide a catalog of and demos of Microsoft products.
- Drivers – lists hardware drivers by category.
- Oldmsdos – contains old DOS tools that can be useful in setup and troubleshooting.
- Sysrec – contains system recovery tools.

The following table lists some important files on the Windows 9x CD:

File	Function
Autorun.inf	Launches the interactive interface for the CD.
Readme.txt	Explains the layout of the CD and gives the locations of other readme files.
Setup.exe	Begins installation of the OS.
Batch.exe	Creates files that can be used for automated Windows 9x installations.
Checklinks.exe	Contains the Link Check Wizard, which can help you find and fix broken links and program shortcuts.
Netmon.386	Contains the Network Monitor, which enables you to monitor network performance remotely for Windows 9x computers.
Regserv.exe	Contains the Microsoft Remote Registry program, which provides a means to view and edit the Windows 9x registry remotely.
Textview.exe	Launches a text viewer that can quickly display text files without having to go through opening and operating a more complex word processing application.
Where.exe	Gives you a tool that you can use from the command line to locate a specific file on your hard drive.

This list doesn't give a comprehensive inventory of the contents of the installation CD but is an overview of what you find there. Any time after you have installed Windows 9x, you can refer back to the CD to access utilities and tutorials on how to use the operating system and the tools that are included with it.

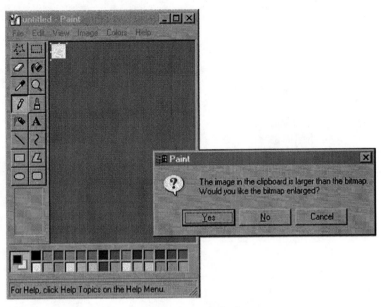

Exhibit 4-5: When prompted, expand the bitmap

Do it!

B-1:   Examining the Windows 9x installation CD

Here's how	Here's why
1 Insert the CD into the CD-ROM drive	If you're using a CD.
What happens after you insert the CD?	
2 Click **Browse This CD** on the Setup menu	Windows Explorer launches, showing the root directory of the CD.
List the files at the root of the CD	
3 Start Windows Explorer	If you're using a copy of the CD files stored at a different location.
Browse to the location of the CD files	
List the files at the root of the main CD directory	
4 Open the winXX folder	Where XX is your version of Windows.

5 Record the following information:

What's the file extension of the majority of files in this folder?

What does this file extension stand for?

How many files in this folder have an .exe file extension?

How many files in this folder have a .com file extension?

6 Double-click **Setup.txt**   The file opens in Notepad.

What's this file's intended use?

7 From Notepad, print Setup.txt

Close Notepad

8 Verify that the file named Intl.txt is included in the folder

Examine Intl.txt

What's this file's intended use?

9 Close Notepad windows   If necessary.

10 Return to the root of the CD in Windows Explorer

Open the Drivers folder

List the categories of drivers contained in the Drivers folder

11 Double-click **Readme.txt**

Print Readme.txt

What URL is mentioned in this file?

What does this URL provide?

12 Return to the root of the CD   In Windows Explorer.

Open the Tools folder

Open Oldmsdos folder

13 Choose **Start**, **Programs**, **Accessories**, **Paint** on the taskbar

You want to create a hard copy of a list of files on the installation CD.

14 Minimize Paint

15 Click the Windows Explorer title bar

To make it the active window.

16 Press (ALT) + (PRINT SCREEN)

To copy the image of the active window, Windows Explorer, onto the clipboard.

17 Restore Paint

Choose **Edit**, **Paste** on the menu bar

Observe the image

You'll probably be notified that the image is larger than the bitmap, as shown in Exhibit 4-5.

18 Click **Yes**

To expand the bitmap.

19 Print the screen shot

Close Paint

Without saving any changes.

20 Remove the CD from the CD-ROM drive

Place it in its protective case

Store it in a safe location

21 What are files with .exe and .com extensions used for?

22 List the steps to take and print a screenshot.

23 What type of information is contained in the Readme.txt file?

24 Name two folders that contain useful utilities for a troubleshooting diskette.

25 What key combination is used to paste a screenshot from the clipboard into the Paint program?

Preparing for installation

Explanation

Before installing Windows 9x, verify that the minimum requirements for the hardware are met. In order for Windows 9x to perform satisfactorily, the PC should meet the recommended requirements. Minimum and recommended requirements for Windows 95 and Windows 98 are listed below:

Minimum and recommended requirements for Windows 95:

- 486DX, 25 MHz or higher processor
- 4 MB of RAM (8 MB is recommended)
- 40 to 45 MB of hard disk storage, depending on the installation

Minimum and recommended requirements for Windows 98:

- 486DX, 66 MHz or higher processor
- 24 MB of RAM (32 MB is recommended)
- From 140 to 315 MB of hard disk storage, depending on the installation

Most likely, you want to install Windows 9x as an upgrade from DOS with Windows 3.x, as an upgrade from Windows 95 to Windows 98, or on a clean hard drive. If you've been having problems with your current operating system and applications, consider doing a clean install rather than an upgrade. *A clean install* ignores any settings in the currently installed OS, including information about installed hardware or software. After a clean install, you must reinstall all hardware and applications. Therefore, before deciding to do a clean install, verify that you have all the application software installation CDs or floppy disks and then back up all data on the drive. Also take the time to verify that the data backup is good and that you have all device driver software.

You don't need to format the hard drive, although you should delete all folders on the hard drive used for the OS or applications, including the \Windows folder, files, and subfolders before you begin the installation. This force Setup to perform a clean install and make certain no corrupted system files or applications remain. If you like, you can also format the hard drive. Do this if you suspect that a virus is present. If you suspect a boot sector virus is present, use the Fdisk/MBR command to rewrite the master boot sector program, and then do a clean install.

After Windows 9x is installed, reinstall all the application software. If you reformatted the hard drive, restore the data from backups. This method takes longer than an upgrade, but you get the advantage of a fresh start, and any problems with corrupted applications or system settings don't carry forward into the new installation.

An *upgrade* installation carries forward as much information as it can about what the current OS knows concerning installed hardware and software, user preferences, and other settings. An upgrade is faster than a clean install, because you don't need to reinstall software and hardware. However, problems with an old installation sometimes carry forward into the upgrade.

You can perform either an upgrade or a clean install with either the Windows 9x for a New PC or the Windows 9x Upgrade CD. If you're doing an upgrade, the old operating system must be in good enough shape to boot up, because you must begin an upgrade from within the currently installed OS.

Performing a clean installation

You can change CMOS settings to specify the order in which system BIOS looks for an OS on the drives on your PC. You might need to change the boot order in CMOS, depending on how you plan to load the OS. Older PCs could boot only from a hard drive or a floppy disk. This meant that, to use a CD-ROM drive, you had to boot these PCs from floppy disks first and then install the CD-ROM drivers. There are more choices with newer PCs, some of which can boot from a hard drive, floppy drive, Zip drive, CD-ROM drive, or other type of drive. These newer PCs have drivers for drive types other than hard drives and floppy drives written into their BIOS, allowing you to boot from a different medium.

Windows 9x comes on a set of floppy disks or on a CD. If you're installing the OS from floppy disks, you can boot from the hard drive or floppy disk. To boot from the floppy disk, make sure the computer is turned off. Then insert the Windows 9x Disk 1, which is bootable, and start the PC. At the A prompt, enter the command Setup.exe. You can also boot from a hard drive, go to a C prompt, and insert the Windows 9x Disk 1 in the floppy disk drive. Enter the command A:\Setup to execute the Setup program on the floppy disk. Either way, the Windows 9x setup screen appears. Follow the directions on the screen.

Note: Your CD-ROM drive might be configured to run a CD automatically when it's first inserted. This Autoplay feature causes the Setup opening menu to appear without your entering the Setup command. To disable the feature, hold down the Shift key while inserting the CD.

If you're installing the OS from a CD, that is, if your PC can boot from a CD-ROM drive, insert the CD in the drive and reboot. If your PC can't boot from a CD, boot from a floppy disk or hard drive, then insert the CD in the CD-ROM drive and enter the command D:\Setup.exe, substituting the drive letter of your CD-ROM drive for D, if necessary.

Note: To speed up the installation, you can copy the files and folders on the Windows 98 CD to a folder on your hard drive and run the Setup program from that folder. Also, having the Windows 98 CD files on your hard drive makes it easier to access the files later when adding Windows components or updating drivers.

Performing an upgrade

If you're doing an upgrade, before you begin the installation, prepare your hard drive by doing these things:

- Verify that you have enough space on the hard drive. Delete unwanted files and temporary directories.

- Run ScanDisk to check and repair errors on the hard drive. From Windows 95, click Start, then choose Programs, Accessories, System Tools, ScanDisk. Scan each logical drive in the system. From a Windows startup disk or from DOS, enter the command Scandisk at the command prompt.

- Run a current version of antivirus software to check for viruses.

- If you're upgrading from Windows 3.x, save configuration files so that you can backtrack to it, if necessary. Save Autoexec.bat and Config.sys, found in the root directory, and all files with .ini or .grp file extensions in the \Windows directory, to a disk. In Windows 3.x, files with the .grp file extension are group files, which contain information about a program group displayed in Program Manager.

- Check Config.sys and Autoexec.bat for potential problems. Verify that any hardware devices using device drivers loaded from these files are working under the old OS, so you know your starting point when troubleshooting problems under the new OS.

Note: The Windows 9x upgrade process moves commands in Autoexec.bat used to load TSRs (Terminate and Stay Resident programs) required for 16-bit Windows programs to Winstart.bat. Look for the Winstart.bat file in the root directory after the installation is done. If setup doesn't find any TSRs to put in the file, the Winstart.bat file isn't created.

- If there are Device drivers, such as QEMM386 (a memory manager by Quarterdeck), loaded from Config.sys or Autoexec.bat and problems arise because they're running during the installation, disable them by converting these lines to remarks or comments. To do this, type REM at the beginning of the command lines. Later, after the installation, you can activate them again by removing REM at the beginning of each line.

- If you are connected to a network, verify that the connection is working. If it is, Windows setup should be able to reestablish the connection correctly at the end of the installation.

- If you're upgrading from Windows 95 to Windows 98, create a Windows 95 rescue disk to use in the event that the installation fails.

- Decide if you want to use FAT16 or FAT32 for your file system. If you choose FAT16, you can later convert to FAT32 using the Windows Drive Converter. After Windows 98 is installed, to access the Converter, click Start, and then choose Programs, Accessories, System Tools, Drive Converter (FAT32). As an alternative, you can use the Run dialog box. For the 16-bit version, enter cvt.exe, and for the 32-bit version, enter cvt1.exe, and then click OK. The Drive Converter Wizard walks you through the process.

- If you're installing Windows on a compressed drive, be aware that the registry can reside on any compressed drive, but the swap file can reside on a compressed drive only if it's compressed using protected-mode software such as DriveSpace. Compressed drives are hard drives that have a portion of their data compressed in order to save space on the drive. DriveSpace marks the area for the swap file as uncompressible. If your drive is compressed with real-mode compression software, such as DoubleSpace, then know that you can't put the swap file on this compressed drive. The best practice is to back up the data and then uncompress the drive. You can later compress it using Windows 98 DriveSpace.

Note: If you used DOS DoubleSpace, available with DOS 6 and 6.2, to compress the drive, type DBLSPACE at the DOS prompt. If you used DriveSpace, available with DOS 6.22, type DRVSPACE. These utilities give you statistics about the compressed drive and also allow you to change the size of the uncompressed part of the drive, called the host drive.

Once you have prepared your hard drive for an upgrade installation, perform the following steps to get to the setup screen:

1 Start the PC, loading the current operating system.

2 Close all open applications, including any antivirus software that's running.

3 Insert the CD in the CD-ROM drive or the floppy disk in the floppy drive. When upgrading from Windows 95 to Windows 98, open the Run dialog box and enter the command `D:\Setup.exe`, substituting the drive letter for the CD-ROM drive or floppy drive in the command line. Click OK.

4 Follow the instructions on the setup screen. When you're given the opportunity to select the folder to install Windows, select the folder that the current OS is installed in; most likely, that is \Windows. If you use the same folder, Setup uses whatever settings it finds there.

Finishing the installation from the setup screen

Once you get to the setup screen, the installation process is the same, no matter whether you're doing an upgrade or a clean install. When installing Windows 9x, you're given the option of creating the Startup disk. Be sure to do that to help prepare for emergencies. During the installation, you're also asked to choose from four setup options:

- **Typical.** This option installs all of the components that are usually installed with Windows 9x. Most often, this is the option to choose.

- **Portable.** Use this option when installing Windows 9x on a notebook computer.

- **Compact.** Use this option if you're short on hard drive space and want the smallest possible installation. No optional components are installed during the installation. After the installation, if you need a component, you can install it by double-clicking the Add/Remove Programs applet in the Control Panel.

- **Custom.** Use this option if you know you need components that aren't normally installed under the Typical installation. You're given the opportunity to select any group of components to be included in the installation.

Windows 9x Setup begins installation in real mode and then switches to protected mode. During real mode, Setup runs ScanDisk, checks for existing Windows software, performs several system checks, loads the extended memory driver, looks for existing TSRs, and starts Windows, if it isn't already started. The Windows logo screen is the first thing the user normally sees during the installation. Setup then switches to protected mode.

Setup creates the registry, getting it ready to contain the hardware information, and then searches for hardware. It loads its own drivers for the detected hardware or, if it can't detect the hardware, requests the drivers from the user. Setup then copies the drivers to the hard drive from the installation source or from a floppy disk, CD or other source provided by the user.

Up to this point, if Setup fails and you reboot the PC, you boot into the old OS. At this point, Setup modifies the boot records on the hard drive to point to the Windows 9x file, Io.sys, rather than to the old OS system files. After this point, if Setup fails and you reboot, you reboot into Windows 9x.

During a normal installation, the PC reboots and Windows 9x is loaded. Some initial startup programs are run to set the time zone and to change existing application programs to Windows 9x. Depending on the hardware present, the PC may reboot again to load new drivers.

During the installation, Setup records information in log files. The primary log file is Setuplog.txt, a text file that's used by Windows to determine how far it got into the installation when it's recovering from a crash. Exhibit 4-6 shows a portion of Setuplog.txt in which the system ran a virus check on CMOS and began checking drives. The Detection Log (Detlog.txt), as shown in Exhibit 4-7, keeps a record of hardware detected.

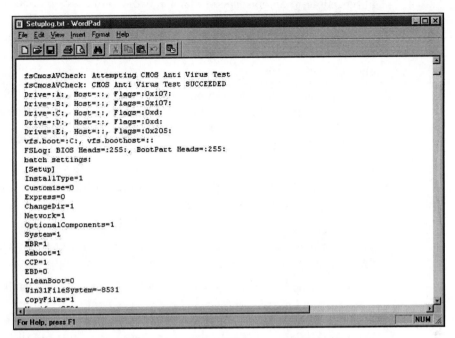

Exhibit 4-6: A sample Setuplog.txt log file

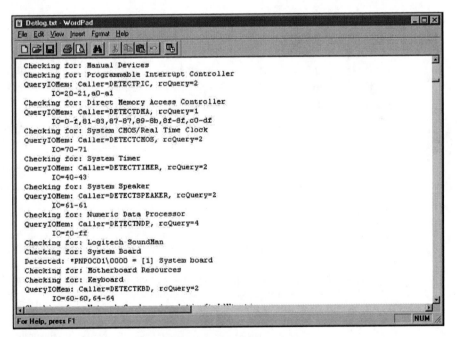

Exhibit 4-7: A sample Detlog txt log file

If the system fails to respond during the hardware detection phase, an entry is recorded in Detcrash.log. Detcrash.log is a binary file used by Windows to help recover from a crash caused by a problem with hardware. Windows doesn't use the contents of Detlog.txt; it's created only for the benefit of the user.

For example, if Setup suspects that a network card is present, because it sees a network driver installed in Config.sys, it records, in Setuplog.txt and Detlog.txt, that it's about to look for the card. If it successfully finds the card, it records the success in Detlog.txt. However, if an error occurs while Setup is searching for the card, an entry is made in the Detcrash.log file.

If the system crashes while trying to detect the network card and Setup is then restarted, it looks at Detcrash.log and Setuplog.txt to determine what it was trying to do at the time of the crash. It skips that step and goes on to the next step, so that it doesn't make the same mistake twice.

Even though Setup might crash several times during the installation process, progress is still being made. By reading the content of the log files, Setup is able to skip steps that cause a problem and move forward.

Note: Be careful not to delete the log files during the installation process, especially if you experienced a crash. Also, restart by using the power on/power off method, so that the ISA bus is fully initialized, which doesn't always happen during a warm boot.

In certain situations you might want to force Setup to begin installation at the beginning instead of looking to Setuplog.txt for the entry point, for example when you think you might have resolved a problem with hardware and want Setup to attempt to find the hardware again. To do that, delete Setuplog.txt to force a full restart.

Customizing setup

Windows and other software store information about an installation on the setup CD or floppy disks in information files. These *information (.inf) files* are text files with an .inf file extension. One .inf file is Msbatch.inf. Information about your installation can be stored in this file, which can then be used to do an automatic, hands-free installation. All the questions that a user must answer during an installation can be answered by entries in this file so that a user has little to do but begin the installation.

You can add several switches to the Setup.exe command that starts the setup process. Some of these switches and descriptions of what they do are listed in the following table:

Switch	Description
Setup /?	Displays help for each command-line switch.
Setup /D	Don't use the existing version of Windows to begin Setup. Use this option if you suspect corrupted Windows system files when upgrading Windows.
Setup /IC	Performs a clean boot. Use this option if you suspect drivers loaded from Autoexec.bat or Config.sys are causing a problem with the installation.
Setup /IH	Run ScanDisk in the foreground so that you can view results. Use this option if setup failed earlier, and you want to check for hard drive corruption.
Setup /L	Load the driver for a Logitech mouse. Use this option if you're using a Logitech Series C mouse.
Setup /IN	Doesn't set up the network.
Setup /IS	Doesn't run ScanDisk.
Setup /PI	Keep hardware settings that aren't default settings. Use this option if a previous try of the installation caused a legacy hardware device to fail.

The following table lists some problems that might occur while installing Windows 9x and what to do about them:

Symptom	Description and solution
An error message about BIOS appears during installation	This is most likely caused by BIOS not allowing changes to the boot sector to protect it from viruses. Disable the feature in CMOS setup.
Windows 9x stalls during the first restart after installation	This is probably caused by legacy hardware not configured correctly. Try the following: Remark (REM) out all entries in Config.sys and Autoexec.bat. Disable the ISA enumerator by commenting out this line in System.ini: Device=ISAPNP.386.
During the first restart after installation, an error message appears with information about a bad or missing file	Probably caused by an error in Config.sys or Autoexec.bat. Try renaming both files so they aren't executed. If this solves the problem, then comment out each line in the file, one at a time, until you know which line caused the problem. You can press F8 during the restart to perform a step-by-step check and also examine the contents of Bootlog.txt.
During the first restart, after the you get an error message about a missing or damaged VxD file	Run Windows setup again and select the option installation, to verify or replace the missing VxD (virtual device driver).
After upgrading from Windows 95 to Windows 98, the startup screen still says Windows 95	This can be caused by one of two problems. The Io.sys file might not have been updated. Use the Sys C: command to replace it. The file Logo.sys is in the root directory, which overrides the logo screen embedded in Io.sys. Delete or rename the file.
"Invalid system disk" error appears during setup	Suspect a boot sector virus. Run a current version during setup of antivirus software. If this error occurs while installing Windows when disk management software such as DiskPro is running, Windows might have damaged the hard drive MBR. To recover from this problem, see the documentation for the disk management software.

Note: For specific error messages that occur during installation and solutions, go to the Microsoft Web site support.microsoft.com and search on the error message.

Configuring the Windows 9x startup with Msdos.sys

In Windows 9x, Msdos.sys is a text file containing several parameters that affect how the OS boots. You can change some of the entries in this file to customize the boot process. The file is a hidden, read-only, system file, so before you can edit it, you must first use the Attrib command at the command prompt or menus from Windows Explorer to make the file available for editing. Also, make a backup copy of the file in case you want to revert to the form it was in before the changes were made.

From a command prompt, follow these steps to change the options in Msdos.sys:

1 Go to an OS command prompt.

2 Go to the root directory of your hard drive by entering:

   `CD\`

3 Make the file available for editing by entering:

   `ATTRIB -R -H -S MSDOS.SYS`

4 Make a backup copy of the file by entering:

   `COPY MSDOS.SYS MSDOS.BK`

5 Use Edit.com to edit the file by entering:

   `EDIT MSDOS.SYS`

6 Save the file and return it to a hidden, read-only, system file by entering:

   `ATTRIB +R +H +S MSDOS.SYS`

The following table lists each entry in the Msdos.sys file and its purpose. You can refer to this table as you read about the various options available when installing and configuring Windows 9x.

Variable name	Description of variable values
AutoScan	0 = Computer doesn't scan hard drive.
	1 = (Default) Prompts the user before running ScanDisk on the hard drive when booting up after the computer isn't shut down properly.
	2 = Automatically scans without prompting the user.
BootMulti	0 = (Default) Boots only to Windows 9x.
	1= Allows for a dual boot. (Press F4 for old OS.)
BootWin	1 = (Default) Boots to Windows 9x.
	0 = Boots to previous version of DOS.
BootGUI	1 = (Default) Boots to Windows 9x with the graphic user interface.
	0 = Boots only to the command prompt for DOS 7.0, the DOS core of Windows 95, or 7.1, the DOS core of Windows 98. Autoexec.bat and Config.sys are executed, and you're in real-mode DOS.
BootMenu	0 = (Default) Doesn't display the Startup Menu.
	1= Displays the Startup Menu.

Variable name	Description of variable values
BootMenuDefault	1 through 8 = The value selected from the Startup Menu by Default. (Normally this value should be 1).
BootMenuDelay	n = Number of seconds delay before the default value in the Startup Menu is automatically selected.
BootKeys	1= (Default) The function keys (F4, F5, F6, F8, Shift+F5, Ctrl+F5, Shift+F8) work during the boot process.
	0 = Disables the function keys during the boot process. (This option can be used to help secure a workstation.).
BootDelay	n = Number of seconds the boot process waits, when it displays the message "Starting Windows 95" or "Starting Windows 98," for the user to press F8 to get the Startup Menu. (The default is 2 seconds).
Logo	1= (Default) Displays the Windows 9x logo screen.
	0 = Leaves the screen in text mode.
Drvspace	1= (Default) Load Drvspace.bin, used for disk compression, if it's present.
	0 = Doesn't load Drvspace.bin.
DoubleBuffer	1= (Default) When you have a SCSI drive, enables double buffering for the drive. (See the drive documentation.)
	0 = Don't use double buffering for the SCSI drive.
Network	1= If network components are installed, includes the option, "Safe mode with network support," in the Startup Menu.
	0 = Doesn't include the option on the Startup Menu. (This is normally set to 0 if the PC has no network components installed. The Startup Menu is renumbered from this point forward in the menu.)
BootFailSafe	1= (Default) Includes Safe mode in the Startup Menu.
	0 = Doesn't include Safe mode in the Startup Menu.
BootWarn	1= (Default) Displays the warning message when Windows 9x boots into Safe mode. Includes Safe mode in the Startup Menu.
	0 = Doesn't display the warning message.
LoadTop	1= (Default) Loads Command.com at the top of conventional memory.
	0 = Doesn't load Command.com at the top of conventional memory. (Use this option when there's a memory conflict with this area of memory.)

Exhibit 4-8 shows a sample Msdos.sys file. The lines containing x's at the bottom of the file are used to ensure that the file size is compatible with other programs.

```
[Paths]
WinDir=C:\WIN95
WinBootDir=C:\WIN95
HostWinBootDrv=C

[Options]
BootMulti=1
BootGUI=1
BootMenu=1
Network=0
;
;The following lines are required for compatibility with other programs.
;Do not remove them (MSDOS.SYS needs to be >1024 bytes).
;xxxxxxxxxxxxxxxxxxxxxxxxxxxxxxxxxxxxxxxxxxxxxxxxxxxxxxxxxxxxxxxxxxxxxa
;xxxxxxxxxxxxxxxxxxxxxxxxxxxxxxxxxxxxxxxxxxxxxxxxxxxxxxxxxxxxxxxxxxxxxb
;xxxxxxxxxxxxxxxxxxxxxxxxxxxxxxxxxxxxxxxxxxxxxxxxxxxxxxxxxxxxxxxxxxxxxc
;xxxxxxxxxxxxxxxxxxxxxxxxxxxxxxxxxxxxxxxxxxxxxxxxxxxxxxxxxxxxxxxxxxxxxd
;xxxxxxxxxxxxxxxxxxxxxxxxxxxxxxxxxxxxxxxxxxxxxxxxxxxxxxxxxxxxxxxxxxxxxe
;xxxxxxxxxxxxxxxxxxxxxxxxxxxxxxxxxxxxxxxxxxxxxxxxxxxxxxxxxxxxxxxxxxxxxf
;xxxxxxxxxxxxxxxxxxxxxxxxxxxxxxxxxxxxxxxxxxxxxxxxxxxxxxxxxxxxxxxxxxxxxg
;xxxxxxxxxxxxxxxxxxxxxxxxxxxxxxxxxxxxxxxxxxxxxxxxxxxxxxxxxxxxxxxxxxxxxh
;xxxxxxxxxxxxxxxxxxxxxxxxxxxxxxxxxxxxxxxxxxxxxxxxxxxxxxxxxxxxxxxxxxxxxi
;xxxxxxxxxxxxxxxxxxxxxxxxxxxxxxxxxxxxxxxxxxxxxxxxxxxxxxxxxxxxxxxxxxxxxj
;xxxxxxxxxxxxxxxxxxxxxxxxxxxxxxxxxxxxxxxxxxxxxxxxxxxxxxxxxxxxxxxxxxxxxk
;xxxxxxxxxxxxxxxxxxxxxxxxxxxxxxxxxxxxxxxxxxxxxxxxxxxxxxxxxxxxxxxxxxxxxl
;xxxxxxxxxxxxxxxxxxxxxxxxxxxxxxxxxxxxxxxxxxxxxxxxxxxxxxxxxxxxxxxxxxxxxm
;xxxxxxxxxxxxxxxxxxxxxxxxxxxxxxxxxxxxxxxxxxxxxxxxxxxxxxxxxxxxxxxxxxxxxn
;xxxxxxxxxxxxxxxxxxxxxxxxxxxxxxxxxxxxxxxxxxxxxxxxxxxxxxxxxxxxxxxxxxxxxo
;xxxxxxxxxxxxxxxxxxxxxxxxxxxxxxxxxxxxxxxxxxxxxxxxxxxxxxxxxxxxxxxxxxxxxp
;xxxxxxxxxxxxxxxxxxxxxxxxxxxxxxxxxxxxxxxxxxxxxxxxxxxxxxxxxxxxxxxxxxxxxq
;xxxxxxxxxxxxxxxxxxxxxxxxxxxxxxxxxxxxxxxxxxxxxxxxxxxxxxxxxxxxxxxxxxxxxr
;xxxxxxxxxxxxxxxxxxxxxxxxxxxxxxxxxxxxxxxxxxxxxxxxxxxxxxxxxxxxxxxxxxxxxs
```

Exhibit 4-8: A sample Msdos.sys file

Instructions for specific upgrades

You've just learned the basic installation process for Windows 9x. Although most actual installations follow this general outline, depending on exactly what version and features you're installing, each type of upgrade has its own issues. This section discusses things to consider when upgrading to Windows 95, 98, and Me from earlier operating system versions.

Installing Windows 9x over DOS and Windows 3.x

If DOS and Windows 3.x reside on the PC prior to installing Windows 9x, you can perform an upgrade or a clean install.

If you choose an upgrade, this is what happens:

- Windows 9x Setup copies information about existing application programs from the .ini files of Windows 3.x into the Windows 9x registry, eliminating the need for you to install the existing programs into Windows 9x.

- These programs are added to the Start menu of Windows 9x.

- Existing programs can find their DLLs in the same Windows\System folder as they did with Windows 3.x. (DLLs, or dynamic link libraries, contain programming routines for common tasks.)

It's possible to install Windows 9x on the same hard drive as another operating system. This is called a dual boot. However, there's usually little need to leave DOS or Windows 3.x on the drive. When upgrading from Windows 3.x to Windows 9x, first start Windows 3.x and enter the Setup command using File Manager.

Upgrading from Windows 95 to Windows 98

Upgrading from Windows 95 to Windows 98 is relatively easy, because the two operating systems are similar. This upgrade isn't as complex as upgrading from DOS with Windows 3.x. Follow these guidelines when upgrading from Windows 95 to Windows 98:

- Check whether your hardware is compatible with Windows 98.
- Use up-to-date virus software and virus definitions to scan for viruses on your hard drive.
- You also need to check software packages and programs for compatibility. You can do this by checking the documentation or the manufacturer's Web site for each program. If you're planning an OS upgrade, a software manufacturer often provides a downloadable *patch*, also called a *service pack*, to make the software compatible with the new OS.
- Make sure you have at least one full backup of your system as it was under Windows 95. If the upgrade to Windows 98 fails for any reason, you can use your Windows 95 backup to restore the system to the point where you were before you attempted the upgrade.

Once you've backed up your system and made sure its hardware and software are compatible with Windows 98, use the following procedure to perform the upgrade:

1. If your system BIOS runs a program to protect the boot sector of your hard drive from viruses, enter CMOS setup and disable the program, because it might interfere with the installation. Remember to turn the program back on after the installation.

2. Start Windows 95 and close any open applications. If you have antivirus software running in the background, close the software. Close any icons open in the System Tray.

3. Insert the upgrade CD in the CD-ROM drive. Click Start, Run and enter D:\Setup in the Run dialog box, where D is the drive letter of the CD-ROM drive, then click OK.

4. When the Setup program opens, it provides a series of windows to guide you through the setup process. All you have to do is follow the prompts and provide any requested information. Always create the emergency startup disk when you're prompted to do so.

5. After Setup is complete, open and test some of the applications you already had installed under Windows 95. Any problem you have with a particular application may be solved by uninstalling and then reinstalling it or by installing any necessary patches to make it work with Windows 98.

6. Once the upgrade from Windows 95 to Windows 98 is complete and you've verified that your system is working, it's a good idea to back up your system again.

Upgrading from Windows 98 to Windows Me

If you're upgrading from Windows 98 to Windows Me, use the same pre-upgrade checklist that's given for the Windows 95 to Windows 98 upgrade in the previous section. Remember to check the compatibility of hardware and software and to back up your system before you begin. To check whether a particular hardware product has been tested for use with Windows Me, go to:

```
http://www.microsoft.com/whdc/hcl/search.mspx
```

In addition to the guidelines in the previous section, do the following before upgrading to Windows Me:

- Uncompress any portions of your hard drive that are compressed. If you aren't sure whether your hard drive is compressed, run ScanDisk, which tells you. Windows Me doesn't install on a compressed hard drive.
- Uninstall power management tools and disk management tools.
- Read the readme.txt file and any other setup information provided on the Windows Me disk.

The steps to upgrade Windows Me are the same as for Windows 98.

Downloading and installing updates for Windows 9x

Between releases of OS versions, manufacturers often produce OS updates in the form of patches or service packs that add features, fix bugs, or address security issues. The Microsoft Web site windowsupdate.microsoft.com/, provides you with a list of updates available for your OS. In Windows 98 and Windows Me, you can access this page by clicking Windows Update on the Start menu. The update process examines your system and recommends available updates for you to select, download, and install following directions on the screen.

Do it!

B-2:   Performing a custom Windows 98 installation

Here's how	Here's why
1 Verify that you don't have any important data on the hard drive	You want to perform a custom installation of Windows 98, during which all data is erased.
2 Format the hard drive	To prepare the hard drive for a clean install of Windows 98.
3 Copy files from the Windows 98 CD to a folder on the hard drive named C:\WIN98CD	
4 Perform a Custom installation of Windows 98	Using the clean install method.
5 Write user documentation as you're performing the installation	To guide an individual step by step through the process of performing a Custom installation of Windows 98.
6 Record each decision you made and all values you entered during the setup process	
7 Give your User Documentation to another student	To perform a critique of it.
Enter the following information:	
Student name:	
Rate the documentation for:	
Clarity of each step:	
What to do if problems occur:	
How to respond to questions asked by setup:	
Any other helpful comments:	
8 What added control do you have when performing a Custom installation compared to a Typical installation?	
9 When would you recommend a Custom installation rather than a Typical installation?	

Topic C: Working with Windows 9x

Explanation

Now that you've learned how to install and upgrade Windows 9x, let's look at some things you need to know about using it. As a PC technician, you need to be familiar with keyboard shortcuts for Windows, as well as how to manage the desktop and use Windows Explorer.

Keystroke shortcuts in Windows

The following table lists a few useful keystrokes to use when working with Windows, including the function keys you can use during startup. You can also use the mouse to accomplish some of these tasks, but keystrokes are faster for experienced typists. Also, sometimes in troubleshooting situations, the mouse isn't usable. At those times, knowing the keystrokes is very valuable.

General action	Keystroke	Description
While loading Windows	F4	Loads a previous version of DOS.
	F5	Starts in safe mode, bypassing config.sys and autoexec.bat and has no network support
	F8 or Ctrl	Displays Startup menu.
	Shift + F8	Provides step-by-step confirmation.
Working with text anywhere in Windows	Ctrl + C	Copies a selected item.
	Ctrl + A	Selects all text.
	Ctrl + X	Cuts a selected item.
	Ctrl + V	Pastes a selected item.
Managing programs	Alt +Tab	Moves from one open application to another.
	Ctrl + Esc	Displays the Start menu.
	Alt + F4	Closes a program window or, if no window is open, shuts down Windows.
	Double click	Opens a program or file.
	Ctrl + Alt + Del	Displays the Task List, which can be used to switch to another application, end a task, or shut down Windows.
Managing files, folders, icons and shortcuts	Ctrl + Shift while dragging a file	Creates a shortcut.
	Ctrl while dragging a file	Copies a file.
	Shift + Delete	Deletes a file without placing it in the Recycle Bin.
	F2	Renames an item.

General action	Keystroke	Description
	Alt + Enter	Displays an item's Properties window.
Selecting items	Shift + click	To select multiple entries in a list, such as file names in Explorer, click the first item and then hold down the Shift key and click the last item you want to select in the list. All items between the first and last are selected.
	Ctrl + click	To select several items in a list that aren't listed sequentially, click the first item to select it. Hold down the Ctrl key as you click other items anywhere in the list. All items you have clicked on are selected.
Using menus	Alt	Activates the menu bar.
	Alt, letter	Activates the menu bar and selects a menu option. The letter must be underlined in the menu.
	Alt, arrow keys	Activates the menu bar and moves over the menu tree.
	Alt, arrow keys, Enter	Activates the menu bar, moves to a menu item, and then selects a menu option.
	Esc	Exits a menu without making a selection.
Managing the desktop	Print Screen	Copies the desktop into the Clipboard.
	Ctrl + Esc	Displays the Start menu and moves the focus to the menu. (Use the arrow keys to move over the menu.)
After the focus is on the Start menu	Alt + M	Minimizes all windows and moves the focus to the desktop.
Working with windows	Ctrl + Tab and Ctrl + Shift + Tab	Moves through tabbed pages in a dialog box.
	Shift + Close or (X) button on a window	Closes current folder and its parent folders.
	F5	Refreshes the contents of a window.
Using the Windows key (labeled with the Windows flag icon)	Win	Displays the Start menu.
	Win + E	Opens Windows Explorer.
	Win + M	Minimizes all windows.
	Win + Tab	Moves through items on the Task bar.
	Win + R	Displays the Run dialog box.
	Win + Break	Displays the System Properties window.
Using the Applications key (labeled with a box and arrow icon)	Application key or Shift + F10	When an item is selected, displays its shortcut menu.

Do it!

C-1: Using keyboard shortcuts

Here's how	Here's why
1 Open Paint	You want to learn about the F1 key, which is the universal keyboard shortcut for launching Help.
Minimize Paint	
2 Open Control Panel	
Minimize Control Panel	
3 Click the desktop	
Press ⌨F1	To open Help for Windows.
4 Close Windows Help	
Restore Paint	
5 Press ⌨F1	To open Help for Paint.
Close Help for Paint	
6 Restore Control Panel	
Press ⌨F1	To open Help for the Control Panel.
7 Press each of the combinations listed below and record the result of each key combination in the column to the right	You want to use the Windows Logo key.
Windows Logo	
Windows Logo + ⌨E	
Windows Logo + ⌨F	
Windows Logo + ⌨R	
Windows Logo + ⌨BREAK	
Windows Logo + ⌨M	
8 Boot the computer	You want to learn to use the keyboard to find, select, open, and print a document when the mouse isn't working.
Unplug the mouse	After the Windows desktop appears.

9	Press (TAB)	Until one of the desktop icons is highlighted.
10	Select **My Computer**	Using the arrow keys.
11	Press (← ENTER)	My Computer opens.
12	Press (TAB)	Until drive A: is highlighted.
13	Select the C: drive	Using the arrow keys.
	Press (← ENTER)	To open drive C:
14	Open Test.txt	(From the current unit folder.) To see the contents of the file displayed in Notepad.
15	Observe the menu bar	Notice on the Notepad window that one letter of each menu item is underlined. For example, in the File menu, the F is underlined.
	Press (ALT) + (F)	The File menu opens. After the menu is open, you can use the arrow keys to move over the menu and select an option by pressing Enter, or you can type the underlined letter of a menu option.
16	Press (ESC)	
17	Press (ALT) + (P)	To select Print. The print dialog box opens.
18	Verify that the correct printer is selected	
19	Activate the Print button	By using the tab key.
	Press (← ENTER)	To send the print job to the printer.
20	Place the cursor at the beginning of the text	You want to practice editing text, using the shortcuts for cutting, copying, and pasting.
	Press (SHIFT)	
	Select the text	Using the arrow keys.
21	Press (CTRL) + (X)	With the text highlighted. To cut the highlighted text from its original location and move it to the clipboard. You can then paste it in another location.
	Release both keys	

22	Press `CTRL` + `C`	To copy a highlighted block of characters to the clipboard. A copy of the highlighted block of characters is placed on the clipboard. You can then paste it in another location.
	Release both keys	
23	Place the cursor to the desired location	To paste text from the clipboard to a new location.
	Press `CTRL` + `V`	
	Release both keys	
24	Open Device Manager	
	View the resources for the mouse	
	Record the following information:	
	What status does Device Manager report about the mouse?	
	What IRQ does the mouse use?	
	According to Windows Explorer, how much space is available on the hard drive?	
25	What key is universally used to launch Help?	
26	What shortcut combination can you use to paste a block of text?	
27	What key combination can you use to switch between open applications?	
28	Is it possible to open the Start menu by pressing only one key?	

Managing the desktop

Explanation

From the Windows 9x desktop, you can make applications automatically load at startup, create shortcuts to files and applications, and make the environment more user-friendly. In this section, you can learn some ways to manage the Windows 9x desktop.

Display settings

To control your display settings, you can right-click anywhere on the desktop and choose Properties from the shortcut menu. The Display Properties window appears, as shown in Exhibit 4-9.

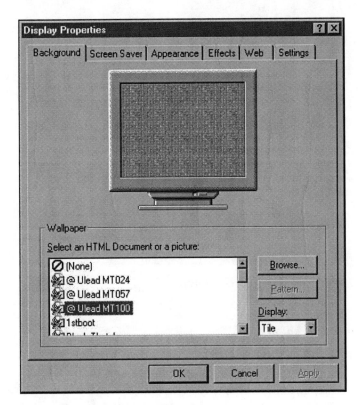

Exhibit 4-9: Changing display settings

Some of the more common things you can change are:

- **Background.** Select desktop wallpaper or pattern.
- **Screensaver.** Select screensaver and change its settings; change power settings for monitor.
- **Appearance.** Pick and customize a color scheme for the desktop.
- **Effects.** Specify icon settings.
- **Web.** Set Active Desktop properties.
- **Settings.** Change color range and display size.

You can also hide and unhide the taskbar at the bottom of the desktop. To do that, click Start, and then choose Settings, Taskbar, Start Menu. The Taskbar Properties window appears. You can also reach this window by right-clicking on the Taskbar and selecting Properties from the shortcut menu. Then click the Taskbar Options tab and select Auto hide, as shown in Exhibit 4-10.

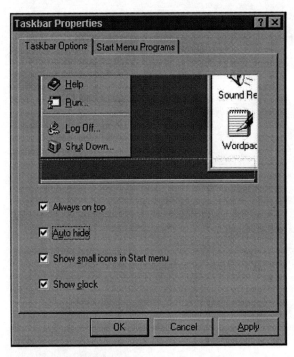

Exhibit 4-10: The Taskbar Options tab

Working with shortcuts

A *shortcut* on the desktop is an icon that points to a program that can be executed or to a file or folder. The user double-clicks the icon to load the software. A shortcut can be created in several ways. One way is through the Start Menu Programs tab on the Taskbar Properties window, as shown in Exhibit 4-10.

From here, click the Add button. The Create Shortcut wizard appears, as shown in Exhibit 4-11. Enter the name of the program you want to create a shortcut to or browse for the file on your computer. In this example, we want to create a desktop shortcut to the Notepad application.

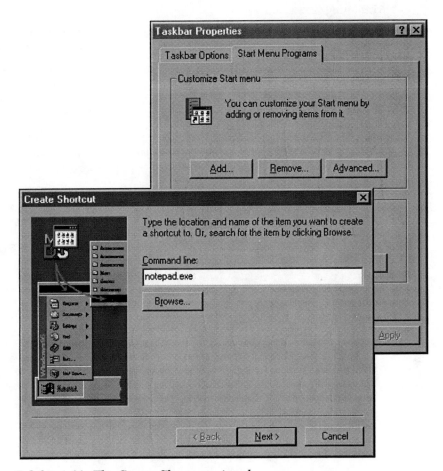

Exhibit 4-11: The Create Shortcut wizard

Once you've entered or selected the name of the program for which you want to create a shortcut, click Next. You're then given the option to select where to place the shortcut. Select Desktop at the top of the folder list to create a desktop shortcut, and then click Next. Follow the directions in the wizard to complete the process. Remember that you can create a shortcut for a program or a data file, name it, and select where to place it (either on the desktop or in the Start menu). If you want a program to load whenever Windows 9x starts, create a shortcut and put the shortcut in the StartUp folder of the Start menu. All items in the StartUp folder are automatically executed when Windows 9x starts.

Note: To edit a shortcut, right-click the shortcut and select Properties from the menu. To delete a shortcut, select Delete from this same menu.

Managing icons

An icon on the desktop can be a shortcut to an application, or it can represent a file that belongs to an application. You can tell the difference between the two by looking for the small bent-arrow shortcut symbol on the icon, as seen in Exhibit 4-12. The icon on the right represents the document file MyLetter1.doc, stored in the \Windows\Desktop folder. The icon on the left is a shortcut to the file MyLetter2.doc, which can be stored anywhere on the drive. Also shown in Exhibit 4-12 are the contents of the \Windows\Desktop folder as seen by Explorer. You can add an icon to the desktop by putting a file in this folder. One way to delete an icon on the desktop is to delete the corresponding file in this folder. However, this method can cause problems for the user.

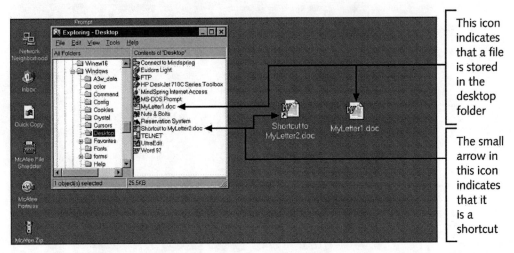

Exhibit 4-12: Shortcut icon and file icon

If you delete a shortcut icon from the desktop or form the \Windows\Desktop folder, such as Shortcut to MyLetter2.doc, the shortcut is gone, but the actual file that the shortcut points to isn't deleted. If you delete a document icon, such as MyLetter1.doc, the document itself is deleted.

An error can occur if the actual document file, MyLetter2.doc, is deleted, but the shortcut to the deleted document remains on the desktop. Exhibit 4-13 shows a sample error message that occurs when this shortcut is used.

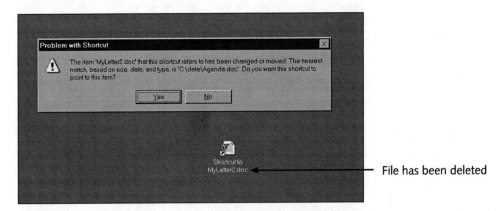

Exhibit 4-13: Error message that shortcut is pointing to a deleted file

Managing files and folders with Windows Explorer

In this section, you will learn how to use Windows Explorer to manage floppy disks and hard drives in Windows 9x. Windows 9x Explorer is the primary tool for managing the files and folders on your hard drive and disks. Open Explorer in Windows 9x (click Start, and then choose Programs, Windows Explorer, or right-click My Computer and choose Explore from the menu) and follow the directions below to manage files and folders. Exhibit 4-14 shows computer resources in the My Computer folder as seen when using Windows Explorer. You can also access My Computer by double-clicking on the icon on the desktop.

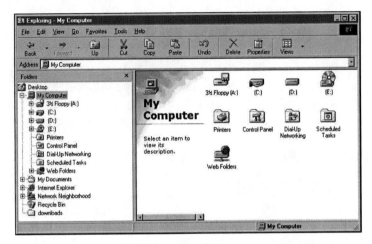

Exhibit 4-14: Using Windows Explorer

Shortcut menu options

The easiest way to manage drives, disks, folders, and files in Windows Explorer is to use the shortcut menus. To access the shortcut menu, right-click the icon representing the item you want to work with. The shortcut menu for the floppy drive is shown in Exhibit 4-15 as an example.

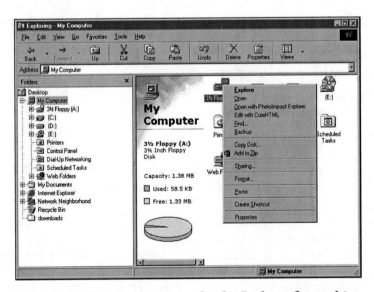

Exhibit 4-15: The shortcut menu for the Explorer floppy drive

Some of the tasks you can perform from a shortcut menu are listed below.

- If you choose Explore, the contents of the selected disk or folder in the floppy drive are shown in the current Explorer window. If you choose Open, the contents of the disk or folder are shown in a separate window.

- The Create Shortcut option creates a shortcut icon for the selected item.

- Choosing Properties brings up a dialog box showing information about the selected item and allows you to change settings for the item.

- If you select a disk or drive, the shortcut menu contains a Format option. Recall that you can use Explorer to format a floppy disk by choosing Format from the shortcut menu.

- The Backup option enables you to make a backup of a disk, and the Sharing option enables you to share a drive, folders, or files with other users on your network.

- For floppy drives, if you choose Copy Disk, a dialog box opens, as shown in Exhibit 4-16, where the disk listed under "Copy from" is the source disk, and the disk listed under "Copy to" is the target disk. Click Start to copy the disk.

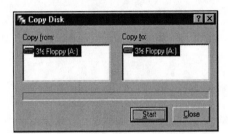

Exhibit 4-16: The Copy Disk window

- The shortcut menu of a folder allows you to create a new file. The menu lists applications you can use to create the file.

- The shortcut menu for files gives you additional options, such as printing and e-mailing the file.

As you can see, some of the options on shortcut menus are the same for files, folders, drives, and disks, and others are specific to the particular item you're looking at. The additional shortcut menu options may vary; depending on what programs you've installed to work with a particular item.

Now let's look in more detail at ways to use Windows 9x Explorer to work with files and folders on your hard drive.

Create a new folder

To create a folder, select the folder you want to be the parent folder by clicking the folder name. For example, to create a folder named Chess under the folder named Games, first click the Games folder. Then click the File menu. Choose New from the menu. Then choose Folder from the submenu that displays. The new folder is created under Games, but its name is New Folder. Click the folder name once to open the text box and highlight the current folder name, New Folder. Type Chess to change the folder name to Chess, as shown in Exhibit 4-17. The maximum depth of folders under folders depends on the lengths of the folder names.

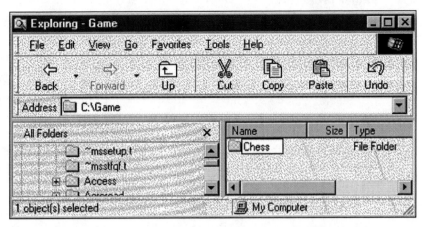

Exhibit 4-17: Editing a new folder's name

Delete a folder

To delete a folder from Explorer is similar to using the RD command from the command line. Right-click the folder and select Delete from the shortcut menu. A confirmation dialog box asks if you're sure you want to delete the folder. If you click Yes, the folder and all of its contents, including subfolders, is sent to the Recycle Bin. Empty the Recycle Bin to free your disk space. Files and folders sent to the Recycle Bin aren't deleted until you empty it.

File attributes

Using Explorer, you can view and change the file attributes, which is similar to using the command-line Attrib command. From Explorer, right-click a file and select Properties from the shortcut menu. The Properties window appears, as shown in Exhibit 4-18. From the Properties window, you can change the read-only, hidden, and archive attributes of the file.

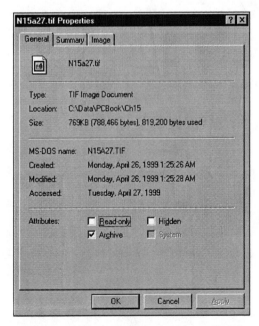

Exhibit 4-18: Properties of a file in Windows 98

Folder properties

You can also view and change the properties assigned to folders. Select the folder and, from the Explorer menu, click View, Folder Options, and then click the View tab. From this window, you can change how and when files are displayed in the folder.

Windows 98 identifies file type primarily by the file extension. In Windows Explorer, by default, Windows 9x hides the file extensions of those files for which it knows which application to use to open or execute the file. For example, just after installation, it hides .exe, .com, .sys, and .txt file extensions but doesn't hide .doc, .ppt, or .xls files until the software to open these files has been installed. To display all file extensions, in the Folder Options windows, uncheck Hide file extensions for known file types.

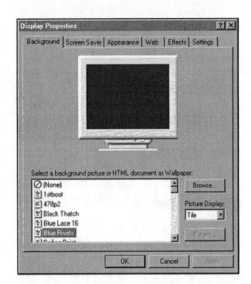

Exhibit 4-19: The Display Properties window

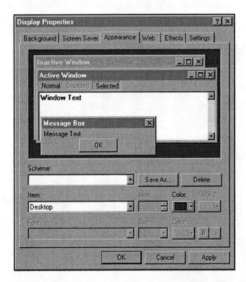

Exhibit 4-20: The Appearance tab of the Display Properties window

Do it!

C-2:   Customizing your desktop

Here's how	Here's why
1 Boot the computer	You want to customize your desktop colors.
Examine the Windows desktop	
Observe the color of the desktop itself, as well as any other features on the desktop	
2 Open Control Panel	
Double-click **Display Properties**	The Display Properties dialog box opens.
3 Click the **Background** tab	
Scroll through the list of backgrounds available to you	
4 Click a background in the list	A preview appears in the monitor graphic at the top of the dialog box, similar to the one shown in Exhibit 4-19.
5 Select different background options	Using the Picture Display list arrow.
6 Click **Apply**	After you find a background that you like.
Verify that the new settings have been applied to your desktop	The Display Properties dialog box should remain open.
If you see a message indicating that the background you selected requires Active Desktop, select a new background	At this point, the color behind the text on the desktop might not match your background.
7 Click the **Appearance** tab	
Click the **Item** list arrow	Notice all the items whose color you can change if you want. For instance, you can select Active Title bar, if you want to change the color of the title bar for the active application.
8 From Item list, select **Desktop**	
From the Color list, select the color you want	To use as your desktop color, as shown in Exhibit 4-20. The exhibit shows you a sample of the color you selected at the top of the dialog box, behind the various sample windows.

9   Click **Apply**

The new color appears behind all the text on the desktop. Note that, if you haven't already selected a background for your desktop, the entire desktop changes to the color you just selected. In this case, because you previously selected a background, the color change affects only the rectangles behind any text on the desktop.

10 Right-click **My Computer** on the Windows desktop

You want to change the name of My Computer.

Choose **Rename**

The text below the My Computer icon is highlighted, ready for you to type a new name for the icon.

11 Enter a new name for the My Computer icon

Can we change it to something else like <student's name> computer. Where <student's name> is your name.

12 Edit the name to read <student's name> computer, where <student's name> is your name

13 What are two ways to open the Display Properties window?

14 What tab in the Display Properties window can you use to change the color of specific items in Windows?

15 What button must you click to make changes to your desktop take effect?

16 Describe how to rename My Computer. Does this change the name of your computer for networking purposes?

17 Can different users have different desktop settings on the same computer? How does Windows know which user is currently using the system?

Topic D: Installing hardware

Explanation

In this section, you will learn how to add new hardware to Windows 9x systems and install 16-bit and 32-bit device drivers, using a CD-ROM drive as an example. You will also learn about Plug and Play support in Windows 9x.

Adding new device drivers

After a device is physically installed in a system, the next step is to install the software necessary to interface with it. This software, called a device driver, is written to interface with the specific device and the specific operating system. Knowing how to install and troubleshoot device drivers is an essential skill of a PC support technician.

Installing and using device drivers under Windows 9x

For Windows 9x, when a new device is installed and you power up the PC, Windows recognizes it and immediately launches the Add New Hardware Wizard. If the wizard doesn't automatically launch, you can manually start it. Go to Control Panel and double-click the Add New Hardware icon, which launches the wizard.

Note: The Control Panel contains several applets, or small programs, that are used to manage Windows. You can view these applets in a list or as icons. Use the View menu in Control Panel to change the way they display.

One step in the wizard is to select the hardware device from a list of devices. If you click OK, Windows uses a Windows driver for the device, or you can click Have Disk to use your own drivers, as shown in Exhibit 4-21. If you have a driver on a floppy disk or CD or have downloaded a driver from the Internet to a folder on your hard drive, click Have Disk and point the wizard to the disk, CD, or folder on the hard drive that contains the driver. Sometimes you must select a folder on the disk or CD for the operating system to use, such as \Win98 to locate the drivers to install under Windows 98.

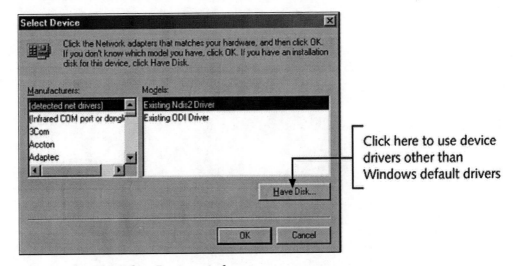

Exhibit 4-21: The Select Device window

Viewing and changing current device drivers

You can view and change current device drivers from the Control Panel. For example, in Windows 98, to view the current video driver, click Start then choose Settings, Control Panel, and then double-click Display. Click the Settings tab to view the currently installed display driver, as shown in Exhibit 4-22.

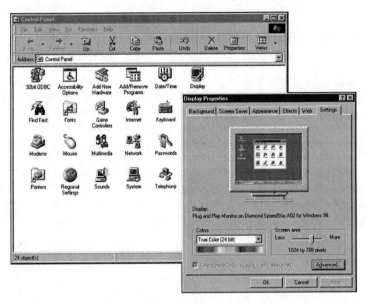

Exhibit 4-22: The currently installed display drivers

To change the video card driver, click Advanced, click the Adapter tab, and then click the Change button. You see the Windows 98 Update Device Driver Wizard. Click Next to see the dialog box, as shown in Exhibit 4-23. The dialog box includes options to let Windows 98 search for a new driver from its list of Windows drivers or to display a list of all the drivers in a specific location, so you can select the driver you want. To provide your own driver, click the second option and then click Next. Then, click Have Disk to provide the new driver from a floppy disk, a CD, or a file downloaded from the Internet.

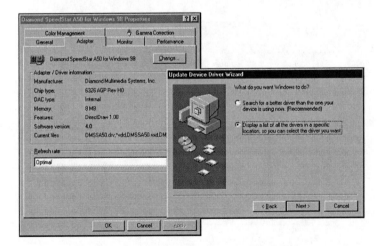

Exhibit 4-23: The Windows 98 update device driver wizard

If the new driver fails, try uninstalling the device and then reinstalling it. To uninstall a device, access Device Manager (click Start, Settings, Control Panel, double-click System, then click Device Manager), select the device and then click Remove, as shown in Exhibit 4-24. Then reboot the PC and allow the Found New Hardware Wizard to launch.

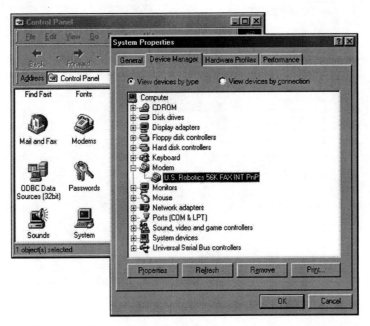

Exhibit 4-24: Use a device manager to uninstall a device driver

Installing a CD-ROM drive with Windows 9x

Now that you have an overview of the process of adding new hardware and device drivers in Windows 9x, let's look at installing a CD-ROM drive as an example and consider how and when you use 16-bit and 32-bit drivers.

To use the 32-bit Windows driver for your CD-ROM drive, click Start, choose Settings, Control Panel, and then double-click Add New Hardware. Click Next when you're prompted to begin installing the software for the new device. Complete the installation by following the directions on the Add New Hardware window.

When Windows 9x starts up after you've installed the CD-ROM drive, it assigns the next available drive letter to the drive. To dictate what the drive letter is, use Device Manager. Click Start, Settings, Control Panel, and then double-click System. Click the Device Manager tab. Select the CD-ROM drive and click Properties, then click the Settings tab, as shown in Exhibit 4-25, where the drive is designated E:. Select a range of letters to be used by the drive and click OK.

Note: When you update or install additional features on application software, some software expects the same drive letter for the CD-ROM drive that was used when it was first installed. Permanently setting the CD-ROM drive letter satisfies the requirements of this software.

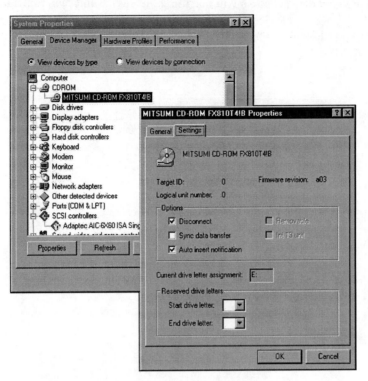

Exhibit 4-25: Installing a CD-ROM drive

Windows 9x supports a wide variety of CD-ROM drives, so most manufacturers assume that Windows provides 32-bit drivers, and ship the accompanying floppy disk with only 16-bit drivers. You use these drivers in a situation where your hard drive has failed and you're booting from the rescue disk. Windows 98 automatically puts its own 16-bit drivers on that rescue disk. These 16-bit drivers supplied by Windows 9x might not work with your CD-ROM drive. If they don't, you use the 16-bit drivers provided by the manufacturer.

Testing the drive

The drive is now ready to use. Press the eject button to open the drive shelf, and place a CD in the drive. Since data on CDs is written only on the bottom, be careful to protect it. Damage to either side of the disk can make it unreadable, but the bottom of the disk is the more sensitive side. Now access the CD using Explorer and the assigned drive letter. If you have a problem reading the CD, verify that the CD is placed in the tray label-side-up and that the format is compatible with your drive. If one CD doesn't work, try another; the first CD may be defective or scratched.

Note: A CD-ROM drive can be set so that, when you insert a CD, software on the CD automatically executes through, a feature called Autorun or Autoplay. To turn the feature on from Device Manager, right-click on the CD-ROM drive and select Properties. From the Properties window, select the Settings tab and then select Auto insert notification. To prevent a CD from automatically playing when the feature is enabled, hold down the Shift key when inserting the CD.

Update your Windows 95 rescue disk to include access to the CD-ROM drive

If you already have a Windows emergency startup disk to start a system in the event of a hard drive failure, you need to update this disk to include tools to access the CD-ROM drive, because Windows 9x is normally loaded from a CD-ROM. When you're recovering from a failed hard drive, you don't have access to the 32-bit Windows drivers on the hard drive. Windows 98 automatically adds the real-mode CD-ROM device drivers to the rescue disk, but Windows 95 doesn't. This section explains how to add this functionality to a Windows 95 rescue disk.

The CD-ROM drive came with a disk that includes the following files:

- Install.exe—the CD-ROM installation program
- Cdtech.sys—CD-ROM device driver
- Instruction files and documentation

Two files are required to access a CD-ROM drive while in real mode: the 16-bit device driver provided by the manufacturer of the CD-ROM drive (or a generic real-mode driver that works with the drive), which in this case is Cdtech.sys, and the 16-bit real-mode OS interface to the driver, Mscdex.exe. The device driver is loaded from Config.sys, and Mscdex.exe is loaded from Autoexec.bat.

If you have run the installation program that came with the CD-ROM drive (Install.exe), then the Autoexec.bat and Config.sys files on your hard drive should already have the correct entries in them. You can add these lines to these same files on your rescue disk, correcting paths to the two files as needed. Copy the two files to your rescue disk so you can access the CD-ROM drive when you boot from this disk, even when the hard drive isn't accessible. For example, on a rescue or boot disk designed to access the CD-ROM drive without depending on any files or commands on the hard drive, the Config.sys file might contain this command:

```
DEVICE = A:\CDTECH.SYS /D:MSCD001
```

The Autoexec.bat file might contain this command line:

```
MSCDEX.EXE /D:MSCD001 /L:E /M:10
```

The explanations of these command lines are as follows:

- Two files needed to manage the drive are Mscdex.exe and Cdtech.sys, which must be copied from this disk into the root directory.
- When the program Mscdex.exe executes, it uses the MSCD001 entry as a tag back to the Config.sys file to learn which device driver is being used to interface with the drive, which in this case is Cdtech.sys.
- To Mscdex.exe, the drive is named MSCD001 and is being managed by the driver Cdtech.sys.
- Mscdex.exe uses Cdtech.sys as its go-between to access the drive.
- Mscdex.exe also assigns a drive letter to the drive. If you want to specify a certain drive letter, use the /L: option in the command line. In our example, the CD-ROM drive is drive E. If you don't use the /L: option, then the next available drive letter is used.
- The /M: option controls the number of memory buffers.
- If the files referenced in these two commands are stored on the floppy disk in a directory different from the root directory, then include the path to the file in front of the filename.

If your hard drive fails and you start up from your rescue disk, once the CD-ROM drivers are loaded and the CD-ROM drive is recognized, you can copy files needed to troubleshoot the system from the Windows 9x CD, which is in drive E. If you decide to reinstall Windows, you can type E:\Setup at the command prompt.

If you have installed 16-bit device drivers from your Config.sys and Autoexec.bat files, when Windows 9x is installed, it often ignores existing Config.sys and Autoexec.bat lines. It turns these lines into comment lines by adding REM to the beginning of the line and handles the CD-ROM drive through its own protected-mode drivers.

Optimizing the CD-ROM cache

Recall that a cache is a location in memory or the hard drive used to store frequently used data. For CD-ROM drives, a memory cache contains data that was recently read from the CD. Recall that Mscdex.exe is the 16-bit OS utility that manages a CD-ROM drive. The 32-bit CD-ROM utility is CDFS (CD file system), which is automatically loaded by Windows 9x if it detects a CD-ROM drive. CDFS has a caching function similar to hard drive caching done by Vcache. It uses a memory cache to speed up reading from a CD. CDFS decides how much memory to use when caching data, based on the speed of the CD-ROM drive and how much memory is installed in the system. You can affect this decision by using the Performance tab in System Properties. Click Start, choose Settings, Control Panel, and then double-click System. In the Properties dialog box, click the Performance tab and then click File System. Click CD-ROM on the File System Properties box, as seen in Exhibit 4-26. By changing the CD-ROM speed in this box, you change the amount of memory allotted to the cache. The amount is displayed in the last sentence on this box.

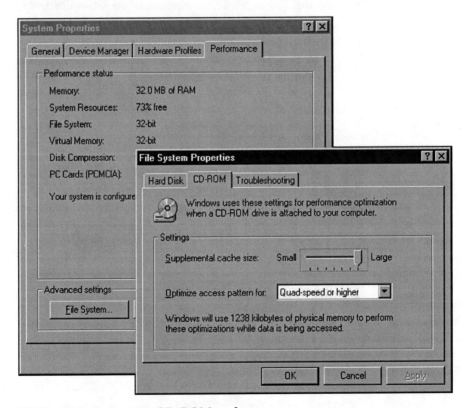

Exhibit 4-26: Optimizing CD-ROM cache

Plug and Play hardware installations

Plug and Play (PnP) is a set of design specifications for both hardware and software that works toward effortless hardware installations. For a system to be truly Plug and Play for Windows 9x, it must meet these criteria:

- The system BIOS must be PnP.

- All hardware devices and expansion cards must be PnP-compliant.

- The OS must support PnP.

- A 32-bit device driver (VxD) must be available (provided by the device manufacturer or Windows).

If all these things are true, hardware installation should be just a matter of installing the new hardware device, turning on the PC, and perhaps providing the 32-bit driver, if it isn't included with Windows 9x. During the boot process, Windows 9x surveys the devices and their needs for resources and allocates resources to each device. Windows 9x is free to assign these resources to the devices and avoids assigning the same resource to two devices. For PnP to work, each device in the system must be able to use whatever resources the OS assigns to it.

PnP components

A Plug and Play OS, such as Windows 9x, provides two main services: resource management and run-time configuration. *Resource management* occurs at startup as system resources are allocated to devices. *Run-time configuration* is an ongoing process that monitors any changes in system devices, such as the removal of a PC Card on a notebook computer or docking and undocking a notebook computer to and from a docking station. The BIOS must be able to recognize these changes during OS run time, that is, any time the OS is running, and communicate them to the OS.

Windows 9x uses four components in implementing PnP architecture:

- *The Configuration Manager* controls the configuration process of all devices and communicates these configurations to the devices.

- *The hardware tree* is a database built each time Windows 9x starts up. It contains a list of installed components and the resources they use.

- *The bus enumerator* locates all devices on a particular bus and inventories the resource requirements for these devices.

- *The resource arbitrator* decides which resources are assigned to which devices.

PnP BIOS

BIOS that is PnP-compliant gathers resource configuration information prior to loading Windows 9x, presenting to Windows 9x details it can use to complete the process. Motherboards manufactured after 1994 most likely contain PnP BIOS. PnP BIOS can also be ESCD (extended system configuration data) BIOS. ESCD BIOS creates a list of configuration changes that you've made manually when installing legacy devices and stores that list on the BIOS chip. Even if the hard drive crashes or you must reload Windows 9x, the configuration changes are still available from the BIOS when it goes through the boot process, and it presents the information to Windows 9x at startup.

To discover if your BIOS is PnP, look for a message about the BIOS type on the startup screen. Information about the BIOS might also be displayed on the CMOS setup screen or written on the BIOS chip, as shown in Exhibit 4-27. You can also use MSD, a 16-bit command-line diagnostic utility, and choose Computer from the menu to get information about your BIOS. The documentation for the motherboard should also say whether the BIOS is PnP.

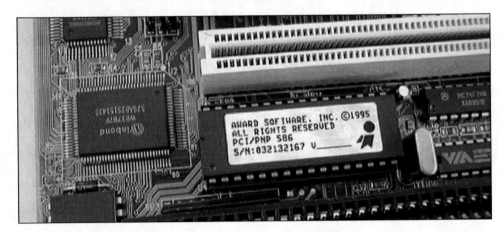

Exhibit 4-27: Plug and Play BIOS

If the BIOS isn't Plug and Play, you can still use Plug and Play Windows 9x software for hardware devices that are Plug and Play. However, you might need to configure the hardware manually or, in some cases, disable the Plug and Play features of the interface card.

Do it!

D-1: Updating drivers with Device Manager

Here's how	Here's why
1 Open Device Manager	
Select your display adapter	From the Display Adapters section.
2 Open the Properties window for your display adapter	
Click the **Driver** tab	
3 Click **Driver File Details**	
Write down the path to the Driver files	
Backup these files to a disk or another directory	So that you can backtrack if necessary.
4 Return to the **Driver** tab	In Device Manager.
Click **Update Driver**	The Update Driver Wizard starts.
5 Click **Next**	In the first wizard dialog box.
6 Click **Search for**	In the second wizard dialog box.
Click **Next**	
7 Check **Specify a location and CD**	In the next wizard dialog box. If you're using the Windows 9x CD.
Clear any other check boxes	
Click **Next**	
8 Type the location of the Windows CD installation file	In the next wizard dialog box.
Click **OK**	After you've specified a location.

9 Click **Next**	Windows searches the location and reports its findings. If the wizard indicates that it has found a file relating to the device you selected in the display adapter.
Verify that you've correctly located the installation files	If the wizard reports that it can't find the file. After Windows locates the drivers, it copies the driver files. If a file being copied is older than the file the system is currently using, you're prompted to confirm that you want to use the older file. Usually, newer drivers are better than older drivers. However, you might want to use an older one if, after having recently updated drivers, you encounter problems. In this case, you might want to reinstall the old driver that wasn't causing problems.
10 Click **Finish**	To complete the installation. After the files have been copied.
11 Restart the computer	If prompted to do so.
12 Identify the display adapter installed on the computer	Using Device Manager.
Search the Web site of the device manufacturer for new video drivers for this adapter	
Install the updated drivers	If you find drivers newer than the one currently in use.
13 Describe the steps required to access Device Manager.	
14 How can you access a device's properties in Device Manager?	
15 What tab in the Properties window allows you to update a driver?	
16 Besides typing the path, what other option do you have to specify a driver's location?	
17 Why would you want to use an older driver?	

Topic E: Installing applications

Explanation

As the bridge between earlier and later versions of Windows, Windows 9x can use both 16-bit and 32-bit software. This section shows you how to install both. Troubleshooting and uninstalling Windows 9x applications are covered elsewhere.

Preparing for software installation

As with installing hardware, there are several things you can do before installing software on Windows 9x to prepare your system and to increase the likelihood that the installation is successful:

- **Check available resources.** Check your computer resources to make sure you have (1) enough space on your hard drive, (2) the minimum requirements for memory, and (3) the proper CPU and video monitor. Read the documentation for the software you're installing and make sure you can fulfill any other requirements of the particular software program. The minimum requirements for the software should be listed in the installation manual. Remember that you shouldn't completely fill your hard drive with software and data, because the operating system needs extra space for temporary files and for the swap file, which changes in size depending on how much space is needed. If your hard drive is too full and you add a new file, the file can't be written all in one place and is split up into pieces (fragmented) and stored wherever there's available space on the hard drive. The system then has to look in several different places on the hard drive to find the whole file, slowing down performance. You can learn more about these performance issues in Windows 9x elsewhere in this document.

  Note: For best performance with Windows 9x, allow a minimum of 100 MB of unused hard drive space for working temporary files used by applications.

- **Protect the original software.** For floppy disks, write-protect the original disks before you begin the installation, that is, set the notch on the disk to open. After the installation is complete, put the original disks or CD-ROM from which you installed the software in a safe place. If you have the original software handy, it's easier for you to reinstall if something goes wrong with the installed software.

- **Back up the registry and system configuration files.** Many older software packages want to edit Config.sys, Autoexec.bat, Win.ini, and/or System.ini files during the installation. Newer software might add its own entries to the Windows registry. Before you begin the installation, make backup copies of all of these files so that you can backtrack if needed.

Performing software installations

To install software designed for Windows 9x, access the Control Panel and double-click the Add/Remove Programs icon. Insert the software CD in the CD-ROM drive or the floppy disk in the floppy disk drive and then click the Install button. Follow directions on the setup screen. If the CD-ROM drive is set to Autorun, a setup screen might automatically appear as soon as you insert the software installation CD in the drive. For older software, click Start and Run, which displays the Run dialog box. Enter the drive and name of the installation program, for example, A:Install or D:Setup. Either way, the installation program loads and begins executing. If the installation program asks you a question you can't answer, you can always abandon the installation and try again later.

Most software asks you for a serial number unique to your copy of the software, which is probably written on the CD-ROM or on the first floppy disk, or it might be stamped on the documentation. Write the serial number on the floppy disk or on the CD case, so that you have it if you lose the documentation later. Copyright agreements often allow you to install the software on only one computer at a time. This serial number identifies the copy of the software that you've installed on this machine.

After the installation is complete and the software is working, update your backup copies of Autoexec.bat, Config.sys, System.ini, Win.ini, and the registry so that they, too, reflect the changes that the application software made to these configuration files.

Troubleshooting software installations

If you are having difficulty with the installation of software in Windows 9x, try the following:

- If an application locks up when you first open it, try deleting all files and folders under \Windows\Temp. A software installation sometimes leaves files and folders in the Windows temporary directories. To conserve space on the hard drive, delete all files and folders under \Windows\Temp.

- Look at the Readme.htm file in the \Windows directory, which points you to the Programs.txt file, also in the \Windows directory. If there's a problem with the software that was known when Windows was shipped, information about the problem and what to do about it might be in these text files. You can also check the Web site of the software manufacturer or the Microsoft Web site for additional insight.

Supporting DOS applications under Windows 9x

Windows 3.x used *PIF (program information file)* files to manage the virtual machine environment for DOS applications and provided a PIF editor to alter these files. Each application had its own PIF that was used to specify the DOS environment that Windows 3.x created for it. If an application had no PIF, Windows 3.x used the settings in _Default.pif in the \Windows\System folder.

Windows 9x manages the environment for DOS applications in a slightly different fashion. Apps.inf contains a section named [PIF95] that contains a master list of settings to be used for all DOS applications listed in the file.

If you want to customize the settings for a DOS application, use the Properties feature of the DOS program file, which creates an individual PIF for the program file and serves as the PIF editor. Right-click the program filename and select Properties from the menu displays. Windows searches for the program's PIF and, if none is found, creates one using default values. If Windows 9x was installed over Windows 3.x, then _Default.pif still exists in the \Windows\System directory, and default values are read from it. Regardless of where the default values come from, any changes made are stored in the PIF for the application. To make the changes, using Explorer, right-click the program filename and select Properties from the shortcut menu. Click the Program tab. (The Program tab isn't present for Windows applications. See Exhibit 4-28.

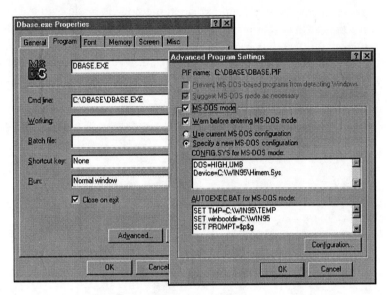

Exhibit 4-28: Properties sheet for DOS

If you select Use current MS-DOS configuration, Windows executes the contents of Dosstart.bat, stored in the Windows folder. *Dosstart.bat* is a type of Autoexec.bat file that's executed in two situations: (1) when you select Restart the computer in MS-DOS mode from the shutdown menu, and (2) when you run a program in MS-DOS mode. This file can be used to load real-mode device drivers, but Set commands aren't executed.

If you select Specify a new MS-DOS configuration, you can make changes to Autoexec.bat and Config.sys files used for this MS-DOS mode only. For example, if the application runs slowly in DOS mode and does a lot of disk accessing, you can add entries to run real-mode SmartDrive here. SmartDrive normally isn't run under Windows 9x, having been replaced by the faster 32-bit Vcache. In this situation, since Windows 9x doesn't manage disk access in MS-DOS mode, loading SmartDrive from this window is appropriate, since Vcache isn't running.

Managing a DOS application memory under Windows 9x

When running DOS applications under Windows 9x, a DOS-like environment must be provided to the application. For example, to provide a DOS environment for the DOS program Edit.com on a PC running Windows 9x, go to Explorer and find the file Edit.com in the \Windows\Command directory. Right-click on the file name and select Properties from the menu that appears. The entries on this Properties Window make up the PIF for this application, which describes the environment that the DOS program uses.

Click the Memory tab, and the Edit.com Properties screen, as shown in Exhibit 4-29, appears, listing the memory options available. From the Memory tab, you can specify how much conventional and extended memory is made available to the application, or leave the settings at Auto, which allows the application to use whatever's available. The last entry on the tab is MS-DOS protected-mode (DPMI) memory. This entry assigns the amount of protected-mode memory allowed the application. If you check Protected in the Conventional memory frame, the OS protects memory used by the OS from the application.

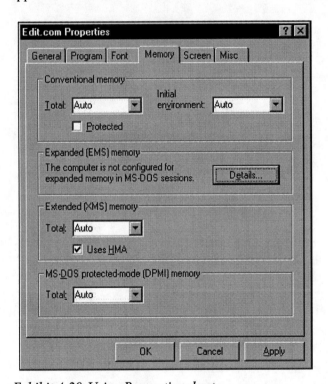

Exhibit 4-29:Using Properties sheets

You can use the default Auto settings to run many DOS applications without any problems. However, sometimes a DOS application has a problem with being given too much memory. Limit the amount of memory given the application by using the Properties sheet, as shown in Exhibit 4-29.

Real mode vs. virtual real mode

An OS that supports protected mode can allow a 16-bit program that's written to work in real mode to run in virtual real mode, sometimes referred to as virtual DOS mode. Exhibit 4-30 shows the difference between real mode and virtual real mode. In virtual real mode, the program "thinks" it's really working in a real-mode environment. It "thinks" that:

- It's the only program running.
- It has all memory available to it, all 1024K of memory addresses that directly point to RAM.
- It accesses data using a 16-bit data path.

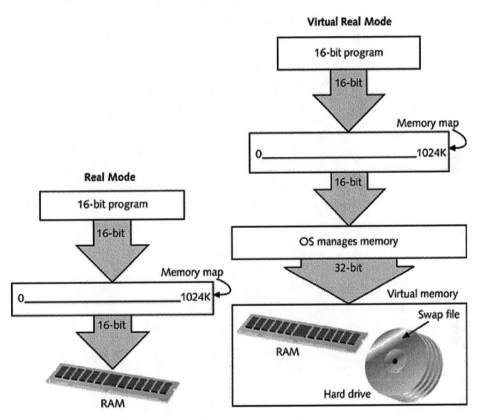

Exhibit 4-30: Virtual real mode provides "DOS in a box"

Underneath this environment, the OS is managing memory for the application. It receives the data in a 16-bit path but is free to use a 32-bit data path to access memory and is also free to use virtual memory for the data.

Recall that there are two types of 16-bit applications: those written for DOS and those written for Windows 3.x. DOS 16-bit applications expect to run in real mode with no other applications running with them. A Windows 3.x 16-bit application expects to allow Windows to manage memory for it and expects that other applications might also be running in a cooperative multitasking environment.

When Windows 9x runs a 16-bit DOS application, ordinarily it runs in virtual DOS mode in a *virtual DOS machine (VDM)*, sometimes called a *DOS box*, rather than in real mode. In a VDM, the application "thinks" it's running in real mode, but the OS is managing hardware resources using 32-bit drivers and providing virtual memory to the application. If you want a DOS application to have a "real" real mode rather than a virtual real mode, access the Properties box for the application. For example, once again using Edit.com as our example of a 16-bit application, right-click the program file name in Windows Explorer. or you can right-click on the shortcut icon to the program, and select Properties. Click the Program tab and click Advanced. The Advanced Program Settings box is displayed, as in Exhibit 4-31. Click MS-DOS mode to run the application in real mode. You can then choose to give the program its own private set of Config.sys and Autoexec.bat settings to be executed before the program runs. This information is stored in the PIF created for the shortcut. When you execute the shortcut or program, Windows 9x shuts down and reboots in real mode before executing the program.

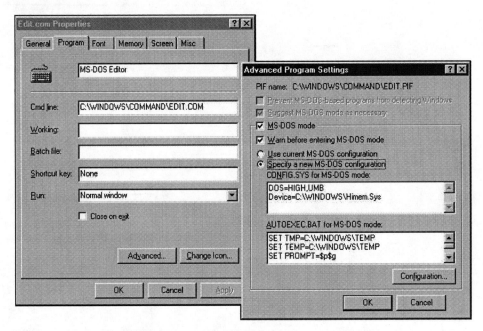

Exhibit 4-31: Real-mode environment

Note: To access real mode in Windows 9x, Click Start, Shutdown. When the Shut Down Windows dialog box appears, select Restart in MS-DOS mode.

Do it!   ## E-1:   Discussing Windows 9x application installation

Exercises

1 _____ is the primary tool for managing files, folders, and disks in Windows 9x.

2 Name three file extensions that Windows Explorer hides by default and three that it doesn't. How does it decide which file extensions to hide?

3 Use the _____ applet in Control Panel when installing 32-bit software designed for Windows 9x. Use the _____ option on the Start menu when installing older 16-bit software.

4 List three things you should do to prepare your system before installing new software.

5 What's virtual real mode? Do you have to use it to handle DOS applications within Windows 9x, or can you run them in "real" real mode?

6 When a 16-bit DOS application runs in a virtual DOS machine, it's sometimes said to be running in a _____.

7 The 32-bit drivers in Windows 9x are often referred to as _____.

Topic F: Memory management

Explanation

Memory management didn't change fundamentally from DOS to Windows 9x. With Windows 9x, memory is still organized as conventional, upper, and extended, as it was under DOS. However, Windows 9x has made some improvements in the allocation of this memory and in the automation of the process that make it easier to manage memory. In effect, Windows 9x, which is mostly a 32-bit OS, resides in extended memory together with its device drivers and applications and only uses base and upper memory for 16-bit components. This section covers some of the other ways memory is managed in Windows 9x.

Device driver memory management

One of the major improvements in memory management in Windows 9x is the new level of 32-bit protected mode drivers. These 32-bit drivers are automatically loaded into extended memory, not conventional or upper memory, when Windows 9x loads, thus eliminating the need to use the older and slower 16-bit drivers loaded from DEVICE= entries in Config.sys.

Windows 9x offers many 32-bit drivers that can replace older 16-bit drivers written for DOS in real mode. These 32-bit drivers are sometimes called *virtual device drivers* or *VxD drivers*; They have .vxd or .386 file extensions and operate in protected mode.

Another memory management improvement in Windows 9x is that it frees up more of conventional and upper memory, because it no longer uses Smartdrv.exe or Share.exe, two TSRs that required a lot of memory below 1 MB. Vcache replaced Smartdrv.exe, a 16-bit driver used to manage disk caching. Vcache is a 32-bit disk caching that's built into Windows 9x. The 32-bit Vshare.386, a part of Vmm32.exe that's automatically loaded when Windows 9x starts, replaced the 16-bit Share.exe.

Note: If you're using all 32-bit drivers and applications in a Windows 9x environment, memory management requires no work on your part. Just let Windows 9x automate the process for you.

Managing memory for 16-bit drivers

If you're using older 16-bit drivers under Windows 9x, search for 32-bit drivers to replace them. Look on the device manufacturer's Web site or the Microsoft Web site. If you can't find replacements, you might need to provide some of the same memory management aids needed by DOS.

You learned about Himem.sys and Emm386.exe, the two files that Windows uses to manage memory above 640K. Windows 9x uses Himem.sys to manage extended memory just as DOS does, but, instead of being loaded from Config.sys, it's automatically loaded by Io.sys without requiring an entry in Config.sys. When using this automatic method, Io.sys doesn't load Himem.sys until after the commands in Config.sys have been executed. If you're using Config.sys to load Emm386.exe, then you must include Himem.sys in Config.sys before the entry for Emm386.exe because Emm386.exe must find Himem.sys already loaded before it can load.

If you need to load a 16-bit device driver into a UMB (upper memory block), then you must have a Config.sys file with these lines in it:

```
DEVICE=Himem.sys
DEVICE=Emm386.exe NOEMS
DOS=HIGH,UMB
```

The DEVICEHIGH command to load the driver into a UMB must appear after these three lines in the Config.sys file. However, if you're using all 32-bit drivers, you don't even need the Config.sys file.

Note: To know whether a driver is 16-bit or 32-bit, look at how Windows loads it. If the driver is a 32-bit driver written for Windows 9x, it's loaded from the registry. System.ini can contain both 16-bit and 32-bit drivers. If the driver's loaded from Autoexec.bat or Config.sys, it's a 16-bit driver written for DOS.

During the Windows 9x installation, Windows 9x setup tries to substitute 32-bit drivers for all 16-bit drivers it finds in use and, if it can, to eliminate the Autoexec.bat and Config.sys files altogether. However, if it can't substitute a 32-bit driver for an older 16-bit driver, it keeps the proper lines in the Config.sys file and sets itself up to use the older driver.

Windows 9x swap file

Windows 9x automates the managing of virtual memory for you, and Microsoft recommends that you allow that. To see what virtual memory options Windows 9x offers, click Start, choose Settings, Control Panel, and then double-click System. Select the Performance tab, and click Virtual Memory to display the dialog box as shown in Exhibit 4-32. These settings are used to tell Windows how to manage the swap file. Unless you have a good reason to do otherwise, check Let Windows manage my virtual memory settings.

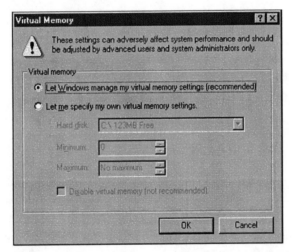

Exhibit 4-32: Options for managing virtual memory in Windows 9X

One reason you might want to manage virtual memory yourself is to make the size of the file permanent in order to prevent Windows from resizing the file, which can slow down performance. To improve performance, first defragment the hard drive so there's plenty of unfragmented space for the file. Then set the maximum and minimum size of the file to the same value, which forces the size not to change. If you have the available hard drive space, set the size to about 2.5 times the amount of RAM.

Notice in Exhibit 4-32 that you can specify the location of the swap file. The name of the swap file in Windows 9x is Win386.swp, and its default location is C:\. You can choose to put the swap file on a compressed drive, but Windows doesn't compress the swap file itself, in order to ensure the safety of the file.

Virtual machine manager

How does Windows 9x provide virtual memory addresses to DOS and 16-bit Windows application programs? By *memory paging*, which involves swapping blocks of memory stored in RAM to the hard drive. The Virtual Machine Manager (VMM) manages memory paging.

As you can see in the Exhibit 4-33, Windows 9x has virtual memory stored in a swap file and provides virtual memory addresses to application programs. In Exhibit 4-33, you see three sets of virtual memory addresses. Each set can contain up to 4 GB of addresses, depending on the amount of virtual memory available. The top set is being used by two 16-bit applications. The second set of virtual addresses is being used by a single DOS application, and a third set of addresses is being used by a 32-bit application. Each virtual machine for DOS has a set of virtual memory addresses. The 16-bit Windows programs share a single set of virtual memory addresses, and each 32-bit program has its own individual set of addresses.

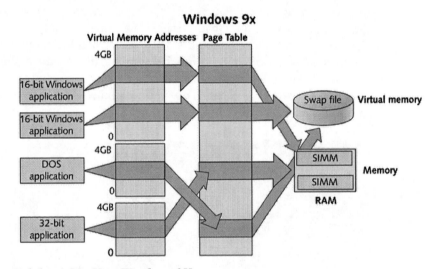

Exhibit 4-33: How Windows 9X manages memory

In Exhibit 4-33, all these virtual addresses map onto the page table, which in turn maps onto either physical memory (RAM) or virtual memory on the hard drive, that is, the swap file. Not all virtual memory addresses in Windows 9x have physical or virtual memory assigned to them. These virtual addresses remain unassigned until an application program uses them.

In Windows 9x, the VMM controls the page table, moving 4K pages in and out of physical RAM. If a program requests memory that the memory manager knows is stored in the swap file, the manager generates a *page fault*, which causes the manager to go to the drive to return the data from the swap file to RAM. This action is called a *page-in*. If RAM is full, the manager takes a page and moves it to the swap file, which is called a *page-out*.

If RAM is full much of the time, the VMM might spend excessive time moving pages in and out of RAM, which can cause excessive hard drive use and a decrease in overall system performance and can even cause the system to lock up or applications to fail. This situation is sometimes called *disk thrashing* and can cause premature hard drive failure. Symptoms of excessive memory paging are:

- Very high CPU use
- Very slow system response
- Constant hard drive use

To avoid excessive memory paging, leave fewer application programs open at the same time or install more RAM.

Getting help from Microsoft

Microsoft offers some excellent support for its products. For those serious about learning to provide professional support for Windows 95 or Windows 98, two good books are Microsoft Windows 95 Resource Kit and Microsoft Windows 98 Resource Kit, both by Microsoft Press.

Microsoft maintains several Web site areas that are valuable sources of information, including software utilities, enhancements, and troubleshooting guidelines.

For general questions and to search the support Knowledge Base, you can go to:

```
support.microsoft.com/default.aspx
```

Click the link to Search the Knowledge Base. Exhibit 4-34 shows a beginning query screen.

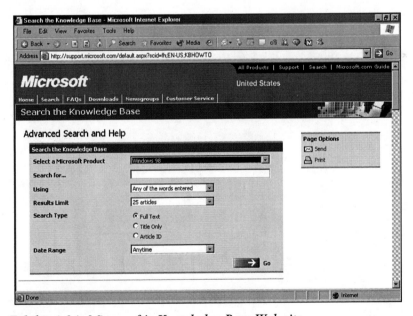

Exhibit 4-34: Microsoft's Knowledge Base Web site

To research specific or general topics about Microsoft products; select the product from the list. Next enter a word or phrase in the Search for box. Change the other options as needed and then click Go. A list of related articles displays. Click the article to display it.

Another useful Microsoft Web site is Microsoft's TechNet, which was developed for IT professionals:

```
www.microsoft.com/technet/default.asp
```

Exhibit 4-35 shows the start page for TechNet, and you can see some of the resources and information this site provides.

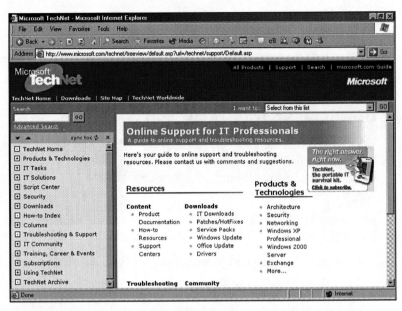

Exhibit 4-35: Microsoft TechNet homepage

The Microsoft Web site (`www.microsoft.com`) contains many links on hardware and software compatibility. These and other Microsoft support links are useful when you troubleshoot Windows 9x.

Do it! **F-1: Discussing Windows 9x memory management**

Exercises

1 How is memory management in Windows 9x similar to memory management under DOS? How is it different?

2 What's a page fault? A page-in? A page-out?

3 Define memory paging. Excessive memory paging can cause what problem? What are some symptoms of this problem?

4 Windows 9x allows for virtual memory to be used to help relieve the RAM. What hardware device is used to create this memory?

5 Virtual memory in reality is a _____ file created by Windows 9x

Unit summary: Installing and using Windows 9x

Topic A In this topic you learned about the Windows 9x **versions** and **architecture**. You learned how Windows 98 differs from Windows 95, about Windows Me and about the Windows 9x **architecture**.

Topic B In this topic, you learned about **installing** Windows 9x. You had an overview of the contents on the **Windows 9x CD** and the steps to be taken to prepare for installation. You learned how to install Windows 9x as a **clean install** and as an **upgrade**. You also learned about the **instructions** for specific upgrades. You learned about downloading and installing **updates** for Windows 9x.

Topic C In this topic, you learned about **keystroke shortcuts** in Windows, managing Windows 9x **desktop** and using **Windows Explorer** to manage **floppy disks** and **hard drives**.

Topic D In this topic, you learned about installing **hardware** with Windows 9x. You also learned about **adding** new hardware and **testing** the **drive**. You had an overview of **Plug and Play** and hardware installations.

Topic E In this topic, you learned about installing **applications** in Windows 9x. You learned about **planning**, **performing**, and **troubleshooting** software installations. You also learned about supporting **DOS applications** under Windows 9x.

Topic F In this topic, you learned about **managing memory** with Windows 9x. You learned about memory management with **device drivers** in Windows 9x and the Windows **swap file**. You also learned about **virtual machine manager** and getting **help** from Microsoft.

Review questions

1 What's the function of the Autorun.inf file included on the Windows 9x installation CD? The Setup.exe file? The Readme.txt file?

2 What are the processor, RAM, and hard disk space requirements for Windows 95? For Windows 98?

3 List at least five things you need to do to prepare your hard drive for an upgrade installation of Windows 9x.

4 What are the four types of installations that you can choose during setup of Windows 9x?

5 Windows 9x installation begins in _____mode and then switches to _____ mode.

6 What are the log files Setuplog.txt, Detlog.txt, and Detcrash.log used for?

7 List the five basic tasks that Setup performs for you during a Windows 95 to Windows 98 upgrade.

8   What type of disk should you always create when prompted to do so during Windows 9x setup? Why is this an important step?

9   Name two things you should do after completing a Windows 9x upgrade.

10   Give two different situations in which Windows keyboard shortcuts might be useful.

11   What's the Windows keyboard shortcut used to display the startup menu while Windows is loading? To go through step-by-step confirmation of startup? To move from one loaded application to another?

12   How do you access the Display Properties window? What are two settings you can change from this window?

13   How is a shortcut icon different from an icon that points directly to a file or program? What happens if you delete a shortcut icon? A file or program icon?

14   When adding hardware to Windows 9x, how do you indicate that you want to use a Windows driver? A manufacturer-provided or downloaded driver?

15   Explain when and why you would use 16-bit and 32-bit drivers when installing a CD-ROM drive with Windows 9x.

16   What Windows component manages the interface to a CD-ROM drive including the CD-ROM cache?

17   Windows _____ automatically puts its own 16-bit drivers on the rescue disk when you create the disk; Windows _____ doesn't, though you can add them to the disk later.

18 What are the four components that Windows 9x uses to implement Plug and Play architecture?

19 How can you determine whether your BIOS is Plug and Play compatible?

20 The component of Windows 9x that handles the basic OS functions such as managing memory is called the _____.

21 For Windows 95 _____ of RAM is recommended while for Windows 98, _____ of RAM is recommended.

22 Checking for viruses is much more important when doing a clean install than with an upgrade. True or false?

23 An operating system upgrade that's downloaded from the Internet is known as a: _____.

24 Of the four-setup options available from the installation screen, the one most often chosen is called _____.

25 What DOS command is used to change a file from being hidden or read-only to one that can be edited?

26 The keyboard shortcuts for copy and for paste are _____ and _____.

27 An icon that points to a program that can be executed or to a file or folder is called a _____.

28 A software utility in Windows 9x that helps in managing disk drives is _____.

29 Technically speaking, a folder is really a _____.

30 For a system to be truly Plug and Play compliant, the hardware and software, including the system BIOS must be Plug and Play capable. True or false?

Independent practice activity

Back up critical Windows 9x files

1   Using Windows 9x Explorer, create a new folder called Win-bak.ini.

2   In the C:\Windows folder select the **System.ini** and **Win.ini** files.

3   Copy these files by pressing **Ctrl + C**.

4   Click the **Win-bak.ini** directory, then paste the copied .ini files into the Win-bak.ini file by pressing **Ctrl + V**.

5   Using Explorer, set View, Options to **Show all files**.

6   Copy C:\Windows\System.dat to C:\ Win-bak.ini. (Do not drag.)

7   Copy C:\Windows\User.dat to C:\ Win-bak.ini. (Do not drag.)

8   Copy C:\Autoexec.bat to C:\Win-bak.ini. (Do not drag.)

9   Copy C:\Config.sys to C:\Win-bak.ini. (Do not drag.)

10   Note that your PC might not have Autoexec.bat or Config.sys. Also, the files System.dat and User.dat hold the registry.

Unit 5

Supporting and troubleshooting Windows 9x

Unit time: 90 minutes

Complete this unit, and you'll know how to:

A Discuss the Windows 9x startup process.

B Troubleshoot the Windows 9x boot process.

C Describe the Windows 9x registry, its organization, and recovery procedures.

D Explain what tools you can use to monitor, control, and troubleshoot Windows 9x.

E Troubleshoot hardware problems, such as missing device drivers.

F Troubleshoot application problems, such as an application that won't start.

G Troubleshoot performance problems, such as an overall slowdown or unexpected errors.

Topic A: Booting Windows 9x

Explanation

In this topic, you will learn about the startup process in Windows 9x, including the differences between booting Windows 95 and booting Windows 98/ME. Finally, you will learn how to cause an application to load at startup. First, though, you'll learn more about important files that Windows 9x uses when booting up.

Files used to customize the startup process

There are several files that Windows 9x uses to control the startup process. Recall that DOS requires Io.sys, Msdos.sys, and Command.com in the root directory of the boot device in order to load. In addition, Autoexec.bat and Config.sys are text files that can contain settings for environmental variables and commands to load drivers and TSRs. Windows 9x supports Autoexec.bat and Config.sys for backward compatibility with DOS.

If Autoexec.bat or Config.sys files are present in the root directory, the command lines in them are executed during the boot. They are used to customize the loading process. Just as DOS uses text files to contain information about what is loaded, Windows 3.x also uses text files to hold custom settings that help control the loading process. These files are called initialization files, and some of the entries in these files are read and used by Windows 9x. However, most Windows 9x settings are stored in the Windows registry rather than in text files.

These text files can be edited with the Edit.com program from the command prompt or any text editor from within Windows. You can use the Windows System Configuration Editor (Sysedit) to edit these files. To use Sysedit, type sysedit in the Run dialog box. The following files are displayed automatically for editing: Autoexec.bat, Config.sys, Win.ini, System.ini, and Protocol.ini. (See Exhibit 5-1.)

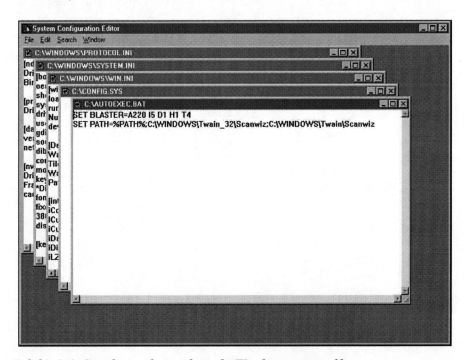

Exhibit 5-1: Sysedit can be used to edit Windows system file

Recall that an initialization file, which has an .ini file extension, is a file used by Windows or application software to store configuration information needed when Windows or an application is first loaded. An application can have its own .ini files and registry and can also store its information in the Windows .ini files and the Windows registry. The following table shows Windows .ini files, which Windows 9x supports for backward compatibility with Windows 3.x:

Windows .ini files	General purpose of the file
System.ini	Contains hardware settings and multitasking options for Windows. The [386Enh] section loads protected mode (32-bit) drivers for older applications, which may cause problems in more recent operating systems.
Progman.ini	Contains information about Program Manager groups.
Win.ini	Contains information about user settings, including printer, fonts, file associations, and settings made by applications.
Control.ini	Contains information about the user's desktop, including color selections, wallpaper, and screensaver options.
Mouse.ini	Contains settings for the mouse.
Protocol.ini	Contains information about the configuration of the network.

The contents of files that have an .ini extension are organized into sections, which are each given a name. Within a section, values are assigned to variables by using this format:

```
[SECTION NAME]
KEY NAME=value
```

Any value to the right of the key name becomes available to Windows or an application software program reading the file; in other words, the key name acts much like the Set command in Autoexec.bat, which assigns a value to a system variable.

System.ini and Win.ini are used by both Windows 3.x and Windows 9x. A sample Windows 9x System.ini file is shown in Exhibit 5-2. The two sections required for the boot process are [boot] and [386Enh]. Windows 3.x kept many more entries in these sections than does Windows 9x, which uses these files only for backward compatibility with older applications.

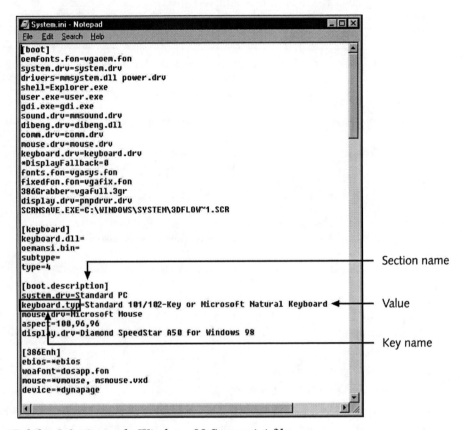

Exhibit 5-2: A sample Windows 98 System.ini file

Initialization files are read only when Windows or an application using .ini files starts up. If you change the .ini file for an application, you must restart the software for the change to take effect. If you want the application to ignore a line in the .ini file, you can turn the line into a *comment* line by putting a semicolon or the letters REM at the beginning of the line.

The maximum file size of .ini files is 64 K, although files greater than 32 K can cause some application software problems. Most applications have a setup program in their program group that is used to make changes to their .ini files.

Note: Sometimes it is necessary to manually edit an .ini file that belongs to an application, but you should normally not edit System.ini or other Windows 9x initialization files. Incorrect changes to these files might result in Windows not running correctly, and Windows sometimes overwrites these files when changes are made to Windows through the Control Panel.

We now turn our attention to studying the Windows 9x startup process, in which these and other files are used.

The Windows 9x startup process

Windows 9x first loads in real mode and then switches to protected mode. With DOS, the two core real-mode system files responsible for starting up the OS, Io.sys and Msdos.sys, remain in memory, running even after the OS is loaded. With Windows 9x, Io.sys is responsible for only the initial startup process performed in real mode. Then, control is turned over to Vmm32.vxd, which works in protected mode, and Io.sys is terminated. Windows 9x includes a file named Msdos.sys, but it is only a text file that contains some parameters and switches that can be set to affect the way the OS boots.

Startup in Windows 9x is a five-phase process, as shown in Exhibit 5-3. We will look at each phase in turn.

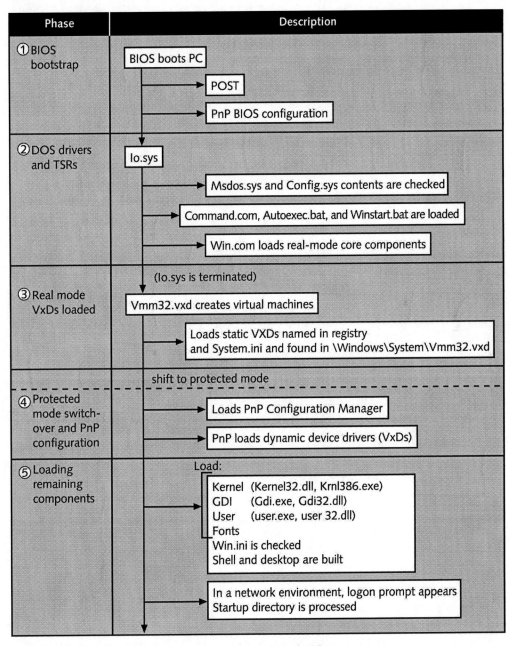

Exhibit 5-3: Windows 9x core components and the loading process

Phase 1: BIOS POST and bootstrap

Startup BIOS begins the process. If the BIOS is a *Plug and Play (PnP) BIOS*, it examines the devices on the system and determines which ones are plug-and-play compliant. BIOS first enables the devices that are not plug and play compliant, and then tries to make the plug-and-play devices use the leftover resources. It also looks to permanent RAM for information about hardware and uses that information to help in configuring PnP devices that have their configuration information recorded there. It performs POST and saves information that the Windows Configuration Manager later uses to complete the hardware configuration.

BIOS looks for a device (hard drive, floppy disk, CD-ROM drive, and so forth) containing the OS and loads Windows 9x. The MBR on the boot device executes the bootstrap loader, which looks for the initial hidden file of Windows 9x (Io.sys).

Phase 2: The OS is loaded

In Phase 2, BIOS turns control over to Io.sys, which creates a real-mode operating system environment. Next, Io.sys checks the text file Msdos.sys for boot parameters. Then Io.sys automatically loads the following drivers if they are present: Himem.sys, Ifshlp.sys, Setver.exe, and Drvspace.bin (or Dblspace.bin).

- Himem.sys provides access to extended memory.

- 16-bit programs use Ifshlp.sys to access the file system.

- Setver.exe is included for backward compatibility with DOS applications that expect all DOS components to be from the same version. Setver.exe "asks" the DOS application what version of DOS it expects to use and presents DOS components to that application as if they were all from that version, even if they are actually from different versions. Setver.exe loads a version table into memory, which has a list of programs and the version number with which they were designed to run.

- Drvspace.bin and Dblspace.bin provide disk compression. One of these two files is loaded only if Io.sys finds Dlbspace.ini or Drvspace.ini in the root directory of the boot drive.

Io.sys also sets several environmental variables to default settings. Entries in Io.sys cannot be edited, but an entry in Config.sys overrides the default entry in Io.sys. Therefore, if you want to use settings different from the default, put the command in Config.sys, which is executed at this point in the load. Here are the default Io.sys entries:

- Files=60

- Lastdrive=z

- Buffers=30

- Stacks=9,256

- Shell=Command.com

- Fcbs=4

Next, Io.sys loads Command.com and follows instructions stored in Autoexec.bat and Winstart.bat. The default assignments made to environmental variables that were stored in Autoexec.bat in DOS are listed below:

- Tmp=c:\windows\temp
- Temp=c:\windows\temp
- Prompt=pg
- Path=c:\windows;c:\windows\command

The Tmp and Temp variables are used by some software to locate where to put their temporary files. You can change any of these by making an entry in Autoexec.bat. Next, Io.sys loads Win.com.

Phase 3: Static VxDs

In Phase 3, Io.sys relinquishes control to the virtual machine manager (VMM) component housed in Vmm32.vxd along with some VxDs. Recall that a VxD is a virtual device driver that works with a VM to provide access to hardware for software running in the VM. Under Windows 3.x, these VxDs were loaded from System.ini and had a .386 file extension. Under Windows 9x, if stored in individual files, they have a .vxd file extension. They are called *static VxDs* because once they are loaded into memory, they remain there. Conversely, *dynamic VxDs* are loaded into and unloaded from memory as needed.

Vmm32.vxd is built specifically for a particular computer when Windows 9x is installed and contains some VxDs critical for a successful boot; each installation of Windows will have a different build of this file. (The VxD drivers that are now included in Vmm32.vxd were listed in the [386enh] section of System.ini under Windows 3.x.) Vmm32.vxd terminates Io.sys and, while still in real mode, loads static VxD device drivers as identified in four different locations. They can be embedded in Vmm32.vxd, named in the registry or System.ini, or stored in the .vxd files in the \Windows\System\Vmm32 directory.

If you suspect a problem with a VxD that is part of the Vmm32.vxd file, then store a new version of the .vxd file in the `\Windows\System\Vmm32` directory. If Windows finds a VxD driver there, it uses that driver instead of the one embedded in Vmm32.vxd. Also, VxD drivers are listed in the registry and in System.ini. Normally, the entries are the same, and entries in System.ini are listed there only for backward compatibility. However, if an entry in System.ini differs from an entry in the registry, the value in System.ini is used.

Phase 4: Protected-mode switchover and PnP configuration

At the beginning of Phase 4, Vmm32.vxd switches to protected mode and loads Configuration Manager. Configuration Manager is responsible for configuring legacy and PnP devices. It will use any information that PnP BIOS might have left for it and loads the 32-bit VxDs for the PnP devices.

Phase 5: Loading-remaining components

In Phase 5, with Vmm32.vxd still in control, the three core components are loaded, and fonts and other associated resources are loaded. Win.ini is checked, and commands stored there are executed to allow for backward-compatibility. The shell and user desktop are loaded. If the computer is working in a networked environment, a logon dialog box is displayed, and the user can log on to Windows 9x and the network. Finally, any processes stored in the Startup directory are performed.

Differences between the Windows 95 and Windows 98/ME boot process

Windows 98 made some minor changes in what happens during startup to speed up the boot process. For instance, Windows 95 waits two seconds while "Starting Windows 95" is displayed so that you can press a key to alter the boot process. Windows 98 eliminated this two-second wait and, in its place, allows you to press and hold the Ctrl key as it loads. If you do that, you see the Startup menu that is also available with Windows 95.

Loading an application at startup

If you want an application to load automatically at startup, you can:

- Place a shortcut in the C:\\Windows\All Users\Startup Menu\Programs\StartUp folder.

- Put the name of the program file in the Load= or Run= line in Win.ini.

- Manually edit the registry key HKEY_LOCAL_MACHINE\SOFTWARE\ Microsoft\Windows\CurrentVersion\Run.

Do it!

A-1:   Discussing the Windows 9x startup process

Exercises

1   List the five phases of the Windows 9x boot process and give a short description of each.

2   Explain how the file Setver.exe is used in Windows 9x.

3   How is a 16-bit driver loaded into a UMB in Windows 9x?

4 What Msdos.sys entry can be used to backtrack from a Windows 9x installation to the underlying version of DOS? What happens when this entry is set to =0? To =1?

5 How is the boot process for Windows 98 different from the Windows 95 boot process?

6 Give three ways you can cause an application to load at startup. Explain how to keep an application from loading at startup.

7 Windows 9x loads a program known as _____ that loads a version table into memory, which has a list of programs and the version number with which they were designed to run.

8 32-bit drivers that are loaded into memory and are never unloaded until the machine is powered off or cold booted are known as _____.

9 Which operating system waits two seconds and displays a message so that you can alter the boot process, Windows 95 or Windows 98/ME?

Topic B: Troubleshooting the boot process

Explanation

In the previous topic, you learned about the steps in the Windows 9x boot process and the files used in the process. When the boot process is not completed correctly, here are the basic steps you go through to troubleshoot it:

1   Check and address any error messages that occur during a normal boot.

2   If you cannot boot to a normal desktop, boot in safe mode and begin troubleshooting there.

3   If you cannot boot by using safe mode, the GUI portion of the OS is not functioning. Boot to the command prompt by using the Startup menu. Use commands at the C: prompt for troubleshooting.

4   If the Startup menu is not accessible, the MS-DOS core of the OS is not functioning. Boot from an emergency startup disk and try to access drive C.

5   If you cannot access drive C, then the hard drive is not accessible.

Error messages

Error messages are your first indications that something is going wrong with the Windows 9x boot process. You can use these messages to figure out how to solve some Windows 9x boot problems. The following table shows error messages that Windows 9x might produce, along with what to do when you see them. Specific errors are covered later in this section:

Error message or problem	What to do
MS-DOS compatibility mode	Windows is using real-mode drivers to access the hard drive rather than the preferred 32-bit drivers. After backing up the Config.sys and System.ini files, remove any references to real-mode drivers for the hard drive in these files.
	The problem might be due to an outdated motherboard BIOS. Consider updating the BIOS.
Bad or missing file Real mode driver missing or damaged	Verify that Config.sys, Autoexec.bat, (root directory of the hard drive) and System.ini (Windows folder) are present and in the right location and also if any files referenced in these two files exist.
Error in Config.sys line xx	Check Config.sys and Autoexec.bat for errors using the step-by-step confirmation option from the Windows 9x Startup menu. To check System.ini, rename the file so that it will not be used and boot with a bare bones version of the file.
	Look in the Win.ini file for applications that are attempting to load at startup but that have been deleted or uninstalled. Check the Load= or Run= lines.
Cannot open file *.inf	This error is caused by insufficient memory. Disable any TSRs running in Autoexec.bat.
	Close any applications that are running or remove them from the Start folder.

Error message or problem	What to do
Insufficient disk space	Run ScanDisk and Defragmenter. Check free space on the hard drive. Delete all files in the temp directory.
Invalid system disk Bad or missing Command.com	Suspect a boot sector virus. Run a current version of antivirus software. Command.com could be missing or corrupted. Restore the file from a backup or an emergency startup disk. To restore all real-mode files needed to begin loading Windows 9x, do the following: (1) boot from a Windows 9x emergency startup disk, (2) to restore Io.sys, Msdos.sys, Drvspace.bin, and Command.com, execute the SYS C: command, and (3) remove the floppy disk and reboot.
Invalid VxD dynamic link call from IFSMGR	This error is caused by a missing or corrupted Msdos.sys file. Restore the file from a backup or from an emergency startup disk.
Missing system files	Run the SYS C: command.
System Registry file missing	Either System.dat or User.dat is corrupted or missing. For Windows 95, restore them by using either System.da0 or User.da0. For Windows 98/ME, run ScanReg.
VxD error returns to command prompt	A VxD file is missing or corrupted. Run Windows Setup from the Windows 9x CD and choose Verify installed components.
Error containing the text "Kernel32.dll"	An error that contains this text probably indicates a corrupted kernel. Try restoring system files. If that doesn't work, reinstall Windows. **Note:** This error may appear at other times, not just during the boot process.

Windows has several tools you can use to help troubleshoot problems with booting. These utilities are listed below.

- **System Configuration Utility** (Msconfig)—Limit what loads during the boot to attain the cleanest possible boot.
- **Device Manager**—Disable a device that you think is causing a problem.
- **Automatic Skip Driver Agent** (ASDA)—Keep Windows from installing a driver that might be corrupted, including built-in Windows drivers.
- **Windows 9x Startup menu**—Includes safe mode, the command prompt, and other troubleshooting options.

Do it!

B-1: Troubleshooting a boot problem

Here's how	Here's why
1 Edit Config.sys	If you're using an installation of Windows 9x that doesn't use a Config.sys file, then create one.
Enter a command line in the file	To cause an error.
Boot the system	
Press F8	During the boot.
Walk through the boot process	To demonstrate how this procedure can be used to diagnose a problem with startup files.
2 Correct the command line in Config.sys	
Boot the system	Walking through each command in the boot process.

The Windows 9x Startup menu

Explanation

Normally, when you load Windows, the message "Starting Windows" appears and then the OS loads. However, you can force the menu to appear rather than the Starting Windows message by tapping the F8 key or holding down the Ctrl key during the boot.

Startup menu options

The Microsoft Windows 9x Startup menu options are:

1 Normal
2 Logged (\BOOTLOG.TXT)
3 Safe mode
4 Safe mode with network support
5 Step-by-step confirmation
6 Command prompt only
7 Safe mode command prompt only
8 Previous version of MS-DOS

We'll take a look at each of these options and describe what to expect when you select the option. Option 4 is displayed if the OS is configured for a network, and Option 8 is displayed if a previous version of DOS was retained during the Windows 9x installation.

Normal

In Msdos.sys, if BootGUI=1, then this option starts Windows 9x. If BootGUI=0, then this option will boot to the DOS 7.0 or DOS 7.1 prompt (the DOS core of Windows 9x). Either way, the commands in Autoexec.bat and Config.sys will be executed.

If a problem appears when you boot in normal mode, but does not appear when you boot in safe mode, then suspect that Config.sys, Autoexec.bat, System.ini, and Win.ini are the source of your problem. To eliminate Config.sys or Autoexec.bat as the source of the problem, boot using the step-by-step confirmation option on the Startup menu. To eliminate Win.ini or System.ini as the source of the problem, use the following procedure:

1   Change the name of the System.ini file in the Windows folder to System.sav.

2   Find the System.cb file in the Windows folder and make a copy of it. Rename the copy System.ini. Do not rename the original System.cb file because you may need it at another time.

3   In the [boot] section of the System.ini file, add this line and then save the file:

```
mouse.drv=mouse.drv
drivers=mmsystem.dll
```

4   Change the name of the Win.ini file in the Windows folder to Win.sav.

5   Restart your computer.

If this works, the problem was in the Win.ini or System.ini files, and you can reexamine these files in detail to determine the exact source of the problem.

Note: If your mouse stops working when you copy the System.cb file and rename it to System.ini, add the following lines in the specified sections of the new System.ini file:

```
[boot]
mouse.drv=mouse.drv
[386Enh]
mouse=*vmouse, msmouse.vxd
```

Logged (\BOOTLOG.TXT)

This option is the same as Normal, except that Windows 9x tracks the load and startup activities and logs them to the Bootlog.txt file. A portion of a sample Bootlog.txt file is shown in Exhibit 5-4. Notice that this file contains information about which components were loaded successfully and which ones were not. This file can be a helpful tool when troubleshooting.

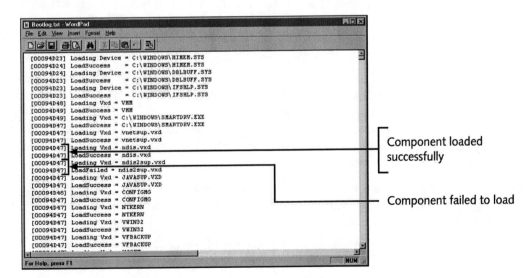

Exhibit 5-4: The Bootlog.txt file

Safe mode

When you are having problems with the Windows 9x boot process but no error message appears during the boot, you can use safe mode to troubleshoot the problems. You can reach safe mode either from the Startup menu or by pressing F5 while Windows is loading. Exhibit 5-5 shows Windows 98 booted into safe mode. Safe mode does not execute entries in the registry, Config.sys, Autoexec.bat, and the [Boot] and [386Enh] sections of System.ini. Also, when you enter safe mode, Windows 98/ME includes support for networks, but Windows 95 does not.

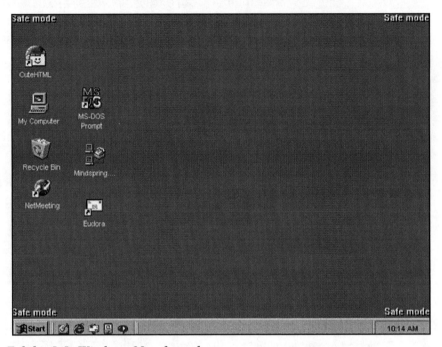

Exhibit 5-5: Windows 98 safe mode

Safe mode starts Windows 9x with a minimum default configuration to give you an opportunity to correct an error in the configuration. For example, if you selected a video driver that is incompatible with your system, when Windows 9x starts, it detects the problem and enters safe mode with a standard VGA driver selected. You can then go to Device Manager, select the correct driver, and restart Windows.

From the Startup menu, you can choose to enter safe mode yourself if you know of a problem you want to correct. For example, if you have previously selected a group of background and foreground colors that makes it impossible to read the screens, you can reboot and choose safe mode. Safe mode gives you the standard color scheme along with the VGA mode. Go to Display Properties, make the necessary corrections, and reboot.

Sometimes you will use safe mode for troubleshooting when you don't know exactly what the problem is. In that situation, once you are in safe mode, use the following checklist:

- Use a current version of antivirus software to scan for a virus.
- Sometimes loading in safe mode is all that is needed. Try to reboot the PC in normal mode.

- If the Safe Recovery dialog box appears, select the option of Use Safe Recovery. Windows 9x will then attempt to recover from previous boot problems. Try to boot again.

- If you were having problems with a device installation before the Windows failure, disable or remove the device in Device Manager. Reboot after disabling each device that you suspect to be a problem.

- If you have just made configuration changes, undo the changes and reboot.

- Look for real-mode drivers or TSRs (programs loaded in Config.sys, Autoexec.bat, or System.ini) that might be causing a problem and disable them by inserting a semicolon or a REM at the beginning of the command line. (Config.sys needs REM only. Use a semicolon for System.ini.)

- Try to boot again. If the problem is still not solved, restore the registry. For Windows 95, overwrite System.dat with System.da0 and User.dat with User.da0 after making backups of these files. For Windows 98/ME, use ScanReg to restore the registry from backups.

- Run ScanDisk to repair errors on the hard drive and optimize the drive. While in safe mode, choose Start, Programs, Accessories, System Tools, ScanDisk. Under Type of Test, select Thorough. (See Exhibit 5-6.)

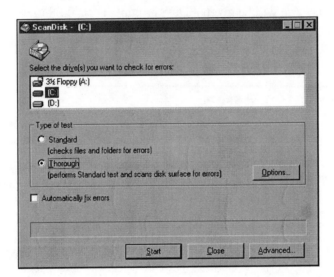

Exhibit 5-6: Use ScanDisk to check the hard drive for errors

- Run the Defragmenter utility to optimize the drive.

- For Windows 98/ME, run System File Checker to verify system files.

- For Windows 98/ME, run the Automatic Skip Driver Agent to skip the loading of any driver that is causing a problem. Reboot and examine the Asd.log file for recorded errors.

- For Windows 98/ME, use the System Configuration Utility to further reduce the system to essentials and reboot. If the problem goes away, restore one item at a time until the problem returns so as to identify the item that is the source of the problem.

- Using Explorer, search for files in system folders that have changed recently. To sort file and folder names by date last modified using Explorer, click Modified. To reverse the sort order, hold down the Ctrl key while clicking Modified. If software or drivers have been installed recently, suspect that they might be the source of the problem.

Safe mode with network support

This option allows you access to the network when booting into safe mode. It's useful if Windows 95 is stored on a network server and you need to download changes to your PC in safe mode.

To eliminate the network connection as a source of a boot problem that you're troubleshooting, first boot in safe mode without network support and then boot in safe mode with network support. If the boot without network support is successful but the boot with network support gives errors, then you can suspect that the network drivers might be the source of the problem. For Windows 98/ME, disable the network card in Device Manager to eliminate the network drivers as the source of the problem.

Step-by-step confirmation

This option asks for confirmation before executing each command in Io.sys, Config.sys, and Autoexec.bat. You can accomplish the same thing by pressing Shift+F8 when the message Starting Windows 95/98 appears.

Command prompt only

This option executes the contents of Autoexec.bat and Config.sys but doesn't start Windows 9x. You will be given a DOS prompt. Type WIN to load Windows 9x. This command executes the file Win.com. There are several switches you can use with the WIN command when troubleshooting the OS. The following table shows these switches:

Command switches	Purpose
WIN /D:M	Starts Windows in safe mode. Excludes all upper memory addresses from real mode drivers.
WIN /D:S	Turns off 32-bit disk access; use this option if there appears to be a problem with hard drive access. Specifies that Windows should not use ROM address space between F000:0000 and 1 MB for a break point. Equivalent to System.ini file setting: SystemROMBreakPoint=FALSE.
WIN /D:V	Instructs Windows not to use memory address F000:0, which is used by BIOS. Specifies that the ROM routine will handle interrupts from the hard disk controller. Equivalent to System.ini file setting: VirtualHDIRQ=FALSE.
WIN /D:X	Instructs Windows that the system BIOS should be used to access the hard drive rather than the OS. Excludes all of the adapter area from the range of memory that Windows scans to find unused space. Equivalent to System.ini file setting: EMMExclude=A000-FFFF.
WIN /D:F	Turns off 32-bit disk access. Equivalent to System.ini file setting: 32BitDiskAccess=FALSE.
WIN /D:N	Enables safe mode with networking.

In a troubleshooting situation, try each switch until you get one that works. You can then identify the source of the problem and can sometimes put entries in the System.ini file to make the switch a permanent part of the load.

Safe mode command prompt only

This option does not execute the commands in Autoexec.bat or Config.sys. You will be given a DOS prompt.

Previous version of MS-DOS

This option loads a previous version of DOS if one is present. You can get the same results by pressing F4 when the message Starting Windows 95/98 appears. This option is not available in Windows 98 SE or Windows ME.

Troubleshooting with the Startup menu

If you have tried using the previous tools, but have not yet identified the source of the problem, use the following checklist to troubleshoot using the Startup menu:

- Try a hard boot. A soft boot might not do the trick, because TSRs are not always "kicked out" of RAM with a soft boot.

- If you have not already done so, try safe mode next.

- Next, try the Step-by-step confirmation option. Look for error messages caused by a missing or corrupted driver file. Try not allowing real-mode drivers to load. Once the problem command within Autoexec.bat or Config.sys is identified, you can eliminate the command or troubleshoot it.

- Use the Logged option next and examine the Bootlog.txt file that is created to see if it identifies the problem.

- Try booting by using the Command prompt only option. From the command prompt, run the real-mode version of ScanDisk, which you will find in the `\Windows\Command folder`, to scan the hard drive for errors. From a command prompt, enter this command: `C:\Windows\Command\Scandisk`. If the Scandisk.exe program on the hard drive is corrupted, use the one on the emergency startup disk.

- For Windows 98/ME, from the command prompt, type Scanreg/Fix and try to reboot.

- For Windows 98/ME, from the command prompt, next type Scanreg/Restore and select the latest known good backup of the Windows 9x registry. Try to reboot.

- From the command prompt, you can use the WIN command with the switches that you saw in the previous table. If one of these commands solves the problem, look for real-mode drivers that might be in conflict, eliminating those that you can. Examine Bootlog.txt for errors and try booting from safe mode again.

- Try booting with the safe mode command prompt only. Remember that when you are in safe mode, the registry is not executed. If you suspect a corrupted registry, restore it to its last saved version. Then try the WIN command, with or without the switches, as necessary.

Using the startup disk for troubleshooting

If you cannot solve the boot problems you are experiencing by using the troubleshooting utilities within Windows or on the Startup menu, use an emergency startup disk to recover from the failed boot.

If you don't have an emergency startup disk, create one on another computer and use it to work with the computer that is having the problem. Before using the startup disk, it's a good idea to check it for viruses on a working computer by scanning it with antivirus software. If you find a virus on the emergency startup disk, destroy the disk and use a working computer to create a new one.

To use the emergency startup disk, place it in the floppy disk drive and turn on the PC. It will boot to a Startup menu or to an A: prompt, depending on the version of Windows 9x you are using. Exhibit 5-7 shows the Startup menu.

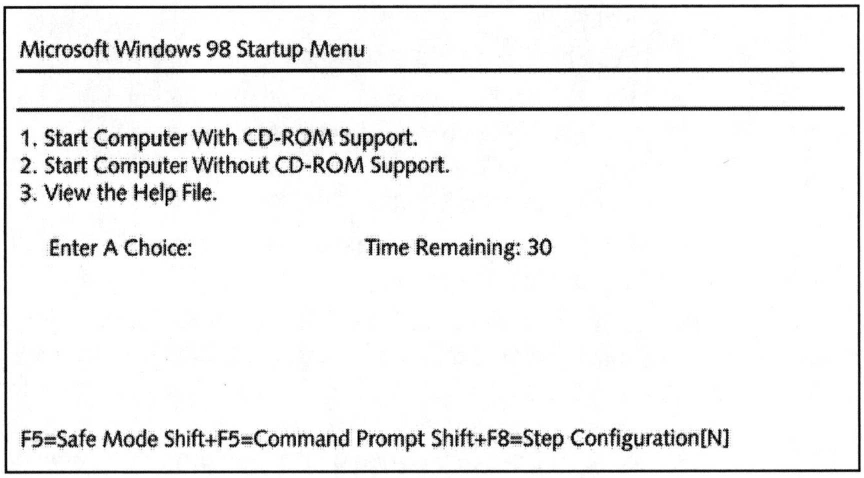

```
Microsoft Windows 98 Startup Menu


1. Start Computer With CD-ROM Support.
2. Start Computer Without CD-ROM Support.
3. View the Help File.

    Enter A Choice:                Time Remaining: 30




F5=Safe Mode Shift+F5=Command Prompt Shift+F8=Step Configuration[N]
```

Exhibit 5-7: Windows 98 rescue disk Startup menu

If you are using a version for which the startup disk boots to a menu, select the first option, which is to start the PC with CD-ROM support. The OS will then examine the system for problems and then provide an A prompt where you can enter commands.

If the system has failed to boot from the hard drive, the first step in troubleshooting at this point is to see if you can access the hard drive. To do that, enter DIR C: at the A prompt. If this step works, then the problem lies in the software that is used on the hard drive to boot, including the OS boot record, OS hidden files, and command interface files. If you cannot access the hard drive, the problem is with the partition table, the Master Boot Record, hard drive, its cabling, or its power source. In this case, you need to examine the hard drive for errors.

Use Fdisk to examine the partition table. If the table is corrupted, most likely you have lost everything on your hard drive. You can try to use the Fdisk /MBR command to restore the Master Boot Record on the drive. If this doesn't work, you can try to create new partitions on the drive and format the drive. All data and software on the drive will be lost. If you cannot use Fdisk on the drive, treat the problem as a hardware problem.

Note: The lack of access to a hard drive does not necessarily indicate that all data is lost, but also note that at some point you have to recognize the need to abandon recovery efforts.

After you have completed troubleshooting the hard drive, eliminating physical problems with the hard drive subsystem, CMOS, and the partition table, the next step is to run the Windows 9x Setup program. When given the opportunity, select Verify installed components. Setup will then restore damaged or missing system files.

Do it!

B-2:   Using the Windows 9x Startup menu

Here's how	Here's why
1 Press (F8)	After your system displays the message "Starting Windows 95/98" during the boot process.
Select **Logged(\Bootlog.txt)**	
2 Open Bootlog.txt	After the boot is complete.
Print out its contents	
3 Shut down Windows	
Reboot the system	
Press (F8)	
4 Select the **Safe Mode** option	
Record the differences in the screen's appearance	
5 Shut down Windows	
Reboot the computer	
Choose **Step-by-step confirmation**	
Press (F8)	
6 Write down each command that executes	

Topic C: The Windows 9x registry

Explanation

In supporting and troubleshooting Windows 9x, you need to understand the role of the registry and .ini files. The registry is a database of configuration information and settings for users, hardware, applications and the OS. Starting with Windows 9x, the registry takes over the essential functions of .ini files.

However, Windows 9x still supports .ini files for compatibility with Windows 3.x and legacy software and hardware devices. Entries that 16-bit Windows applications make in Win.ini and System.ini are not added to the registry because these applications cannot access the registry. Entries made in .ini files by applications that can access the registry are copied into the registry. In this topic, you will examine how the registry is organized, what kinds of information are in the registry, how and why you might edit the registry, and how to recover from a corrupted registry.

How the registry is organized

The registry organizes information in a hierarchical database that has a tree-like, top-to-bottom design. The Windows 9x System.ini file contains setup parameters. Refer to Exhibit 5-2, which shows a portion of the System.ini file. Notice that section names appear in square brackets, key names to the left of the equal signs, and values assigned to these key names to the right of the equal signs. The Windows 9x registry takes on a similar design, but enhances it by allowing for keys to cascade to several levels on the tree. Exhibit 5-8 shows a portion of a Windows 9x registry. Consider names on the left of the window as similar to section names in System.ini; these names are called *keys* by Windows 9x. On the right of the window are value names, such as ScreenSaveTime, and to the right of each name is the *value data* assigned to that name, such as 60. The value names, called values by Windows 9x, are similar to the key names in System.ini, and the value data are similar to the values assigned to key names in System.ini.

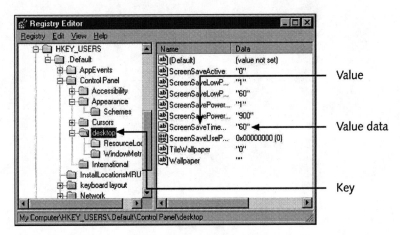

Exhibit 5-8: Structure of the Windows 9x registry

The registry is organized into six major keys, or branches, which are listed in the following table. The registry is contained in two files, System.dat and User.dat, located in the Windows directory as hidden, read-only, system files, although the information forms only a single database:

Key	Description
HKEY_CLASSES_ROOT	Contains information about file associations and OLE data. (This branch of the tree is a mirror of HKEY_LOCAL_MACHINE\ Software\Classes.)
HKEY_USERS	Includes user preferences, including desktop configuration and network connections.
HKEY_CURRENT_USER	If there is only one user of the system, this is a duplicate of HKEY_USERS, but for a multi-user system, this key contains information about the current user preferences.
HKEY_LOCAL_MACHINE	Contains information about hardware and installed software.
HKEY_CURRENT_CONFIG	Contains the same information in HKEY_LOCAL_MACHINE\Config and has information about printers and display fonts.
HKEY_DYN_DATA	Keeps information about Windows performance and plug and play information.

Do it!

C-1: Examining the Windows 95 registry

Here's how	Here's why
1 Examine the Windows 95 registry	To determine if your version of Windows 95 includes support for USB devices.
2 Look in the registry for these two values:	To determine the installed version of the OS.

```
HKEY_LOCAL_MACHINE\SOFTWARE\Microsoft\Windows\▶
   CurrentVersion\Version
```

```
HKEY_LOCAL_MACHINE\SOFTWARE\Microsoft\Windows\▶
   CurrentVersion\VersionNumber
```

OSR 2 with the USB update has
the version and version number:

```
Version "Windows 95" and Version Number "4.03.1212" or▶
   "4.03.1214."
```

3 Print your screen showing the
values for your PC

4 Record whether you have the
USB support installed

Recovering from a corrupted registry

Explanation

Windows 95 has a way to recover from a corrupted registry that is different from the method used by Windows 98/ME. These methods are discussed next.

Windows 95 backup of the registry

Windows 95 maintains a backup copy of the two registry files called System.da0 and User.da0. Each time Windows 95 boots successfully, it makes a backup copy of these two files. If Windows 95 has trouble loading and must start in safe mode, it does not back up the registry.

If Windows 95 does not find a System.dat file when it starts, it automatically replaces it with the backup System.da0. If both System.dat and User.dat are missing, or if the WinDir= command is missing in Msdos.sys, Windows 9x tells you that the registry files are missing and starts in safe mode. It then displays the Registry Problem dialog box. Click the Restore From Backup and Restart buttons. The registry files are restored from System.da0 and User.da0. If these files are also missing, the registry cannot easily be restored. You can either restore the files from your own backups or run Windows 9x Setup. Another option is to look for the file System.1st in the root directory of the hard drive. This is the System.dat file created when Windows 9x was first installed. In an emergency, you can revert to this file.

Windows 98/ME Registry Checker

Windows 98/ME offers a utility called the Registry Checker, which is not available with Windows 95. It automatically backs up the registry each day, and by default, it keeps the last five days of backups. In an emergency, you can recover the registry from one of these backups. You can also tell Registry Checker to make an additional backup on demand, such as when you have just made changes to the registry and want to back up these changes before you make new changes.

To access Registry Checker, choose Start, Programs, Accessories, System Tools, System Information. The Microsoft System Information window opens. (See Exhibit 5-9.) From the menu bar, choose Tools, Registry Checker. Registry Checker tells you if the registry is corrupted and will fix it, if allowed. You can also create a new backup at this time.

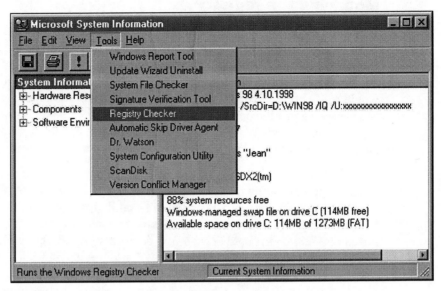

Exhibit 5-9: Accessing the Registry Checker

Backups are kept in cabinet files in the \Windows\Sysbckup folder as rb001.cab, rb002.cab, and so on. To revert to one of these backups, you must first be in MS-DOS mode. For Windows ME, boot from a bootable disk. For Windows 98, boot from a bootable disk or boot to an MS-DOS prompt from the Windows 98 Startup menu (Windows ME does not have this option on the Startup menu). From the MS-DOS prompt (not a DOS box within a Windows session), use the commands in the following table to repair or recover the registry:

Command	Purpose
Scanreg /Restore	Restores the registry from a previous backup. A screen is displayed asking you which backup to use.
Scanreg /Fix	Repairs the corrupted registry. If the problem is inherent to the registry itself, this might work. If the problem is that you want to undo a successful change to the registry, then use the Restore option instead.
Scanreg /Backup	Creates a new backup of the registry at the DOS prompt. Don't do this if the registry is giving you problems.
Scanreg /Opt	Optimizes the registry. ScanReg will look for and delete information in the registry that is no longer used. This reduces the size of the registry, which might speed up booting.
Scanreg /?	Help feature of ScanReg.

Modifying the registry

When you make a change in Control Panel or Device Manager or many other places in Windows 9x, such as when you install software, the registry is modified automatically. For most users, this is the only way they will ever change the registry. However, there are rare occasions when you might need to edit the registry manually. One example would be if you accidentally deleted the device driver for a hardware device but Device Manager says that the device is still installed. Another example would be if the wrong software starts when Windows 9x is loaded and you cannot correct the problem by changing the Startup folder. Both these problems can be corrected by manually editing the registry.

The first step in editing the registry is to back up the two files System.dat and User.dat. Sometimes the files are small enough to fit on floppy disks and can be copied by using Windows Explorer. If the files are too large to copy to a floppy disk, copy them to a different folder on the hard drive or use compression software such as PKZIP to copy them to floppy disks. For Windows 98/ME, use Registry Checker to back up the registry. Third-party utility software such as Norton Utilities (www.symantec.com) has a registry editor that allows for backing up the registry before entering the editor. The following directions use the Windows 9x Regedit utility to edit the registry.

After backing up the registry files, the next step is to use Regedit.exe, located in the Windows folder. You can use Windows Explorer to locate the file, then double-click it, or you can choose Start, Run, and type Regedit in the Run dialog box. When you do, the Registry Editor window opens, as shown in Exhibit 5-10. Open one branch of the tree by clicking on the + sign to the left of the key, and close the branch by clicking on the - sign.

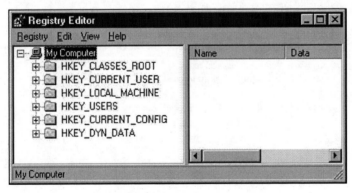

Exhibit 5-10: The six major keys of the registry, as seen in the Registry Editor

To search for an entry in the registry, choose Edit, and then click Find. The Find dialog box is displayed, as shown in Exhibit 5-11, which is ready to find the text "software" in the registry. Enter the key, the value, or the value data, and then click Find Next. You can choose to search keys, values, and/or value data by clicking on the check boxes in the dialog box.

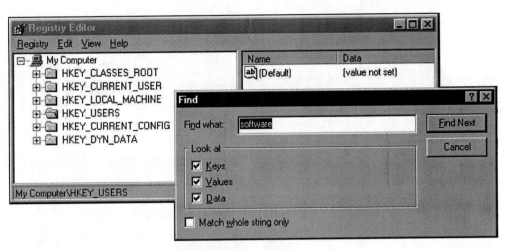

Exhibit 5-11: Searching for entries in the register

For example, suppose that the wrong programs start when you load Windows 9x. First, try to correct the problem without editing the registry. Use Windows Explorer to open the C:\\Windows\All Users\Start Menu\Programs\StartUp folder. Delete any items that you don't want to start when you load Windows. If this does not correct the problem, the problem might be caused by a wrong entry recorded in the registry. Try editing the registry.

First locate Shell Folders, which will be in the following branch: HKEY_CURRENT_ USER\Software\Microsoft\Windows\CurrentVersion\Explorer\Shell Folders. Search for these keys and subkeys one at a time. (Search for HKEY_CURRENT_USER. After you have located it, search for Software, and continue through the list until you come to Shell Folders.)

The value name Startup= in the Shell Folders subkey should be "C:\Windows\Start Menu\Programs\Startup." If the data is incorrect, you can right-click Startup and select Modify from the shortcut menu. Exhibit 5-12 shows the Edit String dialog box that is displayed. Change the value data and then click OK.

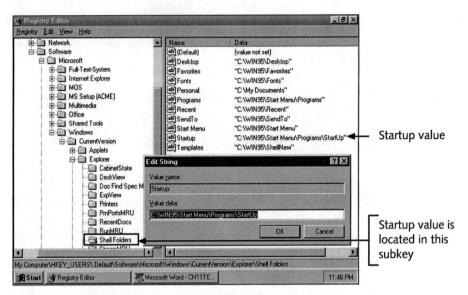

Exhibit 5-12: Editing an entry in the register by using Regedit.exe

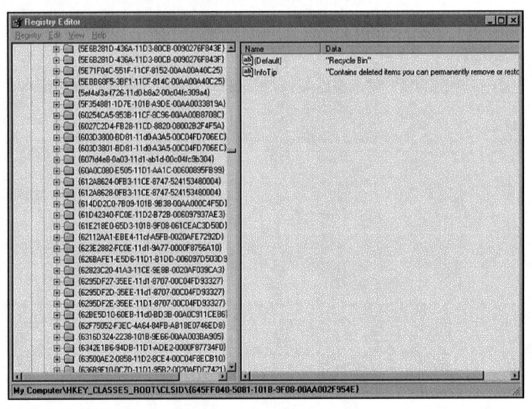

Exhibit 5-13: The Windows registry

Do it!

C-2: Saving, modifying, and restoring the registry

Here's how	Here's why
1 Choose **Start**, **Run**	(On the taskbar.) You'll back up the registry.
Type **scanreg**	
Click **OK**	The Windows Registry Checker utility opens. You might see an MS-DOS prompt briefly and a message indicating that the registry has already been backed up. This is because, once a day by default, the registry is backed up the first time Windows successfully starts.
2 Click **Yes**	To back up the registry again.
3 Click **OK**	(After the backup is complete.) To close the Windows Registry Checker. Windows, by default, stores the last five copies of the registry in the windows\backup folder.
4 Open Windows Explorer	
Locate windows\sysbackup folder	
Determine the name of the backup you just created	By checking the date and time that the file was created.
Record the name, date, and time of this file	
5 Right-click **My Computer**	(On your desktop.) You'll modify the registry.
Verify that the shortcut menu gives you the option of renaming this icon	
6 Right-click **Recycle Bin**	
Verify that the shortcut menu does not give you the option of renaming this icon	In order to rename it, you would have to install and use a special Microsoft utility, named TweekUI, which allows you to make some special changes to Windows.
7 Choose **Start**, **Run**	On the taskbar.
Type **regedit**	
Click **OK**	The Registry Editor opens, displaying the system registry hierarchy in the left pane and any entries for the selected registry item in the right pane.

8	Collapse the registry keys	(To ensure you are searching the entire registry.) You'll find the section governing the Recycle Bin.
	Choose **Edit**, **Find**	On the menu bar.
9	Type **Recycle Bin**	In the search field.
	Notice that you can narrow your search further by limiting which items to search	
	What four ways can you further define your search?	
10	Click **Find Next**	To begin searching the registry.
	What is the first instance of Recycle Bin shown in the right pane?	
11	Press ⌨F3	To find the next instance. The right pane of your Registry Editor should display the two items shown in Exhibit 5-13.
12	Double-click the **Default** entry	The Edit String dialog box opens.
13	Replace "Recycle Bin" with **Trash**	In the Value data field.
	Click **OK**	
14	Verify that "Trash" has replaced "Recycle Bin"	In the right pane.
15	Double-click the **Info Tip** entry	You'll edit the Info Tip for the Recycle Bin.
	Type **This used to be named Recycle Bin**	
	Click **OK**	
16	Note the change in the right pane	
	Close Registry Editor	
17	Choose **Registry**, **Exit**	In the menu bar. Notice that you are not prompted to save the changes to the registry—the changes were saved the instant you made them. This is why editing the registry is so unforgiving. There are no safeguards. You can't undo your work by choosing to exit without saving changes, as you can, for instance, in Microsoft Word.

18 Right-click the desktop

Choose **Refresh**   In the shortcut menu.

Verify that the Recycle Bin icon is
now named "Trash."

19 Move the mouse pointer over the   The new Info Tip appears.
Trash icon

20 Restart **Windows**   You'll restore the previous version of the
registry.

During the boot process, hold   To activate the Startup menu.
down the (CTRL) key

21 Select   (In the Startup menu.) A command prompt
Command Prompt Only   appears.

22 Enter **scanreg**   The Microsoft Registry Checker starts.

23 Press (↵ ENTER)   (To start a registry scan to check for a corrupted
registry.) The Microsoft Registry Checker will
not usually find errors if the registry has been
correctly modified via the Registry Editor. Thus,
assuming you performed the steps in this lab
correctly, the Microsoft Registry Checker will
not find any errors. However, if the Microsoft
Registry Checker detects any corruption in the
registry, it will offer to repair it.

24 Select **View Backups**   After the scan is complete.

Restore the most current saved   By using your knowledge about the registry.
state

25 How often does Windows
automatically save the registry?

26 Where are registry backups
usually stored?

27 What type of safeguards does the
Registry Editor provide to keep
you from making mistakes?

28 What files constitute the registry?
As what type of file are they
saved during backup?

29 In the previous example, how did
you check to make sure that your
registry was restored?

Topic D: Maintenance and troubleshooting tools

Explanation

Windows 9x offers several tools, some of which are listed in the following table, to monitor and improve system performance, control the OS, and to help with troubleshooting. Several of the major tools are covered in this topic:

Tool & file name	Location	Description	Win 95	Win 98/ME
Automatic Skip Driver Agent Asd.exe	\Windows	Automatically skips drivers that prevent Windows from loading and records problems encountered in the log file Asd.log. To run, select Automatic Skip Driver Agent from the Tools menu of the System Information window.		X
Microsoft System Information MSInfo32.exe	\Program Files \Common files \Microsoft shared \Msinfo	Displays system information, including installed hardware and device drivers. To run, choose Start, Programs, Accessories, System Tools, System Information or type Msinfo32.exe in the Run dialog box.	X	X
Hardware Diagnostic tool Hwinfo.exe		Displays the same information as System Information, but in text form. Enter hwinfo/ui in the Run dialog box.		X
Registry Checker Scanreg.exe	\Windows \Command	Backs up, verifies, and recovers the Registry. To run, select Registry Checker from the Tools menu of the System Information window.		X
Windows Update Iexplore.exe	www.microsoft.com /windowsupdate	Download service packs (fixes) for Windows from the Microsoft Web site.	X	X
System options	In Control Panel	Several applets in Control Panel can be used in monitoring and tweaking system performance.	X	X
System Configuration Utility Msconfig	\Windows\System	Allows you to modify the system configuration to help with troubleshooting. To run, select System Configuration Utility from the menu Tools of the System Information window or type Msconfig in the Run dialog box.	X	X
System File Checker Sfc.exe	\Windows\System	Verifies system files. This tool scans for changed, deleted, or corrupted system files and restores them from the originals on the Windows CD-ROM. To run, select System File Checker from the Tools menu of the System Information window.	X	X
System Monitor Sysmon.exe	\Windows	System Monitor tracks the performance of some important system components. To run, click Start, Programs, Accessories, System Tools, System Monitor.		X

Tool & file name	Location	Description	Win 95	Win 98/ME
Microsoft Backup Msbackup.exe	\Program Files \Accessories \Backup	Backs up files and folders to prevent loss when your hard drive fails. To run, choose Start, Programs, Accessories, System Tools, Backup.	X	X
System Recovery pcrestor.bat	On the Windows 98/ME CD in \Tools\Sysrec	Uses a full system backup created by Microsoft Backup to reinstall Windows and restore the system to its state as of the last backup.		X
Dr. Watson Drwatson.exe	\Windows	Traps errors in log files created by applications and takes a snapshot of the system to use for troubleshooting.		X
Schedule Task Wizard Mstask.exe	\Windows\System	Schedule tasks such as MS Backup to run at predetermined times.	X	X
Version Conflict Manager Vcmui.exe	\Windows	Installs Windows files over a newer file that might be in the\Windows folder and subfolders.		X
System Configuration Editor Sysedit.exe	\Windows\System	Text editor to edit files that configure how Windows loads. To run it, enter Sysedit.exe in the Run dialog box. Sysedit automatically opens Protocol.ini, System.ini, Win.ini, Config.sys and Autoexec.bat for editing.	X	X
Task Manager Taskman.exe	\Windows	Run, switchm and end applications, and access the Shutdown menu. To run it, type Taskman in the Run dialog box.	X	X
Signature Verification Tool sigverif.exe	\Windows	Checks system drivers for digital signatures given them by Microsoft, which ensures they have been tested by Microsoft. To run it, use the System Information window.		X
Digital Signature Check	N/A	Identifies drivers that have been digitally signed by Microsoft to verify their integrity. To use it, enable this key in the registry: HKEY_LOCAL_MACHINE\ Software\Microsoft\Driver Signing.		X

As the previous table shows, some tools are available only with Windows 98/ME. Many of these tools are accessed from the Microsoft System Information window. To access this window, choose Start, Programs, Accessories, System Tools, and then click System Information. The dialog box illustrated in Exhibit 5-14 opens. The System Information utility is available under Windows 95, but does not include the tools listed in the previous table.

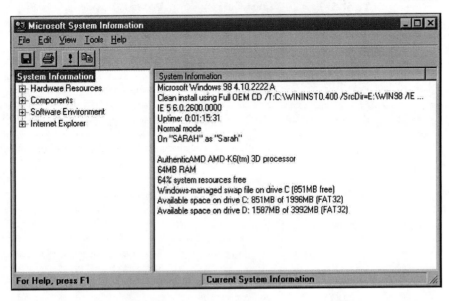

Exhibit 5-14: The System Information window

Note: Windows ME gives a different interface (more "Web" like) for displaying system information. In Windows ME, the capability of sorting on numerous attributes is available.

One tool that is available from the System Information window is the System File Checker, which is illustrated in Exhibit 5-15. To use the utility to restore damaged Windows system files, click Tools on the System Information window and then select System File Checker.

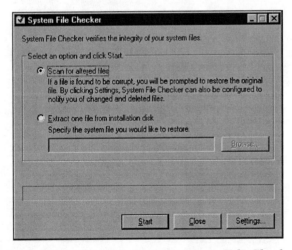

Exhibit 5-15: The Windows 98 System File Checker verifies system files

The same information displayed by the System Information tool can be displayed in text format by using the Hardware Diagnostic tool (Hwinfo.exe). You can use the tool by typing `hwinfo /ui` in the Windows Run dialog box. The Hardware Info window reports information about hardware devices, including drivers used, keys from the registry and how they are used, configuration information, and error and warning information. You can sort and filter the report so that only information about devices with problems is listed.

System applet in Control Panel

To access the System applet in Control Panel, double-click the System icon. The applet offers several tools for performance monitoring and troubleshooting. For example, the Performance tab in Exhibit 5-16 shows a performance report from two computers, one in need of performance tuning and one running at optimal performance. Key messages to look for on this screen (see Exhibit 5-16) are "Some drives are using MS-DOS compatibility" under File System, and "MS-DOS compatibility mode" under Virtual Memory. These messages mean that real-mode drivers are being used, which can slow down performance, especially when used with hard drive access. Exhibit 5-16 indicates that both these components are using 32-bit protected-mode drivers.

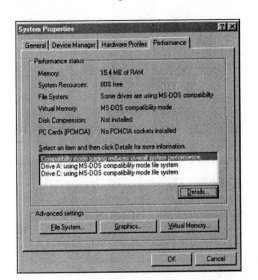 

Exhibit 5-16: The System Properties Performance tab

Whenever you see MS-DOS mode (real mode) drivers being used, see that these drivers are replaced with 32-bit protected-mode drivers. One important tool to use for this process is the file Ios.ini, a text file that contains the Windows 9x Safe Driver List. Windows 9x uses this list to determine if it can safely substitute a protected-mode driver for a real-mode one. Also, if it attempts to make the substitution but fails, it often records the problem in another file, Ios.log. Check this file for information about the problem.

If a real-mode driver is being used, and you believe that a protected-mode driver should be used in its place, first check Ios.log for any error messages. If you don't find an error message, add the real-mode driver name to the safe driver list in the Ios.ini file. Anything following the semicolon on the line is a *comment*. You can also use REM to comment out a line.

Sample lines in the Ios.ini file are:

```
[SafeList]
386max.sys  ;  Qualitas
extrados.pro;  Qualitas Memory Manager
extrados.max;  Qualitas Memory Manager
4dos.com    ;  4DOS shell program
ad-dos.com  ;  Afterdark
ad-wrap.com ;  Afterdark
adi2.com    ;  Afterdark
aspi3x70.sys;  DTC SCSI driver
```

If you're using third-party disk compression software, such as Stacker, make sure to use a 32-bit version of the software. When converting from Windows 3.x to Windows 9x, also upgrade Stacker. If you are still using a 16-bit version of the software, most often an error message about the problem can be found in Ios.log.

System Monitor

System Monitor allows you to monitor how system resources are being used by applications. It can monitor the file system, memory, the kernel, printer sharing services, and network performance data. System Monitor is not automatically installed in a typical installation.

To install System Monitor, open the Control Panel, and double-click Add/Remove Programs. Click Windows Setup, and then select Accessories. To run System Monitor, choose Start, Programs, Accessories, System Tools, System Monitor.

Exhibit 5-17 shows System Monitor tracking the kernel and disk cache hits and misses. Under the File menu, you can add and delete items the monitor is tracking. Use System Monitor to help determine if an application is using an inordinate amount of resources or has a memory leak. A *memory leak* occurs when you exit software and it unloads from memory, but it does not release the memory addresses that it was using for its data back to the OS. Memory leaks can occur when software is corrupted, poorly written, or plagued with a virus. You notice memory leaks when your system gets sluggish after you have launched and exited an application several times before rebooting the system. A reboot releases all memory addresses.

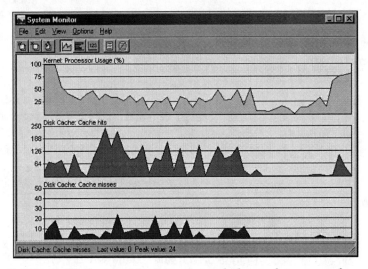

Exhibit 5-17: System Monitor can track the performance of several system resources

System Configuration Utility

Similar to loading Windows in safe mode, the System Configuration Utility (Msconfig.exe) reduces the startup process to its essentials. If starting Windows in this condition eliminates the problem you are troubleshooting, you can use this utility to add items back one at a time until the problem occurs; the source of the problem is related to the last item you added.

To use the utility, do the following:

1 Choose Start, Programs, Accessories, System Tools, System Information. The Microsoft System Information window opens. (See Exhibit 5-9.)

2 From the Tools menu, choose System Configuration Utility. The System Configuration Utility dialog box opens, as in Exhibit 5-18. Another way to access the utility is to type Msconfig in the Run dialog box.

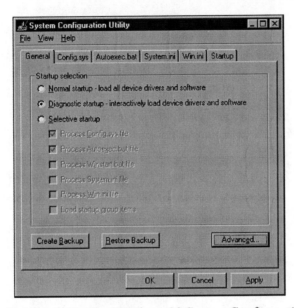

Exhibit 5-18: The Windows 98 System Configuration Utility

3 To diagnose a problem, select Diagnostic startup - interactively load device drivers and software, and then click OK to restart your computer.

4 If this solves the problem, then the clean start was successful. Next, select Selective startup from the screen shown in Exhibit 5-18 and methodically select first one item and then another to restore, until the problem reappears. Begin by restoring all entries in Autoexec.bat and Config.sys, to determine if real-mode drivers and programs loaded from these files are the source of the problem.

5 If the problem still occurs, even with the clean boot, then try these things:

- If you have not already done so, scan for a virus by using a current version of antivirus software.

- Use Registry Checker to check for corrupted system files.

- Use System File Checker to check for corrupted system files.

- Check the CMOS setup screen for wrong settings.

Do it!

D-1:   Modifying system configuration files

Here's how	Here's why
1 Open a command prompt window	You'll edit Msdos.sys using the text editor Edit.com.
2 Enter the following command: `attrib -h -s -r C:\msdos.sys`	 To remove the hidden, system, and read-only status from the Msdos.sys file.
3 Enter **Edit C:\msdos.sys**	The Msdos.sys configuration file opens in the command prompt window. Msdos.sys can be modified to control where Windows files are located and how Windows boots. The [Paths] section indicates on what drive, and in which directory, Windows system files can be found. The [Options] section controls how Window boots.
4 Notice the remarks (or comment lines), which begin with a semicolon	Indicating that extra characters have been added in order to ensure that Msdos.sys is greater than 1,024 bytes in size.
5 Locate the line Boot GUI=1	You can think of the 1 as meaning yes and the 0 as meaning no. Thus, this line tells the system to load a graphical user interface (also known as a GUI).
Change 1 to 0	So that it reads: Boot GUI =0.
What are you instructing the system to do the next time it boots?	
6 Press and release ALT	To activate the menu options in the edit utility that you are using from within the command prompt window.
7 Press F	To activate the File menu.
8 Press S	To save the file.
9 Press and release ALT	
Press F	To access the File menu.
Press X	To exit the edit utility.

10 Enter **exit**   To close the command prompt window.

11 Restart Windows

Describe what happens

Was your prediction from Step 5
accurate?

12 Open a command prompt window   You'll make another change to the Msdos.sys
                                                          file and observe the change.

Enter **edit msdos.sys**

13 Change the BootGUI entry to **=1**

14 Save your changes and exit

Close the command prompt
window

Reboot the system

Observe the boot process

What changed?

15 Open Msdos.sys for editing   To make a third change to the Msdos.sys file
                                                          and observe the change.

16 Place the insertion point under the   In the Doublebuffer line.
"D"

Press (↵ ENTER)

17 Press (↑)   To move the insertion point to the new blank
                                                          line.

Type **Logo=0**

What do you think you just
instructed the system to do?

18 Save your changes

Exit and close the command
prompt window

Reboot the system   Observing the boot process.

What changed?

19	Create a new user Test1 on your system	To practice working with files by using the Sysedit utility.
20	Restart your PC	You'll edit system files.
	Log in as **Test1**	
	Enter password	Windows creates a new user, Test1, making entries in the \Windows\System.ini file and creating a new password file in the Windows folder named Test1.pwl.
21	Log out as **Test1**	
	Log back in as another authorized user on the computer	By using your own name or whatever login you were using on the computer previously.
22	Choose **Start**, **Run**	On the taskbar.
	Type **sysedit**	To examine the Windows\system.ini file by using the System Configuration Utility.
	Click **OK**	The System Configuration Utility opens, displaying five files.
	List the files	
23	Activate the C:\windows\system.ini file window	To bring it to the front.
	Scroll down to the [Password Lists] section	
	Verify that in this section, you see an entry for each user account on this computer	
24	Delete the entry for Test1	By using the Delete or Backspace key.
25	Choose **File**, **Save**	(On the menu bar.) To save changes with the Windows\system.ini window selected.
26	Activate the Windows\win.ini file window	To examine the Win.ini file that is also opened by Sysedit.
27	Choose **Search**, **Find**	On the menu bar.

28 Type **colors**	In the Find dialog box.
Click **Next**	To display the [colors] section of the Windows\win.ini file with the word "colors" highlighted.
29 Press (F3)	To jump to the next instance of the word "colors."

Was there another instance of the word "colors"?

What message do you see?

30 Exit the System Configuration Utility

31 Log out

Log back in as **Test1**

32 Did you have to enter a password?

33 Did test1 show up in the users list?

34 What was the purpose of the Test1 entry in System.ini?

35 What utility can you use to modify the Msdos.sys file?

36 What is the minimum size of Msdos.sys in megabytes?

37 What are the five configuration files you can automatically edit with the System Configuration Utility?

38 Of the five files you listed in the previous question, which two are used by MS-DOS and Windows in real mode?

Security management tools

Explanation

There are several tools and methods in Windows 9x you can use to create, update, and use passwords and *user profiles*. These tools can be used to avoid or address problems caused by unauthorized access to certain machines or computer features.

User profiles

Windows 9x offers user profiles that allow the system to restore user preferences each time a user logs on to the system. A user profile can include software and hardware settings such as how the desktop is displayed, what shortcuts are on the desktop, and what printers or other hardware devices are available for a user. When several users use the same computer, user profiles can be a handy way for each user to keep individual settings. Also, on a network, a roaming profile follows the user from computer to computer on the network. User profiles can be collected into a *group profile* so that changes to the group profile affect all users assigned to that group.

There are many security advantages to having a different profile for each user. When you set a user profile, you also set a logon password that a user must type in when booting up the computer. Each user profile has a different logon password, and the settings of the profile can limit what files, folders, applications, and hardware devices the user has access to. In this way, you can limit what users can do on the PC and on the network. To create user profiles, open the Users applet in the Control Panel. The Multi-user Wizard will step you through the process.

Note: In a network environment, Windows 9x can use policy files to define user, network, and computer settings. A policy file has a .pol file extension; examples are Policy.pol and Config.pol. By using the System Policy Editor, a network administrator can create a policy file that affects the entire network, a group of users, or a single user on the network. The policy file can reside on the network server and is read when Windows 9x first boots. Entries in the policy file override entries in the Windows 9x registry, including those placed there by the User applet.

Screensaver passwords

Sometimes a user will leave his or her computer idle for a period of time, allowing the screensaver to activate. Setting a screensaver password prevents unauthorized users from accessing the computer logged in under an authorized user's profile while the authorized user is away. Once the screensaver password is set and the screensaver activates, you must enter the correct password to close the screensaver and return to the desktop and any open files and applications.

A screensaver password does not protect files on the system. Any user can reboot and access the hard drive without knowing a screensaver password.

To create a screensaver password, select the Screen Saver tab in the Display Properties window. Select a screensaver and check Password protected. To set the password, click the Change button and then enter and confirm a password. (See Exhibit 5-19.) Click OK to save your password and then click OK to exit the Display Properties window.

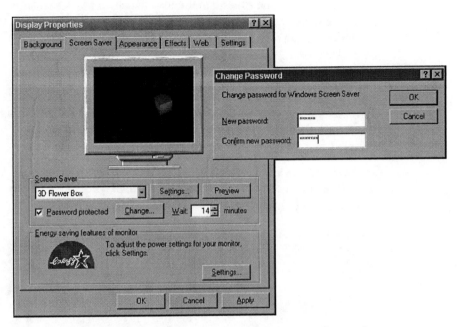

Exhibit 5-19: You must confirm a screensaver password to set it

Drive management tools

Earlier in the unit, you saw the tools ScanDisk and Defrag, both of which check and repair problems with a hard drive, listed as tools to use when troubleshooting the boot process. Defrag doesn't repair problems. It asks you to run ScanDisk if it encounters errors. You can also use these utilities when troubleshooting hard drive problems or even software problems that could be caused by an improperly running hard drive. Even when you're not having problems with your hard drive, it's a good idea to run these utilities occasionally to check the health of the drive and possibly avert future problems.

Defrag

Fragmentation is the undesirable placement of a single file in several cluster locations that are not right next to each other, so that data access time is increased. When a hard drive is new and freshly formatted, the OS writes files to the drive beginning with cluster 2, placing the data in consecutive clusters. Each new file begins with the next available cluster. Later, after a file has been deleted, the OS writes a new file to the drive, beginning with the first available cluster in the FAT. If the OS encounters used clusters as it is writing the file, it simply skips these clusters and uses the next available one. In this way, after many files have been deleted and added to the drive, files become fragmented.

Fragmentation occurs when files are written to a drive in more than one group of contiguous clusters. The clusters that make up a file are together called a *chain*. For a well-used hard drive, it is possible to have a file stored in clusters at 20, 30, 40, or more locations. Fragmentation is undesirable because (1) when the OS has to access many different locations on the drive to read a file, access time slows down, and (2) if the file should become corrupted, recovering a fragmented file is more complicated than recovering a file in one continuous chain.

For these reasons, one routine maintenance task is to periodically *defragment* the hard drive. Windows 9x includes a GUI version of the utility available from the Windows desktop. You can also use third-party software such as Norton Utilities. Regardless of the method used, you should defragment your hard drive every six months or so as part of a good maintenance plan.

Note: To see how badly a drive is fragmented, use Norton Utilities, Windows Disk Defragmenter, or another disk utility to view your FAT. Norton highlights the clusters for each file in a different color so you can easily identify all the clusters that belong to a single file.

To use Windows 9x Disk Defragmenter, choose Start, Programs, Accessories, System Tools. The menu shown in Exhibit 5-20 is displayed. (Two of the other menu items, ScanDisk and DriveSpace, will be discussed next.)

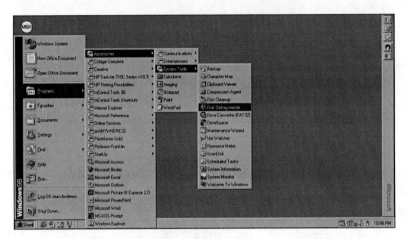

Exhibit 5-20: Windows 98 utilities

Click Disk Defragmenter and select the drive from the dialog box that is displayed. Click OK. When the operation is complete, the message in Exhibit 5-21 appears; click Yes to exit.

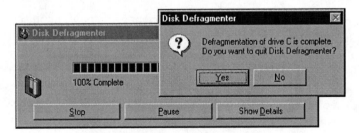

Exhibit 5-21: Disk Defragmenter result

Note: Defragmenting a large hard drive may take a long time, so plan for this before you begin. If you want to watch the progress as it moves through the FAT, click Show Details on the Disk Defragmenter dialog box.

ScanDisk

A directory on either a floppy disk or hard drive is a table holding information about files in that directory or folder. The directory contains the number of the first cluster in the file. The FAT holds the map to all the other clusters in the file. Occasionally, the mapping in the FAT becomes corrupted, resulting either in *lost clusters* or in cross-linked clusters, as shown in Exhibit 5-22. Here, File 3 has lost direction and is pointing to a cluster chain that belongs to File 4. Clusters 29-31 are called *cross-linked clusters* because more than one file points to them, and clusters 15-17 and 28 are called *lost clusters*, or *lost allocation units*, because no file in the FAT points to them.

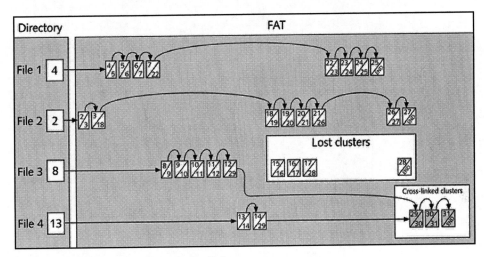

Exhibit 5-22: Lost and cross-linked cluster

To repair cross-linked and lost clusters, use the ScanDisk utility in either MS-DOS mode or from the Windows 9x desktop. For example, in real mode, at the command prompt, enter the command ScanDisk. The screen in Exhibit 5-23 is displayed. When the program finishes scanning the disk, it returns you to a command prompt.

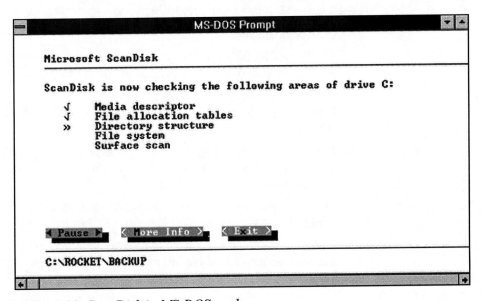

Exhibit 5-23: ScanDisk in MS-DOS mode

From the Windows desktop, choose Start, Programs, Accessories, System Tools, ScanDisk, as shown in Exhibit 5-20. The ScanDisk utility first asks which drive you want to scan and gives you the choice between a standard and thorough scan. The standard scan checks files and folders for errors. The thorough scan does all that the standard scan does plus checks the disk surface. Click Start to begin the scan. Errors are reported as they occur, and final results are displayed as in Exhibit 5-24.

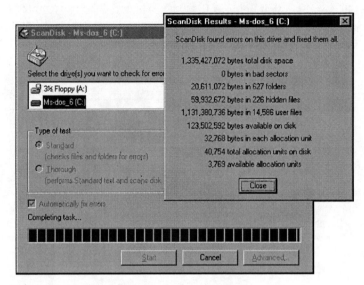

Exhibit 5-24: Scandisk result

Using DOS commands under Windows 9x

A word of caution: Using some DOS commands on a hard drive that uses Windows 9x as the OS may cause damage to a hard drive's file structure. With a Windows 9x upgrade, some of these dangerous commands are erased from the \DOS directory on the hard drive. However, you will find DOS commands that come with Windows 9x stored in the \Windows\ Command directory, and some of these should not be used.

Here are the ones to avoid:

- Don't use disk utility software that does not know about VFAT, long file names or FAT32, including older versions of Norton Utilities and Central Point PC Tools.

- Don't use Fdisk, Format C:, Sys C:, or Chkdsk while in a DOS session within Windows 9x.

- Don't optimize or defragment your hard drive by using software that does not know about long file names; look for the Windows 9x compatibility message on the package.

- Don't run hard drive cache programs unless they are written especially for Windows 9x. Remember that Windows 9x has its own built-in caching software.

- Don't use the older DOS backup programs such as Backup or Msbackup, because the long file name information will not be saved during the backup.

Device Manager

Device Manager gives a graphical view of hardware devices configured under Windows and the resources and drivers they use. By using Device Manager, you can make changes, update drivers, and uninstall device drivers. You can also use Device Manager to print a report of system configuration.

When a device driver is being installed, Windows 9x might inform you that there is a resource conflict, or the device might simply not work. Use Device Manager as a useful fact-finding tool for the resolution of the problem.

Device Manager is one tab on the System Properties window. To access System Properties, right-click the My Computer icon on the desktop and choose Properties from the shortcut menu, or double-click the System icon in Control Panel. From the System Properties window, select the Device Manager tab. The list of devices is displayed, as seen in Exhibit 5-25.

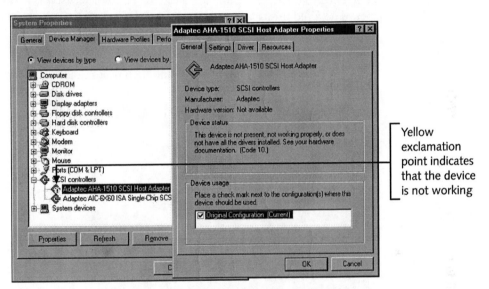

Exhibit 5-25: The properties box of an installed device that is not working

A "+" beside the device name indicates that you can click the device for a list of manufacturers and models installed. The open diamond symbol indicates a SCSI device, and the three-forked symbol is used for USB. Symbols that indicate a device's status are:

- A red X through the device name indicates a disabled device.

- An exclamation point on a yellow background indicates a problem with the device (the device might still be functioning).

- A blue I on a white field indicates that automatic settings were not used and resources have been manually assigned. It does not indicate a problem with the device.

- For Windows ME, a green question mark indicates a compatible driver is installed (not the driver designed for the device), which means the device might not be fully functioning.

To see a better explanation of a problem, select the device and click Properties. The Device Properties dialog box opens, which can give you helpful information about solving problems including I/O addresses, DMA channels, and IRQs used by the device as well as the names of devices that are also attempting to use the same resources.

In fact, before you start hardware installation, you might want to use Device Manager to print a summary of all hardware installed on the PC and resources being used. This printout can be a record of your starting point before the installation as well as a tool to help resolve conflicts during the installation. To print this summary, access Device Manager and click Print. From the Print dialog box, select All Devices and System Summary for a complete listing.

Note: If you have a problem with an installed device, use Device Manager to uninstall the device. Select the device and click the Uninstall button. Then reboot and reinstall the device, looking for problems during the installation that point to the source of the problem. Sometimes reinstalling a device is all that is needed to solve the problem.

Dr. Watson

Dr. Watson is a troubleshooting tool you can use when you are having problems running an application. Dr. Watson is not a repair tool. *Dr. Watson* is a Windows utility that can record detailed information about the system, errors that occur, and the programs that caused them in a log file named \Windows\Drwatson\WatsonXX.wlg, where XX is an incrementing number.

Start Dr. Watson (see Exhibit 5-26) and then reproduce the application error.

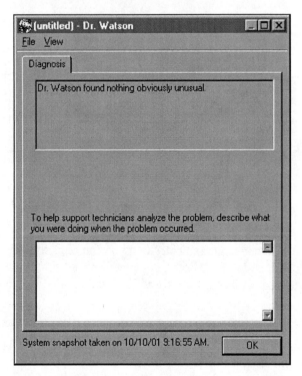

Exhibit 5-26: The Dr. Watson opening window

Then look at the events logged in the Dr. Watson window under the Diagnosis tab. Use this information to check the Microsoft Web site, support.microsoft.com, for the problem and solution. For errors that you cannot reproduce at will, you can load Dr. Watson each time Windows starts by creating a shortcut to Drwatson.exe in the Startup folder.

Windows Help and the Microsoft Web site

Windows Help might provide useful information when trying to resolve a problem. To access the Troubleshooting tool of Windows Help, choose Start, Help, and then click Troubleshooting. The Help information includes suggestions that can lead you to a solution. For example, in Exhibit 5-27, the Hardware Troubleshooter suggests that you check to see that the device is not listed twice in Device Manager. If this were the case, you should remove the second occurrence of the device. Also, the Microsoft Web site, `support.microsoft.com`, has lots of information on troubleshooting.

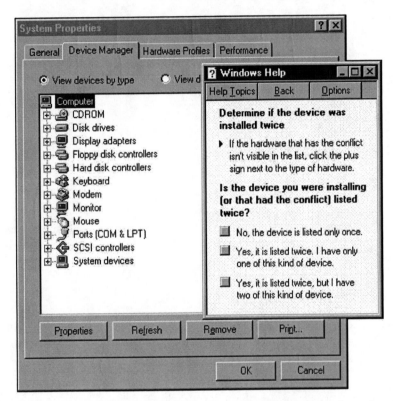

Exhibit 5-27: Troubleshooter making a suggestion to resolve a hardware conflict

Search on the device, an error message, a Windows utility, a symptom, a software application, an update version number, or key words that lead you to articles about the problem and solutions.

Do it!   **D-2:   Optimizing Windows**

Here's how	Here's why
1 Right-click the desktop	To enable a password-protected screensaver.
Choose **Properties**	(On the shortcut menu.) The Display Properties window appears.
2 Select **Screen Saver** tab	
3 From the Screen Saver list, select a screensaver	You can see a preview in the monitor at the top of the dialog box.
4 Try several screensavers	
Choose the one that you like	
5 Click **Settings**	
Customize the appearance of your selected screensaver	
Click **OK**	To save the settings.
6 Click **Preview**	The screensaver appears on your monitor.
7 Press any key or move the mouse	You return to the Display Properties dialog box.
8 Check **Password protected**	You'll assign a password to the screensaver you have selected.
Click **Change**	The Change Password dialog box appears, in which you can specify a password.
9 Type the password	
Retype the password to confirm it	
Click **OK**	You return to the Display Properties dialog box.
10 In the Wait field, change the setting to **one minute**	To specify how long the system will be inactive before the screensaver appears
11 Click **Apply**	To save your settings.
Click **OK**	
Set aside the mouse and keyboard	
12 Wait for one minute	The screensaver appears.
13 Move the mouse	A password dialog box opens.

14 Type your password

Click **OK**   The Windows desktop appears.

15 Re-open the Display Properties
    dialog box

    List the required steps to disable
    the screensaver

16 Disable the screensaver   (Because the Disk Defragmenter utility will
                                          have to start over if interrupted by a screensaver
                                          or other tasks.) You'll defragment drive C: on
                                          your system.

17 Click **Start**

    Choose **Programs**,   To open Disk Defragmenter.
    Accessories, **System Tools**,
    Disk Defragmenter

18 Verify that drive C: is selected

    Click **OK**

19 Continue using Disk   (Even if you see a message indicating that the
    Defragmenter   drive is only slightly fragmented.) A window
                                          appears displaying the progress of
                                          defragmentation.

20 Click **Show Details**   A graphical depiction of the defragmentation
                                          progress appears.

21 Observe the progress window

22 Record the following information
    while the drive is being
    defragmented:

    What unit of division does each
    box represent?

    What does a green box represent?

    What does a red box represent?

    What does a box with a red slash
    through it represent?

    What color represents free space?

23	Click **Yes**	After defragmentation is complete to exit Disk Defragmenter.
24	Open Control Panel	You'll clear temporary Internet files.
	Open Internet Options applet	
25	Click the **General** tab	
	Click **Settings**	(In the Temporary Internet Files section.) The Settings dialog box opens.
26	Click **View Files**	The Temporary Internet Files folder opens, and you can see a list of files in the cache.
27	Drag this window to the side but do not close it	
	Examine the cache	The cache might contain many types of files.
	List four types of files found there	
28	Click **OK**	The Settings dialog box closes and you return to the Internet Properties dialog box.
29	Click **Delete Files**	To delete most files in the cache.
	Click **OK**	To confirm deletion.
30	Click the window that displays the Temporary Internet Files contents	
	Press ⌷F5⌷	(To refresh the window's display.) The list of files is updated to reflect the fact that you just deleted files. Note that all the files have disappeared except for files with names similar to dave@abcnews.go(1).txt. These files are called "cookies."
		Cookies are files that are created by Web servers when you visit a site. Cookies are often used in a good way to help customize content to match your preferences when you revisit a page. However, cookies can also be used to invade the privacy and to secretly send private information from your computer to another computer. Periodically deleting cookies is a good idea.
31	Click **Delete Cookies**	In the Temporary Internet Files section of the Internet Properties dialog box.

32 Click on the window displaying
    the Temporary Internet Files
    contents

    Press (F5)   To refresh.

    Verify that there should be no
    files visible in your Temporary
    Internet cache

33 Click **OK**   To close the Internet Options dialog box and to
                                         close the window displaying the cache.

34 Why should you disable your
    screensaver before defragmenting
    a drive?

35 Why might a drive need
    defragmenting?

36 What Control Panel utility allows
    you to enable the screensaver?

37 What is the name of the Internet
    Explorer cache that contains
    content from Web sites you have
    viewed?

38 What factors might determine the
    size of your Internet cache?

Topic E: Troubleshooting hardware

Explanation

Now that you know about some of the tools used for troubleshooting, you will now learn about the general approaches you should take to troubleshooting problems. Troubleshooting a PC problem begins with isolating it into one of two categories: problems that prevent the PC from booting and problems that occur after a successful boot. Begin by asking the user questions like these to learn as much as you can about the problem:

- When did the problem start?

- Were there any error messages or unusual displays on the screen?

- What programs or software were you using?

- Did you move your computer system recently?

- Has there been a recent thunderstorm or electrical problem?

- Have you made any hardware, software, or configuration changes?

- Has someone else been using your computer recently?

- Can you show me exactly what you did when this problem occurred? (Have the user reproduce the problem and watch each step.)

- Next, ask yourself, "Does the PC boot properly?" If not, then begin troubleshooting the failed boot.

Here are some general tips for troubleshooting hardware devices:

- Try rebooting your computer. The problem with the device may disappear when Windows redetects it.

- Frequent system lockups might indicate corrupted memory modules. Try using memory testing software to check for intermittent memory errors, which indicate the module needs replacing. An example of memory testing software is DocMemory by CST, Inc. (www.docmemory.com).

- For external devices such as monitors, printers, and scanners, try turning on the device before turning on the computer. If you have your computer on and you are rebooting, leave the device on and online.

- If a device doesn't work with one application, try it with another. If the problem occurs only with one application, the problem is probably not with the hardware device but with that application.

- Check Device Manager for errors it reports about the device. If it reports errors, use the Hardware Troubleshooter in Device Manager to help resolve the problem or go to the Microsoft Web site and search on the error message.

- The driver might be corrupted or need updating. Look on the Web for updated device drivers. Search the device manufacturer's Web site or the Microsoft Web site for information about problems with the device and solutions.

- Use Device Manager to uninstall the device and then reinstall it. If you uninstall the device and then reboot, Windows should recognize an uninstalled device and automatically launch the Found New Hardware Wizard. If it doesn't launch, then chances are the device is not working or is not PnP.

- For PnP devices on expansion cards such as sound cards, modems, and network cards, if you uninstall the device in Device Manager and Windows does not recognize the device when you reboot, the device might not be working. The expansion card needs to be reseated or moved to a different expansion slot. If that doesn't work, the card needs replacing.

- If none of these things work, ask yourself what has changed since the device last worked. For example, maybe you have added another hardware device that is conflicting with the one you are using, or maybe you have added software that conflicts with the software that the problem device is using. Try disabling other devices or try uninstalling software that you suspect is causing the problem. Use the Automatic Skip Driver Agent to eliminate other devices that might prevent this one from working.

- The problem might be caused by a lack of resources. If your system is running low on memory or has too many applications open, it might not be able to support a device. A corrupted Windows system file or registry can also cause problems with hardware devices. Try verifying system files or restoring the registry from backup.

- If you still have not resolved the problem, consider it a hardware problem. How to resolve hardware problems is not covered in this course.

Troubleshooting legacy devices and drivers

A device or expansion card that is not PnP is a *legacy device*. Legacy devices are not able to have their resources assigned to them by PnP, and legacy drivers are older 16-bit drivers that cannot be loaded into extended memory.

Legacy 16-bit drivers are loaded from entries in Autoexec.bat, Config.sys, or System.ini files. These entries are created by an install or setup program that comes with the device drivers and is executed when you install the device. If you are having a problem with a legacy device, do the following:

- Make every effort to find a protected-mode driver for the device. Check the Microsoft Web site and the Web site of the device manufacturer.

- If you cannot find a protected-mode driver, check the entries in Autoexec.bat, Config.sys, and System.ini for errors. Try running the install program again.

- If you are attempting to load the driver high and the MEM report says it's not loaded high, check for errors in these command lines: Device=HIMEM.SYS, Device=EMM386.EXE, and DOS=UMB in the Config.sys file. Then look for either the Devicehigh= command in Config.sys or the Loadhigh command in Autoexec.bat.

- Two legacy devices might be in conflict. Use the System Configuration Utility to disable one device or the other to verify the conflict. Also, Device Manager sometimes is aware of a legacy conflict and suggests a substitution for system resources. A hardware technician uses DIP switches or jumpers on a legacy device to configure it to use a different set of system resources.

Conflicts with upper memory addresses

A device might be attempting to use upper memory addresses that the OS is using for a UMB (Upper Memory Block). When the OS creates a UMB, it assigns memory addresses that it "thinks" are not being used by devices. However, some devices don't tell the OS what memory addresses they are using until the device is activated after booting. This delay causes the OS to think that the memory addresses assigned to a device are available, and the OS creates and loads a TSR into the UMB. If this conflict happens, the system might hang, the TSR might not work properly, and/or the device might not work properly.

Try the following approach:

1 Read the documentation that came with the device to find out which memory addresses it is using. Also, try using MSD to display how memory is being used. Once you know the memory addresses being used, you can change the Emm386.exe command line so that this range of addresses is not used.

2 Use the Exclude option for the Emm386.exe command line to exclude certain memory addresses. Do not use the last numeral in the hex address in the command line. For example, suppose you read from the documentation that came with the device that it uses addresses CC000 to CFFFF. To exclude these addresses from the addresses used by UMBs, use this command line:

```
DEVICE=EMM386.EXE NOEMS X = CC00 - CFFF
```

Notice in the command line that the last digit of an upper memory address is omitted in the exclude entry. Reboot your computer to activate the change. The memory conflict problem should then be solved.

Note: When reading the documentation, you will find that most addresses are given in hex rather than decimal form. Sometimes the memory addresses are written without the last hexadecimal numeral. For example, if the documentation says that the device uses C800 through CFFF, interpret this to mean that the upper memory address range is C8000 through CFFFF. Once you have discovered that the two devices use the same memory addresses, find out if one can use alternate addresses. If so, your problem is solved.

Do it!   # E-1:   Discussing troubleshooting hardware

Questions and answers

1 Give at least four problems that can occur with legacy hardware installations and explain how they can be solved.

2 What command in Config.sys is used to instruct the OS to load a device driver high? When might it not work, and how would you solve that problem?

3 You have a network card installed on your computer, and it is working properly. When you install a new scanner card, neither the scanner card nor the network card works. What could cause this problem, and how would you fix it?

Topic F: Troubleshooting applications

Explanation

Remember that Windows 9x supports 16-bit DOS applications, 16-bit Windows 3.x applications, and newer 32-bit applications. This topic looks at problems that can occur with all three types of applications and what to do about them. Problems can be caused by viruses, the application itself, by other applications, by the OS, or by hardware.

Here is the general process to use when troubleshooting problems with applications:

- Address any error messages that appear when using the software.
- If you don't understand the error message, write it down or print it and look it up on the Microsoft support Web site or the Web site of the product manufacturer. Follow the directions given on the Web sites to resolve the problem.
- Read the documentation that came with the application and documents on the manufacturer Web site. Perhaps you are using a function incorrectly.
- A virus might be the source of the problem. Run current antivirus software.
- Consider that data files might be corrupted. Try creating new data files used by the software.
- Consider that the hardware the software is using might have a problem. For the hard drive, run ScanDisk and Defrag and check for free disk space. Delete files in the \Windows\Temp folder. For a device other than the hard drive, try using another application to access the device.
- Try uninstalling and reinstalling the software. Back up the data first.
- Perhaps the problem is caused by a conflict with other software. Software conflicts are addressed later in this section.
- Launch Dr. Watson and then try to reproduce the error with the application. Look in the Dr. Watson log files for clues and search the Microsoft Web site.
- Perhaps OS files are corrupted that the application depends on. Try restoring Windows system files. Check the Microsoft Web site for Windows 9x service packs that might resolve the problem. Install all Windows service packs. You might have to reinstall Windows.

Problems with a software program itself

Suppose the computer boots with no errors, and all but one software package on this computer works correctly. When you try to load the problem software package, however, you get an error message and the software terminates. In this situation, you can probably conclude that the software caused the error. Here are some questions you can ask to troubleshoot the problem:

- **Has this software ever worked?** If it has not, then try installing it again. Maybe wrong information was given during the installation. Be sure you check the requirements for the software. Maybe you don't have enough memory or space on your hard drive to create the necessary working files.
- **When was the last time the software worked?** What happened differently then? Did you get an error message that seemed insignificant at the time? What has happened to your computer since the software last worked? Have you added more software or changed the hardware configuration?
- **Could a virus be causing the problem?** Run a current version of antivirus software.

Consider reinstalling the software even if it has worked in the past. Maybe a program file has become corrupted. Before you reinstall it, however, consider whether reinstallation will erase any data that this software has placed on your hard drive. If you're not sure, back up the data. Maybe you can just copy the data to another directory while you reinstall the program. If the installation does erase the data in the original directory, you can copy one file and then another back to the original directory. If you load the program without the data and it works, but the problem recurs when you put the data back in the original directory, then you've found the corrupted data file that caused the problem.

Software often uses configuration files and scripting files that are specific to a particular PC or user. If you reinstall the software, most likely you will lose the configuration information. Either save the configuration files before you begin or print the contents of the files. See the software documentation for the names and location of the configuration files (file extensions of .ini, .inf, and .cfg are common). Consider that the problem with the software might be a corrupted configuration file.

Note: If an application locks up, press Ctrl+Alt+Del and select the program in the Close Program dialog box. Click End Task.

Uninstalling software

Uninstalling software is clean and easy if the software comes with a well written uninstall program. Use the Add/Remove Program utility in Control Panel to uninstall it. However, some uninstall programs are not that well written, and sometimes a user will simply delete the folders that contain the software, leaving behind DLL files in the \Windows\System directory, entries in the registry, shortcuts on the desktop, and so on for you, the PC technician, to clean up. Even worse, the user or an uninstall program might delete a DLL file needed by another application or make a wrong deletion in the registry. A *DLL (dynamic-link library)* file is a file with a .dll extension that contains a library of programming routines (or mini programs) to perform common tasks.

When software is installed, it can do these things:

- Create new folders that belong to the application only and store files there.
- Store files used only by the application in folders also used by other software. An example is an application's .ini file stored in the \Windows folder.
- Create or overwrite files used by other software. An example is \Windows\ system\CTL3D.DLL, a file used by several applications that might be updated by a software installation.
- Make changes to the Windows registry.
- Make changes to .ini files that belong to Windows.

When software is uninstalled, deleting folders and their contents that belong only to the application is safe. Deleting entire sections in Windows .ini files that are named after the software or a branch in the registry tree that contains the application's name is also safe. But problems might occur when a change is made to a registry entry that other software depends on or when files are deleted that are used by other software.

Exhibit 5-28 shows the results of such an error. The problem, in this case, can be resolved by reinstalling the OCR software.

Exhibit 5-28: The result of an uninstall program deleting a file needed by another application

Sometimes an application is set to automatically launch at startup. After the program is uninstalled, if errors occur when Windows is loaded, look for entries in these places that were not removed by the uninstall program:

- Check the Win.ini file for entries in the Load= and Run= command lines.
- Check the Windows Startup folder for shortcuts.
- Check the registry key HKEY_LOCAL_MACHINE\SOFTWARE\ Microsoft\Windows\CurrentVersion\Run.

Do it!

F-1:   Discussing troubleshooting application problems

Questions and answers

1 Explain the function of DLL files, including what happens if they are deleted or overwritten.

2 Name two ways to end an application that is hung without rebooting the PC.

3 When a software application does not work properly, the first thing to do would be to try:

Topic G: Troubleshooting performance

Explanation

If you have just installed Windows 9x and it is performing slowly, check that the minimum hardware requirements have been met. Perhaps you need to upgrade memory or install an additional hard drive.

How to troubleshoot performance

If Windows 9x was once working fine, but is now generally sluggish, applications are slow to load and run, or the system locks up at unexplained times, do the following:

- Check the hard drive. Run the ScanDisk and Defragmenter utilities. Delete unneeded files and empty the Recycle Bin. Generally clean up the hard drive, making plenty of room for the swap file and temporary files used by applications.
- Suspect a virus. Run a current version of antivirus software. Clean or delete all files that contain viruses. Restore system files.
- Check for applications loaded at startup that are using up system resources. Close applications not currently in use.
- Look for icons in the *System Tray*, the small area on the right side of the taskbar at the bottom of the screen. These icons represent small applets that are loaded at startup and take up system resources. Keep these icons to a minimum.
- Clean up the registry using the Scanreg /opt command.
- Monitor the system by using System Monitor. Look for applications that use an unusual percentage of system resources. Update these applications with the latest versions.
- Remove extraneous software such as fancy screensavers and desktop wallpaper and photos.

Do it!

G-1: Discussing troubleshooting performance

Question and answer

1 Define fragmentation. What problems can it cause? What utility is used to fix it?

2 What tool can you use to look for applications that use an unusual percentage of system resources?

3 What command can you use to clean up the registry?

Unit summary: Supporting and troubleshooting Windows 9x

Topic A   In this topic, you had an overview of **booting** Windows 9x. You learned about the files used to **customize** the startup process and the Windows 9x **startup process**. You also learned about **loading** an application at startup.

Topic B   In this topic, you learned the concepts of troubleshooting the Windows 9x **boot** process. You learned the common **error messages** received while loading Windows 9x and about the Windows 9x **Startup** menu. You also learned how to use a **startup disk** for troubleshooting.

Topic C   In this topic, you learned the organization of the Windows 9x **registry**. You learned how to **recover** from a corrupted registry and how to **modify** the registry.

Topic D   In this topic, you learned about the tools you can use to monitor, control, and troubleshoot Windows 9x. You learned about the **System Applet** in Control Panel, the **System Monitor**, and the **System Configuration Utility**. You learned about tools to manage **security** and to manage a **hard drive**. You also learned about **Device Manager** and **Dr. Watson** utilities and learned to access **Windows Help** and the **Microsoft Web site**.

Topic E   In this topic, you learned about troubleshooting **hardware** in Windows 9x. You learned about troubleshooting **legacy devices** and **drivers**.

Topic F   In this topic, you learned about troubleshooting **applications** in Windows 9x. You learned that the problem could be with the software **program** itself. You also learned how to **uninstall** a software application. You learned that some applications **share files**, such as **DLLs**, which should not be deleted unless you are sure no other application also uses the file.

Topic G   In this topic, you learned to troubleshoot problems with Windows **performance**. You learned how to use **System Monitor** to check what **system resources** are being used. You also learned to use the **Scanreg /opt** command to clean up the **registry**.

Review questions

1 Name three security measures used in Windows 9x.

2 What is a comment line? How is a comment line noted within a file?

3 Explain the purpose of the System Configuration Utility. How would you use it in troubleshooting?

4 The Windows registry takes over the functions of _____ files.

5 Name four configuration files that Windows 9x includes for backward compatibility with legacy software and hardware.

6 The Windows registry is contained in two files, _____ and _____. The Windows 95 backups of these files are called _____ and _____.

7 Which version of Windows includes the Registry Checker? How often does this utility back up the registry?

8 Explain the difference between the Regedit and Scanreg utilities.

9 Name the files that Sysedit automatically displays for editing. Give a short description of each.

10 What is the maximum size of .ini files? Can all applications use .ini files of this size?

11 Place these tools in the order in which you would use them when troubleshooting the Windows 9x boot process: emergency startup disk, safe mode, error messages, and the command prompt.

12 List the options on the Windows 9x Startup menu and give a short description of each. Which option is available for Windows 95 but not for Windows 98, and why? Which option is available for Windows 95/98, but not for Windows ME?
(Answer space continues on next page.)

13 Which Startup menu options execute Autoexec.bat and Config.sys? Which do not?

14 Explain how to eliminate the following files as the source of a boot problem: Win.ini, System.ini, Config.sys, and Autoexec.bat.

15 What is the difference between cross-linked clusters and lost clusters? What utility is used to repair them?

16 What Windows utility allows you to control which drivers are loaded during Windows startup?

17 _____ is a Windows utility that can record detailed information about the system, errors that occur, and the programs that caused them in a log file.

18 Which registry key keeps information about Windows performance and plug and play?

19 Under what circumstances does Windows read initialization files?

20 Should you ever edit .ini files or the Windows registry? If so, when?

21 What parts of the Windows load does safe mode not execute?

22 A troubleshooting mode that contains only a minimum configuration so that a person can check hardware devices is known as _____.

23 Windows 9x, which supports 32-bit (protected) mode processing, actually starts out in 16-bit (real) mode. True or false?

24 The Windows 9x registry is organized as a _____ database, otherwise known as a tree structure.

25 The command line utility that allows for the replacement of a corrupted registry with an older, working version is known as _____.

26 Technicians and users alike should regularly edit the registry manually to ensure that it is working properly. True or false?

27 A screensaver password is not an effective way to secure a computer from unauthorized use. True or false?

28 The main job that the ScanDisk utility performs is to find and correct the links to _____ and _____.

29 _____ is a utility that logs errors in a system with detailed information, but does not help to repair them.

Independent practice activity

Follow these steps to create a new file and then determine which application is associated with it:

1 Right-click **Start** and choose **Explore**.

2 In Windows Explorer, open the **My Documents** folder.

3 Right-click a blank area in the right-hand pane.

4 Choose **New** from the shortcut menu.

5 Click **Text Document**.

6 Name the new file as **associ8.txt**.

7 Double-click **associ8.txt**. What application opens the file?

8 Close the application.

Follow these steps by using Windows Explorer to view and change associations between applications and file types.

1 Open Windows Explorer.

2 Choose **Tools** on the menu bar.

3 Click **Folder Options**.

4 Click the **File Types** tab. Note that the Extension, Content Type (MIME), and the default application associated with a file type (Opens with) are displayed in the **File type details** section.

5 Scroll down the **Registered file types** list box and then click **Text Document**.

6 Record what application opens this type of file by default.

7 With Text Document highlighted, click **Edit**. The Edit File Type dialog box opens. Here you can modify all the information found on the File Types tab. modifying the settings here changes how Windows handles interactions with this file type.

8 In the Actions list box, click **open**.

9 Click **Edit**. The "Editing action for type: Text document" dialog box opens. Here you can specify which application to use to perform an action. If you don't know which one you're going to use or where it is located, you can browse for an application to associate with this file type.

10 Next to the **Application used to perform action** field, click **Browse**.

11 Open the **Program Files\Accessories** directory.

12 Click **Wordpad.exe**.

13 Click **Open**.

14 Return to the Editing action for type dialog box.

15 To associate this application with the selected file type, click the **Application used to perform action** text box.

16 Move the insertion point after the close quotation mark, press the **Spacebar** once and then type **"%1"** including the quotation marks as shown in Exhibit 5-29. The "%1" is a temporary holding place used by Command.com, and tells Windows that Wordpad.exe is to be used to open files of type Text Document.

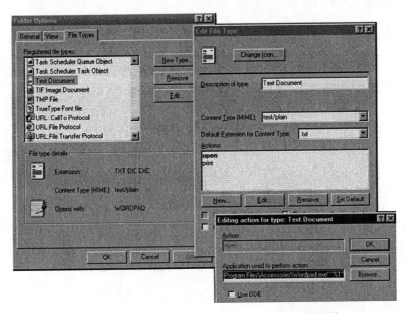

Exhibit 5-29: Change the application associated with a file type

17 Click **OK**. The Editing action for type dialog box closes and you return to the Edit File Type dialog box.

18 Click **Close**. The Edit File Type dialog box closes and your changes are saved.

19 Click **Close** to exit the Folder Options dialog box.

Follow these steps to test the new file association.

1 In Windows Explorer, double-click **associ8.txt**.

2 Record what application opens the file now.

3 Type a sentence in the associ8.txt file.

4 Save the change.

5 Close the application window.

Follow these steps to change the file association back to its original setting.

1 In Windows Explorer, choose **Tools** on the menu bar.

2 Click **Folder Options**.

3 Select the **File Types** tab.

4 Scroll down the **Registered file types** list box, and then click **Text Document**.

5 Click the **Edit** button. The Edit File Type dialog box opens.

6 In the **Actions** list box, click **open**.

7 Click **Edit**. The Editing action for type dialog box opens.

8 Click the **Browse** button, browse to the **Windows** directory.

9 Click **notepad.exe**.

10 Click **Open**.

11 Return to the Editing action for type dialog box.

12 Click **OK** to close the Editing action for type dialog box.

13 Click **Close**. The Edit File Type dialog box closes and your changes are saved.

14 Click **Close** to exit the Folder Options dialog box.

15 In Windows Explorer, double-click **associ8.txt**.

16 Record what application opens the file now.

17 Close the application that was launched.

Follow these steps to add WordPad to the shortcut menu for text files:

1 Return to Windows Explorer and open the Folder Options dialog box.

2 Select the **File Types** tab.

3 In the Registered File Types field, double-click **Text Document**. The Edit File Type dialog box opens.

4 Click **New**. The New Action dialog box opens.

5 In the New Action dialog box, click the **Action** text box.

6 Type **Open with WordPad**.

7 Click **Browse**

8 Browse to the **Program Files\Accessories** directory.

9 Click **wordpad.exe**.

10 Click **Open**.

11 Return to the New Action dialog box.

12 Click the **Application used to perform action** text box, position the insertion point after the close quotation mark, and then press the Spacebar once.

13 Type **"%1"** including the quotation marks.

14 Click **OK**. The Editing action for type dialog box closes.

15 You return to the Edit File Type dialog box.

16 Click **Close**. The Edit File Type dialog box closes and your changes are saved.

17 Close the Folder Options dialog box.

Follow these steps to test the new shortcut menu option.

1 In Windows Explorer, right-click **associ8.txt**.

2 Click **Open with WordPad**. The document opens in WordPad.

3 To remove the **Open with WordPad** option from the shortcut menu, return to the Edit File Types dialog box.

4 In the Actions list box click **Open in WordPad**.

5 Click **Remove**.

6 Click **Yes** to remove this action.

7 Click **Close** to close the Edit File Type dialog box.

8 Save your changes.

9 Then close the Folder Options dialog box.

10 Record the following information.

- What Windows utility is used to manage associations between file types and applications?
- What tab in the Folder Options window lets you modify file associations?
- In Windows, what indicates a file's type?
- Which text editor does Windows normally associate with .txt files?
- How can you open a file in an application when the file's type is not associated with that application?
- Why might you wish to add a second file association?
- Use the Internet to find the definition of MIME and give a brief explanation of its importance.

Follow these steps to update your version of Windows 9x to the most current state.

1 Open your browser.

2 In the address box, enter `windowsupdate.microsoft.com`.

3 Click the **Product Updates** link. You may receive a Security Warning asking if you want to install and run "Windows Update Control."

4 Click **Yes** to install it. The browser displays a message indicating that Microsoft is examining your system and customizing the update selection for your system. Next, a list of available updates is displayed, with the Critical Updates Package selected.

5 Scroll through the available updates and notice that they are grouped into categories and include a brief description indicating the purpose of each update.

6 Click the **Download** link. Depending on your update package and how you are connected to the Internet (28.8 modem, DSL, cable modem, and so forth), downloading might take considerable time.

7 When prompted, confirm the update files you selected.

8 Click the **View Instructions** link and make a note of any special instructions not included in this lab.

9 Close the View Instructions window.

10 Click the **Start Download** link.

11 Your update may require you to accept an End User Licensing Agreement (EULA). If you are prompted to do so, accept the agreement. A window appears indicating the download progress.

12 After the installation process is complete, you will be prompted to restart your computer. Click **Yes** to restart. When your system is in text mode, a message appears indicating that "setup will update configuration files." Next, you might see a message indicating that the update is complete. Windows will then continue to load to the desktop.

Follow these steps to upgrade to the latest version of Internet Explorer:

1 Open Internet Explorer, click **Help**, and then click **About Internet Explorer**. Make a notation of your current version of Internet Explorer.

2 Enter `www.microsoft.com/windows/ie/default.asp`.

3 Click the **Download Now** link to download the most current version of Internet Explorer. Observe a page describing the most current version of Internet Explorer.

4   Verify that the correct language is selected in the **Select a Language** list box, and then click **Go**.

5   Directions for downloading and installing the new version of Internet Explorer appear. Read the directions carefully. Note that you can choose to download the file to your hard drive and execute the downloaded file later, or you can install the update from the Microsoft server.

6   To save time, choose to install from the Microsoft Server across the Internet.

7   Click the link for downloading the latest version of Internet Explorer—for example, **Internet Explorer 6 Service Pack 1**—and then follow the installation directions.

8   If at any time during the process you see a warning about receiving files, check **Always trust content from Microsoft** and then continue.

9   Windows asks whether you wish to save to disk or run from the current location. To indicate that you want to install the file from its current location, click **Open**.

10 The installation wizard launches, ready to guide you through the Internet Explorer upgrade. When the End User Licensing Agreement (EULA) appears, click **Agree** to continue.

11 Next, click **Install Now**.

12 Click **Next**.

13 You are asked if you want to accept additional files to be downloaded as necessary. Click **Yes** to allow the download of additional files. The download process begins and you see a window indicating the progress of the download. When the download is complete, the installation process begins.

14 When the installation is complete, click **Finish** to restart the computer.

15 Start Internet Explorer.

16 Verify that the new version has been installed.

17 Close Internet Explorer.

18 What is the specific version of Windows 9x you are using?

19 Explain how you got your answer for the previous question.

20 Assign a new name for My Computer on your desktop that includes your version of Windows.

21 List the steps required to perform this task.

22 Record the following information.

   • What types of changes are normally associated with an operating system update? What types of changes are associated with an operating system upgrade?

   • Why does Microsoft need to examine your system before displaying update files?

   • What is an EULA?

   • What is the most current version of Internet Explorer?

   • Did you load your new version of Internet Explorer over the Internet or did you save it to the hard drive and run it from there? Why did you choose this option?

Unit 6

Understanding and supporting Windows NT

Unit time: 60 minutes

Complete this unit, and you'll know how to:

A Describe the Windows NT architecture, including the user and kernel modes.

B Install and customize Windows NT.

C Use and support Windows NT.

D Explain the Windows NT boot process.

E Create Windows NT setup and repair disks to repair a Windows NT system.

Topic A: Architecture

Explanation

Windows NT was designed with an architecture different from Windows 9x and provided the Windows OS family's first break with DOS. Windows 2000 and Windows XP also use the Windows NT architecture.

Windows NT was architecturally designed to support multiple users. Windows NT was ported to three non-Intel-based platforms. This port arrangement provides a high level of security, performance, and reliability. In addition, Windows NT offers strong networking features. Windows NT also supports *POSIX (Portable OS Interface)*, a set of standards based on UNIX and adopted by the United States federal government to ensure that operating systems and software can port more easily from one platform to another.

Note: To *port* a program or an OS means the OS or program should work across multiple platforms mostly the same way.

Windows NT was also designed with a strong emphasis on room for improvements and expandability, primarily accomplished by its modular approach to dealing with applications and hardware. Let's begin by looking at the modular approach and then move to a discussion of user and kernel modes in Windows NT.

Windows NT modularity

Here's an analogy to help you understand the modular concept of Windows NT. The idea is to isolate one process from another so that a change in one process has the least possible effect on the other processes. Consider the self-serve restaurant shown in Exhibit 6-1. In the process illustrated in Exhibit 6-1, customers arrive for breakfast, walk to the back of the restaurant, tell the cook what they want, wait for him to cook it, take it back to a table, and eat. Customers are responsible for getting their own drinks, silverware, and so forth. If someone in the kitchen moves the silverware or installs a new and different drink-dispensing machine, every customer must learn a new process so the system can continue to work. This process clearly isn't modular and maximizes the effect that a change in one part of the process has on other parts of the process.

Exhibit 6-1: A non-modular restaurant model

Now consider Exhibit 6-2. A counter has been added, and customers aren't allowed behind this counter. They come to the counter and tell others in the kitchen what they want to eat, and someone in the kitchen brings the food, drink, and silverware to them at the counter. Things work a little better now. When processes change in the kitchen, only employees who work in the kitchen must be retrained. However, there's still a flaw in the efficiency of this design. Every kitchen worker must know how to cook and make drinks and where the silverware is located. This model introduces some benefits of a modular design but still has flaws.

Exhibit 6-2: A partially modular restaurant model

Exhibit 6-3 further refines the process, and our restaurant is now a full-service, highly modular affair. Employees are divided into four groups, each with a different function. The first and second groups of employees, the hosts and hostesses, waiters, and waitresses, interact with the customers, greeting them at the door, showing them their seats, taking orders, and serving food. The second group, the waiters and waitresses, also serve to interface between customers and counter workers. The third group, the counter workers, stand between the kitchen counter and the customer counter, where the drink machines and the silverware are located. The waiters and waitresses pass food requests to the counter workers, who pass the requests to the fourth group, the kitchen workers, who now only prepare the food. When the food is passed back to the counter workers, these workers gather up drinks, silverware, and food and pass them on to the waiters and waitresses, who serve the customers. This model uses a more modular arrangement that provides the benefits of separating processes from each other, even though the overhead (the additional resources needed to implement the new model) is higher than in the other models.

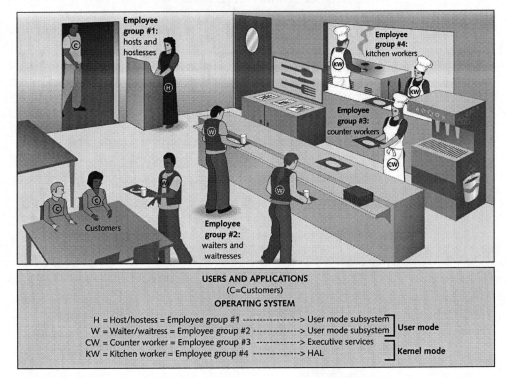

Exhibit 6-3: A high modular restaurant mode

In this model, if the drink machine is upgraded, only the counter workers must be retrained. If the oven or stove in the kitchen is replaced with an altogether new electronic unit, only the kitchen workers change their methods. The counter workers are unaffected. The waiters and waitresses don't need to know how to communicate with the cook, but can focus on customer service. The customer is isolated from the entire process. In comparing Exhibit 6-1 and Exhibit 6-3, at first it looks as though the process has been complicated. There are more workers, and customers now have to wait to be seated. In fact, a new layer of complexity has been added, and two counters are required. However, it turns out that the advantages of the new system outweigh its disadvantages and overhead. Not only can equipment be easily upgraded without having to retrain so many people or reorient customers to the new procedures, but the integrity of the operation is enhanced: because the processes have been separated from each other, they can now be more easily controlled. Standards and procedures can be more easily applied to each segment of the process, because fewer people are involved at each step in the operation, which reduces confusion and improves the overall efficiency of the operation. In summary, the three main reasons to use the highly modular model rather than the non-modular model are:

- To make upgrades of equipment easier (some employees and all customers are unaffected)

- To increase the overall efficiency of the operation (each part of the process involves fewer people than in the other models)

- To ensure the integrity of processes (standards are more easily enforced)

The process of running the restaurant can be viewed as analogous to the way operating systems run a computer: the modular approach is analogous to the Windows NT OS, and the non-modular approaches are analogous to earlier Microsoft operating systems. Customers can be viewed as a combination of users and applications software; employees can be viewed as the OS; the stove, drink machine, silverware stand, and so on, can be viewed as the hardware; and the cook can be viewed as those parts of the OS that relate directly to hardware, system BIOS, and device drivers. The process illustrated in Exhibit 6-1 is most analogous to DOS, in which applications were allowed "behind the counter" to interact directly with BIOS and device drivers, and even to perform some of their own operations with hardware, rather than necessarily turning to the OS to perform hardware operations. For example, in DOS, an application program written to address specific hardware configurations might depend on video RAM always being found at certain memory addresses, and the program could access that RAM directly.

The process illustrated in Exhibit 6-2 is most analogous to a model of the Windows 9x OS, because the customers (the applications) are isolated from some of the interaction with the equipment (hardware) but not all. Notice, for instance, that the silverware stand is still available for customer use; similarly, in Windows 9x, a 16-bit program can interact directly with video memory and other resources.

The process illustrated in Exhibit 6-3 is most analogous to the Windows NT OS, which includes an additional layer between the applications (customers) and hardware (the restaurant equipment); applications (customers) are almost completely isolated from interaction with hardware (restaurant equipment). The access that programs have to system resources is controlled through the two Windows NT modes: user mode and kernel mode.

Modes

Windows NT operates in two modes, user mode and kernel mode, each of which takes advantage of CPU functions and abilities different from the other, as shown in Exhibit 6-4. *User mode* is a non-privileged processor mode in which programs have only limited access to system information and can access hardware only through other OS services. Several *subsystems* or OS modules described in more detail below use it. *Kernel mode* is a privileged processor mode in which programs have extensive access to system information and hardware. Kernel mode is used by two main components: the *HAL* (hardware abstraction layer), and a group of components collectively called *executive services*, which interfaces between the subsystems in user mode and the HAL. Executive services components manage hardware resources by way of the HAL and device drivers. Applications in user mode have no access to hardware resources. In kernel mode, executive services have limited access to hardware resources, but the HAL primarily interacts with hardware.

Memory management is an excellent example of how the user mode subsystems, executive services, and the HAL cooperate in Windows NT. Windows NT provides memory addresses to an application by way of the Win32 user mode subsystem. When an application requests this subsystem to write data to some of these assigned addresses, the subsystem turns to executive services. The component within executive services that manages memory, the virtual memory manager, is responsible for coordinating the interface between the user subsystem and the HAL. The virtual memory manager presents the request to the HAL, which is responsible for the actual writing of the data to memory and responds to the memory manager when finished. The memory manager then reports back to the user subsystem, which, in turn, reports back to the application.

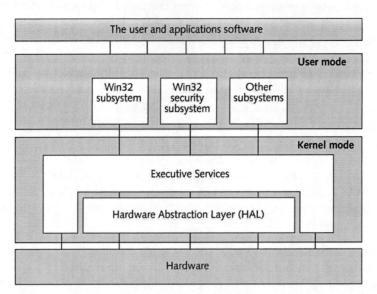

Exhibit 6-4: User mode and kernel mode in Windows NT

Windows NT was designed to port to different hardware platforms easily. Because only the components operating in kernel mode actually interact with hardware, they're the only parts that need to be changed when Windows NT moves from one hardware platform to another. For instance, if the hardware platform changes, the HAL must change. However, the subsystems in user mode require little or no change.

Limiting access to hardware mainly to the HAL increases OS integrity, because more control is possible. With this isolation, an application can't cause a system to hang by making illegal demands on hardware. Overall performance is increased, because the HAL and executive services can operate independently of the applications using them.

On the other hand, Windows NT requires much more robust hardware and can support more powerful applications than either Windows 9x or DOS can. The increased overhead of this OS benefits you only when hardware and applications software are hefty enough to take advantage of the more powerful OS.

User mode

The purpose of the subsystems in user mode is to interface with the user and with applications; the tools you view when running Windows NT are primarily running in user mode. In Exhibit 6-4, note the Win32 subsystem, which is probably the most important user mode subsystem, because it manages all 32-bit programs and provides an environment for these programs, including the user interface, such as the one for Windows Explorer. (32-bit programs are programs written for protected mode using 32-bit code.) The Win32 security subsystem provides logon to the system and other security functions, including privileges for file access. Other subsystems might or might not be running while the Win32 subsystem and security subsystem are running.

All applications relate to Windows NT by way of the Win32 subsystem, either directly or indirectly. Exhibit 6-5 shows how various programs that run under Windows NT interact with subsystems. For instance, each DOS application resides in its own NTVDM. An *NTVDM (NT virtual DOS machine)* is a carefully controlled environment that Windows NT provides in which a DOS application can interface with only one subsystem and can't relate to anything outside the system. All the 16-bit Windows 3.x applications reside in a *Win16 on Win32 (WOW)* environment. Within the WOW environment, these 16-bit applications can communicate with one another, and they can communicate with the WOW, but that's as far as their world goes. Exhibit 6-5 shows three 16-bit Windows 3.x applications residing in a WOW that resides in one NTVDM. Because each DOS application expects to run as the only application on a PC, each has its own NTVDM.

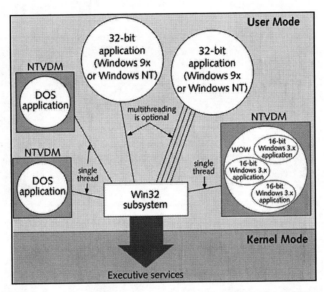

Exhibit 6-5: Environment subsystems in Windows NT user mode

You can see in Exhibit 6-5 that 32-bit applications don't require an NTVDM and can relate to the Win32 subsystem directly, because they're written to run in protected mode. The exhibit shows that 32-bit applications can also use a single line of communication, called single-threading, with the Win32 subsystem or can use multiple lines for interfacing, called *multithreading*, with the Win32 subsystem, depending upon what the process requests. A *thread* is a single task that the process requests from the kernel, such as the task of printing a file. A *process* is a program that's running, together with the system resources assigned to it, such as memory addresses, environmental variables, and other resources. Sometimes a process is called an instance, such as when you say, "Open two instances of Internet Explorer." Technically, you are saying to open two Internet Explorer processes. An example of multithreading is a request from Microsoft Word that the subsystem read a large file from the hard drive while performing a print job at the same time. Single threading happens when the application doesn't expect both processes to be performed at the same time but simply passes one request followed by another.

Kernel mode

The kernel mode of Windows NT is used by executive services and the HAL, which interface more directly with the hardware than do the subsystems operating in user mode. Exhibit 6-6 expands the information from Exhibit 6-4 to show several executive services components operating in kernel mode. Most interaction with the hardware is done by executive services passing requests to the HAL. However, from Exhibit 6-6, you can see that executive services include device drivers, which have direct access to the hardware.

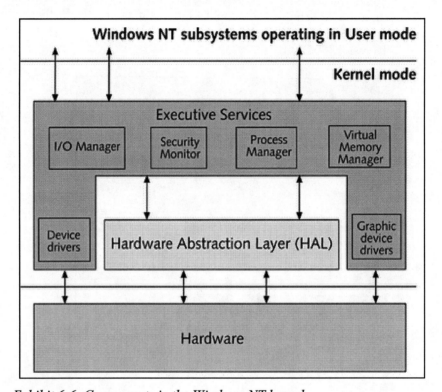

Exhibit 6-6: Components in the Windows NT kernel

Only kernel mode components can access hardware. However, in DOS, applications can access hardware resources directly, or they can use an API call to ask DOS to perform the task. In Windows NT, if a DOS application tried to access the disk directly, Windows NT would shut down the DOS application. But if the DOS application tried to access the disk by passing a DOS API call to the Windows NT NTVDM, it would be allowed to proceed.

Do it!

A-1:   Discussing the architecture

Exercises

1   Which part of the Windows NT architecture makes it possible for Windows NT to port to more than one platform?

2   What are the two modes of the Windows NT architecture?

3   Which of these two modes contains the NTVDM?

4   Why do 32-bit applications not need to reside in an NTVDM?

5   What does HAL stand for?

6   DOS applications can be run in Windows NT by using _____.

Topic B: Installation

Explanation

Because Windows NT differs so fundamentally from Windows 9x, there's no automatic upgrade path from Windows 9x to Windows NT. When you change a PC from Windows 9x to Windows NT, you can install Windows NT in a different folder. No system settings in Windows 9x are transferred to Windows NT. After Windows NT is installed, you must reinstall each application on the PC under Windows NT. Windows NT can be present as the only OS on a PC, or it can be installed on the same PC as Windows 9x in a dual boot configuration.

The main reason that Windows 9x can't be easily upgraded to Windows NT is that the two registries aren't compatible. This incompatibility makes it difficult to transfer information from one to the other. (Remember that a registry is a database containing all configuration information for the OS. Again, realize that Windows NT isn't the next stepping stone beyond Windows 9x but is instead a new road altogether.

Before covering the installation process in detail, let's look at two issues you need to consider before installing Windows NT: how to partition your hard drive and which file system to use.

Hard drive partitions

Windows NT assigns two different functions to hard drive partitions holding the OS, as shown in Exhibit 6-7. The *system partition*, on Intel x86 machines is a primary partition that's been marked active and contains files needed to boot Windows – Ntdetect.com, Ntldr, Boot.ini, and optionally, Bootdd.sys. This is the partition that contains the OS boot record. Remember that the MBR looks to this OS boot record for the boot program as the first step in turning the PC over to an OS. The other partition, called the *boot partition*, is the partition where the Windows NT operating system files are stored. The system partition and the boot partition can be the same partition, or they can be separate partitions. Windows NT is designed to use two partitions in this way so that the Windows NT operating system files don't have to be stored on the same partition that's used to boot the OS. Both partitions can be formatted with either FAT16 or NTFS. However, Windows 9x and DOS can't read files formatted with NTFS. If you want these operating systems to access this partition, you must use the FAT16 file system.

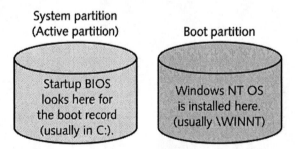

Exhibit 6-7: Two types of Windows NT/2000/XP hard drive partition

Note: Don't be confused by the terminology here. It's really true that, according to Windows NT terminology, the Windows NT OS is on the boot partition, and the boot record is on the system partition, even though that might sound backward. The PC boots from the system partition and loads the Windows NT operating system from the boot partition.

Recall that Windows 9x, using Fdisk, can create two partitions, a primary partition and an extended partition. The primary partition, the C: drive, and the extended partition can contain several volumes or logical drives. Also recall that each FAT16 volume can be no larger than 2 GB. There can be up to four primary partitions on the drive, each containing a single logical drive. However, one of the four partitions can be an extended partition, which means it can have several volumes or logical drives. Each FAT16 volume can be up to 4 GB.

A choice of file systems

Windows NT can work with two types of file systems: the FAT16 file system, which is used by Windows 9x and its predecessors, and the Windows NT file system (NTFS), which doesn't work with Windows 9x or DOS. Windows NT doesn't support FAT32. (Recall that FAT32 was introduced by Windows 95 OSR2 and uses 32 bits for each FAT entry.) Windows NT 4.0 also doesn't support the High Performance File System (HPFS) used by OS/2. If a hard drive is using HPFS, use the Windows NT Convert.exe utility to convert an HPFS partition to an NTFS partition. This program can also convert a FAT16 partition to NTFS.

Note: Even though Windows NT 4.0 doesn't support FAT32, you can use third-party utility software packages, such as FAT32 for Windows NT 4.0 by Winternals (www.winternals.com) to manage the interface, making it possible for Windows NT to read from and write to FAT32.

The FAT16 file system uses three components to manage data on a logical drive: the FAT, directories, and data files. In contrast, the NTFS file system uses a database called the *master file table (MFT)* as its core component. The MFT tracks the contents of a logical drive using one or more rows in the table for each file or directory on the drive. As shown in Exhibit 6-8, the MFT contains in one record, or row, information about each file, including header information (abbreviated H in Microsoft documentation), standard information (SI) about the file (including date and time), file name (FN), security information about the file (called the security descriptor, or SD), and data about the location of the file. Entries in the MFT are ordered alphabetically by file name to speed up a search for a file listed in the table. When a drive is formatted for NTFS, each cluster on the hard drive can range from 512 bytes on smaller disks to 4K on larger disks. Clusters are numbered sequentially by logical cluster numbers (LCNs) from the beginning to the end of the disk.

Referring again to Exhibit 6-8, note that the data area in the MFT record is 2K for small hard drives but can be larger for larger hard drives. For small files, if the data can fit into the 2K area, the file, including its data, is fully contained within the MFT. For small files, all the cluster information for a file can fit into this one data area, including all the cluster numbers for the file. Each cluster number is stored in a 64-bit entry, compared to either 16 bits for FAT16 or 32 bits for FAT32.

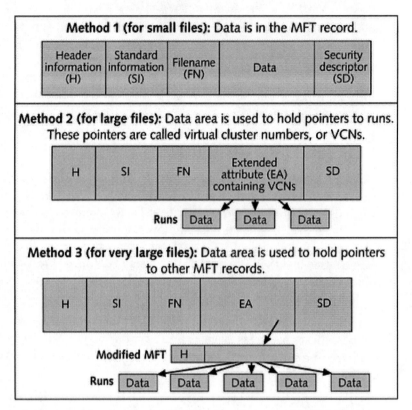

Exhibit 6-8: The Windows NT file system Master File Table

If the file is moderately large and the data doesn't fit into the MFT, the data area in the MFT becomes an extended attribute (EA) of the file, which points to the location of the data. The data itself is moved outside the table to clusters called runs. The record in the MFT for this moderately large file contains pointers to these runs. Each data run, or cluster, assigned to the file is assigned a 64-bit virtual cluster number (VCN). The MFT maps the VCNs for the file onto the LCNs for the drive. This mapping is stored in the area of the MFT record that would have contained the data if the file had been small enough. If the file is so large that the pointers to all the VCNs can't be contained in one MFT record, then additional MFT records are used. The first MFT record is called the base file record and holds the location of the other MFT records for this file.

Advantages of NTFS and FAT16

When choosing between the NTFS file system and the FAT16 file system, consider the advantages that NTFS offers over the FAT:

- NTFS is a recoverable file system. NTFS retains copies of its critical file system data and automatically recovers a failed file system, using this information the first time the disk is accessed after a file system failure.

- NTFS offers increased security over the FAT file system. Security is provided for each file, and auditing information about access to files is more complete.

- NTFS provides added security in the event you boot from floppy disks:
  - If the file system for the active partition of a PC is FAT, you can boot from a DOS or Windows 9x boot disk and bypass the Windows NT security logon. When you use NTFS, you can boot from a DOS or Windows 9x boot disk to an A:\> prompt, but you can't access the hard drive. You can still boot the PC from Windows NT boot disks, but the Windows NT logon is required.
  - If you boot a PC using a DOS or Windows 9x boot disk, you're able to access the hard drive of a Windows NT system that's using the FAT file system, but you can't access an NTFS file system.
  - If you boot a PC using the three Windows NT startup disks, you're able to access the NTFS file system only if you provide an *administrator account* and password. Every Windows NT workstation has an administrator account by default. An administrator has rights and permissions to all computer software and hardware resources and is responsible for setting up other user accounts and assigning privileges to them.

- NTFS supports mirroring drives, meaning that separate copies of data can be kept on two distinct drives to protect against permanent data loss in case of a hard drive crash. This feature makes the NTFS an important alternative for file servers.

- NTFS uses smaller cluster sizes for large partition sizes than does FAT16, making more efficient use of hard drive space when small files are stored.

- NTFS supports large-volume drives. NTFS uses 64-bit cluster numbers, whereas FAT16 uses 16-bit cluster numbers. Because the number of bits assigned to hold each cluster number is so large, the cluster number itself can be a large number, and the table can accommodate very large drives with many clusters. Overall, NTFS is a more effective file system for drives over 1 GB and offers more robust drive compression, allowing compression of individual folders and files.

The advantages of the FAT file system over NTFS include:

- The FAT16 file system has less overhead than the NTFS file system and, therefore, works best for hard drives that have less than 500 MB.

- The FAT file system is compatible with Windows 9x and DOS operating systems. If you plan to use either DOS or Windows 9x on the same hard drive as Windows NT, use the FAT file system so that DOS and Windows 9x can access files used by Windows NT.

- In the event of a serious problem with Windows NT, if you're using FAT16 on the active partition of the drive, you can boot the PC from a DOS or Windows 9x startup disk and gain access to the drive.

You can choose to have Windows NT use NTFS by directing it to convert the hard drive from FAT16 to NTFS or by having Windows NT partition a drive so that one partition of the drive uses the FAT format and the other uses the NTFS format. Windows NT allows you to format logical drives with either FAT16 or NTFS on the same extended partition.

B-1: Discussing file systems

Questions	Answers
1 What two file systems does Windows NT support?	
2 How many bits are used to store a cluster number in the Windows NT NTFS file system?	
3 What's the file system that's common to DOS, Windows 9x, and Windows NT?	
4 What file system can't be read by DOS or Windows 9x but can be used by Windows NT?	
5 Because of the design of the FAT file system, if the FAT16 system is used, hard drive volumes can be up to _____ in size.	
6 What's the main reason that NTFS is more efficient at using hard disk space than FAT16?	
7 Which of these file systems is not supported by Windows NT: FAT16, FAT32, or NTFS?	

Preparing to install Windows NT

Explanation

Before beginning the installation of Windows NT or upgrading from DOS or Windows 9x to Windows NT, you need to prepare for the installation. To determine if your hardware can support Windows NT, begin by searching the HCL. If a device on your system is not on the HCL, contact the manufacturer for a Windows NT driver. If no driver exists, you can't use the device with Windows NT.

Be sure you have enough hard drive space. Windows NT requires about 120 MB of drive space to install itself, and more if the cluster size is large. In addition, a floppy drive and CD-ROM drive are required. For computers without a CD-ROM drive, Windows NT can be installed from a server over a network.

If you're using an Intel-based computer, you can use the *NT Hardware Qualifier (NTHQ)* program found on the Windows NT installation CD-ROM to determine if your system can handle Windows NT. To use Qualifier, boot from a disk onto which you have copied the program, and the utility examines your system to determine if all hardware present qualifies for NT.

Use the following directions to create and use the NT Hardware Qualifier:

Create the NTHQ bootable disk using any computer that has DOS or Windows 9x installed:

1 Insert a bootable disk in the A: drive.

2 To have Windows NT create the Hardware Qualifier disk, from a DOS prompt or from the Run dialog box of Windows 9x, enter this command substituting the drive letter of your CD-ROM drive:

```
D:\Support\Hqtool\MakeDisk.bat
```

3 Using the computer on which you want to install Windows NT, boot from the newly created disk. The following message displays on your screen:

```
Preparing NTHQ
```

You can watch as NT tells you it's creating a RAM drive and copying files to it. Next a screen appears informing you that the log file the utility generates takes several minutes and will be written to the disk and saved as Nthq.txt.

4 Print the log file.

Exhibit 6-9 contains a portion of a sample report from the NTHQ. Note that the two devices listed at the top weren't found in the NTHQ. To determine if these devices work with Windows NT, check the latest HCL on the Microsoft Web site (www.microsoft.com/whdc/hwtest/default.mspx) or contact the manufacturer of each device.

```
Adapter Description: CIRRUS LOGIN PnP V34 MODEM
Adapter Device ID: CIR1000
Listed in Hardware Compatibility List: Not found-check the latest HCL

Adapter Description: OPL3-SAX Sound Board
Adapter Device ID: YMH0024
Listed in Hardware Compatibility List: Not found-check the latest HCL

Adapter Description: S3 Inc. 801/928/964
Listed in Hardware Compatibility List: Yes

Adapter Description: Adaptec AHA-1522
Listed in Hardware Compatibility List: Yes

Adapter Description: Sound Blaster Adapter or compatibles
Listed in Hardware Compatibility List: Yes

Adapter Description: Joystick/game port
Listed in Hardware Compatibility List: Yes
```

Exhibit 6-9: Sample log file from the NT Hardware Qualifier

Installing Windows NT as the only OS

Windows NT comes with three disks that contain a simplified version of Windows NT, enough to boot a PC. If the hard drive doesn't contain an OS, the installation begins by booting from these three disks. After Windows NT loads these three disks, it can access the CD-ROM drive, and installation continues from the CD. The program on the CD executed at that point is Winnt.exe, which is a 16-bit program. A faster version of Winnt.exe on the CD-ROM named Winnt32.exe, a 32-bit program, can sometimes be used instead of Winnt.exe. Winnt32.exe can be run only after Windows NT has already been installed the first time. It's used to upgrade from an older version of NT to a newer version or to reinstall a corrupted version and must be executed from within Windows NT.

The three startup disks can later be used to boot the PC if files on the hard drive become corrupted. You can also create a new set of bootable disks.

Follow these steps to install Windows NT as the only OS:

1 Insert the Windows NT CD in the CD-ROM drive, insert setup disk 1 into the floppy drive, and boot the PC. You're asked to insert disk 2.

2 You see a Welcome to Setup message. You're asked to insert disk 3. Press Enter to continue. Setup lists the mass storage devices it detected. Press Enter to continue.

3 The licensing agreement appears. Scroll to the bottom of the document and press F8 to indicate your agreement and continue.

4 Setup lists hardware and software components it detected. Press Enter to continue.

5 Setup lists existing partitions and space available for creating new partitions. For example, if part of the drive has previously been formatted as drive C with 2047 MB of storage and the other part is still unpartitioned, the following information appears:

```
2442 MB Disk 0 at Id 0 on bus 0 on atapi
C: FAT 2047 MB
Unpartitioned space 394 MB
```

Setup is listing the spaces on the hard drive where it can install the OS, and asking you to make the choice. For this example, highlight Unpartitioned Space, and then press C to create a new partition.

6 Setup asks you for the size of the partition, creates it, informs you it will next format the partition, and prompts you to select a file system for the partition. It then lists the following file systems:

```
Format the partition using the FAT file system
Format the partition using the NTFS file system
```

Select a file system and press Enter.

7 After the formatting is complete, Setup asks for this information:

```
Setup installs Windows NT files onto your hard disk.
Choose the location where you want those files to be
installed: \WINNT
```

The default choice is to install Windows NT in the \Winnt directory. Accept the default by pressing Enter.

8 Setup now asks for permission to examine the hard drive for corruption. You can either allow it by pressing Enter or skip this examination by pressing Esc.

9 Setup tells you that it's copying files to the hard drive. After the copying is complete, the following message appears:

```
Press ENTER to restart your computer
```

When your computer restarts, Setup continues.

10 Up to this point in the installation, all screens appear to be DOS-like with little graphic-user interface and no use of the mouse. When the PC reboots, you're using a true Windows GUI. The opening screen lists the three steps that Windows NT performs to complete the installation:

- Gathering information about your computer
- Installing Windows NT networking
- Finishing Setup

The first item in the list is highlighted. Using the mouse, click Next to continue the installation.

11 Setup offers four options: Typical, Portable, Compact, and Custom. Select Typical and then click Next to continue.

12 Setup requests a name and the name of your organization. Provide them.

13 You're then asked to enter the CD key that identifies the copy of Windows NT being installed. Provide that.

14 Setup then requests a computer name. You're told that the name must be 15 characters or fewer and must be unique for your network. This computer name will later be used to identify this computer on a network. Enter the name, and then click Next.

15 Setup asks for the password for the administrator account. Administrators have full privileges on the workstation. Users have fewer privileges, depending on what the administrator assigns them. If other users who don't have administrator privileges are to use this workstation, or if you're concerned about security at this PC, enter a password, then enter it again to confirm it. If you're the sole user of this PC and security isn't an issue, you don't need to enter a password. Just press Enter.

16 Setup gives you the option to create an Emergency Repair Disk (ERD). Select Yes to create the Emergency Repair Disk, and then click Next to continue.

17 Setup gives you the option to choose what components to install. Since you can later easily install components not installed during the installation, choose Install the most common components.

18 Setup returns to the opening Windows NT setup screen (see Step 11) and continues with Installing Windows NT networking. Click Next to continue.

19 The choices presented are:

```
Do not connect this computer to a network at this time.

This computer will participate on a network:

Wired to the network: Your computer is connected to
the network by an ISDN Adapter or Network adapter.

Remote access to the network: Your computer uses a
modem to connect to the network remotely.
```

For this example, choose Do not connect the computer to a network at this time, and then click Next to continue.

20 Setup returns to the Setup screen (see Step 11). Click Finish to finish Setup. You are asked to select the date and time from the Date/Time Properties sheet. Click Close.

21 Setup automatically detects the correct display adapter. You can change any options on the Display Properties sheet and then click OK.

22 Setup requests that you insert a blank disk labeled Emergency Repair Disk. Insert a blank disk, and then click OK. Setup creates the repair disk.

23 You're instructed to remove the CD and disk from the drives and restart the PC. The installation is done.

Note: If you're having problems with Windows NT detecting your hard drive, the problem might be out-of-date system BIOS. Try flashing BIOS and then attempting the Windows NT installation again.

Installing Windows NT in a dual boot configuration

The Windows NT installation files are stored in the \I386 directory on the CD-ROM drive. If hard drive space is plentiful, you can copy the contents of the \I386 directory and its subdirectories to the hard drive and perform the installation from there. This method is faster, because access to the hard drive is faster than access to the CD-ROM drive. If the computer is connected to a network, the contents of the \I386 directory can be copied to a network server, and the Winnt.exe program can be executed from the server to install Windows NT on the PC, if certain conditions exist.

Remember that Windows NT can coexist on the same PC with either Windows 9x or DOS. The ability to boot from either Windows NT or another OS, such as Windows 9x or DOS, is called a *dual boot*. In a dual boot arrangement, the system partition must be FAT16 rather than NTFS, so that the non-NT OS (Windows 9x or DOS), as well as NT can read it. The main reason for having a dual boot is to accommodate legacy hardware or software that doesn't work under Windows NT.

Note: Remember that Windows NT can't access a FAT32 drive without third-party software. If you're using Windows 98 with FAT32 and want to create a dual boot with Windows NT, first convert to FAT16 or use third-party software to manage the Windows NT and FAT32 interface. Otherwise, Windows NT isn't able to access data on the FAT32 volume. To convert from FAT32 to FAT16, use a third-party utility such as Partition Magic.

Windows NT resides on the boot partition, which can also be formatted for the FAT16 file system and can share the same partition with the other OS or reside on a second partition, such as drive D. You can format this second partition with either FAT or NTFS. If drive D is NTFS, Windows 9x can't read any data stored on that drive. If drive D is a FAT16 partition, either OS can read data from either drive.

After both operating systems are installed, a *Boot Loader menu* appears, asking which OS to boot. The disadvantages of a dual boot are that application software can't be shared between the two operating systems; you must install applications under each OS. Also, you must reboot the PC to move from one OS to the other.

To install Windows NT with Windows 9x loaded, insert the Windows NT installation CD in the drive. If the PC auto detects the CD, you see the Windows NT opening screen. Click Windows NT Setup. If the PC doesn't auto-detect the CD, click Start, Run, and enter this command in the Run dialog box, substituting the drive letter of your CD-ROM drive for D: D:\I386\Winnt.exe. If you want a dual boot, don't choose the same drive that Win 9x is installed on, because this overwrites Windows 9x.

When the PC reboots at the end of installation, it executes the boot loader, which detects two operating systems, and shows a Startup menu (the Boot Loader menu), giving you the choice between Windows NT Workstation Version 4.0 and Microsoft Windows 95 or 98. Select Windows NT Workstation version 4.0, which then loads.

After a Windows NT installation is done, access the Internet and download and install any updates, service packs, and patches from the Microsoft Web site.

Do it!

B-2:   Installing Windows NT

Here's how	Here's why
1 Insert the Windows NT CD in the CD-ROM drive	
Insert setup disk 1	Into the floppy drive.
Boot the system	You're asked to insert disk 2.
2 Observe that the Welcome to Setup message appears	You're asked to insert disk 3.
Press ⏎ ENTER	Setup lists the mass storage devices it detected.
Press ⏎ ENTER	To continue.
3 Observe that the licensing agreement appears	
Scroll to the bottom of the document	
Press F8	To indicate your agreement and continue.
4 Observe that setup lists the hardware and software components it detected	
Press ⏎ ENTER	To continue.
5 Observe that setup lists existing partitions and space available for creating new partitions	For example, if part of the drive has previously been formatted as drive C with 2047 MB of storage, and the other part is still unpartitioned, the following information appears: 2442 MB Disk 0 at Id 0 on bus 0 on atapi C: FAT 2047 MB Unpartitioned space 394 MB
Select Unpartitioned space	To install the OS on the hard disk.
Press C	To create a new partition.
6 Enter the size of the partitions	The setup creates a partition, informs you it will next format the partition, and prompts you to select a file system for the partition.
Select a file system	Setup lists the following file systems: Format the partition using the FAT file system Format the partition using the NTFS file system

7 Press (↵ ENTER)

8 Observe that setup asks for this information: After the formatting is complete.

Setup installs Windows NT files onto your hard disk. Choose the location where you want those files to be installed: \WINNT

Press (↵ ENTER)   To accept the default choice.

9 Press (↵ ENTER)   To examine the hard drive for corruption.

10 Observe that setup tells you that it's copying files to the hard drive

Observe that the message, "Press ENTER to restart your computer," appears   After the copying is complete.

11 Observe that the opening screen lists the three steps that Windows NT performs to complete the installation

The three steps are:
- Gathering information about your computer
- Installing Windows NT networking
- Finishing Setup

Verify that the first item in the list is selected

Click **Next**   To continue the installation, using the mouse.

12 Observe that setup offers four options   These options are: Typical, Portable, Compact, and Custom.

Select **Typical**

Click **Next**   To continue.

13 Observe that setup requests a name and the name of your organization

Enter your and your company's names

14 Enter the CD Key   CD key identifies the copy of Windows NT being installed.

15 Enter the computer name   The computer name must be 15 characters or less and must be unique for your network.

Click **Next**

16	Enter the password for the administrator account	If other users without administrator privileges will be using this workstation, or if you're concerned about security at this PC.
	Enter the password again	To confirm it.
	Press (↵ ENTER)	
17	Select **Yes**	To create the Emergency Repair Disk.
	Click **Next**	
18	Choose **Install the most common components**	To choose what components to install. Setup returns to opening Windows NT setup screen and continues with Installing Windows NT networking.
19	Click **Next**	To continue.
20	Choose **Do not connect the computer to a network at this time**	The choices are: • Do not connect this computer to a network at this time • This computer will participate on a network: • Wired to the network: An ISDN Adapter or Network Adapter connects your computer to the network. • Remote access to the network: Your computer uses a modem to connect to the network remotely.
	Click **Next**	Setup returns to the opening screen.
21	Click **Finish**	To finish Setup.
	Click **Close**	After you're asked to select the date and time from the Date/Time Properties sheet. Setup automatically detects the correct display adapter, and you can change any options on the Display Properties sheet.
22	Click **OK**	Setup requests that you insert a blank disk labeled Emergency Repair Disk.
23	Insert a blank disk	
	Click **OK**	To create a repair disk.
24	Remove the CD and disk from the drives	
	Restart the system	The installation is complete.

Topic C: Supporting Windows NT

Explanation

Recall that Windows NT manages devices, programs, and system resources more efficiently than Windows 9x in many cases and that Windows NT is designed to work with networks and to provide greater security. This section discusses supporting Windows NT, including information on its architecture, how to install hardware and software, and how to handle networking with Windows NT. You will also learn about supporting legacy applications and constructing user profiles for security.

Memory management

Managing memory under DOS and Windows 9x can be complicated because of having to deal with conventional, upper, and extended memory for backward-compatibility. Windows NT eliminates that complexity, because memory is simply memory. In other words, memory addresses are all used the same way. It also loses some backward-compatibility.

The Windows NT memory management model is illustrated in Exhibit 6-10, which shows the NT approach to memory management. The application or device driver says only, "I want memory." It can't say to Windows NT which physical memory or which memory addresses it wants or even the range of addresses that it wants to fall within. Windows NT uses its virtual memory manager to interface between the application or driver and the physical and virtual memory that it controls. Memory is allocated in 4K segments called *pages*. Applications and devices that are written for Windows NT know only how many pages they have. The virtual memory manager takes care of the rest. It's free to store these pages in RAM or on the hard drive in the swap file named *Pagefile.sys*.

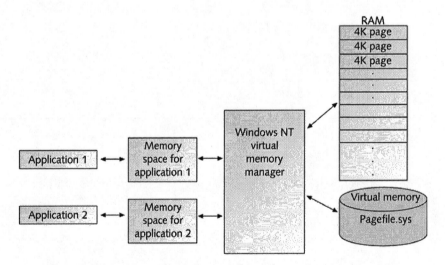

Exhibit 6-10: Windows NT memory management

Installing hardware and software

Hardware and software are installed using the Windows NT Control Panel, as shown in Exhibit 6-11, which looks like and works in a similar way to, that of Windows 9x. With both hardware and software installations, changes are made to the registry. We next look at examples of hardware and software, including how to manage legacy software.

Exhibit 6-11: The Windows NT Control Panel

Note: Windows NT doesn't have a Device Manager. Instead, Windows NT has individual icons for hardware devices in the Control Panel. These icons are used to manage the devices. For a detailed report of the system configuration, use the WinMSD command. At a command prompt, enter WinMSD/a/f. The command creates the report in the current directory.

Installing hardware devices

Windows NT builds its list of available hardware devices each time it's booted. This list isn't kept in the registry permanently. However, when a new hardware device is installed, device driver information is kept in the registry. New hardware devices are installed from the Control Panel, because Windows NT doesn't support Plug and Play and therefore doesn't have an Add New Hardware wizard that automatically launches at startup, as does Windows 9x. The steps below describe the installation of a sound card, because this installation is typical of many hardware devices:

1 To install a sound card, access the Control Panel and double-click the Multimedia icon. The Multimedia Properties dialog box is displayed.

2 Click the Devices tab to see a list of multimedia devices.

3 Select Audio Devices, and then click the Add button. The Add dialog box opens. You can either select a device driver from the list or click Unlisted or Updated Driver to install your own device driver from disk or CD-ROM.

4   If you choose to install your own driver, click Unlisted or Updated Driver, and then click OK. The Install Driver dialog box displays, asking for the location of the driver. As the example shown in Exhibit 6-12 shows, the vendor-provided driver is selected. Several versions of the driver, one for each of the operating systems supported, are located in directories on the CD-ROM that comes with the sound card.

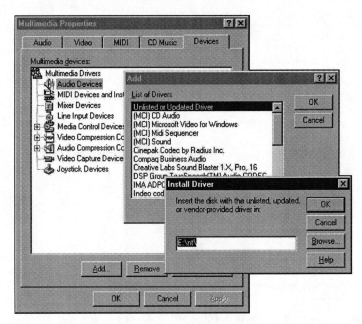

Exhibit 6-12: Installing a device driver

5   On the example CD, the location for the driver is E:\nt\. Enter the path, and then click OK to continue the installation. If Windows NT already has the driver you're installing, the OS gives you the choice to use the driver provided by the vendor or the Windows NT driver.

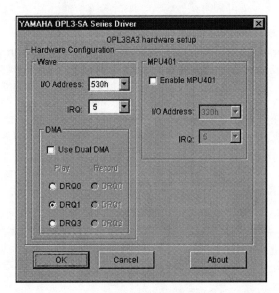

Exhibit 6-13: Windows NT suggests a hardware setup for a new device

6   The driver is copied to the hard drive, and then the hardware setup dialog box displays, as shown in Exhibit 6-13. The suggested I/O address, IRQ, and DMA channels are selected, but you can change these values if you're aware of a conflict. Otherwise, leave the values as suggested and click OK to complete the installation.

7   The Windows NT registry is then updated, and you're asked to restart the PC so that the changes to the registry can take effect.

8   Install the CD Player component of Windows NT to use the new sound card. As with many devices, software is needed to use the sound card. The next step is to double-click the Add/Remove Programs icon of the Control Panel and install the CD Player component of Windows NT in order to use the sound card to play audio CDs. This installation window works just as with Windows 9x.

This example is typical of many hardware installations. The Control Panel was used to install the device driver, and you saw how Windows NT suggests the hardware setup resources to use. Next time the PC boots, the registry contains the location of the sound card device driver, and the *Ntldr (NT Loader)* program loads the device driver by reading this information from the registry. As the driver loads, it looks to the registry for the list of resources that it uses. The Ntldr file is the initially executed Windows NT OS file and is similar to Io.sys in DOS and Windows 9x.

The software to use the CD player is also installed from the Control Panel. This information is now kept in the registry to be used each time the OS loads. The OS uses this registry information to provide the CD Player option under Start, Accessories, Multimedia.

Installing software

Software is installed from the Control Panel using the Add/Remove Programs icon. Installation works very much the same way as under Windows 9x. Access the Control Panel by clicking Start, and then choose Settings, Control Panel. In Control Panel, double-click the Add/Remove Programs icon. The Add/Remove Programs Properties dialog box opens. Any software that installs with a Setup.exe or Install.exe program can be installed using this dialog box. Click Install, and the dialog box requests the location of the setup program.

To add new components to Windows NT that weren't installed when Windows NT was originally installed, click the Windows NT Setup tab of the Add/Remove Programs Properties dialog box. You see a list of all of the Windows NT components. From this list, you can choose to install new components or to uninstall components that are already installed.

Even though it would be convenient if all software running under Windows NT were written in the newer 32-bit code used by Windows 9x and Windows NT, this doesn't always happen. As explained earlier, Windows NT makes provisions for running DOS applications by creating a separate NTVDM for each application, so that each program can run in its native environment. Windows 16-bit applications can run in individual NTVDMs, or several 16-bit Windows applications can run in the same NTVDM so they can share resources.

Do it!

C-1:   Installing a sound card

Here's how	Here's why
1 Open Control Panel	You want to install a sound card.
Double-click **Multimedia**	The Multimedia Properties dialog box opens.
2 Click the **Devices** tab	To see a list of multimedia devices.
3 Select **Audio Devices**	
Click **Add**	The Add dialog box opens.
4 Click **Unlisted or Updated Driver**	If you choose to install your own driver.
Click **OK**	The Install Driver dialog box appears, asking for the location of the driver. As shown in Exhibit 6-12, the vendor-provided driver is selected.
5 Observe that the location for the driver is E:\nt\	In the example CD.
Enter the path	
Click **OK**	To continue the installation. If Windows NT already has the driver you're installing, the OS gives you the choice to use the driver provided by the vendor or the Windows NT driver.
6 Observe that, when the driver is copied to the hard drive, the hardware setup dialog box appears	As shown in Exhibit 6-13.
Click **OK**	To complete the installation.
7 Observe that you're asked to restart the PC so the changes to the registry can take effect	After the Windows NT registry is updated.
8 Install the CD Player component of Windows NT	To use the new sound card.
Double-click **Add/Remove Programs**	In the Control Panel.
Install the CD Player component of Windows NT	To use the sound card to play audio CDs. This installation window works just as with Windows 9x.

Networking

One of the main reasons businesses choose Windows NT as an OS is because of its strong networking features. Remember that there are two versions of Windows NT: Windows NT Workstation and Windows NT Server. In a general PC environment, a workstation is a desktop PC that both accesses a network and works as a standalone PC. In the most general sense, a server is a computer that contains data, software, and security validation files that are accessed simultaneously by workstations on the network. Generally, a server on the network isn't also a workstation. Even though it may have a keyboard and monitor connected to it, a network administrator uses these devices only to administer and monitor the network. The server is solely dedicated to serving the network.

All the functionality offered by Windows NT Workstation is available with Windows NT Server. The primary difference between the two is that Windows NT Server offers the additional functionality of administering and monitoring the network from this centralized location. However, either OS can be configured to work as one node in a workgroup or as one node on a domain.

A *workgroup* is a logical group of computers and users that share resources, as shown in Exhibit 6-14, where the control of administration, resources, and security is distributed throughout the network. A Windows NT *domain* is a group of networked computers that all share a centralized directory database of user account information and security for the entire set of computers, as shown in Exhibit 6-15. A workgroup uses a peer-to-peer networking model, and a domain uses a client/server networking model.

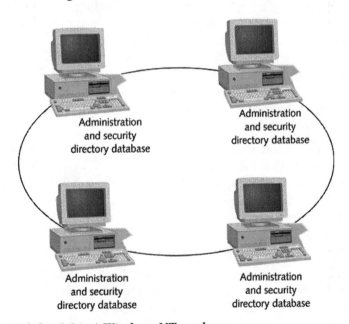

Exhibit 6-14: A Windows NT workgroup

When a group of computers is connected to share resources, you can configure these computers as a network using the *workgroup model*, with the network administered from individual PCs in a workgroup, or use the *domain model*, with the network administered from a centralized location in the domain. Resources, including data, software, and printers, can be shared using either model.

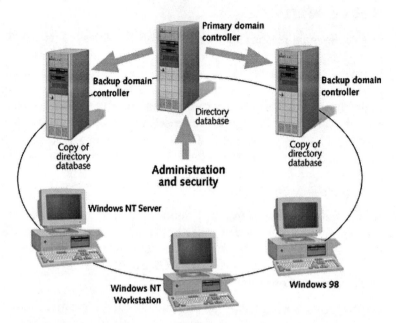

Exhibit 6-15: A Windows NT domain

Also, as you learn about workgroups and domains, remember that, in either case, the group of computers is a logical group, not a geographical group. A workgroup of computers can be in a single building, or it can include PCs in other cities. Distance makes no difference, as long as there's networked connectivity either over phone lines or by other means. PCs are grouped together to share resources. For example, a sales staff member might need to share a marketing database, and the accounting staff of a company might need to share a journals database. People in both groups are spread over several cities. Members of the sales staff make up the sales workgroup, and members of the accounting staff make up the accounting workgroup, so each user can access shared resources within the appropriate group.

When you implement Windows NT Workstation, it's often necessary to set users up in a workgroup with other PCs using Windows NT or Windows 9x and to configure the PCs to be members of a domain controlled by a Windows NT server. Understanding the concepts of workgroups and domains and how they're managed is the first step in learning how to support them.

Using workgroups and domains

In a workgroup, every computer has its own directory database of user accounts and security policies. Each computer in a workgroup manages the accounts on that computer for other users and computers that want to access information on it. If you're a member of a workgroup and want to allow another user on another PC to access files on your PC, you must establish an account for that user. The information about that account is kept only on your PC.

A workgroup can be made up of computers that use either Windows NT Workstation or Windows NT Server. However, PCs that have Windows NT Server installed must be configured as standalone units. A workgroup doesn't require a Windows NT server to be present. Workgroups don't have centralized account management or security. Workgroups are generally used for a small group of workstations, and the PC support person usually manages each user account on each PC in the workgroup.

A domain is used for a large number of workstations, and security for the domain shifts to a business-wide or enterprise function of a network administrator controlling security from a single console.

In a Windows NT domain, a network administrator manages access to the network through a centralized database. In Exhibit 6-15, you see the possible different components of a Windows NT domain. Every domain has a *primary domain controller (PDC)*, which stores and controls a database of accounts. There are three kinds of accounts:

- User
- Group
- Computer

This database is called the directory database or the *security accounts manager (SAM)* database.

An administrator logged on to any workstation or server on the domain can update the directory database by accessing the PDC, but the domain can have only one PDC. One or more read-only backup copies of the directory database can be kept on other computers. Each computer with a backup of the directory database is called a *backup domain controller, (BDC)*. A system can be set up so that whenever the database on the PDC is updated, copies are written to each BDC. This is called replication. In Exhibit 6-15, there are two BDCs, each keeping a copy of the directory database. BDCs use their copy of the SAM database to authenticate users as they log on, thereby relieving the PDC of the burden of authentication functions. This sharing of functions improves performance in domains with many, more than 1000, workstations. Workstations on the domain are shown in the lower part of Exhibit 6-15. A Windows NT network can contain these operating systems functioning in these ways:

- Windows NT Server, functioning as a PDC, a BDC, or as a standalone server, a server on the network that has no domain controller functions.
- Windows 9x, Windows NT Workstation, Windows 2000 Professional, or Windows XP Professional acting as clients on the network.

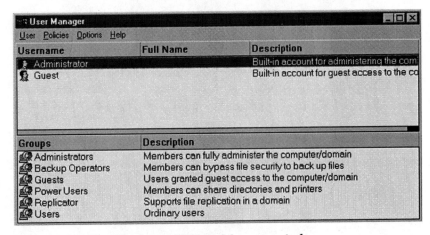

Exhibit 6-16: The Windows NT User Manager window

Do it!

C-2: Managing user accounts

Here's how	Here's why
1 Log on as an administrator	You want to start User Manager.
2 Create a folder named Users in the root directory of the C: drive	Using Windows Explorer.
3 Click **Start**	On the taskbar.
Choose **Programs**, **Administrative Tools**, **User Manager**	The User Manager window appears, as shown in Exhibit 6-16.
Examine the User Manager window	
Answer the following questions:	
Based on your knowledge of Windows NT, what two User accounts are included on a Windows NT system by default?	
Does your system contain any personal user accounts? If so, list them here:	
What user groups are included on your Windows NT system?	
4 Choose **User**, **New User**	From the User Manager menu. You want to add and configure users on a local computer using User Manager.
Observe that the New User window opens	
5 Type a username	The name to be used to log on to Windows NT. For user names, you can use alphanumeric characters, and some symbols (such as "!" and "." but not "\").
6 Type a full name	
Type a description for the account	
7 Enter a password	
Confirm the Password	
Verify that User Must Change Password at Next Logon is checked	

8 Note that User Manager provides
   other options concerning
   password setup

   Record the options   Do not select these options now.

   What other check boxes could you
   select?

9 Click **Groups** at the bottom of   The Group Membership window opens. You
   the New User window   want to add a new user to a user group.

10 Record the following information:

   What group is the New User a
   member of by default?

   How does membership in this
   group differ from membership in
   the Administrator's group?

11 From Not Member of list, select
   Power Users

   Click **Add**   This makes the New User a member of both
                                               Users and Power Users groups.

12 Click **OK**   The Group Membership window closes.

13 Click **Profiles** next to the   The User Environment Profile window opens.
   Groups button

14 Click **Local Path** in the Home   You want to set up the user's home directory
   Directory section of the User   under the C:\Users directory.
   Environment Profile window

   Type   The entry "%username%" tells User Manager to
   C:\Users\%username%   use the account's logon name as the folder name
                                               for the user's home directory.

   Select **Connect**   If you want to place the Home Directory on a
                                               remote system somewhere on the network.

   Specify a drive letter

   Specify a path   In the To section.

15 Click **OK**   The User Environment Profile window closes,
                                               and you return to the User Properties window.

16 Click **OK**   To add this user to the system. You've now
                                               finished adding a user to the system.

17	Repeat this process	To set up accounts for each user in your lab group.
18	Log off as an administrator	You want to examine the settings created for new accounts and discover what you can and can't do with the newly created accounts.
	Log back in using one of your new user accounts	
	What did you have to do when you logged on with your user account?	
19	Open a command prompt window	
	Judging by the command prompt, what folder are you currently working in?	
20	Open User Manager	
	Add a new user account named Test	
	Don't adjust group memberships or profiles	
	When might you not be able to create this account?	
21	Log out	
	Log in as Test	
22	Open a command prompt window	
	What folder are you currently working in?	
23	Open User Manager	
	Add an account called Test1	Without adjusting profiles or group membership.
	Delete the Guest account	
	Why couldn't you create an account?	
	Why couldn't you delete the Guest account?	

24 Log off as Test	You want to configure the lockout feature. The lockout feature is used to lock an account after a user makes several unsuccessful attempts to log onto it. Once an account is locked, an administrator must intervene to make the account accessible again.
Log on as an administrator	
25 Open User Manager	
Choose **Policies**, **Accounts** on the menu bar	The Account Policy window opens.
Observe that the Password restrictions provide four ways to customize a password policy	
Record and explain these options	
26 Click **Account Lockout**	In the section below the Password Restrictions of the Account Policy window.
27 Set the Lockout after field to **3 bad logon attempts**	
28 Select **Forever** in the Lockout Duration section	This option tells Windows NT to keep the account locked until the administrator unlocks it.
29 Click **OK**	To close the Account Policy dialog box.
30 Log off as an administrator	You want to lock and unlock an account.
Log on as Test	Using an incorrect password.
What message appears at the fourth logon attempt?	
31 Log on as an administrator	
Open User Manager	
32 Double-click **Test** account	
Clear **Account Locked-out**	
Click **OK**	
33 Log off as an administrator	
Log back on as Test	
Explain what happens	

34 Besides adding and deleting users,
what other tasks can you perform
with User Manager? List five.

35 Besides the Administrators group,
what other group has permission
to add and delete users? What
group doesn't?

36 List the steps required to change
the group an account belongs to.

37 What setting determines the
current directory when the
command prompt window opens?

Topic D: The boot process

Explanation   Understanding the boot process and making changes to it are critical when supporting Windows NT. (Windows 2000 and Windows XP use this same boot process.) In this topic you'll learn what happens during the boot and how to solve boot problems.

Understanding the boot process

The following is a look behind the scenes with a description of each step in the boot process. As you read, the following table shows an outline of the boot sequence for Intel-based computers:

1 **BIOS executes POST.** First, startup BIOS performs POST, which happens just as it would regardless of the OS present. After POST, BIOS turns to the hard drive to load an OS. BIOS looks for the partition information at the beginning of the hard drive.

2 **BIOS executes the MBR program.** The first thing in the partition information that BIOS needs is the MBR containing the master boot program. The master boot program is the very first thing written in the first sector of a hard drive. The partition table follows the master boot program, and both are stored in the master boot sector. BIOS executes this master boot program, which examines the partition table, looking for the location of the active partition on the drive, and then turns to the first sector of the active partition to find and load the program in the boot sector of that active partition. So far in the boot process, nothing in Windows NT is different from other operating systems.

3 **The MBR program executes the OS boot program.** Remember that, when DOS or Windows 9x boots, the OS boot sector contains the name of the initial OS load program, Io.sys. When Windows NT is installed, it edits this boot sector of the active partition, instructing it to load the Windows NT program, Ntldr, at startup, instead of Io.sys. It does this even when the PC is configured for a dual boot.

4 **The boot program executes Ntldr.** With the execution of Ntldr, Windows NT then starts its boot sequence. This program is responsible for loading Windows NT and performing several chores to complete the loading process. It then passes off control to the OS.

5 **Ntldr changes the processor mode and loads a file system.** Up to this point, the CPU has been processing in real mode; every program had complete access to system resources. Windows NT doesn't process in real mode. Ntldr is a 32-bit program and begins by changing the CPU mode from real mode to a 32-bit mode called *32-bit flat memory mode*, in order to run its 32-bit code. Next, a temporary, simplified file system called the *minifile system* is started, so that Ntldr can read files from either a FAT or an NTFS file system.

6 **Ntldr reads and loads the boot loader menu.** Ntldr then is able to read the Boot.ini file, a hidden text file that contains information needed to build the Boot Loader menu. The menu is displayed, and the user can make a selection or, after the preset time expires, the default selection is used.

7 **Ntldr uses Ntdetect.com.** If Ntldr is to load Windows NT as the OS, Ntldr runs the program Ntdetect.com, which checks the hardware devices present and passes the information back to Ntldr. This information is later used to update the Windows NT registry concerning the last known good hardware profile used.

8 **Ntldr loads the OS and boot time device drivers.** Ntldr then loads Ntoskrnl.exe, Hal.dll, and the *System hive*. The System hive is a portion of the Windows NT registry that includes hardware information that's now used to load the proper device drivers for the hardware present.

9 **Ntldr passes control to Ntoskrnl.exe.** Ntldr then passes control to Ntoskrnl.exe, and the boot sequence is complete.

10 **An operating system other than Windows NT is chosen.** If a selection was made from the Boot Loader menu to load an OS other than Windows NT, such as DOS or Windows 9x, Ntldr doesn't load Ntdetect.com or complete the remaining chores to load Windows NT. Instead, Ntldr loads and passes control to boot sector of that OS. This is stored in a file. For Windows or DOS, this file is called Bootsect.dos.

The following table lists the steps in the Intel-based CPU boot process:

Step	Description	Performed by:
1	POST is executed.	Startup BIOS
2	MBR is loaded, and the master boot program within the MBR is run.	Startup BIOS
3	The boot sector from active partition is loaded, and program in this boot sector is run.	MBR program
4	Ntldr (NT Loader) file is loaded and run.	Boot sector program
5	The processor is changed from real mode to flat memory mode, in which 32-bit code can be executed.	Windows NT loader
6	Minifile system drivers are started so files can be read.	Windows NT loader
7	Read Boot.ini file and build the Boot Loader menu described in the file.	Windows NT loader
8	If the user chooses Windows NT, run Ntdetect.com to detect hardware present; otherwise, run Bootsect.dos.	Windows NT loader
9	Ntldr reads information from the Registry about device drivers and loads them. It also loads Hal.dll and Ntoskrml.exe.	Windows NT loader
10	Ntldr passes control to Ntoskrml.exe; load is complete.	Windows NT loader

Note: When repairing a corrupted hard drive, a support person often copies files from one PC to another. However, the Bootsect.dos file contains information from the partition table for a particular hard drive and can't be copied from another PC.

The files needed to boot Windows NT successfully are shown in the following table. In the table, references to \winnt_root follow Microsoft documentation conventions and mean the name of the directory where Windows NT is stored, which is \Winnt by default.

File	Location
Ntldr	Root directory of the system partition (usually C:\)
Boot.ini	Root directory of the system partition (usually C:\)
Bootsect.dos	Root directory of the system partition (usually C:\)
Ntdetect.com	Root directory of the system partition (usually C:\)
Ntbootdd.sys*	Root directory of the system partition (usually C:\)
Ntoskrnl.exe	\winnt_root\system32 directory of the boot partition
Hal.dll	\winnt_root\system32 directory of the boot partition
Registry	\winnt_root\system32\config of the boot partition
Device drivers	\winnt_root\system32\drivers of the boot partition

Note: *Ntbootdd.sys is used only with a SCSI boot device.

Do it!

D-1:   Discussing the boot process

Exercises

1 What's the first Windows NT program that's loaded and run when Windows NT is booted?

2 Like the previous versions of Windows 9x, Windows NT begins booting with the CPU in real mode. True or false?

3 When repairing a corrupted hard drive, what file can't be copied from another PC? Why?

4 What's the System hive?

Topic E: Troubleshooting

Explanation

In this topic, you'll learn about troubleshooting Windows NT, including the boot process and some diagnostic tools that you can use for maintenance and troubleshooting. Many of the general troubleshooting tips from other applications apply to Windows NT as well. Since you've just learned about the Windows NT boot process, let's begin with a discussion of troubleshooting that process.

Troubleshooting the boot process

Listed below are the things you can do and the order in which you should do them to troubleshoot a failed Windows NT boot. Remember that Windows NT doesn't have a safe mode, as does Windows 9x, and several of the useful troubleshooting utilities of Windows 9x are missing from Windows NT.

To recover from a failed Windows NT boot, do the following:

- If the Windows NT Startup menu appears (it appears if it thinks there's a problem you need to know about), use the Last Known Good configuration to return to the last registry values that allowed for a successful boot. Any configuration changes since the last good boot are lost.
- If you can't boot from the hard drive, boot using the three boot disks that came with the OS. If you don't have these three disks, you can create them on another PC that's working. Check for corrupted boot and system files that you can replace.
- Boot from the three disks and select the option, "To repair a damaged Windows NT version 4.0 installation."
- Try reinstalling Windows NT into the same folder it currently uses. Tell the Setup program that this is an upgrade.
- As a last resort, if you're using the NTFS file system and you must recover data on the hard drive, move the hard drive to another system that's running Windows NT and install the drive as a secondary drive. You might then be able to recover the data.

Last Known Good Configuration

Each time Windows NT boots and the first logon is made with no errors, the OS saves a copy of the hardware configuration from the registry. This is called the Last Known Good Configuration. All hardware configuration sets stored in the registry, including the Last Known Good Configuration, are called control sets. The next time the PC boots, if an error occurs, it can use the Last Known Good Configuration.

The key in the registry that contains the Last Known Good Configuration is:

```
HKEY_LOCAL_MACHINE\HARDWARE
```

If Windows NT detects the possibility of a problem, it adds the Last Known Good Configuration option to the Windows NT Startup menu. You can select this Last Known Good Configuration option to revert back to the control set that was used for the last good boot. For example, if you install a new device driver, restart Windows NT, and find that the system hangs; then you can use the Last Known Good Configuration option to revert back to the previous configuration.

Because the configuration information isn't saved to the Last Known Good Configuration control set until after the logon, if you're having trouble with the boot, don't attempt to log on. Doing so causes the Last Known Good Configuration to be replaced by the current control set, which might have errors.

For example, if you've installed a new video driver and you restart Windows, but the screen is very difficult to read, don't log on. Instead, press the reset button to reboot the PC. When given the choice, select Last Known Good Configuration from the Startup menu.

To prevent hard drive corruption, if you're having problems booting Windows NT, wait for all disk activity to stop before pressing the reset button or turning off the PC, especially if you're using the FAT file system.

If you accidentally disable a critical device, Windows NT decides to revert to the Last Known Good Configuration for you. You aren't provided with a menu choice.

Reverting to the Last Known Good Configuration causes the loss of any changes made to the hardware configuration since the Last Known Good Configuration was saved. Therefore, it's wise to make one change at a time to the hardware configuration and reboot after each change. That way, if problems during booting are encountered, only the most recent change is lost. When installing several hardware devices, install them one at a time, rebooting each time.

Note: If you're having problems booting in Windows NT, don't log on, because if you do, you overwrite your previous Last Known Good Configuration.

Boot disks

With Windows 9x and DOS, any single disk could be formatted as a boot disk or system disk. Windows NT is different. It requires three disks to hold enough of Windows NT to boot. However, formatting a single disk just to hold data or software can be done using Windows Explorer.

When Windows NT formats a disk, the boot sector is written to boot the Ntldr program instead of Io.sys, as in DOS and Windows 9x. To format a disk, use Windows NT Explorer. Right-click the 3½ Floppy (A:) line in Windows Explorer and choose Format from the shortcut menu. The dialog box shown in Exhibit 6-17 is displayed.

The only file system available for a floppy disk is FAT. Note in the exhibit that there's no option to make the disk a system disk or boot disk. If you try to boot from a disk that has been formatted by Windows NT, this error message appears:

```
BOOT: Couldn't find NTLDR
Please insert another disk
```

Windows NT comes with a set of three disks that are initially used to boot the machine before the installation continues from the CD-ROM. After the OS is installed, you can use these disks in an emergency to boot the OS. These three disks come with Windows NT, but you can make extra sets. The set of boot disks is the same no matter what PC you're using. The disks contain no special information about your system.

If the original three disks to boot Windows NT become corrupted or lost, you can make extra copies using Winnt32.exe, if you're running Windows NT or using Winnt.exe, if you're running another OS, such as DOS or Windows 9x. You don't have to be working on the PC where you intend to use the disks in order to make them, since the disks don't contain unique information for a specific PC.

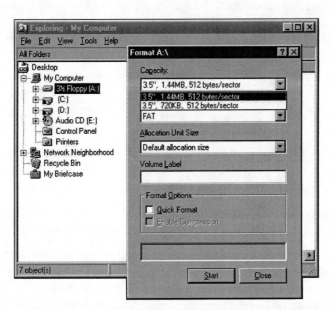

Exhibit 6-17: Windows NT dialog box used to format a disk

Creating Windows NT setup disks: Proceed as follows to create boot disks using Windows NT:

1 Click Start, Run and then enter the path and Winnt32.exe with the /OX parameters. These parameters say to create only the set of three disks, without performing a complete installation. Note the E:\I386\winnt32.exe/ox entry in the Run dialog box of Exhibit 6-18. This is the command line from within Windows NT used to create the disks when drive E contains the Windows NT installation CD.

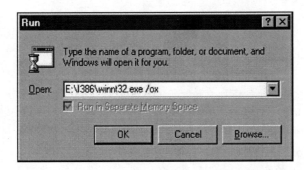

Exhibit 6-18: Use Winnt32.exe to create a set of boot disks

2 The program asks for the location of the installation files. In this example, you enter E:\I386. You're then prompted to insert three disks. The program creates the disks beginning with disk 3, then 2, then 1.

Windows NT doesn't have a safe mode, so if the PC can't boot Windows NT from the hard drive, these three disks can be used to load Windows NT, which loads using a generic VGA mode. After Windows NT is loaded, use the Emergency Repair Disk to restore critical system files to their state at the time the last update was made to the Emergency Repair Disk.

Emergency Repair Disks

A fourth important disk is the *Emergency Repair Disk (ERD)*, which does contain information unique to your OS and hard drive. You're given the opportunity to create the disk during installation. Always create and update this disk, because it's the record of critical information about your system that can be used to fix a problem with the OS.

The ERD enables restoration of the Windows registry on your hard drive, which contains all the configuration information for Windows.

The files on the ERD are shown in the following table. Files stored on the ERD are also written to the hard drive during the installation process. Using Windows Explorer, you can see the files listed in the \winnt_root\repair folder:

File	Description
Setup.log	A read-only, hidden system file that's used to verify the files installed on a system.
System._	A compressed file containing part of the registry.
Sam._	A compressed file containing some of the security part of the registry.
Security._	A compressed file containing some of the security part of the registry.
Software._	A compressed file containing software information in the registry.
Default._	A compressed file containing part of the registry.
Config.nt	The Windows NT version of Config.sys used in creating a command window.
Autoexec.nt	The Windows NT version of Autoexec.bat.
Ntuser.da_	A compressed file containing information about authorized users of the system.

After the installation, you can create a new ERD or update the current one by using the Rdisk.exe utility in the \winnt_root\system32 folder. You should update the disk any time you make any major changes to the system. For example, you install hardware or software. To use the Rdisk.exe utility, click Start, Run, and then either click Browse or enter the path to the utility. Adding the /S to the command bypasses the dialog and directly saves the ERD. The /S switch also copies the SAM onto the floppies.

If Windows NT is stored on the D: drive, the command line is:

```
D:\WINNT\System32\rdisk.exe /s
```

First, files are updated in the \winnt_root\repair directory, and then you're given the opportunity to create a new ERD.

Recovering from a failed boot

In the case of problems with the OS, there are several things you can do to attempt to load Windows NT from the hard drive, which are beyond the scope of this book. However, in the case of a hard drive failure, you can boot from the set of three boot disks that come with the Windows NT CD or that you made using either Winnt.exe or Winnt32.exe. The Windows NT programs on these disks may also request that you provide the ERD. Insert the first boot disk and reboot. You're prompted to insert disk 2, followed by disk 3. The Setup menu in Exhibit 6-19 is then displayed. Select the option to repair a damaged installation by pressing R and follow the directions on screen.

```
Windows NT Workstation Setup

Welcome to Setup.
The Setup program for the Microsoft(R) Windows NT(TM) OS version 4.0
prepares Windows NT to run on your computer.

        *To learn more about Windows NT Setup before continuing, press F1
        *To set up Windows NT now, press ENTER
        *To repair a damaged Windows NT version 4.0 installation, press R
        *To quit Setup without installing Windows NT, press F3
```

Exhibit 6-19: Windows NT Workstation Setup menu

Do it!

E-1: Creating setup and repair disks

Here's how	Here's why
1 Log in as an administrator	
2 Open the command prompt window	
Make the directory containing the Windows NT setup files the current directory	In most cases, you find the files for systems with Intel compatible processors in the \i386 directory on the Windows NT installation CD.
3 Enter **winnt32 /ox**	At the command prompt. The Windows NT 4.00 Upgrade/Installation utility window opens.
4 What does the message say about copying files?	
5 Specify the path to the Windows NT setup files	Typically, the i386 directory on the installation CD.
Click **Continue**	
6 Label the disk **Setup Disk 3**	When prompted.
Insert the disk	
Click **OK**	Setup files are written to each disk.
Repeat the procedure for Disks 2 and 1	

7 Remove Disk 1	When the last disk is finished, the utility closes, and you return to the command prompt window.
8 Open a command prompt window	You want to create the Emergency Repair Disk.
9 Enter **Rdisk / S**	At the command prompt. The Repair Disk Utility opens and begins by notifying you that it's saving the configuration, which should only be used to recover a bootable system in case of failure.
10 What options are included in this utility?	
11 Label a floppy disk "ERD" Insert the floppy disk Click **Create Repair Disk**	To create an Emergency Repair Disk. Windows formats the floppy, examines the system's configuration, and creates an ERD that matches the system's current configuration.
12 Remove the ERD Click **Exit** Close the command prompt window	
13 Use Windows Explorer	To display the contents of each disk. You want to examine the contents of the disks you've created.
Answer the following questions: On Setup Disk 1, what files with .exe extensions are included? On Setup Disks 2 and 3, what file extensions are used? Name five files that are included on the ERD. What types of information do you think these files contain?	

14 What command do you use to create Windows NT setup disks when using DOS?

15 Why might it be convenient to copy the files on the Windows NT installation CD to a hard drive shared over the local network?

16 In what directory are Windows NT setup files for Intel-based computers stored?

17 When should you create a new ERD?

18 Why should you safeguard your ERD?

Making repairs

Next, you'll use your set of Emergency Repair Disks to repair a Windows NT Workstation that won't boot correctly. The ERD enables restoration of the Windows registry on your hard drive, which contains all the configuration information for Windows. However, keep in mind that you can't boot from the ERD. To boot up a damaged Windows NT machine, you still need the Windows NT CD or the set of three boot disks that come with the CD.

Do it!

E-2:   Repairing a Windows NT Workstation

Here's how	Here's why
1 Log on as an administrator	To display hidden files, because system files aren't displayed by default.
2 Open Windows Explorer	
Select the root directory of drive C:	In the left pane.
Choose **View**, **Options** on the menu bar	The Options dialog box opens.

3 Click the **View** tab

   Select **Show All Files**

   Clear **Hide file extensions for known file types**

   Click **OK**   To apply the changes and close the Options window. Hidden files are now visible in Windows Explorer.

4 Right-click **boot.ini**   In the right pane.

   Choose **Properties**   The Boot.ini Properties dialog box opens.

5 Clear **Hidden**

   Clear **Read-only**   So that the files appear and you can make changes to them.

6 Click **OK**   The Boot.ini Properties dialog box closes, and you return to Windows Explorer.

7 Right-click **boot.ini**

   Choose **Open**   To open Boot.ini in Notepad.

8 Delete the line that begins "Default="

9 Choose **File**, **Save**   Windows NT is now damaged.

10 Attempt to boot your system   To verify that Windows NT is damaged.

   Record the boot process

   What do you see?

11 Insert the ERD   You want to boot from the ERD.

   Boot the system

   Describe what happens

12 Insert the Windows NT   You want to repair the system.
   Workstation installation CD in the CD-ROM drive

13 Insert setup Disk 1

   Reboot the system

14 Insert Disk 2   When prompted.

15	Press `R`	At the Windows NT setup menu. To repair the installation. Setup displays a list of tests that it performs in order to find the problem.
16	Press `← ENTER`	With Continue selected. To proceed as though you have no idea what the problem is.
17	Press `← ENTER`	To allow setup to detect disk controllers.
18	Insert Disk 3	When prompted.
	Press `← ENTER`	Setup detects your hard disk controller and loads the drivers needed for this controller as well as other drivers needed to access critical devices.
19	Press `← ENTER`	After Setup detects other drives to allow Setup to load drivers.
	Press `S`	If Setup fails to detect a necessary drive.
	Follow instructions provided by the instructor	To enable your device.
20	Press `← ENTER`	If Setup notifies you that it has discovered large hard drives. Setup asks if you have the ERD.
21	What does Setup attempt if you don't have the ERD?	
22	Press `← ENTER`	To indicate that you have the ERD.
23	Insert the ERD	When prompted.
	Press `← ENTER`	
24	Press `← ENTER`	To let Setup examine the hard drives. Setup examines the hard drive and then displays a warning about restoring the registry.
25	What might occur when you restore the registry?	
26	Select all components except Security and SAM	Using the up and down arrow keys and the Enter key. Setup displays a list of registry components and system files it can repair and also lists those that appear to be corrupt or missing. To repair Windows NT, Setup overwrites these selected files with good copies.
	Select **Continue**	
	Press `← ENTER`	If you overwrite the SAM, which contains username and account information for all users, only default user accounts are restored to the system.

27 Press (A)   If you're informed that the files don't match the original files. To continue replacing all files anyway.

28 Remove the ERD and the CD   After the repair process is finished.

29 Press (← ENTER)   To reboot the PC.

Log on to Windows NT with your username and password

30 Access the Internet   After Windows NT is restored.

Check for the latest service packs for this workstation

Install the latest service packs

What service packs did you install?

31 Recall that the Windows 9x ERD is bootable. Is the Windows NT ERD bootable?

32 In theory, is there any hope of successfully completing the repair process if you don't have an ERD? Explain.

33 In the repair process, what step(s) must not be skipped so that the CD-ROM drive is detected?

34 What happens to user accounts you created after installing Windows NT if you restore the security and SAM files during the repair process?

35 What should you do immediately after you restore the system to a bootable state?

Unit summary: Understanding and supporting Windows NT

Topic A   In this topic, you learned about the Windows NT **architecture**. You learned about the **modular** concept of Windows NT and the two Windows NT modes: **User mode** and **Kernel mode**. You learned that user mode has several subsystems, with the **Win32 subsystem** being the most important. You also learned the kernel mode is used by two main components: **HAL** (hardware abstraction layer) and **executive services**.

Topic B   In this topic, you learned how to install Windows NT. You learned about the **hard drive partitions** and how to choose between the two available **file systems: NTFS** and **FAT16**. You also learned to **prepare** to install Windows NT by searching the **HCL** for **compatible hardware**. You also learned the steps needed to install Windows NT as the **only OS** and as the **second OS** on the hard drive in a **dual boot** configuration.

Topic C   In this topic, you learned how to perform support tasks for Window NT. You learned about **memory management** in Windows NT. You then learned how to install **hardware** and **software**. You learned that Windows NT doesn't support **Plug and Play**. You also learned the concepts of Windows NT **networking** and how a network can be set up in a **workgroup** configuration or as a **domain**.

Topic D   In this topic, you learned about the Windows NT **boot process**. You also learned what **files** are needed for the boot process and the **location** of these files on the hard drive.

Topic E   In this topic, you learned about **troubleshooting** Windows NT. You learned how to troubleshoot the **boot process**. Then you learned the types of **diagnostic tools** you can use for **maintenance** and **troubleshooting** Windows NT. You learned how to create the disks required to **recover** from a **failed boot**: three **boot disks** and the **Emergency Repair Disk** (ERD).

Review questions

1   What are the two versions of Windows NT 4.0?

2   Why can't a 16-bit device driver work under Windows NT?

3   What layer of Windows NT is most responsible for interacting with hardware?

4   What's one reason that interaction with hardware is limited to only one or two components of the OS?

5 Can an application or device driver specify which physical memory or memory addresses it wants in Windows NT? Why or why not?

6 Before you install Windows NT, how can you determine if the OS supports all the hardware on your PC?

7 What's one function of a backup domain controller in a Windows NT domain?

8 In a Windows NT workgroup, where is access to an individual workstation on the network controlled?

9 In a Windows NT domain, where is access to an individual workstation on the network controlled?

10 What's the term for the 4K segments in which Windows NT allocates memory?

11 How many floppy disks are needed in order to boot Windows NT from disk?

12 In what two places can the Windows NT virtual memory manager store memory pages?

13 A dual boot results in bother operating systems being loaded into RAM. True or false?

14 A 4K segment of RAM managed by Windows NT is called a _____.

15 A _____ is a group of networked computers that share a centralized directory database of user account information and security for the entire set of computers.

16 Unlike DOS and Windows 9x, Windows NT requires ____ boot disks.

17 What useful information is contained on a Windows NT Emergency Repair Disk?

18 What's one reason to upgrade from Windows 98 to Windows NT?

19 If you have Windows 98 installed on a PC using FAT32 and you're creating a dual boot with Windows NT, what must you do first so that Windows NT can access the entire hard drive?

20 Windows NT is installed using a system partition and a boot partition. Which of these partitions must be the active partition of the hard drive?

Independent practice activity

Follow these steps to install incorrect display drivers, try to recover with the Last Known Good Configuration option, and boot using the VGA Only mode to correct problems with the display drivers.

1 Boot Windows NT.

2 Log on as an administrator.

3 Right-click the desktop.

4 Choose **Properties**.

5 Click the **Settings** tab.

6 Click **Display Type**.

7 Click **Change**

8 Select the proper adapter from the lists or click **Have Disk**

9 Browse to the location of the setup files provided by your instructor.

10 If necessary, insert the Windows NT Workstation installation CD or point to its location.

11 If necessary, select the correct adapter and then click **OK**.

12 Click **OK** after the drivers have been set up successfully.

13 Click **Close** to exit the Display Type dialog box. You return to the Display Properties dialog box.

14 Click **Apply**. The Display Properties dialog box closes, and you're asked if you want to restart the system.

15 Click **Yes** to restart the system. Windows boots, and a message appears indicating that a new display has been adjusted.

16 Click **OK**. The Display Properties dialog box opens, where you can adjust the color and resolution to suit your preference.

17 Click **Test** to test the settings.

18 Click **OK** on the Testing Mode warning message. You see a test bitmap, which is a series of colored and shaded boxes on a green background. The test pattern disappears after five seconds.

19 If you could read the test bitmap display, Click **Yes** to keep the settings. Otherwise, repeat the test using different display settings until you can read the test bitmap.

20 Click **Apply** on the Display Properties window. The settings are applied to your desktop.

21 Click **OK** to close Display Properties.

Follow these steps to make the display unreadable.

1 Boot Windows NT.

2 Log on as an administrator.

3 Right-click on the desktop.

4 Choose **Properties** from the shortcut menu. The Display Properties dialog box opens.

5 Select the **Settings** tab.

6 Click **Display Type**. The Display Type dialog box opens.

7 Record your current display adapter.

8 Click **Change**. The Change Display dialog box opens.

9 Select the Manufacturer and Display adapter.

10 Click **OK**. The Third-party Drivers warning appears.

11 Click **Yes** to continue.

12 Next, specify the location of the installation files for this adapter.

13 If necessary, insert the Windows NT Workstation installation CD or point to the location of the Windows NT setup files using the Browse button.

14 Select the file.

15 Click **OK**.

16 Click **OK** after the drivers have been installed successfully.

17 Click **Close** to exit the Display Type dialog box. You return to the Display Properties dialog box.

18 Click **Close**. The Display Properties dialog box closes, and you're asked if you want to restart the system.

19 Click **Yes** to restart the computer.

Follow these steps to observe the results of changing the display.

1 Observe the boot process.

2 Record the point at which the display became unreadable.

3 Press **Ctrl** + **Alt** + **Del** to access the Logon dialog box.

4 Press the **Tab** key four times (five times if you log onto a domain controller).

5 Press **Enter** twice. To shut down the system.

Follow these steps to restore video on a failed system.

1 Restart the system.

2 After the Windows NT Start Up menu appears, press spacebar to activate the **Last Known Good** option.

3 Select **Original Configuration**.

4 Press **Enter**.

5 Did this solve the display problem?

6 Explain why or why not.

7 Restart your system.

Follow these steps to correct the display problem.

1 Boot the system.

2 At the Windows NT Start Up menu, select **Windows NT Workstation (VGA Only)**

3 Press **Enter**.

4 Log in to Windows NT as an administrator.

5 Now that you know how to change display adapters, change your adapter back to the one recorded above, where you configured the incorrect adapter.

6 Reboot the system.

7 Select **Windows NT Workstation** at the Start Up menu.

8 Verify that you can read the display.

Unit 7

Installing and using Windows 2000

Unit time: 60 minutes

Complete this unit, and you'll know how to:

A Describe new features of Windows 2000 Professional and explain the differences between basic and dynamic disks.

B Plan and perform a Windows 2000 Professional installation.

C Manage and configure Windows 2000 Professional, including the Start menu and taskbar.

D Install hardware and applications with Windows 2000 Professional.

Topic A: Architecture

Explanation

Windows 2000 is the culmination of the evolution of Microsoft operating systems from the 16-bit DOS operating system to a true 32-bit, module-oriented operating system, complete with desktop functionality, user-friendly Plug and Play installations, and other easy-to-use features. Windows 2000 comes in several versions, some designed for the desktop and others designed for high-end servers. Windows 2000 Server, Advanced Server, and Datacenter Server are networking server operating systems. Windows 2000 Professional is the next generation of Windows NT Workstation, and has become popular as a corporate desktop OS. While taking advantage of the user-friendly features of Windows 98, Windows 2000 is based on Windows NT technology and is committed to leaving behind the compromises that Windows 9x made with legacy hardware and application software. In addition, Windows 2000 introduces many new features, including a new approach to managing hard drive storage, called dynamic storage. In this unit, you learn about the architecture of Windows 2000, how to install the OS as well as hardware and applications with it, and how to use it.

Windows 2000 uses the same architecture as Windows NT. However, Windows 2000 supports Plug and Play and the FAT32 file system. In addition, Windows 2000 has a safe mode and Device Manager, while Windows NT doesn't.

New features

A feature new of Windows 2000 is *Active Directory*, a directory database service that allows for a single point of administration for all shared resources on a network. Active Directory can track the location of files, peripheral devices, databases, Web sites, users, services, and so forth. It uses a locating method similar to that used by Internet users. Windows 2000 Server versions provide Active Directory, and Windows 2000 Professional acts as an Active Directory client, or user of the directory.

A Windows NT client/server network has one primary domain controller and may have one or more backup domain controllers. A Windows NT network cannot have more than one primary domain controller, which maintains the only copy of the directory database that can be edited. When the directory database is changed, such as when a new user is added to the network, only the directory database on the primary domain controller is updated. The primary domain controller updates the directory databases on the backup domain controllers. With Windows 2000, a network can have any number of domain controllers, each keeping a copy of the directory that can be edited, as shown in Exhibit 7-1. An administrator can update the directory on any one of these domain controllers, which then communicates the change to the other domain controllers.

When both Windows NT and Windows 2000 domain controllers are on the same network, conflicts can result because of the differences in the way the domain controllers work in each OS. For this reason, Windows 2000 runs in two modes: mixed mode and native mode.

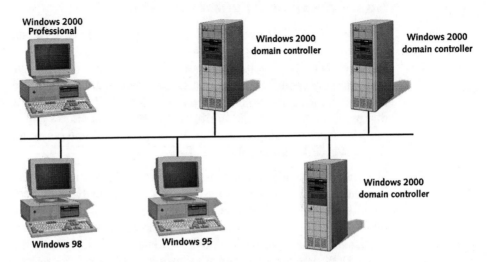

Exhibit 7-1: Windows 2000 allows for multiple domain controllers

Native mode is used when no Windows NT domain controllers are present, and *mixed mode* is used when there's at least one Windows NT domain controller on the network. Mixed mode is necessary in a situation where a network is being upgraded from Windows NT to Windows 2000, and some servers have received the upgrade but others haven't. When installing Windows 2000 Server, the installer can choose mixed mode during the installation process and later migrate to native mode by using the Microsoft Management Console (MMC). Once you've changed a domain to native mode, you can't change back to mixed mode.

Windows 2000 includes several new diagnostic and recovery tools, including Recovery Console, safe mode (similar to Windows 98 safe mode), and File Protection, which prevents system files from being corrupted or erased. For backups, Windows NT provides a backup utility to tape only, but Windows 2000 allows backups to tape, Zip drives, recordable CD-ROMs, and external hard drives. Windows 2000 supports the Internet Printing Protocol (IPP), so that users can print directly to a printer's URL anywhere on the Internet. In addition, several other features new to Windows 2000 are designed to support and improve Internet services for users.

Basic disks and dynamic disks

Windows 2000 offers two ways to configure a hard drive: as a basic disk or dynamic disk. A *basic disk* is the same as the configuration used with DOS, Windows 9x, and Windows NT. By default, Windows 2000 uses basic disk configuration. With basic disk, you generally create partitions of a set size, which aren't changed. If you want to change the size of a partition, you either have to reinstall Windows, if Windows is installed on that partition, or use special third-party software that allows you to change the size of a partition without losing your data. Within partitions, you create logical drives, sometimes called basic volumes, of set size.

Dynamic disks, which are new to Windows 2000, don't use partitions or logical drives. Instead, they use *dynamic volumes*, which are called dynamic because you can change the size of a volume dynamically, or perform any disk and volume management without rebooting the operating system. Data to configure the disk is stored in a disk management database that resides in the last 1 MB of storage space at the end of a hard drive. DOS, Windows 9x, and Windows NT can't read dynamic disks. Dynamic disks are compatible only with Windows 2000 and Windows XP.

A dynamic volume is contained within a dynamic disk and is a logical volume similar to a logical drive in a basic disk. There are three types of dynamic volumes:

- A *simple volume* corresponds to a primary partition on a basic disk and consists of disk space located on a single physical disk.

- A *spanned volume* appears as a simple volume but can use space from two or more physical disks. It fills up the space allotted on one physical disk before moving on to the next. This increases the amount of disk space available for a volume. However, if one physical disk on which data that's part of a spanned volume fails, all the data in the volume is lost.

- A *striped volume* also can use space from two or more physical disks and increases the disk space available for a simple volume. The difference between a spanned volume and a striped volume is that a striped volume writes to the physical disks evenly rather than filling up allotted space on one and then moving on to the next. This increases disk performance as compared to access time with a spanned volume.

Exhibit 7-2 illustrates the difference between basic disk and dynamic disk organization. A basic disk or a dynamic disk can use any file system supported by Windows 2000 (FAT16, FAT32, or NTFS). Once Windows 2000 is installed, you can use the Windows 2000 Disk Management utility to switch from basic to dynamic or dynamic to basic and change the file system on either type of disk.

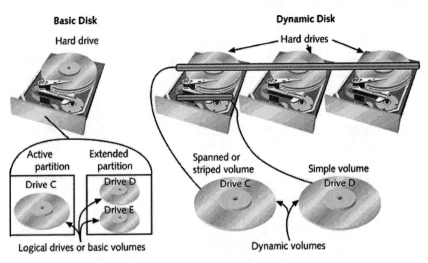

Exhibit 7-2: Difference between basic disks and dynamic disks

Do it!

A-1:   **Discussing the architecture**

Exercises

1   Explain the difference between Windows 2000 native mode and mixed mode.

2   Basic disks divide a hard drive into _____, but dynamic disks divide hard drives into _____.

3   Explain the difference between a spanned volume and a striped volume.

4   Dynamic Disks allow for Windows 2000 to manage 2 or more _____ disks at a time. (physical or logical)

5   The use of dynamic disks is possible under any of the file systems supported by Windows 2000, FAT16, FAT32, or NTFS. True or false?

Topic B: Installation

Explanation This topic looks at installing Windows 2000 on a system with a newly installed hard drive, that is, a clean installation, and also installing Windows 2000 as an upgrade from Windows 9x or Windows NT, that is, an upgrade installation. Just as with Windows NT, Windows 2000 can be installed to be dual-booted with another OS. Before any type of installation, verify that your system meets the minimum requirements for Windows 2000. You must have at least 650 MB of free space on your hard drive, at least 64 MB of RAM and a 133 MHz Pentium-compatible CPU or higher. As you read the following instructions, notice how the installation process is similar to that of Windows NT Workstation.

Planning the installation

Windows 2000 has its roots in Windows NT. Like Windows NT, it doesn't use system BIOS to interface with hardware devices. For that reason, a hardware device must be designed specifically to interact with Windows 2000. Use the hardware compatibility list (HCL) to determine if all the hardware devices in your system qualify for Windows 2000. A version of the HCL is on the Windows 2000 CD in the \Support folder. However, to see the latest version of the list, check the Microsoft Web site at `www.microsoft.com/whdc/hcl/default.mspx`. Don't assume that, because a device is compatible with Windows NT, it work with Windows 2000. There are some instances in which this isn't the case, so check the HCL for Windows 2000 to be sure.

Note: Microsoft sometimes puts last-minute documentation in a Release Notes file in the root directory of an installation CD. Check the directory for Readme.htm and search it for information that might be important for the installation.

Software applications must also qualify for Windows 2000. To verify that all the applications you intend to use on the Windows 2000 PC are certified to work with Windows 2000, search the list of compatible software applications list at the following Web site:

```
www.microsoft.com/windows2000/professional/howtobuy/
upgrading/compat
```

If an application isn't on the list, it might still work with Windows 2000. You can verify that by checking with the application manufacturer's Web site or technical support, or you can just install the application under Windows 2000 and test it yourself.

Support for ACPI

The Advanced Configuration and Power Interface (ACPI) standards developed by Intel, Microsoft, and Toshiba apply to system BIOS, the OS, and certain hardware devices and software to control when a device goes into an inactive state in order to conserve power. To take full advantage of Windows 2000 power management abilities, your system BIOS must be ACPI-compliant. If you have BIOS that isn't ACPI-compliant and you try to install Windows 2000, it doesn't install ACPI support and installs an older HAL that doesn't support ACPI. If you later flash your BIOS to make it ACPI-compliant, you have to reinstall Windows to include ACPI support.

Some BIOS manufacturers offer a BIOS upgrade to make older systems compliant. Most types of system BIOS made after January 1999 are compliant. To learn if your BIOS is compliant, when you're upgrading from Windows 98 to Windows 2000, you can check for the ACPI feature under the Windows 98 Device Manager. Look for ACPI, Advanced Configuration and Power Management Interface, in the Device Manager list of devices. Because Windows 95 and Windows NT don't support ACPI, it isn't listed under these OS installations. You can also check the Web site of the BIOS manufacturer or the Microsoft Web site.

Microsoft calls ACPI-compliant BIOS a "good BIOS" and puts it on the Good BIOS list. The Microsoft site allows you to search for ACPI-compatible computers. When you search by model and manufacturer, the Microsoft Web site tells you if the system is compatible with Windows 2000 and sometimes provides a link to the BIOS Web site where you can download an upgrade to the BIOS. If you're upgrading BIOS, do that before you begin the Windows 2000 installation. If the system isn't ACPI-compliant, you can still install Windows 2000, but you cannot use some of the power management features.

Note: For Microsoft links to hardware and software, and BIOS compatibility checks, see this URL:

```
www.microsoft.com/windows2000/professional/howtobuy/upgrading/
compat/default.asp
```

Selecting a file system

When selecting a file system for an upgrade or replacing Windows 2000 with an existing OS, plan the installation by assuming that you have a basic disk. Later, after Windows 2000 is installed, you can switch to dynamic disk if you like.

Plan which partition on the hard drive to hold Windows 2000 and what file system to use on that partition. Windows 2000 supports the FAT16, FAT32, and NTFS file systems. For compatibility with Windows 98, use the FAT32 file system. For compatibility with DOS or Windows 95, use FAT16, and for the most security, use NTFS. If the hard drive isn't yet partitioned or formatted, Windows 2000 does that for you during the installation. As an alternative, you can also use Fdisk to create a partition before you begin the installation. Create only a single partition and then, after the installation, you can use Disk Management to create other partitions.

Note: The NTFS file system supports *encryption*, encoding files so they can't be deciphered by others, compression, reducing the size of files and folders, and disk quotas,, limiting the hard drive space available to a user. If you want to use any of these features, use NTFS because they aren't supported by FAT file systems.

The following table summarizes which file systems are supported by which operating systems. You need this information when planning your Windows 2000 installation. Windows versions not discussed in this unit are included for comparison:

OS	FAT16	FAT32	NTFS
DOS	X		
Windows 95	X	X (for OSR2)	
Windows 98	X	X	
Windows NT	X		X
Windows 2000	X	X	X
Windows XP	X	X	X
Windows 2003	X	X	X

Installing Windows 2000 on networked computers

If you're installing Windows 2000 on a networked PC, consider where the Windows 2000 installation files are stored. You can install the OS from a CD in the computer's CD-ROM drive, or you can store the files on a file server on the network and perform the installation from the file server. If you're doing multiple installations on the network, consider using a file server. Copy all the files from the \i386 folder on the Windows 2000 CD to a folder on the file server, and then share that folder on the network. Later, during the installation, when you're ready for the CD, point the setup program to the file server folder instead.

Automated installation options

Windows 2000 offers a number of options for installation that can be automated without requiring someone to sit at the computer responding to the questions that Setup asks during the installation process.

One method is called an *unattended installation* and is performed by storing the answers to installation questions in a text file or script that Windows 2000 calls an *answer file*. A sample answer file is stored on the Windows 2000 CD. If you must perform many installations on computers that have the same Windows 2000 setup, it might be worth your time to develop an answer file to perform unattended installations.

Another option is drive imaging. After the installation, use the sysprep.exe utility to remove configuration settings such as the computer name that uniquely identifies this PC. Then clone the entire hard drive to a new PC using third-party drive-imaging software.

Note: To learn how to create an unattended installation of Windows 2000, go to the Microsoft Support Web site (support.microsoft.com) and search on the Microsoft Knowledge Base article Q216258. You can also search the Web site for other articles on this subject.

When installing Windows 2000 on a network, just as with other operating systems, you need to know how to configure the computer to access the network. You should know these things before you begin the installation:

- The computer name and workgroup name for a peer-to-peer network
- The username, user password, computer name, and domain name for a domain network
- For TCP/IP networks, how the IP address is assigned, either dynamically or statically

If the computer gets its IP address from a DHCP server when it first connects to the network, then the IP address is dynamically assigned. When an IP address is permanently assigned to the workstation, the address is statically assigned. If the IP address is statically assigned, then have the IP address to assign the workstation. DHCP servers are used to assign IP addresses when a computer connects to a network.

Upgrade or clean installation

If you're installing Windows 2000 on a new hard drive, then you're doing a clean installation, but if Windows 9x or Windows NT is already installed on the hard drive, then you have three choices:

- You can perform a clean installation, overwriting the existing operating system and applications.
- You can perform an upgrade installation.
- You can install Windows 2000 in a second partition on the hard drive and create a dual-boot situation.

There are advantages and disadvantages to each of these options.

Clean installations

If the hard drive doesn't have a lot of important data on it, or if the data can be backed up, a clean installation that overwrites the existing installation has some advantages.

One advantage is that you get a fresh start. With an upgrade, problems with applications or the OS might follow you into the Windows 2000 load. If you erase everything, that is, format the hard drive, then you're assured that the registry and all applications are as clean as possible.

The disadvantage is that, after Windows 2000 is installed, you must reinstall application software on the hard drive and restore the data from backups. If you do a clean installation, you can choose to format the hard drive first or simply do a clean installation on top of the existing installation. If you don't format the drive, the data is still on the drive, but the previous operating system settings and applications are lost.

If you decide to do a clean installation, verify that you have all the application software CDs or floppy disks and software documentation. Back up all the data and verify that the backups are good. Then, and only then, format the hard drive or begin the clean installation without formatting the drive. If you don't format the hard drive, be sure to run a current version of antivirus software before you begin the installation.

Upgrade installations

All versions of Windows 9x and Windows NT Workstation 3.51 and higher can be upgraded to Windows 2000. The advantages of upgrading are that all applications and data are carried forward into the new Windows 2000 environment, most OS settings carry forward, and the installation is faster. If you perform an upgrade, you must begin the installation while you're in the current OS. If you're working from a remote location on the network, you can't do an upgrade.

Note: You can't upgrade a compressed Windows 9x drive. You must first uncompress it before you can upgrade to Windows 2000 Professional.

Creating a dual boot

Don't create a dual boot unless you need two operating systems, such as when you need to verify that applications and hardware work under Windows 2000 before you delete the old OS. Windows 2000 doesn't support a second operating system on the same partition, so you must have at least two partitions on the hard drive. All applications must be installed under each operating system.

Note: Recall that Windows NT/2000/XP can support up to four partitions on a hard drive. All four can be primary partitions, which can have only one logical drive, or one of the partitions can be an extended partition, which can have several logical drives. For the first primary partition, the active partition, that drive is drive C. For a dual boot with Windows 2000, one OS is installed in the active partition on drive C, and the other OS is installed on another logical drive.

You must decide what file system to use for the Windows 2000 partition: FAT16, FAT32, or NTFS. If you choose to use a dual boot with DOS, use FAT16 for the Windows 2000 partition, so that DOS can read the partition. For Windows 9x, use either the FAT16 or FAT32 file system, not NTFS, so that Windows 9x can read the Windows 2000 partition.

Windows 2000 uses the latest version of NTFS that was first introduced by Windows NT Server 4.0, NTFS Version 5.0 (NTFS5). Windows NT Workstation 4.0 uses NTFS4. The NTFS5 version includes numerous enhancements over previous versions, but can't be read by Windows NT Workstation 4.0 unless Windows NT 4.0 Service Pack 4 is applied. For this reason, if you create a dual boot between Windows 2000 and Windows NT using NTFS for both operating systems, you can encounter the following problems:

- The file system data structures might not be the same.
- Disk utilities, such as Chkdsk under Windows NT, might not work on the drive.
- Windows NT isn't able to read encrypted files and folders.
- You can't use Windows 2000 to repair a damaged Windows NT 4.0 NTFS partition. Windows NT 4.0 allows access to an NTFS drive only from within Windows NT 4.0 and not from any other OS.

For these reasons, using a dual boot between Windows 2000 and Windows NT isn't recommended.

Features new to NTFS under Windows 2000 include file and folder encryption (protects from unauthorized access), disk quotas (control user disk space), and mount points (add a remote volume to a system without using a drive letter). These features weren't included in Windows NT and might cause conflicts if you set up Windows 2000 and Windows NT as a dual boot.

Planning an upgrade from Windows 9x to Windows 2000

So far you've learned that there are many similarities in structure between Windows 2000 and Windows NT. When you're upgrading from Windows 9x to Windows 2000, the Windows 2000 registry isn't compatible with the Windows 9x registry. Therefore, during an upgrade, Windows 2000 can't easily import settings from the Windows 9x registry, even though it attempts to do so. Because of the difference in structure between the Windows 9x registry and the Windows 2000 registry, transfer of information from one to the other isn't as complete as with an upgrade from Windows NT. Until you've performed the upgrade, you don't know exactly what Windows 2000 was able to import from Windows 9x, though Setup might inform you or ask for additional help in some cases.

To test your system and be alerted to potential problems, it's a good idea to run the Check Upgrade Only mode of Windows 2000 Setup, which doesn't actually install Windows 2000 but instead just checks for compatibility and reports any upgrade issues with hardware or software. Run the utility to produce the report, Upgrade.txt, which is stored in the C:\Windows directory.

Hardware compatibility

One issue to consider in upgrading from Windows 9x to Windows 2000 is that Windows 2000 doesn't import drivers from Windows 9x, because they're generally not compatible. As you learned earlier, a hardware device must be designed to be compatible with Windows 2000. If you want to install a device for which there's no device driver included in Windows 2000, you might have to download a driver from either the Microsoft site or the manufacturer's Web site.

Check for compatibility and make sure you have the required device drivers before you begin your Windows 9x-to-Windows 2000 upgrade. Windows 2000 attempts to carry over installed hardware devices that are compatible with Windows 2000, asking for new drivers where necessary; it ignores and doesn't install incompatible devices. If Setup can't find a critical driver, such as the driver to control a hard drive, it cancels the upgrade.

Another thing you need to know is that Windows 2000 deletes all the Windows 9x system files and replaces them with Windows 2000 system files in the same directory.

Software compatibility

Basically, the main advantage in performing an upgrade from Windows 9x to Windows 2000 rather than doing a clean install of Windows 2000 is that you don't have to reinstall software that's compatible with Windows 2000. If an application was written for Windows 9x, it may or may not be compatible with Windows 2000. Windows 9x applications store registry data differently from Windows 2000 applications and may rely on APIs specific to Windows 9x. If an application doesn't work after you upgrade to Windows 2000, try reinstalling it. If that doesn't work, check the software manufacturer's Web site for a patch or upgrade.

Planning an upgrade from Windows NT to Windows 2000

Upgrading to Windows 2000 from Windows NT is much easier than upgrading from Windows 9x. However, here are some considerations you need to be aware of before performing the upgrade:

- You must install networking on Windows NT 3.51 machines before upgrading, or you won't be able to log on to Windows 2000.

- If you're upgrading from Windows NT using NTFS, Setup automatically upgrades to the Windows 2000 version of NTFS.

- If you're upgrading from Windows NT using FAT16 or Windows NT with third-party software installed that allows it to use FAT32, Setup ask you whether you want to upgrade to NTFS.

Hardware compatibility

Generally, most hardware devices and their corresponding drivers that worked under Windows NT also work under Windows 2000, although some third-party drivers might need to be updated for Windows 2000. As always, it's a good idea to check the HCL on the Microsoft Web site or run the Check Upgrade Only mode of Windows 2000 Setup.

Software compatibility

Nearly all applications that run with Windows NT Workstation 3.51, and later, run with Windows 2000 without modification. Here are some exceptions:

- Antivirus software and third-party network software, both of which must be removed before upgrading to Windows 2000.

- Some disk management tools.

- Custom tools for power management, which are replaced in Windows 2000 by ACPI. Windows 2000 also provides minimal support for APM (Advanced Power Management), which also must be removed before the upgrade. Windows 2000 considers APM a legacy tool, uses it only on notebook computers, and uses only enough APM features to support the battery on a notebook computer. With ACPI-compliant BIOS, the BIOS senses information about the system and turns that information over to the OS to make decisions and manage the power management functions of the system.

- Custom solutions that are workarounds for Windows NT not supporting Plug and Play, which are unnecessary in Windows 2000, because it provides complete support for Plug and Play.

- Software to monitor and control a UPS (uninterruptible power supply).

Now that you've learned about advantages and disadvantages to installing Windows 2000 as a clean install and as an upgrade, including issues to consider with specific upgrades, let's look at step-by-step procedures for how to do both.

Note: When installing Windows from across the network to a remote PC, you can perform only a clean installation. In this situation, run the Winnt.exe setup program. When working at the local computer, to perform a clean installation, you can boot from the Windows CD or run Winnt32.exe from a command prompt. If you want to perform an upgrade, you must execute the Winnt32.exe program from within Windows. In any case, the program executed is called Setup in Windows documentation.

Do it!

B-1: Preparing for installation

Here's how	Here's why
1 Using the Microsoft Web site, research whether your computer qualifies for Windows 2000	
2 Record the device/application name, version, and if it qualifies for Windows 2000 for each of the following items:	
System board BIOS	
Video card	
Modem card (if present)	
Sound card (if present)	
Printer (if present)	
Network card (if present)	
CD-ROM drive (if present)	
DVD drive (if present)	
SCSI hard drive (if present)	
Any other devices that are present	
Application 1	(Any application that is present, such as Word.)
Application 2	
Application 3	
3 Print the Web pages showing whether each hardware device and application installed on your PC qualifies for Windows 2000	

Performing a clean installation

Explanation

The Windows 2000 package comes with documentation and a CD. For United States distributions, the package includes a floppy disk to provide 128-bit data encryption.

If your PC is capable of booting from a CD, then insert the CD and turn on the PC. The Welcome to the Windows 2000 Setup Wizard screen appears, as shown in Exhibit 7-3. Select Install a new copy of Windows 2000, then click Next, and then proceed to Step 6 below. However, if your PC doesn't boot from a CD and you have a clean, empty hard drive, first create a set of Windows 2000 setup disks to boot the PC and to begin the installation process. The remaining installation is done from the CD.

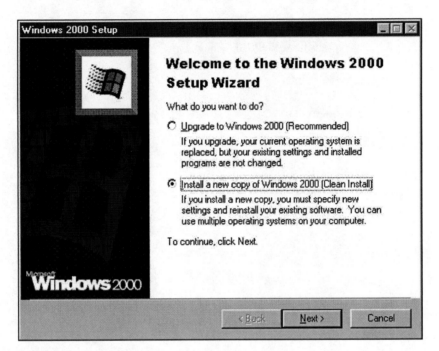

Exhibit 7-3: The Setup Wizard

To make the four setup disks, follow these directions:

1 Using a working PC, format four floppy disks.

2 Place the Windows 2000 CD in the CD-ROM drive and a formatted floppy disk in the floppy disk drive. For Windows 9x, click Start, Run and enter this command in the Run dialog box: `D:\bootdisk\makeboot.bat A:`, substituting the drive letter of the CD-ROM drive for D: and the letter of the floppy drive for A:.

3 Insert new disks in the drive, as requested. Label the disks Windows 2000 Setup Disks 1, 2, 3, and 4.

4 Now begin the Windows 2000 installation. Boot the PC from the first setup disk created above. You're asked to insert each of the four disks in turn and then asked to insert the Windows 2000 CD.

5   The Windows 2000 license agreement appears. Accept the agreement, and the Welcome screen appears, as shown in Exhibit 7-3. The setup process is now identical to that of booting directly from the CD. Save the four floppy disks, in case you have future problems with Windows 2000.

6   Windows 2000 searches the hard drive for partitions and asks which partition to use. If the partitions aren't created, you need to create partitions using the interface provided by setup. You're asked to decide which file system to use. If the hard drive has already been formatted with the FAT16 or FAT32 file system, you're asked if you want to upgrade to the NTFS file system. Be aware that, if you convert the file system to NTFS, you can't revert to FAT16 or FAT32. You can also convert from FAT16 or FAT32 to NTFS after the installation is complete. If the hard drive is already partitioned and contains a partition larger than 2 GB, and if you select the FAT file system, then Windows 2000 automatically formats the drive using the FAT32 file system. It puts the entire partition into one logical FAT32 drive.

7   During the installation, you're given the opportunity to change your keyboard settings for different languages, enter your name and company name, and enter the product key found on the CD case. You're also given the opportunity to enter date and time settings and an administrator password. Be sure to remember the password. It's required when you log on to the system later to set up new users and perform other administrative tasks. If you forget it and no one else has administrator privileges, you might have to reinstall Windows 2000.

8   If Setup recognizes that you're connected to a network, it provides the Networking Settings window to configure the computer to access the network. If you select Typical settings, then Setup automatically configures the OS for your network. After the installation, if the configuration isn't correct, you can make changes.

9   At this point in the installation, you're asked to remove the Windows 2000 CD and click Finish. The computer then restarts. After Windows 2000 loads, it completes the process of connecting to the network. You're asked questions about the type of network (for example, does the network use a domain or workgroup?). When the configuration is complete, verify that you have access to the network if there is one.

Performing a clean installation over another OS

Using Windows 9x, if your PC automatically detects a CD in the CD-ROM drive, follow these directions to do a clean install when another OS is already installed:

1 Using antivirus software, scan memory and your hard drive for viruses. Turn off antivirus protection and close applications and services before you install.

2 Insert the Windows 2000 CD in the CD-ROM drive. If your PC detects the CD, a window opens with the message "This CD-ROM contains a newer version of Windows that the one you are presently using. Would you like to upgrade to Windows 2000?" Answer No. The Install Windows 2000 window appears (see Exhibit 7-4).

3 Click Install Windows 2000. The Windows Setup Wizard opens, as shown in Exhibit 7-3. Select Install a new copy of Windows 2000 (Clean Install). You're asked to accept the license agreement, which is displayed. Enter the product key from the back of the CD case, and you're given the opportunity to select special options. After a reboot, the installation process continues as described above.

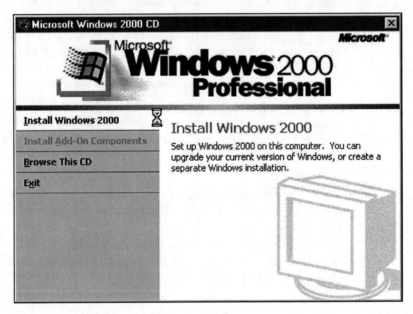

Exhibit 7-4: Windows 2000 Setup window

If your PC doesn't automatically recognize a CD, then insert the CD in the CD-ROM drive and do the following:

1 Click Start, Run. In the Run dialog box, enter the command: `D:\i386\winnt32.exe`. Substitute the drive letter of the CD-ROM drive for D:.

2 The Windows 2000 Setup Wizard appears, as shown in Exhibit 7-3. Select Install a new copy of Windows 2000 (Clean Install). The installation process continues as described above.

Upgrade installation

To upgrade your operating system from Windows 9x or Windows NT using the Windows 2000 CD, first prepare for the installation by doing the following:

1 Verify that all devices and applications are Windows 2000-compatible. Download and install any patches or upgrades from hardware or software manufacturers.

2 Using antivirus software, scan memory and your hard drive for viruses.

3 Back up all critical system files and data files. Back up the registry in case you need to backtrack to the current installation. If you have important data on your hard drive, back up the data.

4 Close all applications and services and disable any virus-scanning software. If the hard drive is compressed, decompress the drive.

You're now ready to perform the upgrade. Do the following:

1 Insert the Windows 2000 CD in the CD-ROM drive. If your system is set to detect the CD automatically, it runs the setup program and shows a message asking if you want to upgrade your computer to Windows 2000. Answer Yes, and the installation process begins. If Windows doesn't detect the CD, then click Start, Run, enter `D:\i386\winnt32.exe` in the Run dialog box, and then click OK. Substitute the drive letter of the CD-ROM drive for D:. On the Welcome to Windows 2000 Setup Wizard Screen, select Upgrade to Windows 2000 (Recommended). Follow the directions on the screen.

2 Windows 2000 Setup performs the upgrade in two major stages: the Report phase and the Setup phase. During the Report phase, Windows 2000 Setup scans the hardware, device drivers, current operating system, and applications for compatibility. Also, in the Report phase, you're given the opportunity to provide third-party DLL files that make a device driver or application Windows 2000-compatible, if Setup recognizes that the device driver or application doesn't work without the fix. Next, Setup generates a report of its findings. If findings indicate that an unsuccessful installation is likely to happen, you can abandon the installation and perhaps check with hardware and software manufacturers for fixes. In the Report phase, Setup also creates an answer file that it uses during the Setup phase, installs the Windows 2000 boot loader, and copies Windows 2000 installation files to the hard drive.

3 The PC reboots and the Setup phase begins, which has two parts: the Text mode and the GUI mode. In the Text mode, Setup installs a Windows 2000 base in the same folder that the old OS is in, usually C:\Windows for Windows 9x and C:\WINNT for Windows NT. This target folder can't be changed at this point. Setup then moves the Windows registry and profile information to <windir>\setup\temp, where <windir> is the path to the Windows folder, which most likely is C:\Windows\setup\temp.

4 The PC reboots again, and the GUI mode of Setup begins. Setup reads information that it saved about the old Windows system and makes appropriate changes to the Windows 2000 registry. It then migrates application DLLs to Windows 2000 and reboots for the last time. The upgrade is now done.

Note: During installation, Windows 2000 records information about the installation to a file called Setuplog.txt. This file is useful when troubleshooting any problems that occur during installation. You can also press Shift+F10 to get a command prompt during the installation.

Backing up the system state

After you've completed installing Windows 2000, do the following:

1   Access the Internet and download and install all OS service packs, updates, and patches.

2   Verify that all hardware is working and install additional devices, such as printers, as needed.

3   Create user accounts for Windows 2000. You can also install any additional Windows components at this time.

4   Verify that the system is functioning properly and back up the system state. This backup of the system can later be used to help you recover the OS in the event of system failure.

Windows 2000 calls the files critical to a successful operating system load the *system state data*. This includes all files necessary to boot the OS, the Windows 2000 registry, and all system files in the <SystemRoot> folder, the folder in which Windows 2000 is installed. For an upgrade of Windows 9x, the folder is most likely C:\Windows, the original Windows folder before the upgrade. For a clean install or an NT upgrade, the default folder is C:\WINNT. When you perform a backup of the system state data, you can't select which of these files you want to back up, because Windows 2000 always backs up all of them. Here's the process:

1   Click Start, and then choose Programs, Accessories, System Tools, Backup. The Backup dialog box opens. Click the Backup tab, as shown in Exhibit 7-5.

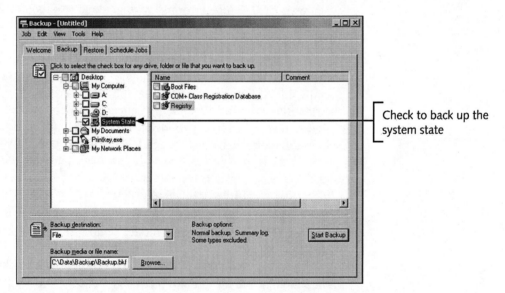

Exhibit 7-5: Back up the Windows 2000 registry and all critical system files

2   Check the System State box in the list of items you can back up. Notice, in Exhibit 7-5, that the system state includes the boot files and the registry. It also includes the COM+ (Component Object Model) Registration Database, which contains information about applications and includes files in the Windows folders.

3   Select the destination for the backup. You can back up to any medium, including a folder on the hard drive, a Zip drive, a tape drive, or a network drive. Click Start Backup to begin the process.

Later, if you have problems with a corrupted Windows 2000 installation, you can click the Restore tab in the Backup window, as shown in Exhibit 7-5, to restore the system to its state at the last backup.

Note: When you back up the system state, the registry is also backed up to the folder <SystemRoot>\repair\RegBack. If you later have a corrupted registry, you can copy files from this folder to the registry folder, which is <SystemRoot>\System32\Config.

Do it!

B-2:   Installing or upgrading to Windows 2000

Here's how	Here's why
1 Obtain a list of devices in the system and detailed system specifications	Such as processor speed and drive capacity. To plan and prepare for a Windows 2000 Professional installation on your computer.
If no list currently exists, use Device Manager or SANDRA to compile one	
2 Make another list of important applications	
Check to see if they're compatible with Windows 2000	
If you find any that aren't compatible, check to see if any patches or upgrades are available to make them compatible	
3 Check each system specification and device against both the Hardware Compatibility List and the system requirements list for Windows 2000	Most likely your system is compatible with Windows 2000. However, in the future, when working on other systems, you might discover significant incompatibilities. In such a case, you have to decide whether or not upgrading to Windows 2000 is really an option. If you decide to go ahead with the upgrade, you then have to decide which applications or hardware you need to upgrade before upgrading the operating system.
Check using the following URL:	The Windows 2000 installation CD also offers a Check Upgrade Only mode that you can use to check for incompatibility issues in your system before you actually install the OS. However, the information on the Microsoft Web site, which you're using in this step, is often more current and easier to access.

```
www.microsoft.com/windows2000/server/howtobuy/upgrading▶
   /compat/default.asp
```

4 Record the following information:

Does your system qualify for Windows 2000?

If not, what hardware or application doesn't qualify?

Will you install using FAT32 or NTFS? Explain your decision

5 From the manufacturers or the Microsoft Web site for both installed applications and hardware, download all necessary drivers, service packs, and application patches

Record a summary of the components you're required to install to make your system compatible with Windows 2000

6 Gather any network-specific information in preparation for the installation

Answer the following:

If you're connected to a network.

If you're using a TCP/IP network, how is your IP address configured?

For a static IP address, what's the IP address?

What's the workgroup name or domain name of the network?

What's your computer name?

7 Verify that you have the correct CD key for your installation CD

The CD key, which is provided with the Windows 2000 installation CD, usually consists of a set of alphanumeric characters.

8 Review the information you've collected so far

Decide whether to do a clean installation or an upgrade

For instance, if all the important applications on your system are compatible with Windows 2000, an upgrade probably saves time, because it leaves compatible applications in working condition. On the other hand, if you know that you have to install new applications anyway because of incompatibilities, you might choose to perform a clean installation.

Do you want to perform a clean install or an upgrade?

Give a brief explanation as to why you chose the option you chose

9 Back up any critical data files

That is, any work you or others have stored on your computer that you can't afford to lose during the installation process.

Where did you back up critical data files to?

If you have critical data files on the PC.

10 Record if you're performing the installation from (a) the Windows 2000 CD, (b) files stored on your hard drive, or (c) a network drive

11 Run antivirus software

To scan the computer's memory and hard drive for viruses, before you insert the installation CD or run the setup files from a location on your hard drive or network.

Disable any automatic scans

After the scan is complete.

Close the antivirus program

Before beginning installation.

12 Begin the installation

The Setup program starts. This program guides you through the actual installation.

Run WINNT32.exe from the \I386 folder

Using the Run command on the Start menu. If the Setup program doesn't begin automatically.

Did Setup start automatically for you, or did you have to use the Run command?

13 Observe that Setup informs you that you're running an older version of Windows and asks whether you want to upgrade to Windows 2000

   Click **Yes**   To continue.

   Follow the instructions in the Setup program   Note that, although Setup initially uses the word "upgrade," you're given the option of doing an upgrade from Windows 98 or a fresh installation of Windows 2000.

14 Accept the EULA (end user license agreement)

   Click **Next**

15 Enter the CD key   When prompted.

   Click **Next**   Setup examines your system and reports any situations that could cause problems during installation.

16 Continue the installation   Even if some problems are reported, you have done your homework during planning and likely have the solution.

17 Review the Hardware Compatibility List   If you wish to review it again, as you're given the opportunity to review the Hardware Compatibility List.

   Click **Next**   To continue.

18 Specify your file system   Either NTFS or FAT32.

   Select **FAT32**

   Click **Next**   The system begins to copy files for the installation. Then the text portion of the installation, which provides a DOS interface rather than a Windows GUI, begins.

   Observe that this portion of the installation includes the following:

   • Examining hardware

   • Deleting old Windows files, if applicable

   • Copying Windows 2000 operating system files

   • Automatically rebooting your computer

19 Observe that, after your computer reboots, the Windows 2000 Setup portion begins.

Observe that this part of the installation includes the following:

- Verifying the file system

- Checking the file structure

- Converting the file system to NTFS, if applicable

- Automatically rebooting again

20 Choose **Windows 2000 Professional**   On the startup menu.

Verify to see a message indicating that the conversion was successful   If you converted your file system to NTFS.

21 Observe that the system installs software for detected devices

22 Provide the requested network information   When prompted.

Observe that Setup performs some final setup tasks, including the following: After you've specified how your network is configured.

- Configuring the Startup menu

- Registering components

- Upgrading programs and system settings

- Saving settings

- Removing temporary files

23 Observe that the computer reboots   You're now able to log on as an administrator and install any new applications or devices.

24 Verify that the system is working correctly

25 Record any differences you noted
    between the preceding installation
    steps and your own experience

    Record any decisions you made
    during the installation process

    Record any information you
    entered during the installation
    process

26 Name five things you should do
    before you start the installation
    process.

27 How can you find out if your
    video card works with Windows
    2000?

28 What type of installation can save
    time because it usually retains
    system settings and leaves
    applications in working
    condition?

29 What step is critical to ensure that
    you don't lose important data
    during installation?

30 What step can you take to help
    speed up the actual installation
    process?

Topic C: Using Windows 2000

Explanation

You've learned how keyboard shortcuts and Windows Explorer help you in using Windows 9x. Much of the information you learned about using Windows 9x applies to Windows 2000 as well. However, there are important differences and improvements that you need to know about, including how to manage the desktop and how to increase the security of files and resources. As with any version of Windows, additional Windows components can be installed using the Add/Remove Programs applet in Control Panel.

Managing the desktop

There are two basic ways to set up your desktop. One is the classic Windows style, used in Windows 95 and later versions, in which you single-click to select an item and double-click to open it, and all your desktop content is offline and localized to your computer. The second is to use Active Desktop, which allows you to set your desktop to behave like a Web page and include Web content.

To activate Active desktop, right click anywhere on the desktop and select Show Web Content from the shortcut menu. Because Active Desktop uses considerable system resources, it isn't recommended for most situations.

Managing shortcuts

You've learned how to create and manage desktop shortcuts and icons in Windows 9x and about keystroke shortcuts when using Windows 9x. You can use that same information with Windows 2000. As a reminder, here are three different ways to create a shortcut in Windows 2000:

- Select (single-click) the file, folder, or program in Explorer or in a My Computer window. From the File menu, choose Create Shortcut.
- In Windows Explorer, from the File menu, choose New, Shortcut.
- Right-click on the file, folder, or program to which you want to create a shortcut and choose Create Shortcut from the menu.

Once the shortcut is created in the same folder as the file it pertains to, drag the shortcut to the desktop.

Managing the Start menu

As you know from your own experience, the Start menu in Windows shows frequently used files and programs. This enables you to access these items quickly rather than having to search for them in Windows Explorer or with the Find command.

There are many ways you can customize the Start menu. For example, you can set the Program menu to display only recently used applications and show an arrow at the bottom by which you can expand the menu and access programs that weren't initially shown. To make this change:

1   Click Start, and then choose Settings, Taskbar and Start Menu.

2   The Taskbar and Start Menu Properties window opens. Check Use Personalized Menus, as shown in Exhibit 7-6.

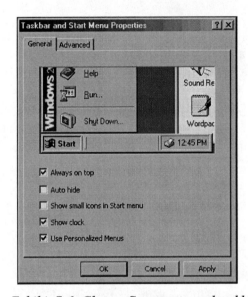

Exhibit 7-6: Change Start menu and taskbar options

3   Click Apply to execute the change, and then click OK to close the window.

4   Click Start and point to Programs. Only recently used programs are displayed, as shown in Exhibit 7-7.

5   Notice, in Exhibit 7-7, that there is a small double chevron at the bottom of the personalized menu. You can access programs not shown on the personalized menu by clicking the chevron. The complete menu appears with the programs that weren't shown on the personalized menu shaded in a lighter color.

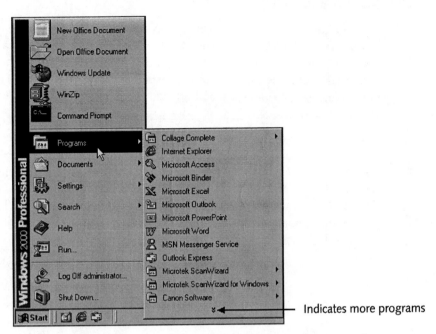

Indicates more programs

Exhibit 7-7: A personalized menu shows only recently accessed programs

Notice, in Exhibit 7-6, that you selected the personalized menus option from the General tab of the Taskbar and Start Menu Properties window. The Advanced tab offers additional options for customizing the Start menu, as shown in Exhibit 7-8. From this window, you can add, remove, and sort Start menu items as well as add commands or tools that aren't usually shown on the Start menu. As an alternative to using personalized menus, you can even choose to display the Programs menu as a scrolling list. The scrolling list under Start Menu Settings offers a variety of options. To activate an option, scroll through the list and check the items that you want, and then click Apply and OK.

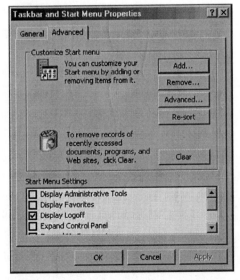

Exhibit 7-8: The Advanced tab offers many ways to customize the Start menu

Managing the taskbar

As with the Start menu, the taskbar in Windows 2000 offers more options for customization than were available with earlier versions of Windows. One option that was available with Windows 9x, auto-hiding the taskbar, works the same way with Windows 2000. The taskbar can show status information, provide quick links to common programs and files, and include an address bar in which to type paths and URLs to go to.

The General tab of the Taskbar and Start Menu Properties window, as shown in Exhibit 7-6, offers options to auto-hide the taskbar or to set it always to be on top of whatever windows are open. You can reach additional options for customizing the taskbar by right-clicking it and selecting options from the shortcut menu. For example, to add toolbars to the taskbar, right-click it, point to Toolbars, and then choose the desired toolbar from the menu that appears, as shown in Exhibit 7-9.

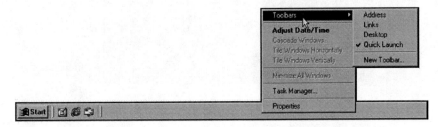

Exhibit 7-9: Use this shortcut menu to add toolbars to the taskbar

Exhibit 7-10 shows the taskbar with toolbars added. Notice the system tray (systray) on the right side of the taskbar that contains icons indicating the status of several currently running services such as the sound controls.

Exhibit 7-10: Adding toolbars to the taskbar

Do it!   **C-1:   Managing the Start menu**

Here's how	Here's why
1 Click **Start**	
Choose **Settings, Taskbar and Start Menu**	The Taskbar and Start Menu Properties window opens.
2 Check **Use Personalized Menus**	As shown in Exhibit 7-6.
3 Click **Apply**	To execute the change.
Click **OK**	To close the window.
4 Click **Start**	
Choose **Programs**	Only recently used programs are displayed, as shown in Exhibit 7-7.
5 Observe a small double chevron at the bottom of the personalized menu	See Exhibit 7-7.
Click the chevron	To access programs not shown on the personalized menu. The complete menu appears with the programs that weren't shown on the personalized menu shaded in a lighter color.

Topic D: Hardware and application management

Explanation

This topic discusses how to install hardware and software and includes special considerations for legacy hardware and software. As with Windows 98, Windows 2000 has an Add New Hardware wizard that automatically launches when new hardware is detected, and software is best installed from the Add/Remove Programs icon of Control Panel.

Installing hardware

Windows 2000 can automatically detect and install Plug and Play devices, as long as you also have Plug and Play BIOS and drivers and devices that are Plug and Play compliant. If a device is Plug and Play, Windows 2000 automatically does the following:

- Identifies the device you're installing.
- Determines what system resources the device needs and assigns them, so that there are no conflicts with other devices.
- Configures the device as necessary.
- Loads any device drivers that are needed to run the device.
- Informs the system of any changes in configuration.

For PnP devices, the Add New Hardware Wizard automatically launches at startup. Any user can complete the installation, if the following are true: installing the device drivers can be done without user input, all files necessary for a complete installation are present, the drivers have been digitally signed, and there are no errors during installation. If any of these conditions doesn't exist, the installation is abandoned until someone with administrator privileges logs on.

Most devices that are designed to work with Windows 2000 are Plug and Play compatible. If a device isn't Plug and Play, you can use the Add/Remove Hardware applet in Control Panel to install the device, if you're logged on with administrator privileges.

If you're using the Add/Remove Hardware Wizard, you have to provide information, such as where the driver for the device is located. Some devices that don't work with Windows 2000 may be completely incompatible and not work at all. After a device is installed, if you have a problem with the device, you can attempt to update the device driver as follows:

1   In the Control Panel, double-click the System icon.

2   The System Properties window opens. Select the Hardware tab, as shown in Exhibit 7-11.

3   Click the Device Manager button. The Device Manager opens, as shown in Exhibit 7-11. Expand the device class tree by clicking the plus sign, and locate the device for which you want to update a driver. For this example, we're using the floppy disk drive.

4   Right-click the floppy drive and select Properties from the shortcut menu, as shown in Exhibit 7-11.

5   The Floppy disk drive Properties window opens, as shown in Exhibit 7-12. On the Driver tab, click Update Driver. The Update Device Driver Wizard is displayed. Follow the directions on the screen to update the driver, if an update exists.

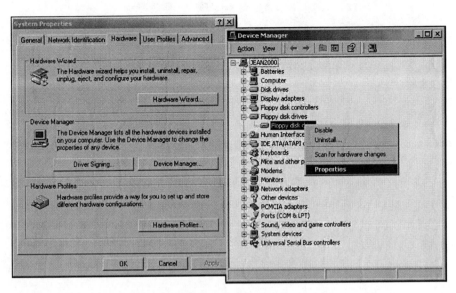

Exhibit 7-11: Use Device Manager to access a device's properties

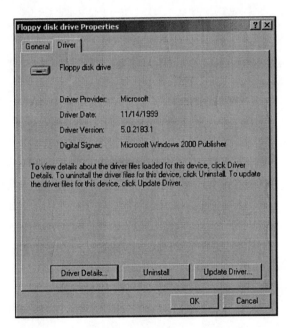

Exhibit 7-12: A device's Properties window provides a way to update its drivers

Note: You must be logged on with administrator privileges to make changes from the Device Manager.

Do it!

D-1: Updating a device driver

Here's how	Here's why
1 Open Control Panel	
2 Double-click the **System** icon in the Control Panel	The System Properties window opens.
3 Select the **Hardware** tab	As shown in Exhibit 7-11.
4 Click **Device Manager**	The Device Manager opens, as shown in Exhibit 7-11.
Click the plus sign	To expand the device class tree.
Locate the device for which you want to update a driver	For this activity, use the floppy disk drive.
5 Right-click the floppy drive	
Choose **Properties** from the menu, as shown in Exhibit 7-11	The Floppy disk drive Properties window opens, as shown in Exhibit 7-12.
6 Click **Update Driver**	The Update Device Driver Wizard is displayed.
Follow the directions on the screen to update the driver	If an update exists.

Installing applications

Explanation

The process of installing applications in Windows 2000 isn't much different from in earlier versions of Windows. If you're familiar with the installation wizards and setup programs that were used with Windows 9x, you should recognize all but a few minor details of these same components in Windows 2000.

The Windows 2000 Add/Remove Programs utility looks significantly different from that of Windows 9x, and it provides more options. From the Windows 2000 Add/Remove Programs window, you can change or remove presently installed programs, as shown in Exhibit 7-13; add new programs from a CD-ROM, a floppy disk, or from Microsoft over the Internet, and add or remove Windows components. Note that, in Exhibit 7-13, the menu in the upper-right corner is expanded for you, showing how you can sort the view of presently installed programs.

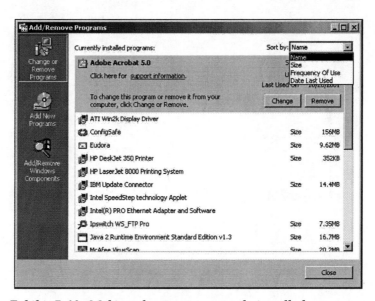

Exhibit 7-13: Making changes to currently installed programs

Do it!

D-2:   Installing and using support tools

Here's how	Here's why
1 Log on as an administrator	To install Windows 2000 Support Tools.
2 Open Windows Explorer	
In the Windows 2000 installation files on your hard drive, navigate to the Support\Tools directory	
Double-click **Setup.exe**	The Setup Wizard launches and welcomes you.
3 Click **Next**	To continue.

4 In the User Information window, enter your name and organization in the appropriate fields

Click **Next**   To continue.

5 In the Select an Installation Type window, select **Typical Installation**

Click **Next**   To continue. The Begin Installation window appears to let you know that the wizard is ready to begin copying files.

6 Click **Next**   To continue. The Installation Progress window appears and displays a progress bar informing you of the progress of the installation. When the installation is complete and the Start menu is set up, the wizard indicates that the installation was successful.

7 Click **Finish**   To exit the wizard.

8 Double-click the **Administrative Tools** icon in the Control Panel   To open the Administrative Tools window and to familiarize yourself with the Error and Event Message Help tool.

9 Double-click **Event Viewer**   To launch the Event Viewer.

10 Click **System Log**   In the left pane of Event Viewer.

    View the event entries in the right pane

11 Double-click any warning or error events   Otherwise, double-click an information event.

    Observe that, when you double-click any event, the Event Details window opens

    Read the information in this window

    Record the Event ID number and description

12 Click **Start**

    Choose **Programs, Windows 2000 Support Tools, Error and Event Messages**   The Error and Event Messages Help window opens.

13	Click the **Search** tab	
14	Click **Type in word(s) to search for**	
	Type the Event ID number recorded in Step 11	
	Click **List Topics**	The Select Topic field displays all Help topics that refer to this Event ID number.
15	Select the item whose title matches the event description recorded in Step 11	In the Select Topic field.
16	Click **Display**	Information about the highlighted item is displayed in the right pane.
	Record the explanation of the event and the relevant user action	If the information is provided.
17	Choose **Start**, **Programs**, **Windows 2000 Support Tools**, **Tools Help** on the taskbar	Tools Help opens in a familiar Help window. You want to find and print information about a particular support tool.
18	Click the **Search** tab	(If necessary). You want to use the Search tab to find information about the executable file for the Windows 2000 System Information tool, which provides information on the hardware resources and software environment for your system. The name of this file is "msinfo32.exe."
	Type **msinfo32.exe**	In the box labeled: Type in the word(s) to search for.
	Click **List Topics**	Topics related to msinfo32.exe are displayed in the Select topic pane.
19	Double-click the topic ranked second	Information on msinfo32.exe is displayed in the right pane.
20	Choose **Options**, **Print** on the Tools Help menu bar	The Print dialog box opens.
	Select a printer and change any settings	If necessary.
21	Click **Print**	To print the information on msinfo32.exe. Keep the printed information handy.

22	Launch System Information	Following the directions in the Help information you printed above. You want to record information about your system's software environment using the System Information tool.
23	Double-click **Software Environment** in the left pane	To display a list of subcategories.
	Record the subcategories	
24	Click **Program Groups** in the left pane	The program groups for Windows are displayed, showing the software that's installed on the system.
	What five program groups are always added for each user?	
25	Click **Startup Programs** in the left pane	
	Are the programs listed associated with your Start menu, or are they the programs that launch automatically when you log on to the system? Explain	
26	What directory contains the files necessary to set up Windows 2000 Support Tools?	
27	What support tool allows you to search for information based on the Event ID numbers used in Event Viewer?	
28	What Windows 2000 Support Tool offers information about all other support tools?	
29	What's the executable file for the System Information tool?	
30	Can you run all of the Support Tools by selecting them from the Start menu?	

Unit summary: Installing and using Windows 2000

Topic A   In this topic, you learned about the Windows 2000 **architecture**. You learned the **new features** of Windows 2000 and the concepts of **basic** and **dynamic disks**.

Topic B   In this topic, you learned how to **plan** and **perform** the Windows 2000 installation. You learned the features of **upgrade** and **clean installation**. You also learned about planning an upgrade from **Windows 9x to Windows 2000** and from **Windows NT to Windows 2000**. You learned how to perform a clean installation when the hard drive has as operating system installed and the concepts of backing up the **system state**.

Topic C   In this topic, you learned how to manage and use Windows 2000. You learned about managing the **desktop**, including managing **shortcuts**, managing the **Start** menu, and managing the **taskbar**.

Topic D   In this topic you learned how to install **hardware** and **applications** with Windows 2000. You also learned how to install the Windows 2000 **support tools**.

Review questions

1 What's required before Windows 2000 can provide full power management functionality?

2 Name three manufacturers responsible for the initial development of ACPI?

3 What three file systems does Windows 2000 support?

4 When you print to a printer URL on the Internet, what protocol are you using?

5 If you're installing Windows 2000 on a new hard drive and your system can't boot from a CD, how do you begin the installation?

6 If you want to access a hard drive using either DOS or Windows 2000, what file system must you use?

7 If you install Windows 2000 on an 8 GB hard drive, use a single partition for the drive, and choose not to use the NTFS file system, what file system will Windows 2000 automatically use?

8 What file must you create before you can do an unattended installation of Windows 2000?

9 If your BIOS isn't ACPI-compliant, what should you do before you install Windows 2000?

10 List the operating systems that qualify for a Windows 2000 upgrade.

11 What Windows 2000 tool can be used to switch between a basic disk and dynamic disk organization for a hard drive?

12 What was the first Windows OS to support FAT32?

13 Which Windows OS doesn't support FAT32?

14 If an administrator is concerned about security on a system, which file system is appropriate?

15 How do you access System Properties in Windows 2000?

16 Can you perform an upgrade of Windows 2000 from a remote computer on the network? Explain your answer.

17 List the steps necessary to access the Windows 2000 Backup utility.

18 For a person to be able to install hardware, what privileges or permissions must be assigned to his or her user account?

19 Explain how you would use My Computer to create a desktop shortcut.

20 Explain how to uninstall a device in Windows 2000.

21 When backing up the system state, where does Windows 2000 store a copy of the registry?

22 NTFS is a more secure file system, because it supports _____ while the others do not.

23 The Windows 2000 OS supports _____, a feature of Windows 9x that was not available to Windows NT.

24 The configuration of the Windows 2000 operating system, known as the Windows Registry in Windows 9x and Windows NT, is referred to as the _____.

25 The desktop feature that causes your desktop to feel and act like a Web page is called _____.

26 An address bar can be added to the Windows 2000 taskbar. True or false?

27 Like Windows NT, Windows 2000 doesn't support Plug and Play. True or false?

28 In Windows 2000, the taskbar can be customized to include commonly used _____.

Independent practice activity

You want to use Windows 2000 Help to look up information on various topics related to the operating system. Follow these steps to use the main features of Windows 2000 Help:

1 Log on to your computer as an administrator.

2 Close or minimize any applications that start automatically, so that the desktop is active.

3 Press **F1**. Note that, to avoid having to make the desktop active, you could choose to click Start on the taskbar and then click Help. Windows 2000 Help launches. The Windows Help interface is similar to a Web browser.

4 Record what four tabs are available in Windows Help.

5 Record what the five menu bar items are.

6 If no one has used Windows Help on your computer before, the Contents tab is visible. If Help has been opened previously, the most recently used tab is visible. Click the Contents tab, if it isn't already visible.

7 Move the mouse pointer over the Introducing Windows 2000 Professional topic in the left pane.

8 Note that the pointer becomes a hand, as it does in Internet Explorer when you move it over a link.

9 Notice that when you point to the topic, the topic becomes underlined, like a hyperlink.

10 Click **Introducing Windows 2000 Professional** in the left pane. The topic Introducing Windows 2000 Professional expands in the left pane, displaying subtopics.

11 Verify that the right pane hasn't changed yet.

12 Click **Tips for new users**. Subtopics are displayed in the right pane.

13 Scroll the right pane to get a sense of the information provided there.

14 Click **locate lost files** in the right pane. The topic expands to show a description of what it contains, as well as a link to more information under Overview for locating lost files.

15 Click **Overview for locating lost files**. The right pane displays a list of locations where lost files might be found, along with steps for looking for files in each of these locations. Note that the list begins with the most likely locations for lost files, with less likely possibilities at the bottom of the list.

16 Record the possible locations for lost files.

17 The Windows Help toolbar contains buttons similar to those found in a Web browser, including a Back button (a left-facing arrow), which you can use to display a previous topic. Click the **Back** button in Windows Help. The Tips for new users topic is again displayed in the right pane.

Follow these steps to use the Index and Search features.

1 Click the **Index** tab. If this is the first time the Index has been used, Help displays a small box with a flashlight icon and the message, "Preparing index for first use." At the top of the Index tab is a text box where you can type keywords you want to search on. Below the textbox is a list of all possible Help topics.

2 Type **los** in the text box.

3 As you type, record what happens to the list of topics.

4 Finish typing **lost files** into the text box. Verify that the list of topics below the text box now includes lost files.

5 Select the topic, **lost files**, in the list of topics.

6 Click the **Display** button at the bottom of the pane to display the topic.

7 Record what Windows prompts you to do.

8 In the list of topics, click **locating**.

9 Click **Display**. The Topics Found dialog box appears, displaying two topics. These topics should look familiar to you.

10 In the Topics Found dialog box, click **Locating lost files** (if necessary to select it.)

11 Click **Display**. The Topics Found window closes and information on locating lost files is displayed in the Help window's right pane.

12 Record how the information currently displayed compares to the information recorded earlier.

13 Now click the **Search** tab. Note that the Search tab looks similar to the Index tab, except that it doesn't automatically display topics.

14 Search for Help is an alternative to browsing the Index for a topic. You simply type a topic into the Search box and click the List Topics button. Keep search topic strings as short as possible to focus your search better.

15 Type **lost files** in the textbox at the top of the tab.

16 Click **List Topics**. A list of topics is displayed below the text box.

17 Record if the Search tab returns more topics than the Index tab or fewer.

18 Click **Tips for new users**.

19 Click **Display**.

20 Record how the display in the right pane changes.

Follow these steps to record a list of topics that you want to refer to again without having to search for them on the Favorites tab.

1 Click the **Favorites** tab.

2 The topic, "Tips for new users," is listed at the bottom of the tab, below a blank pane.

3 Click **Add** to add this item to your list of favorite topics.

Follow these steps to troubleshoot non-functioning DOS applications:

1 Click the **Contents** tab in the Help window.

2 In the left pane, locate and click **Troubleshooting and Maintenance**. A list of subtopics appears below "Troubleshooting and Maintenance" in the left pane.

3 In the list of subtopics, click **Windows 2000 troubleshooters**.

4 Observe that a table appears in the right pane, with a list and description of Windows troubleshooting tools.

5 In the chart, click **MS-DOS programs**.

6 The Windows Troubleshooter for MS-DOS programs starts in the right pane of Windows Help. The Troubleshooter asks you for details about the problem you're troubleshooting, so that it can provide a solution tailored to that problem. For this portion of the activity, assume the following:

- You have only one DOS application that isn't working.
- The NTVDM subsystem is working.
- The program works when it's the only program running.

7 To troubleshoot the problem, click the appropriate option buttons for the specified scenario.

8 Use the Next button to advance through the Troubleshooter screens. Notice that the Troubleshooter also provides buttons that you can use to go back to a previous screen and to start over at the beginning of the process.

9 Record what solution the Troubleshooter offers for your problem.

10 Click **Start Over** to troubleshoot a slightly different problem. This time, assume the following:

- No DOS applications work.
- The NTVDM works.
- The program doesn't run by itself.
- The program runs in Safe Mode.

11 Record the following information:

- Record what conclusion the Troubleshooter reaches.
- Record what two options are offered to correct the problem temporarily?

12 Record the following information:

- What type of program is Windows Help similar to?
- What two Help search tabs operate in similar ways? What are the differences between them?
- What are two ways to launch Windows Help?
- What tool, accessible from Windows Help, takes you step by step through the process of diagnosing and perhaps repairing common problems?
- Are troubleshooters ever launched automatically? Explain.

Follow these steps to install the Windows 2000 Setup Manager:

1 Open Explorer.

2 Select the C: drive.

3 Create a new folder named **Deploy**.

4 Using Explorer, navigate to the Support\Tools directory in the Windows 2000 installation files on your hard drive or on the Windows 2000 setup CD.

5 Double-click **Deploy.cab**.

6 Follow directions on screen to copy **contents of Deploy.cab** to the Deploy directory on drive C:

Follow these steps to create an unattended installation answer file.

1 Verify that the C:\Deploy directory is still open in Windows Explorer.

2 Double-click **setupmgr.exe**. The Windows 2000 Setup Manager Wizard starts and displays a welcome message.

3 Click **Next** to continue.

4 In the New or Existing Answer File section, select **Create a new answer File.**

5 Click **Next**.

6 In the Product to Install section, select **Windows 2000 Unattended Installation**.

7 Record what other types of products this wizard supports.

8 Click **Next** to continue.

9 In the Platform Type section, select **Windows 2000 Professional**.

10 Click **Next** to continue.

11 In the User Interaction Level section of the wizard, select **Fully Automated**.

12 Click **Next** to continue.

13 In the License Agreement section, accept the EULA.

14 Click **Next** to continue.

15 In the Customize the Software section, specify the user name and the organization name.

16 Click **Next** to continue.

17 In the Computer Names section, type the computer name.

18 Click **Add**. Note that you can use the answer file you're creating to install Windows 2000 on several computers, as long as the computers' hardware configurations are identical.

19 Click **Next** to continue.

20 In the Administrator Password section, specify the Administrator password for this computer. Confirm the password.

21 Click **Next** to continue.

22 In the Display Settings section of the wizard, specify **Preferred Video Settings**. These settings include color, screen area, and refresh rate and depend on the settings supported by the video cards in the computers on which the unattended installation is performed.

23 Click **Next** to continue.

24 In the Network Settings section, select the correct Network Type and Settings for your network.

25 Click **Next**.

26 In the Workgroup or Domain section, specify whether the computer is part of a workgroup or domain.

27 If the computer is a part of a domain, specify the Administrator user name and password account.

28 Click **Next** to continue.

29 In the Time Zone section, specify your time zone and then click **Next**.

30 In the Additional Settings section, you can select additional settings that are required for other devices. These settings include telephone information, regional settings, such as country and currency, the preferred language for menus and other operating system features, and printers that you might want to install automatically. Click the **No, do not edit the additional settings**.

31 Click **Next** to continue.

32 In the Distribution Folder section, you can specify whether you want to install the operating system from a CD or to create a distribution folder, typically on a network location. When you use a distribution folder, all necessary source files are copied to that location. Choose to install from a CD. Click the option button, indicating installation from a CD.

33 Click **Next** to continue.

34 In the Answer File Name section, specify the name (sysprep.inf) and location for the answer file you're creating (the Sysprep folder at the root level of the drive on which Windows is to be installed.)

35 Click **Next** to continue.

36 Click **Finish** to exit the wizard and close Windows 2000 Setup Manager. The wizard creates the answer file in the specified location.

37 Install Windows 2000 using the answer file you just created and record the following information.

38 Where were the installation files located?

39 How did you launch the installation process?

40 How did you tell Setup to use your answer file?

41 What, if anything, did you have to do while the installation was in progress?

42 What error messages, if any, did you see? What did you do about them?

43 Record the following information:

44 What type of file does the Windows 2000 Setup Manager Wizard create, and what's this file used for?

45 Before the wizard was developed, how was this type of file created?

46 What other operations does this wizard support?

47 Could you use the Setup Manager Wizard to create a file to assist an unattended installation that automatically creates an account on a Windows domain? Explain.

48 If you choose to create a distribution folder, why won't the Windows 2000 Professional installation CD be necessary during the unattended installation?